More praise for
Gay Talese and
HONOR THY FATHER

"A marvelous piece of work, showing how a good journalist can catch a man just as he is ready to reconsider his past and is anxious to find someone who will listen."
Newsweek

"Mr. Talese's insight will do more to help us understand the criminal than any amount of moral recrimination."
The Times Literary Supplement

"A family saga as important as any we've seen in this country."

PETE HAMILL
Book World

"A blockbuster."

Publishers Weekly

Also by Gay Talese:

UNTO THE SONS
THY NEIGHBOR'S WIFE
THE KINGDOM AND THE POWER
THE BRIDGE
FAME AND OBSCURITY
NEW YORK—A SERENDIPITER'S JOURNEY
THE OVERREACHERS

HONOR THY FATHER

Gay Talese

IVY BOOKS • NEW YORK

Ivy Book
Published by Ballantine Books
Copyright © 1971, 1981 by Gay Talese

An explanation about this book and how it was researched will be found in the Author's Note, which follows the final chapter.

ISBN 0-8041-1058-1

Printed in Canada

First Ballantine Books Edition: March 1992
Fourth Printing: November 1992

For CHARLES, JOSEPH, TORY, and FELIPPA
in the hope that they will understand
their father more, and love him no less . . .

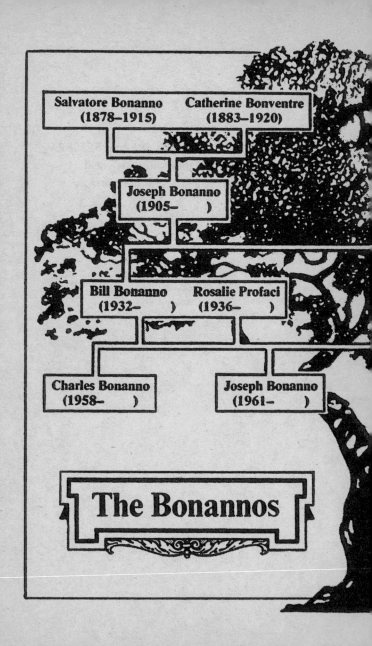

Salvatore Bonanno
(1878–1915)

Catherine Bonventre
(1883–1920)

Joseph Bonanno
(1905–   )

Bill Bonanno
(1932–   )

Rosalie Profaci
(1936–   )

Charles Bonanno
(1958–   )

Joseph Bonanno
(1961–   )

The Bonannos

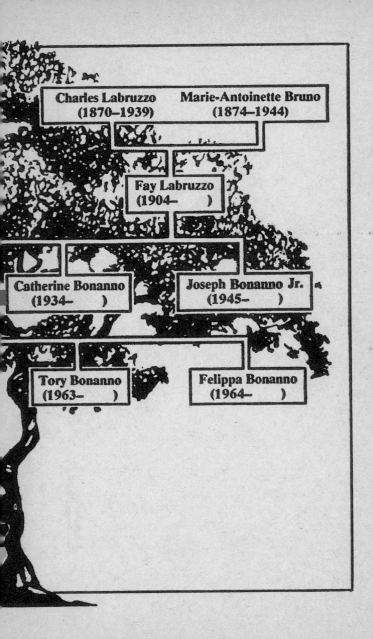

CONTENTS

AUTHOR'S GLOSSARY

JOSEPH BONANNO Patriarch of family. Born in 1905 in western Sicilian town of Castellammare del Golfo. An anti-Fascist student radical in Palermo after Mussolini came to power in 1922, Bonanno fled Sicily and entered United States during Prohibition. Decades later, a millionaire, Bonanno was identified by U.S. government as one of top bosses in American Mafia.

FAY BONANNO Wife of Joseph Bonanno. Born Fay Labruzzo in Tunisia of Sicilian parents who later emigrated to United States and settled in Brooklyn. There, in 1931, she married Joseph Bonanno.

SALVATORE (BILL) BONANNO Eldest son of Joseph and Fay Bonanno, born 1932.

CATHERINE BONANNO Daughter of Joseph and Fay Bonanno, born 1934.

JOSEPH BONANNO, JR. Younger son of Joseph and Fay Bonanno, born 1945.

ROSALIE BONANNO Wife of Bill Bonanno, whom she married in 1956. Born Rosalie Profaci in 1936; niece of Joseph Profaci.

JOSEPH PROFACI Millionaire importer of olive oil and tomato paste. Until death from cancer in 1962, boss of Brooklyn organization with close ties to organization headed by Joseph Bonanno. Born Villabate, Sicily, 1897.

JOSEPH MAGLIOCCO His sister married to Joseph Profaci; after Profaci's death, Magliocco, a longtime aide, succeeded to leadership of Profaci organization. Suffered fatal heart attack in December 1963.

JOSEPH COLOMBO Succeeded Magliocco; negotiated uncertain peace within factionalized Profaci organization following Gallo brothers revolt of 1960, but organization never regained power it had during 1950s and 1940s under Profaci. Colombo in 1970 started Italian-American Civil Rights League; in 1971, at League outdoor rally, Colombo was shot by black man posing as photographer.

STEFANO MAGADDINO   Boss in Buffalo area. Native of Castellammare del Golfo, distant cousin of Joseph Bonanno, but enemy of Bonanno since 1960s.

GASPAR DI GREGORIO   Magaddino's brother-in-law, loyal member of Joseph Bonanno organization for years—until in 1964, disenchanted by elevation of thirty-two-year-old Bill Bonanno in organization, led internal revolt that led in mid-1960s to so-called Banana War. Magaddino, among others, backed Di Gregorio's cause.

FRANK LABRUZZO   Brother of Fay Bonanno and loyal captain in Joseph Bonanno organization.

JOSEPH NOTARO   Loyal captain in Bonanno organization.

JOHN BONVENTRE   Cousin of Joseph Bonanno and veteran officer in organization who in 1950s returned to native Sicily to retire. In 1971, in Italian government's anti-Mafia drive, Bonventre was cited as leader and exiled with other alleged mafiosi to small island off northeast coast of Sicily.

FRANK GAROFALO   Loyal Bonanno captain; returned to peaceful retirement in Sicily in 1950s, where he died natural death.

PAUL SCIACCA   Bonanno member who quit organization in 1964 dispute, joined Di Gregorio's faction.

FRANK MARI   Bonanno member who joined Di Gregorio and became identified as top triggerman against Bonanno loyalists during Banana War in mid-1960s.

PETER MAGADDINO   First cousin of Stefano Magaddino, the boss in Buffalo; Peter Magaddino left Buffalo and supported Joseph Bonanno, his boyhood friend in Sicily, in the dispute with Di Gregorio's faction.

SALVATORE MARANZANO   Old-time Sicilian boss from Castellammare del Golfo; friend of Joseph Bonanno's father. In 1930, Maranzano organized group of Castellammarese immigrants in Brooklyn to fight against New York organization headed by Joe Masseria, a southern Italian who wanted to eliminate Sicilian clan. This feud, extending from 1928 until 1931, became known as the Castellammarese War and is referred to in Chapter 12.

THE MAFIA   Called by several names—and never *Mafia* by members—is of ancient origin in Sicily. In United States it became organized along modern business lines after completion of Castellammarese War in 1931. At that time it realigned itself into a national brotherhood of approximately 5,000 men belonging to twenty-four separate organizations (''families'') located in major cities in every region of the United States. In New York City, where an estimated 2,000 of the 5,000 members were in residence, five ''families'' were established, each headed by a family boss, or don. In 1931, at the age of twenty-six, Joseph Bonanno was the youngest don in the national brotherhood.

THE COMMISSION Of the twenty-four bosses, nine take turns serving as members of the commission, which is dedicated to maintaining peace in the underworld; but it is supposed to restrain itself from interfering with the internal affairs of any one boss. Occasionally it cannot resist, and then—as with the Bonanno affair in the mid-1960s—there is trouble. Before the Bonanno affair, however, the commission members subordinated their differences and kept the nine-man membership intact. The commission included the following:

JOSEPH BONANNO NEW YORK.

JOSEPH PROFACI NEW YORK.

VITO GENOVESE Succeeded to leadership of New York–based organization once headed by Lucky Luciano, who, after being sentenced in 1936 to long prison term, was deported to Italy in 1946. Frank Costello, who tried to take over the Luciano organization, was discouraged when his skull was grazed with a bullet in 1957.

THOMAS LUCCHESE New York. Took over leadership of organization headed by Gaetano Gagliano, who died of natural causes in 1953.

CARLO GAMBINO New York. Close to Lucchese; their children intermarried. Gambino heads organization formerly controlled by Albert Anastasia, who was fatally shot in a Manhattan barbershop in 1957.

STEFANO MAGADDINO Buffalo. Born in 1891 in Castellammare del Golfo, he is senior member of commission.

ANGELO BRUNO Boss of organization centered in Philadelphia.

SAM GIANCANA Boss of organization centered in Chicago.

JOSEPH ZERILLI Boss of organization in Detroit.

ORGANIZED CRIME It is most often assumed by newspaper readers that the Mafia is all there is to organized crime in America, when in fact the Mafia is merely a small part of the organized crime industry. There are an estimated 5,000 mafiosi belonging to twenty-four "families"; but federal investigators estimate that there are more than 100,000 organized gangsters working full-time in the crime industry— engaged in numbers racketeering, bookmaking, loansharking, narcotics, prostitution, hijacking, enforcing, debt collecting, and other activities. These gangs, who may work in cooperation with Mafia gangs or may be entirely independent, are composed of Jews, Irish, blacks, Wasps, Latin Americans, and every ethnic or racial type in the nation.

Because the Mafia, made up almost entirely of Sicilians and southern Italians, has since Prohibition been more ethnically tight and cohesive than most other gangs, its influence and notoriety has been considerable in organized crime circles. But during the 1960s, as old-style Mafia bosses became older and their sons lacked the interest or talent to replace them and had better options in the larger American society, the Mafia structure is now disintegrating as have the great Irish gangs of the late 1800s and the great Jewish cliques of the 1920s (of which only Meyer Lansky remains supreme today). The blacks and Latin Americans have shown signs of emerging in the 1960s as a dominant force to overthrow the last vestiges of white rule of ghetto rackets.

This book is a study of the rise and fall of the Bonanno organization, a personal history of ethnic progression and of dying traditions.

AUTHOR'S FOREWORD

THIS BOOK EVOLVED out of my father's embarrassment—my Italian-born father's embarrassment over the fact that gangsters with Italian names invariably dominate the headlines and most television shows dealing with organized crime. My father, a proud and consummate custom-tailor who immigrated from Italy in 1920 and prospered on the resort island of Ocean City, New Jersey—where I was born during the winter of 1932—always encouraged me to take pride in my ethnic heritage, a heritage he identified with such names as Michelangelo and Dante, Medici and Galileo, Verdi and Caruso. But as I grew up in the early 1940s, the Italian names I saw most frequently on the front pages were those belonging to the reputed leaders of the Mafia—Charles ("Lucky") Luciano and Al Capone; Vito Genovese, Carlo Gambino, Frank Costello, Thomas ("Three-Finger Brown") Lucchese, and Joseph ("Joe Bananas") Bonanno.

Whenever my father saw me reading articles about such individuals he would shake his head and say things like: "It's all exaggerated! The press will do anything to sell newspapers." At times he denied the very existence of the Mafia, suggesting it was the creation of publicity-craving FBI agents, or Senate committeemen seeking higher office, or Hollywood moguls and other mythmakers pandering to the American public's historic addiction with villains and fugitives, with Little Caesars and Godfathers—all to the discredit of millions of law-abiding Italian-Americans like himself. Inevitably this aroused within me a curiosity about the Mafia that would in time lead me to its doorstep, and ultimately beyond the portal into the private world of one of the Mafia's leading families, that headed by "Joe Bananas" himself.

How this came about is detailed in my Author's Note, which

follows the final chapter of this book. But I must quickly confess
that the completion of this book did not terminate my interest,
nor the American public's interest, in the endlessly fascinating
world of organized crime. Although many of the people I write
about or whom I interviewed while researching *Honor Thy Father* have since been murdered, or have died from occupational
stress, most of the book's main characters are still very much
alive—including the octogenarian Joseph Bonanno (the *only*
Godfather dating from the boom years of Prohibition who *is* still
alive); his eternally loyal son, Bill Bonanno, the principal character in my book who has so far survived the ambitions of rival
factions; and the Bonanno family lawyer, Albert J. Krieger, who
in 1992 took on extra work to defend the alleged *mafioso* John
Gotti against Federal charges of racketeering and the murder of
an ex-Godfather named Paul Castellano.

All of this publicity—together with the recordings of gangsters' voices that investigators have collected—has left little
doubt about the true existence of the Mafia; and even my octogenarian father in New Jersey, whom I visit regularly, is beyond
issuing denials about the roles Italian-Americans play within
organized crime circles.

But my father, and most other Italian-Americans I know, is
far less embarrassed now than before by the prominence of Italian names in crime headlines. The lowly status of Italian-
Americans during the World War II period when I was growing
up—a period in which Italy was a battlefield enemy of the Allies,
and when Italian-Americans' ethnic pride was almost limited to
cheering for the baseball star, Joe DiMaggio—has now in the
1990s been altered greatly by the assimilation and success of
Italian-Americans into all levels of American life, and by the
swiftness with which Italian-Americans will strike back at any
American who attempts to associate them generally with the
notoriety of the Mafia.

As I was writing this Author's Foreword during the winter of
1992, Governor Mario Cuomo of New York had just learned
that, in a secretly recorded telephone conversation between Arkansas' Governor Bill Clinton and a woman friend, Clinton was
heard saying that Cuomo "acts" at times like a *mafioso*.

Cuomo's reaction was immediate. He condemned the remark
not only as an insult to Italian-Americans but as an assault on

all ethnic minorities; and his statement, widely distributed and applauded by the press nationwide, prompted quick and profuse apologies from the Arkansas governor. There were now approximately twenty million Americans with Italian roots in the United States. They were unquestionably a formidable political force.

PART ONE

THE DISAPPEARANCE

1

KNOWING THAT IT is possible to see too much, most doormen in New York have developed an extraordinary sense of selective vision: they know what to see and what to ignore, when to be curious and when to be indolent; they are most often standing indoors, unaware, when there are accidents or arguments in front of their buildings; and they are usually in the street seeking taxicabs when burglars are escaping through the lobby. Although a doorman may disapprove of bribery and adultery, his back is invariably turned when the superintendent is handing money to the fire inspector or when a tenant whose wife is away escorts a young woman into the elevator—which is not to accuse the doorman of hypocrisy or cowardice but merely to suggest that his instinct for uninvolvement is very strong, and to speculate that doormen have perhaps learned through experience that nothing is to be gained by serving as a material witness to life's unseemly sights or to the madness of the city. This being so, it was not surprising that on the night when the Mafia chief, Joseph Bonanno, was grabbed by two gunmen in front of a luxury apartment house on Park Avenue near Thirty-sixth Street, shortly after midnight on a rainy Tuesday in October, the doorman was standing in the lobby talking to the elevator man and saw nothing.

It had all happened with dramatic suddenness. Bonanno, returning from a restaurant, stepped out of a taxicab behind his lawyer, William P. Maloney, who ran ahead through the rain toward the canopy. Then the gunmen appeared from the darkness and began pulling Bonanno by the arms toward an awaiting automobile. Bonanno struggled to break free but he could not. He glared at the men, seeming enraged and stunned—not since Prohibition had he been so abruptly handled, and then it had been by the police when he had refused to answer questions; now he was being prodded by men from his own world, two burly men wearing black coats and hats, both about six feet tall, one of whom said: "Com'on, Joe, my boss wants to see you."

Bonanno, a handsome gray-haired man of fifty-nine, said nothing. He had gone out this evening without bodyguards or a gun, and even if the avenue had been crowded with people he would not have called to them for help because he regarded this as a private affair. He tried to regain his composure, to think clearly as the men forced him along the sidewalk, his arms numb from their grip. He shivered from the cold rain and wind, feeling it seep through his gray silk suit, and he could see nothing through the mist of Park Avenue except the taillights of his taxi-cab disappearing uptown and could hear nothing but the heavy breathing of the men as they dragged him forward. Then, sud-denly from the rear, Bonanno heard the running footsteps and voice of Maloney shouting: "Hey, what the hell's going on?"

One gunman whirled around, warning, "Quit it, get back!"

"Get out of here," Maloney replied, continuing to rush for-ward, a white-haired man of sixty waving his arms in the air, "that's my client!"

A bullet from an automatic was fired at Maloney's feet. The lawyer stopped, retreated, ducking finally into the entrance of his apartment building. The men shoved Bonanno into the back seat of a beige sedan that had been parked on the corner of Thirty-sixth Street, its motor idling. Bonanno lay on the floor, as he had been told, and the car bolted toward Lexington Ave-nue. Then the doorman joined Maloney on the sidewalk, arriv-ing too late to see anything, and later the doorman claimed that he had not heard a shot.

Bill Bonnano, a tall, heavy, dark-haired man of thirty-one whose crew cut and button-down shirt suggested the college student that he had been in the 1950s but whose moustache had been grown recently to help conceal his identity, sat in a sparsely furnished apartment in Queens listening intently as the tele-phone rang. But he did not answer it.

It rang three times, stopped, rang again and stopped, rang a few more times and stopped. It was Labruzzo's code. He was in a telephone booth signaling that he was on his way back to the apartment. On arriving at the apartment house, Labruzzo would repeat the signal on the downstairs doorbell and the younger Bonanno would then press the buzzer releasing the lock. Bonanno would then wait, gun in hand, looking through the peephole to be sure that it was Labruzzo getting out of the elevator. The furnished apartment the two men shared was on the top floor of a brick building in a middle-class neighborhood, and since their apartment door was at the end of the hall they could observe everyone who came and went from the single self-service elevator.

Such precautions were being taken not only by Bill Bonanno and Frank Labruzzo but by dozens of other members of the Joseph Bonanno organization who for the last few weeks had been hiding out in similar buildings in Queens, Brooklyn, and the Bronx. It was a tense time for all of them. They knew that at any moment they could expect a confrontation with rival gangs trying to kill them or with government agents trying to arrest them and interrogate them about the rumors of violent plots and vendettas now circulating through the underworld. The government had recently concluded, largely from information obtained through wiretapping and electronic bugging devices, that even the top bosses in the Mafia were personally involved in this internal feud and that Joseph Bonanno, a powerful don for thirty years, was in the middle of the controversy. He was suspected by other dons of excessive ambition, of seeking to expand—at their expense and perhaps over their dead bodies—the influence that he already had in various parts of New York, Canada, and the Southwest. The recent elevation of his son, Bill, to the number three position in the Bonanno organization was also regarded with alarm and skepticism by a few leaders of other gangs as well as by some members of Bonanno's own gang of about 300 men in Brooklyn.

The younger Bonanno was considered something of an eccentric in the underworld, a privileged product of prep schools and universities whose manner and methods, while not lacking in courage, conveyed some of the reckless spirit of a campus activist. He seemed impatient with the system, unimpressed with the roundabout ways and Old World finesse that are part of Mafia tradition. He said what was on his mind, not altering his tone when addressing a mafioso of superior rank and not losing his sense of youthful conviction even when speaking the dated Sicilian dialect he had learned as a boy from his grandfather in

Brooklyn. The fact that he was six feet two and weighed more than 200 pounds and that his posture was erect and his mind very quick added to the formidability of his presence and lent substance to his own high opinion of himself, which was that he was the equal or superior of every man with whom he was associating except for possibly one, his father. When in the company of his father, Bill Bonanno seemed to lose some of his easy confidence and poise, becoming more quiet, hesitant, as if his father were severely testing his every word and thought. He seemed to exhibit toward his father a distance and formality, taking no more liberties than he would with a stranger. But he was also attentive to his father's needs and seemed to take great pleasure in pleasing him. It was obvious that he was awed by his father, and while he no doubt had feared him and perhaps still did, he also worshiped him.

During the last few weeks he had never been far from Joseph Bonanno's side, but last night, knowing that his father wished to dine alone with his lawyers and that he planned to spend the evening at Maloney's place, Bill Bonanno passed a quiet evening at the apartment with Labruzzo, watching television, reading the newspapers, and waiting for word. Without knowing exactly why, he was mildly on edge. Perhaps one reason was a story he had read in *The Daily News* reporting that life in the underworld was becoming increasingly perilous and claiming that the elder Bonanno had recently planned the murders of two rival dons, Carlo Gambino and Thomas (Three-Finger Brown) Lucchese, a scheme that supposedly failed because one of the triggermen had betrayed Bonanno and had tipped off one of the intended victims. Even if such a report were pure fabrication, based possibly on the FBI's wiretapping of low-level Mafia gossip, the younger Bonanno was concerned about the publicity given to it because he knew that it could intensify the suspicion which did exist among the various gangs that ran the rackets (which included numbers games, bookmaking, loan-sharking, prostitution, smuggling, and enforced protection). The publicity could also inspire the outcry of the politicians, provoke the more vigilant pursuit of the police, and result in more subpoenas from the courts.

The subpoena was dreaded in the underworld now more than before because of a new federal law requiring that a suspected criminal, if picked up for questioning, must either testify if given immunity by the court or face a sentence for contempt. This made it imperative for the men of the Mafia to remain inconspicuous if they wanted to avoid subpoenas every time there were newspaper headlines. The law also impeded the Mafia leaders' direction of their men in the street because their men, having to be very cautious and often detained by their caution and evasiveness, were not always where they were supposed to be at the appointed hour to do a job, and frequently they were unavailable to receive, at designated telephone booths at specific moments, prearranged calls from headquarters seeking a report on what had happened. In a secret society where precision was important, the new problem in communications was grating the already jangled nerves of many top mafiosi.

The Bonanno organization, more progressive than most partly because of the modern business methods introduced by the younger Bonanno, had solved its communications problem to a degree by its bell-code system and also by the use of a telephone answering service. It was perhaps the only gang in the Mafia with an answering service. The service was registered in the name of a fictitious Mr. Baxter, which was the younger Bonanno's code name, and it was attached to the home telephone of one member's maiden aunt who barely spoke English and was hard of hearing. Throughout the day various key men would call the service and identify themselves through agreed-upon aliases and would leave cryptic messages confirming their safety and the fact that business was progressing as usual. If a message contained the initials "IBM"—"suggest you buy more IBM"— it meant that Frank Labruzzo, who had once worked for IBM, was reporting. If the word "monk" was in a message, it identified another member of the organization, a man with a tonsured head who often concealed his identity in public under a friar's robe. Any reference to a "salesman" indicated the identity of one of the Bonanno captains who was a jewelry salesman on the side; and "flower" alluded to a gunman whose father in Sicily was a florist. A "Mr. Boyd" was a member whose mother was known to live on Boyd Street in Long Island, and reference to a "cigar" identified a certain lieutenant who was never without one. Joseph Bonanno was known on the answering service as "Mr. Shepherd."

One of the reasons that Frank Labruzzo had left the apartment that he shared with Bill Bonanno was to telephone the service from a neighborhood coin box and also to buy the early edition of the afternoon newspapers to see if there were any developments of special interest. As usual, Labruzzo was accompanied by the pet dog that shared their apartment. It had been Bill Bonanno who had suggested that all gang members in hiding keep dogs in their apartments, and while this had initially made it more difficult for the men to find rooms, since some landlords objected to pets, the men later agreed with Bonanno that a dog made them more alert to sounds outside their doors and also was a useful companion when going outside for a walk—a man with a dog aroused little suspicion in the street.

Bonanno and Labruzzo happened to like dogs, which was one of the many things that they had in common, and it contributed to their compatibility in the small apartment. Frank Labruzzo was a calm, easygoing, somewhat stocky man of fifty-three with glasses and graying dark hair; he was a senior officer in the Bonanno organization and also a member of the immediate family—Labruzzo's sister, Fay, was Joseph Bonanno's wife and Bill Bonanno's mother, and Labruzzo was close to the son in ways that the father was not. There was no strain or stress between these two, no competitiveness or problems of vanity and ego. Labruzzo, not terribly ambitious for himself, not driven like Joseph Bonanno or restless like the son, was content with his secondary position in the world, recognizing the world as a much larger place than either of the Bonannos seemed to think it was.

Labruzzo had attended college, and he had engaged in a number of occupations but had pursued none for very long. He had, in addition to working for IBM, operated a dry-goods store, sold insurance, and had been a mortician. Once he owned, in partnership with Joseph Bonanno, a funeral parlor in Brooklyn near the block of his birth in the center of a neighborhood where thousands of immigrant Sicilians had settled at the turn of the century. It was in this neighborhood that the elder Bonanno courted Fay Labruzzo, daughter of a prosperous butcher who manufactured wine during Prohibition. The butcher was proud to have Bonanno as a son-in-law even though the wedding date, in 1930, had to be postponed for thirteen months due to a gangland war involving hundreds of newly arrived Sicilians and Italians, including Bonanno, who were continuing the provincial discord transplanted to America but originating in the ancient mountain villages that they had abandoned in all but spirit. These men brought to the New World their old feuds and customs, their traditional friendships and fears and suspicions, and they not only consumed themselves with these things but they also influenced many of their children and sometimes their children's children—among the inheritors were such men as Frank Labruzzo and Bill Bonanno, who now, in the mid-1960s, in an age of space and rockets, were fighting a feudal war.

It seemed both absurd and remarkable to the two men that they had never escaped the insular ways of their parents' world, a subject that they had often discussed during their many hours of confinement, discussing it usually in tones of amusement and unconcern, although with regret at times, even bitterness. *Yes, we're in the wagon wheel business*, Bonanno had once sighed, and Labruzzo had agreed—they were modern men, lost in time, grinding old axes. This fact was particularly surprising in the case of Bill Bonanno: he left Brooklyn at an early age to attend boarding schools in Arizona, where he was reared outside the family, learned to ride horses and brand cattle, dated blonde girls whose fathers owned ranches; and later, as a student at the University of Arizona, he led a platoon of ROTC cadets across the football field before each game to help raise the American flag before the national anthem was played. That he could have suddenly shifted from this campus scene in the Southwest to the precarious world of his father in New York was due to a series of bizarre circumstances that were perhaps beyond his control, perhaps not. Certainly his marriage was a step in his father's direction, a marriage in 1956 to Rosalie Profaci, the pretty dark-eyed niece of Joseph Profaci, the millionaire importer who was also a member of the Mafia's national commission.

Bill Bonanno first met Rosalie Profaci when she was a young student attending a convent school in upstate New York with his sister. At that time he had a girl friend in Arizona, a casual American girl with a flair for freedom; while Rosalie was appealing, she also was demure and sheltered. That the young couple would meet again and again, during summer months and holidays, was largely due to their parents, who were very close and whose approval was bestowed in subtle but infectious ways whenever Rosalie and Bill would converse or merely sit near one another in crowded rooms. At one large family gathering months before the engagement, Joseph Bonanno, taking his twenty-year-old daughter Catherine aside, asked her privately what she thought of the likelihood that Bill would marry Rosalie. Catherine Bonanno, an independent-minded girl, thought for a moment, then said that while she was extremely fond of Rosalie personally she did not feel that Rosalie was right for Bill. Rosalie lacked the strength of character to accept him for what he was and might become, Catherine said, and she was about to say something else when, suddenly, she felt a hard slap across her face, and she fell back, stunned, confused, then burst into tears as she ran, never before having seen her father that enraged, his eyes fiery and fierce. Later he tried to comfort her, to apologize in his way, but she remained aloof for days although she understood as she had not before her father's desire for the marriage. It was a wish shared by Rosalie's father and uncle. And it would be fulfilled the following year, an event that Catherine Bonanno would regard as a marriage of fathers.

The wedding, on August 18, 1956, had been extraordinary. More than 3,000 guests had attended the reception at the Astor Hotel ballroom in New York following the church wedding in Brooklyn, and no expense was spared in embellishing the occasion. Leading orchestras were hired for the dancing, and the entertainment included the Four Lads and Tony Bennett. A truckload of champagne and wine was sent as a gift by a distributor in Brooklyn, and it was arranged through Pan American Airways to have thousands of daisies flown in from California because that flower, Rosalie's favorite, was then unavailable in New York. The guest list, in addition to the legitimate businessmen and politicians and priests, included all the top men of the underworld. Vito Genovese and Frank Costello were there, having requested and received inconspicuous tables against the wall. Albert Anastasia was there (it was the year before his murder in the barbershop of the Park-Sheraton Hotel), and so was Joseph Barbara, whose barbecue party for nearly seventy mafiosi at his home in Apalachin, New York, three weeks after the murder, would be discovered by the police and would result in national publicity and endless investigations. Joseph Zerilli had come with his men from Detroit, and so had the Chicago delegation led by Sam Giancana and Tony Accardo. Stefano Magaddino, the portly old don from Buffalo, cousin of Joseph Bonanno, was given an honored table in front of the dais, and seated near him were other relatives or close friends of the Bonannos and Profacis. All of the twenty-four semi-independent organizations that formed the national syndicate were represented at the wedding, meaning that there were men from New England to New Mexico, and the group from Los Angeles alone totaled almost eighty.

Bill Bonanno, smiling next to his bride on the dais, toasting the guests and being toasted in turn, often wondered during the evening what the FBI would have done had it gotten its hands on the guest list. But there was little chance of that since the list, in code, had been in the careful custody of Frank Labruzzo and his men who were posted at the door to receive the guests and to escort them to their tables. There were no intruders on that night. There was not really a great deal of public concern over the Mafia in 1956. The Kefauver hearings of 1951 were already forgotten, and the Apalachin fiasco was one year away. And so the wedding and reception proceeded smoothly and without incident, with Catherine Bonanno as the maid of honor; and Joseph Bonanno, elegant in his cutaway, presided over the gathering like a medieval duke, bowing toward his fellow dons, dancing with the women, courtly and proud.

After the reception, during which the bridal couple had received in gift envelopes about $100,000 in cash, Bill Bonanno and his bride flew to Europe for a honeymoon. They stayed for a few days at the Ritz Hotel in Paris, then at the Excelsior in Rome; they received special attention in each place and were ushered quickly through customs at the airport. Later they flew to Sicily, and as the plane slowly taxied toward the terminal building in Palermo, Bill Bonanno noticed that a large crowd had gathered behind the gate and that a number of carabinieri were among them, standing very close to Bonanno's aging, baldheaded uncle, John Bonventre, who seemed rather grim and tense. Bonanno's first thought was that Bonventre, who had once served in the United States as an underboss in the Bonanno organization, was about to be deported from his native Sicily, to which he had gone the year before to retire, having taken with him from America a lifetime's supply of toilet paper, preferring it to the coarse brands produced in Sicily. After the plane stopped but before the door opened, a stewardess asked that Mr. and Mrs. Bonanno please identify themselves. Slowly, Bill Bonanno raised his hand. The stewardess then asked that the couple be the first to leave the plane.

Walking down the ramp into the hot Sicilian sun, mountains

rising in the distance behind sloping villages of tan stone houses,
Bonanno sensed the crowd staring at him, moving and mur-
muring as he got closer. The old women were dressed in black,
the younger men had fixed dark expressions, children were mill-
ing everywhere, and the statuesque carabinieri, flamboyantly
dressed and brandishing gleaming silver swords, stood taller
than the rest. Then the uncle, Bonventre, bursting with a smile
of recognition, ran with arms outstretched toward the bridal
couple, and the crowd followed, and suddenly the Bonannos
were surrounded by clutching, kissing strangers, and Rosalie,
blushing, tried without success to conceal the awkwardness she
felt in the center of swarming unrestrained affection. Her husband, however, seemed to enjoy it thoroughly, reaching out with
his long arms to touch everyone that he could, leaning low to
be embraced by the women and children, basking in the ado-
ration and salutations of the crowd. The carabinieri watched
impassively for a few moments, then stepped aside, clearing a
path that led toward a line of illegally parked automobiles waiting to take the couple to the first of a series of celebrations that
would culminate with a visit on the following day to Castellammare del Golfo, the town in western Sicily where Joseph Bonanno was born and where the earlier Bonannos had long ruled
as *uomini rispettati*—men of respect.

Rosalie had hoped that they would also visit her father's birthplace, a town just east of Palermo called Villabate, but her husband, without ever explaining why, indicated that this was
impossible. Moments after he had landed at Palermo his uncle
had whispered a message just received from the United States
from the elder Bonanno insisting that the couple avoid Villabate.
A number of friends and distant relatives of the Profacis still
living in Villabate were then struggling with a rival gang for
control over certain operations, and there had already been seven
murders in the past ten days. It was feared that the enemies of
Profaci's friends in Villabate might seek revenge for their dead
upon Bill Bonanno or his wife, and although Rosalie persisted
in her request to see Villabate, her husband managed to avoid
the trip after making endless excuses and offering a busy itin-
erary of pleasant distractions. He was also relieved that Rosalie
had not questioned, nor had even seemed to notice, the quiet
group of men that followed them everywhere during their first
day of sightseeing in Palermo. These men, undoubtedly armed,

were serving as bodyguards for the Bonanno couple, even sitting outside the couple's hotel door at night to guarantee that no harm would come to them in Sicily.

The journey to Castellammare del Golfo, sixty miles west of Palermo, was the highpoint of the Sicilian visit for Bill Bonanno. As a boy he had seen on the walls at home framed photographs of his father's town, and he later noted references to it in history books and travel guides, although the references were very brief and superficial—it was as if the writers, with few exceptions, had quickly driven through the town without stopping, perhaps being intimidated by one published report claiming that eighty percent of Castellammare's adult male population had served time in prison.

There was no social stigma attached to this, however, because most of the local citizens regarded the law as corrupt, representing the will of invaders who had long sought to control the islanders and exploit the land through the conqueror's law. As with most of Sicily, the history of Castellammare had been turbulent for centuries, and Bonanno remembered reading that the island was conquered and reconquered no less than sixteen times—by Greeks, Saracens, and Normans, by Spaniards, Germans, and English, by various combinations and persuasions ranging from Holy Crusaders to Fascists. They had all come to Sicily and did what men do when away from home, and the history of Sicily was a litany of sailor's sins.

As the caravan of cars arrived at Castellammare, having driven for two hours along narrow mountain roads above the sea, Bill Bonanno felt a sudden sense of familiarity with the landscape that was beyond mere recognition from pictures. He felt united with all that he had imagined for years, all that he had heard as a boy from the reminiscing men gathered around his father's dinner table on Sunday afternoons. The town was actually quite beautiful, a tranquil fishing village built along the bottom of a mountain, and at the very tip of the land, on a jagged rocky edge splashed by waves, stood the old stone castle that gave the town its name. The castle, built many centuries ago by the Saracens or Aragons, no one was absolutely certain, had served as the town's lookout for spotting invading ships; but now it was a decaying structure of no purpose, and the elder Bonanno and the other men had recalled playing in it as boys.

Near the castle, along the small beach, were the fishermen,

weatherworn and ruddy, wearing black berets; they were pulling in their nets as the Bonanno party passed but were too busy to notice the line of cars. In the town square, near a church built four hundred years ago, were many men walking slowly, arm in arm, making many gestures with their hands. The stone houses, most of them two or three stories high with balconies in front, were arranged in tight rows along narrow cobbled roads over which was heard the clacking sounds of donkeys pulling colorfully painted wagons between the motor traffic. Here and there, sunning themselves in front of their doors, were groups of women, the unmarried ones seated with their backs to the street, possibly following a fashion inherited a thousand years ago when the Arabs occupied Sicily.

In front of one particularly well-constructed house on Corso Garibaldi, a crowd had gathered. When the procession of cars was spotted, the people stepped up to the curb, waiting. They were about thirty in number, dressed in dark clothes except for the children, one of whom held a bouquet of flowers. They were standing in front of the home where Joseph Bonanno was born, and the arrival of his son was regarded as an event of historical proportions. An indication of the Bonanno family status in Castellammare was the fact that the ceremony surrounding Joseph Bonanno's baptism in 1905 had marked the end of a shooting war between the local mafiosi and those in the neighboring village of Alcamo; and when Joseph Bonanno's father, Salvatore Bonanno, died in 1915, he was buried in the most prominent plot at the base of the mountain.

After the bridal couple was greeted by, and disentangled themselves from, the embracing crowds and had coffee and pastry with their cousins and *compari*, they went to the cemetery; and Bill Bonanno, standing before a large gravestone that exhibited a proud picture of a man with a handlebar moustache, sensed something more about his own father's relationship to the past. The eyes looking out from the gravestone were penetrating and dark, and Bill Bonanno could readily accept what he had heard of his grandfather's persuasive power, although he found it difficult to believe that this authoritative-looking photograph was of a man who had died at thirty-seven. His grandfather seemed to be a tall man—lean and tall unlike Sicilians. Perhaps this is because the Bonannos were not Sicilian by origin. Hundreds of years ago they had lived in Pisa, according to Joseph Bonanno, and had left rather hastily following a dispute with the ruling family. Joseph Bonanno, who kept a family coat-of-arms hanging in his home in the United States, a shield decorated with a panther, had compiled a history of his ancestry that claimed kinship with Charles Bonanno, engineer of the Leaning Tower of Pisa.

After Bill Bonanno returned from his honeymoon in September 1956, he urged his father to visit Castellammare. And a year later the elder Bonanno visited the town. But the recollection of the pleasant experiences of that trip was somewhat negated by certain events that followed in 1957 and other subsequent events. There was the publicity attached to the Anastasia murder and the Apalachin meeting, and in 1963 there was the Senate testimony of Joseph Valachi, the Mafia defector, who identified Joseph Bonanno as his sponsoring godfather and as the leader of one of New York's five "families" as well as a member of the nine-man national commission. Also in 1963 there was the dissension within Bonanno's organization, internal differences between a few old friends who had left Castellammare forty years before. And now, in October 1964, hiding in the apartment, Bill Bonanno, the son, was a partner in the tension and intrigue.

He was tired of it, but there was little he could do. He had not seen Rosalie or his four young children in several days, and he wondered about their well-being and wished that his relationship with his in-laws, the Profacis, had not declined as it had in recent years. He and Rosalie had now been married for seven years, and much had happened since their honeymoon, too much, and he hoped that he could repair the damage. What was required, he felt, was a new start, a second attempt in another direction, and he thought that they were moving toward this earlier in the year, in February, when they moved into their new home, a ranch-type house on a quiet tree-lined street in East Meadow, Long Island. They had finally left Arizona, which Rosalie had come to hate for a number of reasons, not the least of which was a certain woman in Phoenix, and they came East to live for a few months in the mansion of Rosalie's uncle Joe Magliocco in East Islip, Long Island, before getting their own home. The time spent at Magliocco's place was hectic, not only for them but also for their children.

The mansion was on a sprawling estate protected by high

walls and trees and by watchdogs and gunmen. After the death
of Joseph Profaci in 1962, Joe Magliocco, a muscular fat man
weighing 300 pounds, had taken over the Profaci operation,
including its control over the Italian lottery in Brooklyn. (Rosalie's father, Salvatore Profaci, was also dead at this point; he
was killed before her wedding due to an explosion he had caused
while working on an engine in his motorboat.) Magliocco, an
impulsive man who lacked organizational ability, had also inherited many problems when he took over, the worst of which
was an internal revolt of younger members led by the Gallo
brothers. The dissension caused by the Gallo faction was still
unresolved when Rosalie and Bill Bonanno moved in with Magliocco in 1963, and they sensed that things were becoming almost desperate for Magliocco in the late summer and fall of that
year—men were coming and going at odd hours, the dogs were
on constant alert, and Magliocco was rarely without his bodyguard even when walking short distances through his estate.

One morning in December, as the Bonannos' two-year-old
son, Joseph, was crawling through the dining room, he reached
between the china closet and the wall and pulled the trigger of
a rifle that had been left standing there. The rifle blast blew a
hole in the ceiling, hitting through the upper floor not far from
where Magliocco lay sleeping. The fat man bolted out of bed,
yelling, and Rosalie, who had been feeding her newly born infant in another part of the house, began to scream. The big house
suddenly vibrated with a flurry of bodies running in panic, chasing and shouting—until the little boy was discovered downstairs,
sitting on the rug wearing his red pajamas, stunned but safe,
with a smoking rifle at his feet. Two weeks later, Joe Magliocco
died of a heart attack.

2

On hearing Frank Labruzzo ring the downstairs bell, Bill Bonanno pressed the buzzer and then watched through the peephole of the apartment door. He saw Labruzzo step out of the elevator with newspapers under his arm, and he could tell by the pale expression on Labruzzo's face that something had gone wrong.

Labruzzo said nothing as he entered the apartment. He handed the papers to Bonanno. On the front page of every one in large headlines at the very top, was the news:

JOE BANANAS—CALL HIM DEAD

JOE BONANNO IS KIDNAPED BY TWO HOODS IN NEW YORK

MOB KIDNAPS JOE BANANAS

FBI JOINS KIDNAPER SEARCH

Bill Bonanno felt feverish and dizzy. He sank into a chair, his mind racing with confusion and disbelief. The headlines, large letters spreading across the entire page, more prominent than the war in Vietnam and the social revolution in America, seemed to be screaming at him and demanding a reply, and he wanted to react quickly, to run somewhere to do something violent, hating the feeling of being helpless and trapped. But he forced himself to sit and read every paragraph. Most of the newspaper articles suggested that Joseph Bonanno was already dead, possibly encased in concrete and resting in a river. There was some speculation that he was being held hostage until he made certain concessions, and there was even a theory that the kidnaping was a hoax arranged by Joseph Bonanno himself as a way of avoiding an appearance before a federal grand jury meeting in Manhattan later in the week.

17

The younger Bonanno discounted the last point as absurd. He was convinced that his father had intended to appear before the grand jury as he had before others in the past—revealing nothing, of course, but at least appearing and pleading his innocence or seeking refuge in his constitutional rights. Bill Bonanno also did not believe that his father would have attempted anything so tricky as a staged kidnaping without first consulting with Labruzzo and himself.

He watched Labruzzo pacing back and forth through the room like a caged animal. Labruzzo still had said nothing. Normally calm, he seemed at this moment nervous and fearful. Aware that he was being observed, Labruzzo turned and, as if trying to reestablish his position as a cool man under pressure, said almost casually, "Look, if it's true that he's dead, there's nothing we can do about it."

"If it's true," Bonanno replied, "they're going to be looking for us next."

Labruzzo was again silent. Bonanno got up to turn on the television set and the radio for late news. He wondered if the location of their apartment was known to outsiders, and he also tried to figure out which men from his own organization might have collaborated in his father's capture, feeling certain that it had been handled partly from the inside. How else would they have known that Joseph Bonanno had planned to spend the night at Maloney's place? Everything had been done so neatly, the two gunmen appearing on Park Avenue just as the elder Bonanno stepped out of a cab, and Maloney, getting out first, running ahead through the rain and not seeing anything until after it had happened. Maloney might have been part of the deal, Bonanno thought, Maloney or one of the lawyers in his firm who knew of Joseph Bonanno's plans.

Bill Bonanno, like his father, was suspicious of most lawyers. Lawyers were servants of the court, part of the system, which meant that they could never be trusted entirely—or they were Mafia buffs, men who enjoyed being on the fringe of the gangster's world, who were fascinated no doubt by the occasional glimpses they got into the secret society. Sometimes they even became involved in Mafia intrigue, giving advice to one don or another, and shifting sides as the odds changed—it was a kind of game with them. And no matter which faction won or lost, the lawyers survived. They lived to accompany their clients to

the courthouse, and they later made statements to the press—
they were a privileged clique, highly publicized, highly paid,
often crooked but rarely caught, *they* were the untouchables.
Bonanno remembered having heard years ago of how the Mafia
dons had complained among themselves about the exorbitant
fees charged by certain lawyers after the police raided the Apalachin conference. A few dons claimed to have paid about
$50,000 each for their legal defense, and since much of this was
paid in cash, as the lawyers had requested, the mafiosi could
only guess at the amount on which no taxes were paid. While
Bonanno did not know Maloney or his legal partners personally
or professionally, he nevertheless suspected the worst until evidence proved otherwise—they were lawyers, after all, they lived
off other people's misery.

As for the men who provided the muscle in the kidnaping,
Bonanno assumed that they had the approval of the Mafia's national commission, which had recently suspended Joseph Bonanno from its membership. He also assumed that they acted
under the personal direction of the Mafia boss in Buffalo, the
senior member of the commission, seventy-three-year-old Stefano Magaddino, his father's cousin and former friend from Castellammare. Magaddino's apparent bitterness toward the elder
Bonanno was a subject often discussed within the Bonanno organization in 1963 and 1964. It was believed to be based partly
on the fact that Magaddino, whose territory extended from western New York into the Ohio Valley and included links with Canadian racketeers in Toronto, felt threatened by Joseph
Bonanno's ambitions in Canada. For decades the Bonanno organization had worked in partnership with a group of mafiosi in
Montreal, sharing most profitably in the importation of untaxed
alcohol as well as in gambling and other illegal activities, including the control of the pizza trade and various protection
rackets in Montreal's large Italian community. In 1963, when
Joseph Bonanno applied for Canadian citizenship, Magaddino
interpreted this as further evidence that Bonanno's Canadian
interests were going to extend into Magaddino's territory, and
he was overheard one day complaining of Bonanno: "He's
planting flags all over the world!"

Even though Bonanno's petition for Canadian citizenship was
denied and was followed by his expulsion, Magaddino's suspicions persisted. The feeling was not based on any one issue,

Bonanno's men believed, but was inspired by a combination of fear and jealousy. They remembered Magaddino's dark mood on the night of Bill Bonanno's wedding reception in 1956, how he had stood near the dais surveying the great gathering of mafiosi who had come from all parts of the nation out of respect for Joseph Bonanno, and Magaddino said in a loud voice to a man at his table: "Look at this crowd. Who the hell's going to be able to talk to my cousin now? This will go to his head."

Bill Bonanno also sensed how little Magaddino thought of him, and how upset the Buffalo boss had become when the elder Bonanno sanctioned his elevation to number three man in the Bonanno organization and overlooked a member that Magaddino considered more worthy of promotion—Magaddino's own brother-in-law, Gaspar Di Gregorio. Di Gregorio had been a member of the Bonanno organization for thirty years, and until recent months Bill Bonanno believed that Di Gregorio was one of his father's most loyal followers. He was a quiet, unassuming gray-haired man of fifty-nine who ran a coat factory in Brooklyn and was virtually unknown to the FBI. Born in Castellammare, he fought alongside the elder Bonanno in the famous Brooklyn gang war of 1930, and a year later he was the best man when Joseph Bonanno married Fay Labruzzo. He was also Bill Bonanno's godfather, a friend and adviser during the younger Bonanno's years as an adolescent and student, and it was difficult for Bonanno to figure out when and why Di Gregorio had decided to pull away from the Bonanno organization and lure others with him. Di Gregorio had always been a follower, not a leader, and Bill Bonanno could only conclude that Magaddino had finally succeeded after years of effort to use Di Gregorio as the dividing wedge in the Bonanno organization. Di Gregorio took with him perhaps twenty or thirty men, perhaps more—Bill Bonanno could only guess, for there was no easy way for him to know who stood where at this point. Maybe fifty of the 300-man Bonanno family had defected in the last month, influenced by the commission's decision to suspend the elder Bonanno and encouraged by Magaddino's assurance that the commission would protect them from reprisals by Bonanno loyalists.

No matter what the situation was, Bill Bonanno knew that he could only wait. With his father gone, perhaps dead, it was important that he remain alive to deal with whatever had to be done. To venture outdoors at this point would be foolish and maybe suicidal. If the police did not spot him, Magaddino's men might. So Bonanno tried to suppress the fury and the despair that he felt and to resign himself to the long wait with Labruzzo. The phone was ringing now, the third code call in the past five minutes—the captains were reporting in from other apartments, available for any message he might wish to leave with the answering service. He would call in a few moments to let them know that he was all right.

It was noon. Through the venetian blinds he could see that it was a dark, dreary day. Labruzzo was sitting at the kitchen table drinking coffee, the dog at his feet. The pantry was well stocked with canned goods and boxes of pasta, and there was plenty of meat and sauce in the refrigerator. Bonanno, a fair cook, would now have lots of practice. They could exist here easily for several days. Only the dog would miss the outdoors.

Bonanno and Labruzzo lived in confinement for nearly a week, sleeping in shifts with their guns strapped to their chests. They were visited at night by the few men they trusted. One of these was a captain named Joe Notaro. He had been close to the Bonannos for years and was respected for his judgment and caution. But on his first visit to the apartment, Notaro admitted with regret and embarrassment that he had probably been indirectly responsible for the elder Bonanno's capture.

He recalled that on the day of the kidnaping he was sitting in his car discussing Joseph Bonanno's plans for the evening with another officer, speaking in a tone loud enough to be heard by the driver. Notaro's driver was a meek little man who had been with the organization for a number of years and had never been taken seriously by the members. As Notaro was later astonished to discover, the driver was then working as an informer for the Di Gregorio faction. The driver had apparently held a grudge against the organization ever since one of the captains had taken away his girl friend, and Joseph Bonanno was too preoccupied at the time with other matters to intercede in the driver's behalf. The fact that the offending captain was later sentenced to a long jail term on a conspiracy charge in a narcotics case had not soothed the driver's wounded ego. After Bonanno's capture, the driver had disappeared, and Notaro just learned that he was now driving for Di Gregorio's group.

Among other bits of information picked up by Notaro and his
fellow officers from their sources around town—from bookmakers and loan sharks, from the men who work in nightclubs
and in related businesses linked socially to the underworld—
was that Joseph Bonanno was not yet dead and was being held
by Magaddino's men at a farm somewhere in the Catskill Mountains in upstate New York. The FBI and the police were reported
to be concentrating their efforts in that area, and they had also
visited Bonanno's home in Tucson and were keeping watch on
the late Joe Magliocco's mansion, considering it an ideal hideaway because of its protective walls and the private dock. As
for the status of the organization, Bonanno's officers believed
that more than 200 men were still loyal and that their morale
was high. Most of the men were remaining indoors, the officers
said, and were sleeping in shifts and doing their own cooking
in their apartments and rented rooms. Bonanno and Labruzzo
were told that at one apartment the men had complained at
dinner the previous evening that the spaghetti had a metallic
taste—they later learned that the cook, while vigorously stirring
the meat sauce, had knocked his pistol out of his chest holster
into the pot.

With each visit the officers brought the latest papers, and Bonanno and Labruzzo could see that the kidnaping episode was
continuing to receive enormous coverage. Pictures of the younger
Bonanno appeared in several papers, and there was speculation
that he too had been taken by his father's enemies, or that he
was hiding in New York or Arizona, or that he was in the protective custody of federal agents. When a reporter had telephoned FBI headquarters to verify this, an agency spokesman
refused to comment.

The headline writers were having fun with the story, Bonanno
could see—YES, WE HAVE NO BANANAS—and reporters were also
keeping a close watch on his wife and children at home in East
Meadow, Long Island. One paper described Rosalie as leaning
out of a window to reply to a reporter, in a "trembling voice,"
that she knew nothing of her husband's whereabouts, and her
eyes were said to be "red-rimmed" as if she had been crying.
Another newspaper, describing her as very pretty and shy, said
she had spent part of the afternoon in a beauty parlor. A third
paper reported that Bonanno's seven-year-old son, Charles,
while playing on the sidewalk in front of the house, had been

approached by a detective asking questions about his father but the boy replied that he knew nothing. Bill Bonanno was very pleased.

He had trained his children well, he thought. He had cautioned them, as his own father had once cautioned him, to be careful when speaking with strangers. He did not want his children to be curt or disrespectful to anyone, including the police, but he warned them to be on guard when asked about matters pertaining to their home or parents, their relatives, or the friends of relatives. He had also conveyed to his children his disapproval of tattletales. If they saw their brothers, sisters, or cousins doing something wrong, he had said, it was improper for them to go talebearing to adults, adding that nobody had respect for a stool pigeon, not even those who gained by such information.

Sitting quietly in the apartment, after Notaro had left and Labruzzo was sleeping, Bonanno remembered an incident earlier in the year when his advice to his children seemed to boomerang. The family was spending the day at a relative's home in Brooklyn, and during the afternoon one of the aunts complained that the little wagon she kept in the backyard for hauling laundry had been taken and that the children, who had been playing with it earlier, claimed not to know who had taken it out of the yard. Bonanno then approached the children, lining them up for questioning, and when none gave any information about the wagon, he said in a forceful tone that he was going to take a walk around the block and that when he returned he wanted to see the wagon back in the yard. He did not care who had taken it, there would be no punishment; he just wanted it back. After his walk, Bonanno returned to the yard. The children were out of sight, but the wagon had reappeared.

While Bonanno was not overly concerned about his children's well-being during his absence, knowing Rosalie's capabilities as a mother, he was worried about the loneliness and anxiety that she would undoubtedly feel each night after the four children went to sleep. Her mother, who lived forty-five minutes away in Brooklyn, would certainly visit; but Mrs. Profaci did not drive a car, and it would not be easy for her to arrange transportation. Her relatives, as well as most relatives on the Bonanno side of the family, were hesitant about appearing at Bill Bonanno's home, fearing the publicity and the police investigation that might follow. Bonanno's sister, Catherine, who feared

neither publicity nor the police, would have been a great comfort
to Rosalie but she lived in California with her husband and young
children. Bonanno's mother was probably in Arizona, or else
living in seclusion with friends. And his eighteen-year-old
brother, Joseph, Jr., was a student at Phoenix College. Knowing
Joseph, he doubted that he was attending classes very often.
Joseph was the wild one of the family, a drag racer, a bronco
rider, a nonconformist who was so thoroughly undisciplined that
he could never become a member of the organization, Bill Bonanno felt sure. The elder Bonanno had been on the run during
much of his younger son's adolescence, dodging the Kefauver
committee or the McClellan committee or some other investigation or threat; and Joseph, Jr. had been left under the super-
vision of his mother, who could not control him. In any case,
Joseph, Jr. was now in Phoenix, and Rosalie was in Long Island,
and Bill Bonanno only hoped that she could manage things alone
and not crack under the continued pressure that she had been
forced to face in recent years.

He knew that Rosalie would probably be surprised if she knew
his thoughts at this moment, having heard her accuse him so
often of caring only about "those men" and never about her.
But he was sincerely concerned about her, and was also aware
of a certain guilt within himself which would be hard to admit,
at least to a wife. That he loved her he had no doubt, but the
responsibilities that he felt toward his father's world, and all that
had happened to him because of it, had destroyed a part of him,
perhaps the better part. He knew that he could not justify much
of what he had done with regard to Rosalie since their marriage,
nor would he try. To himself he saw it all as a temporary escape
from the tight terrifying world that he had inherited, an indul-
gence to his restlessness between the brief moments of action
and interminable hours of boredom, the months of waiting and
hiding and the machinations attached to the most routine act,
like making a telephone call or answering a doorbell—in such a
strange and excruciating world, he had done some damnable
things, but now he could only hope that his wife would concentrate on the present, forgetting the past temporarily. He hoped
that she would run the home efficiently, borrowing money from
her relatives if necessary, and not become overly embarrassed
by what she read in the newspapers, saw on television, or heard
in the street. This was asking a lot, he knew, particularly since

she had not been prepared as a girl for the life she was now leading. He remembered her description of how her family had sought to protect her from reality and how accustomed she had become as a girl to finding holes in the newspapers around the house, sections cut out where there had been photographs or articles dealing with the activities of the Profaci organization.

His homelife as a boy had been different. His father had never seemed defensive about any aspect of his life, seeming only proud and self-assured. The elder Bonanno had somehow suggested the nature of his life so gradually and casually, at least to Bill, that the ultimate realization of it was neither shocking nor disillusioning. As a boy Bonanno had noticed his father's rather odd working hours. His father seemed either to be home all day and out at night or to be at home constantly for weeks and then gone for weeks. It was very irregular, unlike the routines of the fathers of the boys Bill had first gone to school with in Long Island. But he was also aware that his father was a busy man, involved in many things, and at first this awareness satisfied his curiosity about his father and seemed to explain why his father kept a private office in the house.

During this period of Bill Bonanno's life, in the 1940s, his father had a cheese factory in Wisconsin, coat factories and a laundry in Brooklyn, and a dairy farm in Middletown, New York, on which were forty head of cattle and two horses, one named after Bill and the other after Catherine. The family's home was in Hempstead, Long Island, a spacious two-story red-brick Tudor-style house with lovely trees and a garden, not far from East Meadow, where Rosalie and Bill now lived. The family moved to Hempstead from Brooklyn in 1938, and Bill attended school in Long Island for four years, until a serious ear infection, a mastoid condition that required operations, led to his being transferred to schools in the dry climate of Arizona. His father selected a boarding school in Tucson and would come to Arizona with his wife to visit Bill for the entire winter, renting an apartment there at first, later buying a house. Within four or five years Bill gradually became aware of the many men who frequently visited his father there, men who seemed respectful and deferential. These were many of the same men he remembered seeing around the house as a boy in Long Island; and he also recalled a particular cross-country automobile trip that the Bonanno family had taken years before, when Bill was about

eight years old, traveling from New York to California, visiting
the Grand Canyon and other sites, and in every large city in
which they stopped his father seemed to know numbers of people, friendly men who made a great fuss over young Bill and his
sister.

After Bill Bonanno got his driver's license, which was obtain-
able at sixteen in Arizona, his father sometimes asked him to
meet certain men arriving at the Tucson train station or the airport, men Bill knew well now and had become fond of—they
were like uncles to him. When he eventually began to recognize
these same men's photographs in newspapers and magazines
and to read articles describing them as thugs and killers, he
concluded, after a brief period of confusion and doubt, that the
newspapers were uninformed and prejudiced. The characterization of the men in the stories bore little resemblance to the
men he knew.

Perhaps his first personal involvement with his father's world
occurred while he was a student at Tucson Senior High School
in 1951, on a day when he was called out of class and told to
report to the principal's office. The principal seemed upset as
he asked, "Bill, are you in any kind of trouble with the law?"

"No," Bonanno said.

"Well, there are two men from the FBI in my outer office,"
the principal said, adding, "Look, Bill, you don't have to talk
to them if you don't want to."

"I have nothing to hide," he said.

"Would you prefer that I be present?"

"Sure, if you want to."

The principal led Bill Bonanno, who was seventeen, into the
outer office and introduced him to the agents, who asked if he
knew anything about the disappearance and possible murder of
the Mafia boss Vincent Mangano. Bill Bonanno said that he
knew nothing about it. He had heard that name before, but it
had been in connection with James Mangano, who had an asthmatic daughter and had rented the Bonannos' Tucson home one
summer when they were away. The agents took notes, asked a
few more questions, then left. Bill Bonanno returned to his
classroom somewhat shaken. He felt the eyes of the other students on him, but he did not face anyone as he took his seat; he
felt separated from his classmates in a way that he had not felt
before.

It was a feeling, he was sure, that Rosalie never had as a girl, and he even wondered if she had it now. She seemed totally unaware and naïve about his world. While he occasionally interpreted this as self-protectiveness on her part, a determination to ignore what she disapproved of, he also believed sometimes that his wife was genuinely remote from reality, as if her parents had really fulfilled their ambition to separate Rosalie from the embarrassing aspects of their past. But this could not be entirely true, for if they had really wished to separate her from themselves they would never have condoned her marriage to him. Still, for whatever reason, his wife's quality of detachment irritated him at times, and he hoped that now, following his father's disappearance, she would respond to the emergency and do nothing foolish or careless. He hoped, for example, that when she left their house with the children she would remember to lock the front and back doors and would be certain that all the windows were securely bolted. He was worried that FBI men, posing as burglars, would break into the house and infest the interior with electronic bugs. They often did this, he had heard. They would enter a house and overturn a few pieces of furniture and plow through the bureau drawers and closets, giving the impression that they were thieves looking for valuables, but what they really were doing was installing bugs. Once the agents got into a house, he knew, it was nearly impossible to detect their little handiwork, conceding that in this area the FBI was very creative and clever. He knew of a case in which the agents had even bugged a house *before* the carpenters finished building it. It happened to Sonny Franzese, an officer in the Profaci organization; the agents had apparently gone to the construction site of Franzese's new home in Long Island after the workmen had left for the day, inserting bugs into the framework and foundation. Franzese later wondered why the agents knew so much about him.

Bill Bonanno kept an electronic debugging device in his closet at home, a kind of plastic divining rod with an antenna that was supposed to vibrate when sensing bugs, but he was not sure how trustworthy it was. If the agents did get into his house, he was sure that they could find some things that would serve as evidence against him. They would find a few rifles in the garage and pistols in his bedroom bureau. They might find a false identification card or two and various driver's licenses and passports.

They would discover his vast collection of quarters, several dollars' worth neatly packed in long thin plastic tubes that fit into the glove compartment of his car and were used for long-distance calls at telephone booths. The agents would probably help themselves to the excellent Havana cigars that he remembered having left on the top of his bedroom bureau, in a jar that also contained Q-tip cotton swabs on sticks that he used for draining his left ear in the morning, the infected ear that had gotten him to Arizona, where he wished he was at this moment. The agents might be interested in some of the books in his library, which included three books on the FBI and all the books about the Mafia, including ones by Senators Kefauver and McClellan. They would find several other books that he suspected would be over the agents' heads—the Churchill volumes, books by Bertrand Russell, Arthur Koestler, Sartre, and the poetry of Dante. But there was one book that they would surely like to thumb through—the large photo album of his wedding. The album, which consisted of several photographs of the reception, including the crowded ballroom scene at the Astor, would identify most of the distinguished guests; and what the album failed to reveal, the movie of the wedding, packed in a tin can at the bottom of a bookshelf, *would* reveal. There was more than 2,000 feet of home-movie film on the wedding, and he and Rosalie had enjoyed looking at it from time to time during the past seven years. The wedding event, the extravagance and splendor of it, probably marked the highpoint of Joseph Bonanno's life, the pinnacle of his prestige; and a social historian of the underworld, should one ever exist, might describe the event as the "last of the great gangster weddings," coming before the Apalachin exposure and other vexations had put an end to such displays.

One of the things that most fascinated Bill Bonanno about the film, after he had seen it three or four times, was what it revealed about the caste-consciousness of the mafiosi who attended, and no doubt the FBI would be equally interested if it could review the film. By observing the way that a mafioso dressed, one could determine his rank within the organization. The lower-echelon men, Bonanno had noticed, all wore white dinner jackets to the wedding, while the middle-level men, the lieutenants and captains, wore light blue dinner jackets. The top men, the dons, all were dressed in black tuxedos, except, of course, the principal males in the wedding party, who wore cutaways.

* * *

On November 5, which was Bill Bonanno's thirty-second birthday and was fifteen days after the elder Bonanno's disappearance, five of the Bonanno officers decided that they had had all the confinement they could stand—they needed a short vacation. Bill Bonanno agreed. It did not appear that their enemies planned an armed confrontation at this time, not with so many police on the alert, and Bonanno also welcomed a change of scenery. He sent word to Rosalie through one of his men that he was alive. The question facing Bonanno now was where to go to find rest and relaxation and not attract attention. He and his men could not fly south because the airports were too well patrolled and, even with their disguises, they might be spotted. He also did not want to venture too far from New York because there was always the chance of some new development concerning his father. They would have to use their cars, traveling at night. After a few hours of thought, Bonanno decided that they should visit the ski country of New England. None of the men had ever been on skis, nor did they intend to try. They merely wished to experience again the act of movement, to travel over open roads in the brisk outdoors, to clear their minds, recharge the batteries of their cars, and walk their dogs away from the repressive environment of New York.

They left that evening within the first hour of darkness. Two men to a car, they planned to meet at a large motel near Albany. Bonanno's green Cadillac was parked a block away, under a lamplight. He approached it slowly and carefully, alert for any movement or sound around the car or along the dark street. Labruzzo followed several feet behind, holding the dog on a leash with his left hand and keeping his right hand free for his gun.

Lowering a suitcase to the ground, Bonanno walked around the car, which was covered with dust and a few fallen leaves. He examined the front fenders and the hood for fingerprints, as he always did before unlocking the door, in an attempt to detect any bombs planted within the vehicle. Confident that the car had not been touched since he had left it, he got in and turned on the ignition. The car started up immediately, which did not surprise him, for he had always maintained it to perfection, changing the batteries and other engine parts long before they ceased to function properly.

Sitting in the car waiting for Labruzzo, stretching his long thin legs and pressing his broad back against the cold soft leather seats, he felt a renewed sense of appreciation for the car, its powerful engine idling quietly, its gleaming dashboard adorned with a stereo. It was a big comfortable car for a tall heavy man of his size, and he guessed that his weight had increased by ten or fifteen pounds during the last few weeks of tension, confinement, and overeating. He was probably between 235 and 240 pounds, and he felt it. Though his legs were still lean and though his large frame could easily support extra weight, his face could not; and as he leaned toward the rearview mirror, he saw that he bore little resemblance to his recent newspaper photos. His lower jaw and cheeks were heavier, and with his beard, his plain glass horn-rimmed glasses, and the snap-brim hat that he wore as part of his disguise, he imagined that he looked like a jazz musician, a fat jazz musician. The image repulsed him. He hated being overweight, imagining that almost every extra pound he put on over 225 went to his face, especially the lower part of his face, making him jowly, squarish, double-chinned; it emphasized his heavy beard and deemphasized his attractive features, his strong cheek bones, his deep-set gentle brown eyes, his delicately arched eyebrows. In his present condition, in fact, the upper portion of his face seemed mismatched with the lower part—if a line were drawn across the middle of his face below his nose, the upper part would appear to belong to a man ten years younger than the part below: above the line the eyes were innocent, trustworthy, and the skin was light and clear; below the line was the heavy dark jaw, and the folds of flesh and puffiness of the middle-aged man that Bill Bonanno would become should he live that long.

After Frank Labruzzo deposited the dog in the back seat and the gun under the front seat, the two men began the slow ride through the side streets of Queens that Bonanno knew so well. Within a half hour they were rolling smoothly on the highway, saying little as they listened to the stereo, the lights of the city behind them. Bonanno was delighted to be leaving New York. He had never liked the city very much, and recently he had come to hate it. He often wondered why so many mafiosi, men with roots in the sunny agrarian lands of southern Europe, had settled in this cold polluted jungle crowded with cops and nosy newsmen, with hazards of every conceivable nature. The Mafia bosses in the South, or in the Far West, in places like Boulder, Colorado, undoubtedly lived a much better life than any of the five dons with organizations centered in New York City. The don in Colorado probably owned a trucking business or a little nightclub and, with only ten or twelve men under his command, ran a few gambling parlors or a numbers racket on the side. He worked regular hours, probably played golf every afternoon, and had time in the evening for his family. His sons would graduate from college, becoming business executives or lawyers, and would know how to steal legally.

The five dons in New York each commanded forces of between 250 and 500 men, meaning that approximately 2,000 mafiosi—forty percent of the national membership of 5,000—were in New York fighting the traffic and one another. The New York dons never felt secure no matter how much power they had. Why did they remain? Bonanno knew the answer, of course. New York was where the big money was. It was the great marketplace, the center of everything. Each day a million trucks came rolling into or out of New York—it was a hijacker's paradise, a town of tall shadows, sharp angles, and crooked people from top to bottom. Most New Yorkers, from the police to the prostitutes, were on the take or on the make. Even the average citizen seemed to enjoy breaking the law or beating the system in some way. Part of the success of the numbers racket, which was the Mafia's most lucrative source of income, was that it was illegal. If the lawmakers would legitimize numbers betting it would hurt business because it would deprive customers of that satisfactory sense of having beaten the system, of having outwitted the police and the august judiciary, with the mere placing of a bet. It was the same satisfactory sense that people got forty years ago when they dealt with their bootlegger or were admitted into an all-night speakeasy.

New York was also a marvelous place in which to hide. One could get lost in the crowds of New York, could blend in with the blurring sights, movement, shadows, and confusion. People tended to mind their own business in New York, to remain uninvolved with the affairs of their neighbors, and this was a great asset for men in hiding. Bonanno knew that one of his father's captains, a man named John Morale, had been hiding from federal authorities for twenty years and was still in circulation, living most of the time at his home in a neighborhood of nondescript houses in Queens. Morale came and went at odd hours, never following a predictable routine, and his family had been trained in ways that would not expose him by word or act.

Bonanno's father once concealed himself for more than a year in Brooklyn, during the gangland discord of 1929–1930, a time when a rival boss had issued a "contract" for his death. Bill Bonanno was sure that if his father was still alive he could hide indefinitely in New York because he possessed the necessary discipline. Discipline was the main requirement. Disguises and hideaways, false identification cards, and loyal friends were important, but individual discipline was the essential factor, combining the capacity to change one's routine, to adjust to solitude, to remain alert without panicking, to avoid the places and people that had frequently been visited in the past. When his father went into hiding in 1929, a time when he had been actively courting Fay Labruzzo, he suddenly and without explanation stopped appearing at her home. She heard nothing from him for several months and assumed that their engagement was terminated. Then one of her brothers-in-law noticed that the window shades of the building directly opposite the Labruzzo home, on Jefferson Street in Brooklyn, had been down for a long time, and later he saw the glimmer of rifle barrels poised behind the small opening at the bottom of the shades, obviously waiting for Bonanno to appear in front of the Labruzzo home.

Bill Bonanno was confident that, if he had to, he could hide in New York for a very long time. He believed that he had discipline, that he would not panic if the search parties were getting close, that he had a certain talent for elusiveness. Even now, driving at night on the New York Thruway, obeying the speed limit, he was aware of every car that followed him, the arrangements of their headlights in his rearview mirror. Whenever he passed a car he observed its body style, the license plate, tried to get a look at the driver, and his alertness intensified whenever a car behind him gained speed to pass. He tried to maintain a certain distance between himself and the others, shifting lanes or reducing speed when necessary. Since he had carefully studied the road map before the trip, as he did before every trip, he knew the exits, the detours, the possible routes of escape.

Whenever he planned to remain in a single town or certain area for a few days, he familiarized himself not only with the streets but also with the hill formations and arrangements of trees along certain roads that might temporarily obscure his car as he drove it from the view of drivers behind him. He actually charted out zones of obscurity into which he would drive when he felt he was being followed, particular places where the road dipped or curved and was joined by an alternate route. Whenever he sensed that he was being tailed in Long Island, for example, he led his possible pursuers into Garden City, where he was intimately familiar with several short curving roads that linked with other roads, and he knew several places where the roads dipped, then rose, then dipped again, stretches where his car vanished from sight for several seconds if his followers were keeping at a subtle distance. He also knew perhaps seven ways to get into and out of Garden City, and anyone who followed him into that city—whether federal agents or unfriendly *amici*—was almost sure to lose him.

Another reason that Bonanno had confidence in his ability to hide was that loneliness did not bother him. He had adjusted to it as a teen-ager in Arizona when he lived alone in a motel room, later in his parents' home, each year between fall and winter while his parents were in New York—an arrangement made necessary by his eviction at the age of fifteen from his boarding school dormitory because one day he had led a group of classmates, who were supposed to be visiting a museum, into a film house showing the controversial *Forever Amber*. He remembered how embittered he was by the punishment, which permitted him to attend classes but prohibited his remaining on campus at night. He was also surprised by his father's lack of influence with the headmaster, who had accepted generous gifts from the Bonannos in the past, including large shipments of cheese for the school from the factory in Wisconsin, and also butter when it was scarce because of World War II rationing. His parents, remaining in New York because of his father's activities, could do nothing after the eviction but arrange for him to stay at the Luna Motel, which was owned by a friend of the elder Bonanno and was close to a bus stop where Bill could get a ride to school.

In angry response to his punishment, Bill withdrew his horse from the school's stable. He kept the animal in a yard behind the motel. The horse and a miniature Doberman pinscher, the same type of dog that was in his car now as he drove upstate,

were his main companions during those months his parents were
away, and he became very independent and self-reliant. Each
morning he got up by himself and made his own breakfast. He
spent many evenings alone in the motel room listening to the
radio. He remembered the sound of the fast-talking Gary Moore
on the Jimmy Durante show and the reassuring voice of Dr.
Christian. Occasionally at sunset he took long rides on his horse
through the Arizona desert, passing the ranches of the rich, the
smoking mud huts of the Zuñi tribesmen, the dusty wranglers
and bronco riders who nodded toward him as he passed.

He had first ridden a horse as a three-year-old boy in Long
Island, riding on weekends with his father and the other men.
Many of Bonanno's men were superb horsemen, having ridden
as small boys in Sicily where horses and donkeys were the main
means of transportation; and Bill had many photographs of himself galloping with the mafiosi on weekends through the woods
in Long Island. His father insisted from the beginning that he
ride a full-sized horse, not a pony, and his pride in his equestri-
anship compensated to a degree for his lack of achievement as
an athlete when he got to high school.

It was not his ear ailment so much as his parents' travel sched-
ule that limited his participation in organized sports. He wanted
to join the football team at Tucson Senior High School, but he
was with his parents in New York when football practice began
in August. In the winter and spring, when his parents were in
Arizona, he spent considerable time with his father after school
hours. His life was one of extremes: either he was entirely alone,
or he was encircled by his family and his father's friends. There
were times when he wanted to escape the extremes, and not
long after his eviction from boarding school he took some money
and ran away. He boarded a bus for New York, a five-day journey, and on arriving at the terminal on Forty-third Street off
Broadway he took another bus upstate to the family farm in
Middletown, which was close to where he was driving at this
moment on the New York State Thruway, and he was tempted
now to pull off the main road and briefly revisit the farm that
his father had since sold. He resisted the temptation, although
he continued to think about his visit to the farm many years ago,
remembering how upset the farmers were when he arrived, saying that his father had telephoned and had just flown to Tucson
in an attempt to find him.

Within a few days the elder Bonanno arrived at the farm, angry at first, but then his anger subsided. He admitted that he had also run away at fifteen, in Sicily, and he thought that perhaps such experiences were part of a boy's growing up. He nevertheless talked his son into returning to school in Tucson, where a new yellow Jeep would await him.

Once back in Arizona, Bill also arranged to visit a doctor. He had had stomach pains sporadically during the year, and after a medical examination it was determined that he had an ulcer.

3

By most people's definition the trip by Bonanno, Labruzzo, and the other men through New York State into New England would hardly qualify as a vacation: it consisted largely of driving hundreds of miles each day and remaining in motels at night, watching television, and talking among themselves.

After Albany they drove through Bennington, Vermont, and continued on up to Burlington along Lake Champlain. They then headed east into New Hampshire, then south two days later into Massachusetts. The travel route was charted each morning by one of the men who was a native New Englander, and they met each night at predetermined places before they registered, in pairs, at separate motels which were close to one another and had suites with kitchenettes.

They shopped for groceries at local stores and, after walking the dogs, gathered at night in Bonanno's suite where the cooking was done. Bonanno had brought with him in his attaché case various spices and herbs and also a paperback edition of James Beard's cookbook. Each night he cooked and the other men cleaned up afterward. He was impressed with the modernization of motels since his boyhood days at the Luna—in addition to the streamlined kitchenettes there were the ice-making machines, body vibrators installed in the beds, wall-to-wall carpeting, color television, and cocktail lounges that provided room service.

The most relaxing part of the trip for Bonanno was the act of driving—moving for dozens of miles without pausing for a traffic jam or even a signal light—and observing the tranquillity of small towns and imagining the peaceful existence of those who occupied them. Occasionally he passed cars driven by young people with skis strapped onto the roofs and college emblems stuck to the windows and the Greek letters of fraternities that he could identify, and he was constantly reminded of how far he had drifted from the campus life he had known a decade ago.

It had been a gradual drifting, occurring so slowly over the years that he did not really know when he had crossed the border into his father's world. During most of his college career, which had begun in the summer of 1951 and had extended irregularly through 1956, he lived a kind of dual existence. At certain times, particularly when his father seemed to be at odds with other bosses or to be hounded by federal agents, he had felt both a desire and a responsibility to stand by his father, to lend verbal and emotional support even though his father had not requested it, saying instead that he wanted Bill to remain in school concentrating on his studies. And there were times when Bill's interests seemed to be centered entirely around the campus—he attended classes punctually, joined student groups, supported the football team. He was gregarious and generous, was popular with his classmates; he always had a car and a girl.

But as a student he had limited powers of concentration, seeming to lose interest in subjects that he could not master quickly. He had grown accustomed in high school to making the grade with a minimum of effort because of his superior education in boarding school, but in college this advantage did not exist. He was also distracted by an increasing awareness of his father and by the conflicts that he began to recognize in himself. While he did not want to inherit his father's problems, did not want to be identified with gangsterism and suffer the social ostracism that resulted from exposure in the press, he also did not want to separate himself from his father's circumstances or feel apologetic or defensive about his name, particularly since he did not believe that his father was guilty of crimes against society. Sometimes the reverse was true, society was using such men as Joseph Bonanno to pay for the widespread sins in the system. In any case, no matter how damaging the consequences might be to himself, he could not turn against his father, nor did he really want to. His emotional link with his father was very strong, exceeding the normal bond of filial fidelity. It was more intense, more unquestioning, there was a unity in the tension they both shared and a certain romanticism about the risks and dangers involved, and there was also a kind of religious overtone in the relationship, a combination of blind faith and fear, formality and love. The many long periods of separation had in a strange

way drawn them closer, had made each visit an event, a time of
reunion and rejoicing, and during their months apart Bill's
youthful imagination and memory had often endowed his father
with qualities approximating a deity, so impressive, absolute,
and almost foreign was the elder Bonanno in person.

Joseph Bonanno was handsome in ways both strong and serene; he had soft brown eyes, a finely etched face, and a benign
expression that was evident even in photographs taken by the
police. Considering that police photographers and the tabloid
cameramen were rarely flattering and usually made Mafia suspects appear grim and sinister, Bill thought it remarkable that
his father seemed gracious and composed in nearly every one
of the hundreds of news photos and police posters that were
displayed in recent years—including the latest ones circulated
since his disappearance. *Never let anyone know how you feel*,
Joseph Bonanno told his son, and Bill tried to follow the advice.
He remembered an occasion years ago when he accepted an
invitation to appear on Alumni Day at his old boarding school:
after he delivered a pleasant little speech to the students expressing the hope that his own children might one day benefit from
the school's fine principles, he walked across the stage smiling
and shook the hand of the headmaster who had evicted him from
the dormitory.

During the drive through New England he remembered several incidents from his past that had seemed inconsequential
when they occurred, but now in retrospect they revealed the
double life he led as a boy, the private battles he fought without
knowing he was fighting. He knew then only that his life was
dominated by a soft-spoken man in silk suits who arrived in
Arizona every winter from New York and put an end to Bill's
loneliness, speaking in oracles, offering ancient remedies for
contemporary ailments. He remembered his father directing him
into the desert sun every afternoon to sit on a chair and tilt his
head in such a way as to expose his left ear to the heat, saying
that it would stop the draining; which it had. He remembered a
summer day in Long Island when his sister cut her leg badly
climbing a fence, and his father carried her into the house, placed
her on a table, and squeezed lemon juice into the wound, mas-
saging it in a special way that stopped the bleeding, and after
the wound healed, there was no scar. He recalled how his father
arranged with a judge to free him without penalty after he was

caught speeding without a license when he was thirteen, and he remembered being extricated from other situations, too, boyish pranks or minor crimes during his hot-rodding days in high school, which was about the time he became curious and even intrigued by his father's world.

He often wondered how he would measure up to the men around his father. Sometimes he heard them speaking casually about the danger they faced, or the jails that might await them, and he wondered if he would have been that calm in the circumstances.

The idea of jail both worried and fascinated him in those days, and he remembered when he was once arrested as a high school student. He and a group of boys were at a football game, behaving boisterously throughout the afternoon. They were pushing, shouting, and tossing paper cups, which so irritated other spectators that the police finally evicted them from the stadium and charged them with disorderly conduct. They spent the night in jail, an experience that Bill found interesting during the first hour, but then it quickly palled. And yet he realized that his offensive behavior was deliberate, he really wanted to end up in jail, and he was also somewhat satisfied later that he had remained cool and controlled during confinement.

News of the incident did not reach his father, although his teachers learned of it and were disappointed and surprised. Unlike some boys in the junior class, Bill Bonanno was not thought of as troublesome or rebellious. He was regarded as a student leader; he was president of the student antiliquor club, an organizer of the blood drive, an editor on the magazine. He did not smoke cigarettes, because of a promise he had made one day to an elderly woman he met in a café, a tubercular recuperating in Tucson, that he would avoid the habit. After asking for his pledge in writing on a paper napkin, she handed him a five-dollar bill; he kept his word along with the money and napkin from that day on.

Despite the appearance of propriety and leadership in high school, there were nights when he indulged his restlessness by traveling with a gang of Mexican youths who specialized in stealing Cadillac hubcaps and other auto accessories that could be resold to used-car dealers, junk yards, or to motorists. Some gang members became involved in the summer of 1950 with an older group of gunrunners along the Mexican border, a risky and exciting operation that appealed to him, but he could not pursue it because he had to go East with his parents in June.

He remembered that trip as a strange, tense journey of long silences and new insights into his father's way of life. He had expected his father to let him drive much of the way through Arizona into Texas and onward toward New York, as his father had done during previous trips to New York for the summer, but on the trip in 1950 his father would not relinquish the wheel, and in addition to his mother and baby brother, there was one of his father's men in the car. The route his father followed was different from what had been familiar in the past; they drove through El Paso and Van Horn, avoiding the customary visit to Dallas, and then remained for two days in Brownsville, Texas, where other men arrived to speak with his father. He remembered while stopping for the night in St. Louis that his mother and father were not registered together at the hotel; the elder Bonanno and his companion took one room, and Mrs. Bonanno and the two sons shared a suite elsewhere in the hotel. They left St. Louis in the middle of the night and drove toward Wisconsin, not along the usual roads toward New York.

Through June and most of July they remained in Wisconsin, living in motels or cabins near the lakes north of Green Bay, not arriving in New York until the end of July. Then they settled in a house on the north shore of Long Island, living in seclusion except for the visits of men. It was a mournful summer in which conversations seemed leveled to a whisper and dinner was served every night without the usual clattering of plates or rattling of silver. Bill asked no questions. But he knew what was happening—his father and many of his father's friends were feeling the pressure of the Kefauver committee, and they were trying to avoid subpoenas that would summon them to testify before the Senate and the television cameras.

Although the main target of the committee was Frank Costello, whose appearance was marked by his ill temper under the hot lights as the cameras focused on his nervously tapping fingertips, other names were mentioned in the press that Bill Bonanno was personally familiar with. Joseph Profaci was prominently cited on the Senate crime charts, and so was Joseph Magliocco.

While Joseph Bonanno was also mentioned, he did not receive great attention, and he successfully avoided an appearance before the investigators. Nevertheless, Bonanno was deeply disturbed by the publicity he did get, because it was the first time in years that he was openly associated with organized crime. The elder Bonanno was especially upset because the exposure introduced his daughter to the charges against him, and Catherine, who was then sixteen, broke down and cried for days. But the revelation did not diminish her affection for him. She, like Bill, was filled with compassion, and she actually felt closer to her father than she had before.

After that summer Bill left New York to begin his final term at Tucson Senior High. He borrowed a company car from the Bonanno cheese factory, and accompanied by a school friend, he drove quickly across the country, loving the buoyant sense of escape he felt behind the wheel. He arrived in Arizona a week before classes began. Then he drove an additional 1,200 miles alone to San Antonio to visit a girl he was fond of, the sister of a classmate from his boarding school days. Her father, an industrialist in Michigan, raised polo ponies, and Bill remembered riding them during the visit, galloping over the turf imagining the good life of men in white helmets and jodhpurs, swinging mallets through the sky.

His final year in high school dragged on listlessly, the single memorable event being his father's graduation gift, a new Chevrolet Bel Air hardtop. He began at the University of Arizona that June, contemplating a degree in prelaw, but soon he switched to agricultural engineering, believing it would provide a useful background for the day when he would inherit part of his father's share in a large cotton farm north of Tucson. On reaching twenty-one, he would have in his own name not only land but certain income-producing properties that his father, a skillful real estate speculator, had acquired since coming to Arizona. Bill looked forward to earning his own money, for his father had always been tight about allowances, an inconsistent trait in an otherwise generous man. It was typical of his father to buy him a new car but to provide so little spending money that Bill was usually out of gas.

As a result Bill was compelled to take part-time jobs after school, which was what his father wanted; the elder Bonanno abhorred idleness, and one of his favorite expressions was *the best way to kill time is to work it to death*. Bill had begun working during his early teens, and during his college days he worked at night at a drive-in hamburger stand, where he met a pretty blonde waitress, a divorcee with whom he had his first sexual affair.

Before this time, his experience consisted largely of heavy petting with girls like the one in San Antonio and quick ejaculations into a town tart who first seduced him in the projection room of the Catalina movie house in Tucson on a day no film was shown. Although he had had opportunities with other girls and could have used his parents' home, he never took full advantage of their many absences. He was somewhat puritanical in those days, incapable of sexual activity in his mother's linen, and he did not even hold parties there with his young friends because there was the possibility that outsiders might snoop through his father's things.

The affair with the divorcee was conducted at her apartment, continuing for more than a year without his parents' knowledge. While there had never been talk of marriage he was very possessive of her, and he became infuriated when he heard that she had dated, in his absence, a jockey who was in Arizona for the racing season. The fear of losing her, the first girl he thought he had ever truly had, and the shocking realization that she could make love to him and then date other men filled him with despair. For the first time in his life he recognized his capacity for violence.

He remembered waiting for her in the apartment, then seeing her come up the path with two tiny men, both tailored to the toes in an expensive but flashy way, their small suntanned faces drawn tight across their cheek bones. As she opened the door, laughing at something one of them had said, Bill stepped forward, towering over them, shouting. When one of the men yelled back, Bill grabbed him and shook him, then began to slap him hard against the wall as the girl screamed and the other jockey ran.

Soon the police arrived to arrest Bill for assault. Later in court, however, it had somehow been arranged, perhaps through his father's influence, to have the case heard by a judge who was then rumored to be having an affair with another man's wife. Whether the judge feared that his own indiscretion might be exposed if he ruled harshly in the case, Bill never knew; he knew only that the case against him was dismissed.

The end of the romance was part of a depressing year in

general. He was doing poorly in college; the girl in San Antonio informed him that she was going steady with a Texas football star; and then his father suffered a heart attack and left Tucson to recuperate in a quiet spot near La Jolla, California. Bill was again alone in the house through the winter and spring, and through another session of summer school.

He spent part of the summer at an ROTC camp, preparing for a commission in the army. He adapted easily to the routine of military discipline, and he was soon promoted to drill sergeant in the cadets' elite marching unit, the Pershing Rifles. On the firing range he was a superb marksman with a rifle or pistol—he had had previous target practice at boarding school and was on familiar terms with guns since his boyhood days, when he noticed them bulging from beneath the jackets of men who came to visit his father. But it was after leaving New York for Arizona that he had become most aware of guns, seeing them carried openly and casually by people in cars or on horseback by ranchers, wranglers, and Indians, and he sometimes felt that he was on the set of a cowboy film. And he liked the feeling.

He also liked the clothes, becoming quickly accustomed to wearing boots, hip-hugging pants, and string ties, and his father did the same in Arizona. So did some of his father's men during their extended visits, although the fatter ones always looked uncomfortable and comical in these clothes, their Western buckles lost under their bellies. Nevertheless, a kinship of sorts probably did exist between these men and the legendary American cowboy, Bill thought, impressed by the similarity between the tales of the old West and certain stories he had heard as a boy involving gun battles between mounted mafiosi in the hills of western Sicily. He had heard that his grandmother in Castellammare sometimes packed a pistol in her skirts, a kind of Ma Barker, and the Sicilians of that region today still honor the memory of the bandit Giuliano, a leader of a gang of outlaws who shared what they stole with the poor.

Although Giuliano was a hero in western Sicily he might easily be regarded elsewhere as a common thief—it depended largely on one's point of view, and the same could be said when appraising the life of any man, the activities of any group, the policies of any nation. If Bill Bonanno had learned anything from reading the memories of great statesmen and generals it was that the line between what was right and wrong, moral or

immoral, was often thin indeed, with the final verdict written by
the victors. When he went to ROTC camp, and later into military
service with the Army Reserves, he was trained in the technique
of legal killing. He learned how to use a bayonet, how to fire an
M-1 rifle, how to adjust the range finder of a cannon in a Patton
tank. He memorized the United States military code, which in
principle was not dissimilar from the Mafia's, emphasizing honor,
obedience, and silence if captured. And if he had gone into combat and had killed several North Koreans or Chinese Communists
he might have become a hero. But if he killed one of his father's
enemies in a Mafia war, where buried in the issues was the same
mixture of greed and self-righteousness found in all the wars of
great nations, he could be charged with murder.

In the Mafia today were many American veterans of World
War II, one a decorated infantryman who became Joseph Bonanno's bodyguard. This veteran wore a metal plate in his forehead and had several scars on his body as a result of combat
against the Germans. He had fought in the North African campaign and also participated in the invasion of Sicily in which the
Americans employed local mafiosi as intelligence agents and
underground organizers against the Nazi and Fascist forces.
Many such agents were rewarded with lawful authority by the
Allies after the war, a fact documented in many books about the
Mafia that Bill had read; some of them became the mayors of
towns and officials in the regional government because of their
strong antifascism and hatred of Mussolini. During the Fascist
regime in Italy, Mussolini sponsored a campaign of terror against
the Mafia, torturing many Mafia suspects and without a fair trial
killing many more. When Mussolini himself was captured and
killed, Bill remembered the satisfied reaction of his father and
his father's friends. His father was forced out of Sicily during
his days as a student radical because he had opposed certain
Fascist policies, and as a result he settled in the United States.
Otherwise he might have remained in his native land, and Bill
wondered what it would have been like if he, too, had been born
and had remained in Castellammare. Perhaps life would have
been better. Perhaps it would have been worse.

Although the trip through New England taken by Bill Bonanno, Frank Labruzzo, and the other men was pleasantly uneventful and restful, there gradually developed within Bonanno

a slight nagging feeling that he could not explain. It was as if he had forgotten something, was ignoring an obligation, compromising a trust, was somehow failing to fulfill all that his father might have expected of him. Whatever it was, he reasoned that it must be relatively unimportant, otherwise he would have no difficulty in defining it; and yet it continued to bother him as he drove south along Massachusetts Bay and then headed west toward Concord.

It was getting dark. Soon he and Labruzzo would be stopping at a motel where they would be joined later by the other men for dinner. They had now been on the road for a week, and during that time there had been nothing in the newspapers or on the radio to indicate that the situation had changed in New York. The gangs apparently were still remaining out of sight. There had been no message on Bonanno's answering service requiring an immediate response. The government's search for his father had revealed no clues. Some police officials believed that Joseph Bonanno was still hiding in the Catskills, others believed he was dead. Bill did not know what to believe, and during the past few days he had managed not to think too much about it. Maybe that was what was bothering him. He did not know.

After dinner he wandered off by himself to walk the dog along a narrow dirt road near the highway, leaving the men seated around the television set in his suite. They were watching a crime serial called "The Untouchables," which was based loosely on the Mafia and had angered many Italo-Americans around the nation because the scriptwriters tended to give Italian names to the gangster roles. But the real-life gangsters enjoyed watching the show, Bonanno knew, although they appreciated it on a different level than the producers had intended. The gangsters saw this show, along with others like the FBI series and Perry Mason, as broad comedy or satire. They laughed at lines that were not intended to be funny; they mocked the dim-witted caricatures of themselves; they hooted and jeered the characters representing the FBI or the police, turning television watching into a kind of psychodrama. They seemed mostly to enjoy the Perry Mason serial, whose murder mysteries they could usually solve before the second commercial and whose courtroom scene at the end of each show—a scene in which a prime suspect always collapses under cross-examination and jumps to his feet proclaiming his guilt—they found ridiculously amusing.

Returning to the motel, uncomfortably cold and unaccustomed to the eastern climate after so many winters in Arizona, Bill thought of Rosalie and the children, wishing that he could call them. If only Rosalie were reachable at a phone that was not tapped, he would call her at this moment, and as he thought about this he slowly became excited—he was clarifying what it was that had been bothering him.

He recalled a conversation with his father four months ago in late July immediately after the elder Bonanno had been evicted from Montreal and had returned to the United States. At that time Joseph Bonanno recounted his legal hassle with the Canadian immigration authorities, the frustration of appearing all day in the Montreal courthouse and then not being able to reach Bill at night to talk freely on an untapped phone, and he said that should they ever again be separated for an extended period, they should have some system that would permit them to communicate. Joseph Bonanno then devised a plan—a workable system, Bill had thought at the time, but during the hectic months that followed, culminating in his father's disappearance, Bill had forgotten about his father's proposal. Now, on this November night in Massachusetts, it came back to him.

The plan specified that if they lost contact without explanation, Bill was to go to a particular telephone booth in Long Island on each Thursday evening at eight o'clock sharp until the elder Bonanno was able to call him there. The booth was located next to a diner on Old Country Road between Hicksville and Westbury, and Joseph Bonanno kept a record of that number as he had of dozens of other booths that he had used in the past at prearranged times to speak with one of his men. This specific booth was selected for his son because it was not far from Bill's home and because it had not been used so often in the past that it was likely to be under police surveillance. The booth was also chosen because there was a second telephone booth near it that could be used if the first was busy.

Excitedly, entering the motel, Bill announced to the other men that he was returning to New York early the next morning. He explained the reason, adding that the next day, November 12, was a Thursday. But the men thought it unlikely that the elder Bonanno would call; even if he was alive and unharmed and had not forgotten his arrangement of four months ago, he would probably be too cautious or otherwise unable to make the call, they said. Bill, however, would not be discouraged. If his father was alive, he would make the call, Bill said. If he did not make it this Thursday, then he would make it next Thursday, or the Thursday after that, and Bill said he would be there every time, just in case, until he was convinced that his father was dead. He also pointed out, in a low tone that seemed almost self-accusatory, that when they had left New York a week ago, on the night of November 5, it was a Thursday, and perhaps he had already missed one of his father's calls.

It was agreed that they would return to New York. The other men were to go directly to their apartments, informing the subordinates that they were back in town, while Bonanno and Labruzzo would go on to Long Island.

They arrived in New York shortly before 7:00 P.M., the distant skyline glowing softly in the early-evening light, the last of the commuter traffic moving swiftly out of the city. At a quarter to eight, Bonanno and Labruzzo arrived at the diner on Old Country Road. They turned into the parking lot, stopping near the booth. It was glass-paneled and trimmed in green aluminum, and it was empty. They sat in the car for a few minutes, the motor running, and headlights off. Then, at five before eight, Bonanno got out, walked into the booth, and stood waiting.

He was relieved that the coin slot was not covered with the familiar yellow sticker reading "out of order"; and after depositing a coin and getting the reassuring sound of a dial tone, he replaced the receiver. The condition of coinbox phones was of vital importance to him and the other men, and he knew how infuriated they had all been at one time or another by malfunctioning phones and how they swore vengeance on the petty thieves who tamper with outdoor phones. Whenever they discovered one that was jammed or broken into, they reported it to the telephone company and later checked back at the booth to be certain that the repairs had been made and also to be sure that the number had not been changed. If it had been, they recorded the new number on a private list they kept in their cars—a list containing not only the telephone numbers and booth locations, but also an identifying number that distinguished one booth from another. These last numbers were memorized by the Bonanno men as faithfully as baseball fans memorized the numbers on the backs of players, and the system had greatly reduced the organization's communications problem in recent years. It had enabled the elder Bonanno, for example, to use his home telephone, which was tapped, to call his son's home, where the phone was also tapped, and to engage his son in a folksy conversation in Sicilian dialect into which he slipped two numbers that indicated he wished to speak privately with Bill: the first number identified the locale of the booth that Bill was to go to, the second established the hour to be there. Then, just before the appointed hour, Joseph Bonanno would go to a booth, would dial his son at the other booth, and they would speak freely without worrying about being tapped.

This system was similar to what Joseph Bonanno had proposed in July, except that Bill had been told then to go automatically to booth number 27—the one near the diner—each Thursday at 8:00 P.M. and to wait—as he was now waiting on this night in November. He felt chilly and cramped within the four glass walls that pressed him from all sides. He must go on a diet, he thought; he was becoming too large for phone booths. Raising his left arm, he looked at his watch, a diamond-studded gold watch given him months ago by a few of his father's men. It was 7:59.

The silence in the booth was intense, reminding him of boyhood moments waiting in a confessional, fretful seconds before the stern priest slapped open the sliding screen. At 8:00 his senses were so sharp and expectant that he could almost hear ringing sounds piercing deep within his mind, and, looking down at the green plastic instrument, he searched for the slightest sign of vibration. But it hung motionless, quiet in its cradle.

He looked through the glass doors, seeing the parked car with Labruzzo behind the wheel. Labruzzo sat perfectly still, but the dog was jumping in the back, paws against the closed window. Bonanno then heard sounds coming from behind him—three men were leaving the diner, talking and laughing, getting into a station wagon. They did not look in his direction. Soon they were gone. He waited. Finally, he looked at his watch.

It was 8:04. It was all over for tonight, he thought. If his father did not call on the dot, he would not call at all. He also knew that his father would not want him to linger and possibly attract attention. So he reluctantly pulled open the door of the booth and walked slowly toward the car. Labruzzo flashed on the headlights. They drove in silence back to the apartment in Queens.

* * *

The rest of the week and the weeks that followed through November into December were for the most part monotonous. Bonanno and Labruzzo resumed housekeeping in their hideaway. They ventured out at night, remaining indoors during the day.

On Thursdays, however, their mood changed. Each Thursday was the highpoint of their week; it began in the morning with a sense of anticipation and it heightened during the late afternoon, building with each mile of the trip to the booth. The trip was taking on a strange, almost mystical, meaning for Bonanno and Labruzzo—it was becoming an act of faith, a test of fidelity, and the booth, a solitary glowing structure in the vacant darkness, was approached almost reverentially. They drove slowly up to it, neither man speaking. Then Bill, after getting out of the car, would stand in the bright enclosure for two minutes—from 7:59 to 8:01. Conceding the silence, he would step out, betraying no emotion as he walked to the car. There was always another Thursday ahead, another visit to be made to the telephone booth that might finally link them to Joseph Bonanno.

The longer the government search continued without a trace of his father or the discovery of a bullet-riddled body, the more encouraged Bill Bonanno became. It was now six weeks since the disappearance, and if the elder Bonanno had been killed, that fact would presumably have already circulated through the underworld by his father's ecstatic rivals, or it would at least have been hinted at in Mafia gossip. But so far the speculation about Bonanno's death was largely limited to the newspapers, whose information came from the government, which was no doubt becoming embarrassed by its inability to find Bonanno after so much searching.

The younger Bonanno was also now encouraged by his own efforts during his father's absence. Quickly recovering from the initial shock, he assumed the responsibility of trying to hold the organization together by eluding his potential captors and by demonstrating always a sense of confidence and optimism. In spite of his youth, he believed that he was now accepted by most of the men as their interim leader; their attitude toward him had changed considerably from what it had been when he first joined the outfit in the mid-fifties as "JB's kid" and when the respect shown him was in deference to the name. Aware of that situation, his father had contemplated denying him a place in the "family" and having him join the organization headed by Albert Anastasia. Anastasia, a close friend of Joseph Profaci, came to know Bill during Bill's summer vacations from college, occasionally taking him to the Copacabana, and he would eagerly have found a spot for him. It might have been advantageous for Anastasia, for it would have fostered closer ties with both the Bonanno and Profaci groups and perhaps ultimately formed a tight three-family alliance that could have dominated the two larger gangs in New York, one headed by Vito Genovese, the other by Thomas Lucchese.

But Joseph Bonanno finally decided that he wanted his son with him, sensing perhaps the Mafia hierarchy's growing dissatisfaction with Anastasia, an autocratic and ambitious man with a tendency to overstep his boundaries—a tendency that would cost him his life. So Bill Bonanno, having quit college without a degree, followed in his father's path, although he straddled two worlds for a while—operating legitimate businesses in Arizona, including wholesale food market and real estate trading firms, while being affiliated with the Bonanno organization, whose small southwestern branch was involved in bookmaking and other illegal gambling activities.

Bill did not enjoy his involvement with his father's world during these years; he had no objection to it on moral grounds, but he resented his lowly status among his father's men. Whether Bill was in New York or Arizona, his father gave him little to do, and he invariably dismissed Bill's suggestions promptly. His father seemed to be constantly second-guessing him, questioning him, and Bill resented it. He remembered one occasion when he fought back, losing his temper completely and screaming uncontrollably at his father; and he remembered the look of shock on his father's face. The elder Bonanno apparently had never been shouted at before in such an unrestrained manner, and he did not know how to react, at least not toward his own son. Bill quickly tried to pass over the situation, saying, "Look, I was born to lead, not to follow." After a pause, his father replied with quiet firmness: "Before you can lead, you must learn to follow."

After that, Bill managed to control his temper in front of his father, and although he did not refrain from disagreeing in private when he felt justified, he learned to follow orders. When he was told to be at a certain place at a certain time, he was there at the precise moment, remaining until he was instructed to leave. He remembered one morning when he drove his father to a drugstore and was told to wait outside. He waited for one hour, then a second hour. Then he left the car and looked into the drugstore and saw his father seated at a booth talking with another man, drinking coffee. Bill returned to the car and continued to wait. The afternoon passed, extending into early evening. Finally, twelve hours after he had entered the drugstore, his father walked out. He nodded toward Bill but did not apologize or explain what had taken so long.

Now, years later, looking back on that incident and similar incidents, Bill realized how his father had tested his patience and discipline, seeing how he would respond to a condition that was necessary and common in the organization and yet was unnatural to most men. In Bill's case, however, waiting had been no problem. He spent most of his life waiting, especially for his father, waiting as a teenager in Arizona for his father's reappearances each winter, as expectantly and hopefully as he was waiting now. His past had prepared him for the present, he thought, and he believed that he was now truly disciplined, capable of withstanding the worst that might come along, and this possibility pleased him very much.

He was also pleased by the behavior of the men during this ordeal. While it was true that maybe fifty or even seventy members had defected to join Gaspar Di Gregorio's faction, that number was low considering the fact that the Mafia's national commission had ousted his father and had urged a mass walkout of the men and also the fact that none of the men knew for sure whether Joseph Bonanno would ever return. Bill was particularly indebted to his uncle who during the last six weeks had been a source of strength as well as a sensitive and compatible friend.

Bill did not have to prove anything to Labruzzo, his mother's brother, a man who had become like his own brother, understanding by instinct. Though they were twenty years apart and had lost touch during Bill's years in Arizona, they shared the knowledge of a similar past and were united on so many personal levels. Bill was intimately familiar with the neighborhood in which Labruzzo grew up, the Brooklyn house in which he lived, the almost exotic Sicilian exiles that were Labruzzo's par-

ents, Bill's grandparents. Labruzzo's father, domineering and
proud, was not unlike the elder Bonanno in some ways, and Bill
sensed the conflict in Frank Labruzzo and recognized it in himself.

To be born of such foreign fathers and to remain loyal to them
throughout one's lifetime, was to bear the burden of being an
outsider and being alienated from much of America. Bill thought
that the only thing that might have separated Frank Labruzzo
and himself from their present circumstances would have been
total rebellion, a complete break with their fathers' past and
present, but for the younger Bonanno and Labruzzo this was
not possible. They were too close, too involved, were the products of people who believed intensely in family loyalty; and
although they themselves were a generation removed from the
clannish hills of western Sicily and had both had the benefit of
higher education, they were still influenced by certain values of
the old country and they sometimes felt like strangers in their
native land. They were fractional Americans, not yet totally
acceptable nor receptive to the American majority, and Bill believed that they were also different from the sons of most other
Italian immigrants—they were less malleable, more deeply defined, more insular.

He remembered how insular Frank Labruzzo's neighborhood
in Brooklyn had been. Except for the absence of a mountain, it
could have passed for a Sicilian village. The dialect and manner
of the people were the same, the cooking was the same, the
interior of the homes seemed the same. The old women wore
black, mourning death on two continents, and the unmarried
young women lived under the watchful eyes of their parents,
who missed nothing. Bill recalled hearing from his mother and
her sisters how strict his grandfather Labruzzo had been during
their courting days, not permitting them to wear lipstick or eyebrow pencil or cut their hair in the contemporary fashion or
smoke or be outdoors after dark. Charles Labruzzo, who neither
spoke nor wrote English despite living in America for thirty-
two years, made few concessions to the modern world except
for the purchase of an automobile, which he drove without a
license.

Charles Labruzzo was born in 1870 in the western Sicilian
town of Camporeale, in the hilly interior southeast of Castellammare, into a family of sheepherders and cattle raisers. A strap-

ping broad-shouldered man, he worked as a blacksmith in Camporeale, married a local girl, and sired the first of his twelve children. Then one night, after a violent fight with an uncle who tried to cheat him out of his inheritance, he abruptly left Sicily for Tunisia, thinking that he had killed the uncle during an exchange of body blows. Later his wife joined him in Tunisia, continuing to let him believe that he was wanted for murder in Sicily though she was aware of his uncle's recovery; she had had enough of Sicily and knew that by withholding the information she could avoid going back.

After a few years in Tunisia—during that time was born their daughter Fay, Bill's mother—the Labruzzos immigrated to the United States. Industrious and shrewd, Charles Labruzzo prospered in America in the butcher business and in real estate investing. On Jefferson Street in Brooklyn, during the 1920s, he owned a comfortable home with a large backyard in which he kept chickens and a milk-bearing goat; a commercial building leased to a clothing manufacturer; and a four-story tenement in which he rented apartments. His butcher shop was on the ground floor of the tenement and under it was a pipeline through which flowed wine from his home two doors away. He was the envy of several Sicilians in the neighborhood, and his quick temper and touchiness contributed to his unpopularity. The sight of him chasing someone down the street, swearing in Sicilian, was not uncommon, and once after a painter standing on a ladder yelled down an insult, Labruzzo grabbed a shotgun, aimed it at the painter and forced him to jump thirty feet to the sidewalk. The panicked man, after landing without injury, ran for cover.

Labruzzo was often intercepted and calmed down during his angry pursuits by a soft-spoken young man who offered to settle his difficulties, wanting nothing in return except peace and quiet in the neighborhood. The man was Joseph Bonanno. Charles Labruzzo knew the Bonanno name from the old country, and he liked the younger man's style, his self-assurance, and he was delighted later when Bonanno married his daughter—and in 1932 presented him with a grandson, Salvatore Vincent Bonanno, who would be known as Bill.

The child was born during an otherwise miserable year in Labruzzo's life. He had just lost a leg during an operation for diabetes, and he became bitter and depressed, drinking great quantities of wine and cursing his fate. He banged his crutches

angrily against the walls of his room when he wanted one of his
daughters to attend to his needs, and his only unintimidated
companion during this period was a pet chicken who followed
him everywhere and slept on his bed at night, often on his chest.
Whenever the Bonannos came to visit and left young Bill for a
few days, the old man was pleased.

Bill remembered his grandfather as a heavy white-haired man
sitting in the sun in front of the house reciting Sicilian prov-
erbs—ancient truths from a stoical society—and occasionally
the old man would send him to a nearby tavern for a container
of beer or into a drugstore for a single cigarette, which could be
bought for a penny. When his grandfather wished to go up to
his room, Bill would tuck his shoulder under the stump of his
grandfather's leg, and they would slowly climb each step; although the weight was borne by the crutches, Bill was providing
moral support, and he liked the appearance of being needed and
being close.

Sometimes when the old man was asleep, the youngest son,
Frank, would take Bill for walks, looking after him as he would
later in life. Frank Labruzzo was then in his twenties, working
at odd jobs during the Depression years, including part-time
work as an undertaker in a funeral parlor partly owned by Joseph
Bonanno. Bill remembered how horrified his grandmother was
when she heard that Frank had become a mortician and how she
screamed whenever he entered the house, warning him not to
touch anything. Frank would merely shrug in his casual way,
not offended by her attitude or embarrassed by his work, which
he preferred to working in a butcher shop.

Frank Labruzzo never did work for his father; he was attracted
instead to the activities of his brother-in-law, Joseph Bonanno.
Bonanno's existence seemed glamorous and exciting. He wore
fine clothes, drove a new car. He was in touch with the outside
world.

On Thursday evening, December 17, Bill Bonanno and Frank
Labruzzo paid their weekly visit to the phone booth on Long
Island. It was the sixth consecutive Thursday they had gone
there. In a week it would be Christmas Eve, and on the way to
the booth the two men wondered aloud if the holiday truce would
be observed by the various gangs this year as it had been in the
past. Under normal circumstances it would be—all organization

members would temporarily forget their differences until after January 1—but since the Bonanno loyalists were technically suspended from the national union, neither Bill nor Frank knew for sure whether the holiday policy would now be followed with regard to their people. They would have to anticipate the worst, they decided and both men assumed that they would not be spending Christmas with their wives and children.

At 7:55 P.M. they pulled into the parking lot near the diner and parked a few feet away from the booth. It was a cold night, and Bill, turning off the radio, sat waiting in the car with the window partly open. The sky was dark and cloudy, the only reflection came from the big neon sign above the diner. There were three cars parked in front of the diner, and except for a few customers seated at the counter and an elderly couple at a table, it was empty. The food must be terrible, Bill thought, for the diner had never seemed busy during any of his visits, although he conceded the possibility that it had a late trade, maybe truck drivers, which might explain the large parking lot. Many people thought that places patronized by truckers must be serving good food, but Bill believed that the opposite was probably true. He had eaten at hundreds of roadside places during his many motor trips across the country, and most of the time he had observed the truckmen eating chicken soup and salted crackers, and he was willing to bet that most of them suffered from nervous stomachs and hemorrhoids.

He looked at his watch. It was exactly 8:00. He and Labruzzo sat silently as the seconds ticked away. He was about to conclude that it was another uneventful Thursday. Then, the telephone rang.

Bill slammed against the door, bounced out of the car, ran into the booth with such force that it shook. Labruzzo ran after him, pressing against the glass door that Bill had pulled shut. Bill heard a woman's voice, very formal, sounding far away—it was the operator repeating the number, asking if it corresponded to the telephone number in the booth.

"*Yes*," Bill replied, feeling his heart pounding, "yes it is."

He heard muffled sounds from the other end, then silence for a second, then the sound of coins dropping into the slot, *quarters*, six or seven quarters gonging—it was long distance.

"Hello, Bill?"

It was a male voice, not his father's, a voice he did not recognize.

"Yes, who is *this*?"

"Never mind," the man replied, "just listen to me. Your father's OK. You'll probably be seeing him in a few days."

"How do I know he's OK?" Bill demanded, suddenly aggressive.

"Where the hell do you think I got this number from?" The man was now irritated. Bill calmed down.

"Now look," the man continued, "*don't make waves!* Everything's OK. Just sit back, don't do anything, and don't worry about anything."

Before Bill could respond, the man hung up.

4

THE EXCITEMENT, THE ecstasy, that Bill Bonanno felt was overwhelming, and during the drive back to Queens he heard the conversation again and again, and he repeated it to Labruzzo. *Your father's OK, you'll probably be seeing him in a few days.* Bill was so happy that he wanted to go to a bar and have a few drinks in celebration, but both he and Labruzzo agreed that despite the good news they should remain as careful and alert as they had been before. They would follow the advice of the man on the telephone, would sit back and wait; in a few days Joseph Bonanno would reappear to make the next move.

Yet, in the interest of efficiency, Bill thought that some preparation for his father's return was necessary; he felt, for example, that Maloney, his father's attorney, should be informed immediately of this development. Bill reasoned that Maloney would be his father's chief spokesman after the reappearance, an event that would undoubtedly cause a circus of confusion and complex legal maneuvering in the courthouse, and Maloney would have to plan the elder Bonanno's strategy for the interrogation by the federal grand jury. Bill also felt a touch of guilt about Maloney, since Bill had been very suspicious of him after the incident on Park Avenue. The veteran lawyer was forced to appear on five or six occasions since then before the grand jury to defend himself against government implications that he was somehow involved in the kidnaping, and Bill imagined that Maloney's reputation as a lawyer had suffered as a result. On the following day, Bill Bonanno drove to a telephone booth and called Maloney's office.

"Hi, Mr. Maloney, this is Bill Bonanno," he said, cheerfully, picturing the old man jumping out of his chair.

"Hey," Maloney yelled, "where are you? *Where's your dad?"*

"Hold on," Bonanno said, "take it easy. Go to a phone outside your office, to one of the booths downstairs, and call me at this number." He gave Maloney the number. Within a few minutes the lawyer called back, and Bonanno recounted all that he had been told the night before.

But Maloney was dissatisfied with the brevity of the details. He wanted more specific information. He wondered on what day the elder Bonanno would appear, where he would be staying, how he could be reached now and through whom. Bill said he did not know anything other than what he had already told, adding that as soon as he knew more he would contact Maloney at once. When Maloney persisted with more questions, Bonanno cut him off. He had to run, he said. He hung up.

He returned to the apartment. Labruzzo had arranged for certain men to be there that evening, having already informed them of the news. The pace was quickening, there was activity, anticipation, and Bill Bonanno was confident that soon a few things would be resolved, soon he and the other men might get some relief from the wretched routine of hiding. The reappearance of his father should stabilize the organization to a degree and lessen the uncertainty. His father had undoubtedly come to some terms with his captors or he would not be alive; the next hurdle was the government. His father would appear before the grand jury, and Bill and the other men who were sought would probably do the same. They would come out of hiding, would accept their subpoenas, and after consulting with their lawyers, they would present themselves in court. If their answers displeased the judge, they might be sentenced for contempt, but at this juncture they had few alternatives. Their terms could be for a month, a year, or more, but it would not be intolerable so long as some stability was reestablished within the organization and perhaps their status regained in the national brotherhood. Hopefully they would not enter prison as underworld outcasts. Their existence behind bars was much easier when they were known to be members in good standing; they were accorded a respect not only by the other prisoners but also by the prison guards and certain other workers, men for whom favors could be done on the outside. The "man of respect" serving time also knew that during his confinement he need not worry about his wife and children; they were being looked after by organizational representatives, and if they required help they received it.

While Bill Bonanno sat in the living room of the apartment reading the afternoon papers, Labruzzo took a nap, undisturbed by the noise from the television. It was too early for the evening news, and neither man had paid much attention during the last few hours to the series of quiz shows, soap operas, or comedies that monopolized the screen.

Suddenly, there was an interruption of the program—the announcement of a special news bulletin. Bill Bonanno looked up from his newspaper. He expected to hear that war was declared, Russian bombers were on the way. Instead he heard the announcer say *Mafia leader Joseph Bonanno, who was kidnaped and believed to have been killed by rival mobsters in October, is alive. Bonanno's attorney, William Power Maloney, made the announcement today. Maloney also said that his client would appear before the federal grand jury investigating organized crime, at 9:00 A.M. on Monday, and . . .*

Bill Bonanno was stunned. Labruzzo came running in to watch. Bonanno began to swear quietly. Maloney had not only called a press conference but had also identified him as the source of the information. Bonanno buried his head in his hands. He felt heat racing through his body, his sweat rising and seeping through his shirt. He knew he had made a horrible mistake in talking to Maloney in the first place, then in not swearing him to secrecy. Now he did not know what was ahead for his father. He recalled the words of the man on the phone saying *don't make waves . . . don't do anything.* And, stupidly, he had done it. He had possibly ruined everything, for the announcement would make page one all over the country, would drive the elder Bonanno deeper into hiding, and it would intensify the investigation, activating those agents who had been lulled into thinking that Joseph Bonanno was dead.

The television set displayed a picture of Maloney, then a picture of the Park Avenue apartment house, and suddenly Bill was sick of the whole episode—reaching for a heavy glass ashtray on a nearby table, he threw it hard at the set, hitting the screen squarely in the center. It exploded like a bomb. Thousands of tiny pieces of glass sprayed the room, tubes popped, wires curled and burned in varicolored flame, sparks flared in several directions—a remarkable little fireworks show of self-destruction was playing itself out within the twenty-one-inch screen, and Bonanno and Labruzzo watched with fascination until the interior of the set had nearly evaporated into a smoldering hole of jagged edges and fizzling filament.

A week passed, nothing happened. Joseph Bonanno did not make the appearance before the grand jury that Maloney had predicted, and the lawyer was summoned to explain in court. The younger Bonanno and the other men remained in hiding. On Thursday evening, Christmas Eve, Labruzzo and the others slipped away to meet with their families at the homes of relatives or friends most remote from police surveillance. Bonanno told Labruzzo that he was meeting Rosalie at the home of one of the Profacis in Brooklyn, but this was not true. He was sure that Rosalie's movements would be carefully watched by agents during the holidays, making it too risky to meet her, and he also felt so miserable that he really preferred being alone.

At 8:00 P.M. he visited the telephone booth in Long Island, expecting it to remain silent, and it did. Not wanting to return to the apartment, he kept driving through Queens. It was snowing, and there were Christmas lights strung on many of the houses that he passed. He decided to drive into Manhattan, to take a walk through Times Square, lose himself in the crowd.

Finding a parking space on a side street east of Broadway, he locked the car, began to walk through the snow and slush. He was glad that he had not forgotten his rubbers but wished he had left his gun in the glove compartment. The gun had become such a natural part of his anatomy in recent months that he was usually unaware of carrying it. But he did not feel like returning to the car now; so he continued to walk with the gun strapped to his chest under his jacket. His blue cashmere overcoat was warm and light, and his gray fedora was slightly forward on his head and pushed down so that it would not blow off in the wind. He had never felt comfortable in hats; as a boy he hated them because they messed up his long wavy hair, a source of great pride, and although his hair was now short he still reacted negatively to hats, tolerating them only as part of a disguise.

He walked uptown under the bright marquees of the Broadway cinemas, past a noisy jazz band in the Metrodome bar. He smelled the hot dogs cooking on Nedicks' sidewalk grill, felt the

distant nearness of a thousand people all around him, watched
their faces changing color as they walked under the lights; their
tourist faces seemed satisfied, peaceful, unconcerned, so distant
from the tiny private province of hell that he had inherited. On
Fifty-third Street, waiting for a traffic light to change, a mounted
policeman galloped within a few feet of him, and he inhaled the
familiar aroma of a horse. Then he crossed to the other side of
Broadway, walking downtown past Jack Dempsey's and Lindy's,
then past the Astor Hotel, where he paused momentarily.

The hotel seemed unchanged, even the red-coated doorman
whistling for a cab seemed familiar. Bill remembered again the
wedding reception and remembered, too, how excited and concerned his father was on the following morning when he found
out that a piece of Bill's luggage was missing just as the bridal
couple's car was being loaded on the sidewalk outside the hotel.
Then Frank Labruzzo quickly deduced that the doorman had
mistakenly put that suitcase in the limousine that had just pulled
away from the curb with Joseph Barbara and some of the men
from upstate New York. Bill remembered the sight of Labruzzo
running after Barbara's limousine, which had fortunately stopped
for a traffic light; Labruzzo rapped on the rear fender, inviting
frowns from the men within, but they stopped when they recognized him and graciously returned the suitcase. They had no
idea that it contained about $100,000 in gift envelopes.

Bill passed the Astor thinking of Rosalie—and, remembering
that a Western Union office was two blocks away, he walked to
it and sent her a Christmas telegram with flowers. Tired of walking in the slush, he approached a cinema on Forty-second Street
and, without looking up to see what was playing, bought a ticket.
He spent the next three hours watching a double feature, a
slightly risqué foreign film followed by a second-rate Western.
When he came out at 1:00 A.M., it had stopped snowing but had
gotten colder. Broadway was no longer crowded, and the prostitutes and homosexual hustlers were more conspicuous.

He got into his car, drove along the West Side Highway toward the Battery Tunnel, passing the hulking silhouettes of ocean
liners docked along the piers. In Queens he passed many houses
with parties in progress, with people standing in crowded rooms
holding drinks, trimming trees, or dancing; his block, which
was in a Jewish neighborhood, was relatively quiet. He circled
the block twice to be sure he was not being followed. Then,

locking his car, he crossed the street ready to reach for his gun at the sound of movement behind the bushes or trees. But everything was silent and still.

Unlocking his apartment door he could hear a noise from the television set, a new one that Labruzzo had bought. Bill always left the television on after leaving the apartment, thinking the noise might discourage anyone from breaking in. He watched a late-late show until 4:30 A.M. Then he went to bed. He considered it the worst Christmas Eve of his life.

He woke up on Christmas Day shortly before noon. Hearing the dog's impatient growl, he got out of bed and opened a can of chopped meat. The apartment seemed strangely empty without Labruzzo. He turned on the television set, then peeked through the venetian blinds. It was cloudy, the streets were covered with slush, and the small patches of snow along the sidewalk had already been darkened by polluted air. He started to think about his children, what they were doing at this very moment in East Meadow, but he quickly blocked these thoughts from his mind.

He continued to look out the window at the few people on the street, bundled up in coats and mufflers and boots, looking drab and unhealthy, and he wished, as he so often did, that he were back in Arizona. And suddenly, he became consumed with a desire to go there. It might seem absurd, but at this moment he did not care. He had been existing in absurdity for several weeks, and a trip to Arizona did not seem in the least irrational, the more he thought about it. There was nothing for him to do in New York during the holidays, no one that he could see, and he still considered Arizona his home. His younger brother would be there, on holiday vacation from Phoenix Junior College, and a few of his father's friends would also be there. He could get some money while there, could also check on the condition of his father's house and various properties.

He decided to go. He went to a telephone booth and called a young man who was available to the organization for odd chores and asked him to help with the driving. Bill spent the rest of Christmas Day in the apartment. He went to bed early and awoke at 4:00 A.M. Accompanied by his dog, Bill picked up the man at a nearby corner and began the 2,600-mile journey to Arizona.

* * *

In more than twenty years of shuttling back and forth between New York and Arizona, beginning in 1942 as a ten-year-old student in Tucson, Bill Bonanno had gained an intimate sense of American geography, a familiarity with winding back roads and small bridges and endless towns stretching from the industrial marshes of the northeastern coast to the dusty flatlands of the West. He had developed an ear for regional dialogue, an eye for the folkways of people, a taste for the kitchen specialties of hundreds of roadside restaurants. He knew the varying prices of gasoline, the tolls of tunnels, the graffiti on mountain rocks, the prayers on billboards. He was attuned to the chatter of disc jockeys, the changing rhythms of regional radio. Without consulting a map he could travel through back roads in each state, knowing the best ways to avoid overpopulated centers, rush-hour traffic, icy roads, radar traps.

The state he knew best, of course, was Arizona. He had covered every corner of it by car, horse, or on foot, or in the small airplane that he had learned to fly years ago, a plane owned by one of his father's partners in a cotton farm that was located forty miles north of Tucson. Bill had flown the plane low along the Mexican border between mesas, skimming the tops of cactus plants and Indian reservations, and he had flown westward to the California line, eastward toward El Paso.

He had driven his car up into the White Mountains of northeastern Arizona to go trout fishing, and he had gone deer hunting along the northern Arizona border into Utah. After his marriage to Rosalie in 1956, he returned to Arizona and lived during the next seven years in various parts of the state, beginning in the high regions near the Grand Canyon, in the scenic city of Flagstaff. With an altitude of nearly 7,000 feet, Flagstaff was a center for winter sports activity. It also was the locale of Northern Arizona University, and shortly after Rosalie and Bill settled in Flagstaff they registered for courses there. The people of Flagstaff were outgoing and hospitable, and almost immediately the Bonannos made friends with other couples, were being invited home to dinner, and were reciprocating. And not long after Bill's first few deposits in the local bank, the word spread through the community of 15,000 that he was a man of means.

He invested in real estate and in a small radio station in the nearby town of Holbrook. He joined the Kiwanis Club, was a leader in the March of Dimes campaign and other charity drives, and in his entire life he had never felt more relaxed and free. He was 260 miles from Tucson, was remote from New York in every way. His calls and visits to his father were becoming less frequent, less expected. The elder Bonanno, leading a relatively easy life of his own at this time, was not very demanding.

In Tucson, where he listed his occupation as that of a retired cotton broker, Joseph Bonanno went unchallenged. The limited publicity he had received during the Kefauver days was now forgotten, and he was considered socially acceptable by nearly everyone in town. He lived in a comfortable, unostentatious home on East Elm Street, where he often entertained politicians, priests, and business investors who sought his financial support. He was often seen walking through the business district wearing Western clothes, smiling easily, and being pleasant with everyone he met. His wife participated in civic activities and charities, and she usually attended Mass each morning. Joseph Bonanno was traveling out of state less often, his interests in New York, Wisconsin, and elsewhere were adequately handled by partners or subordinates, and in October 1957 he found time for a short vacation in Sicily, where he revisited old friends and relatives in Castellammare.

But shortly after his return to the United States, an event happened that suddenly changed the life-style and image of both Bonanno and his son, an event that within hours of its public disclosure would destroy the tranquillity and social acceptance that the Bonannos had enjoyed, replacing it with rejection and national notoriety. It happened on November 14, 1957, in the upstate New York village of Apalachin, with a police raid on a gathering of nearly seventy "delegates" to a Mafia "summit meeting" held in the home of Joseph Barbara. The purpose of the session, according to the later analysis of crime experts, was to discuss pressing problems in the underworld—the tendency of some members to become involved in narcotics despite the opposition of the dons (who opposed it partly on moral grounds, partly from fear of long imprisonment, and also because they wanted nothing to do with the erratic Cuban and Puerto Rican gangsters and undisciplined youths who were running so much of the operation); the unresolved issues following the murder of Albert Anastasia, who had persistently intruded upon the Caribbean gambling enterprises that were in the Florida Mafia's domain; the practice of certain dons to initiate more members into their "families" despite a national policy opposed to new membership in the interest of maintaining balance between the individual organizations. There were other subjects under discussion, too, but the whole session came to an abrupt end when it was discovered that the police were observing Barbara's home. Several of the men ran out to their cars and drove quickly down the road toward the highway but were intercepted by the police roadblock. Other men dashed into the woods, ripping their clothes on tree branches and vines, and many managed to escape. But most of them were caught, and while no guns were found, a search of their pockets uncovered almost $300,000 in cash. The men's explanation that they had visited Barbara's home because they had heard he was ill and wished to cheer him up was jocularly reported in the press, and although the conviction of twenty-one of the men was later reversed by the court of appeals, it did generate months of highly publicized trials and editorial comment that exposed and embarrassed the men. It also assisted the federal agencies in their efforts to obtain more funds from Congress for combating organized crime and more cooperation from the courts with regard to the use of wiretapping and bugging.

Among those named by the police as having visited Barbara were Joseph Profaci, Joseph Magliocco, and Joseph Bonanno. Rosalie was at home alone in Flagstaff when word of the raid was announced; Bill had gone off for a weekend of deer hunting near Utah, and the news was two days' old when he returned to his anxious wife waiting in seclusion. She had received numerous calls from relatives during the weekend, including several cryptic messages from the elder Bonanno, who had somehow slipped past the state police in New York and was now waiting impatiently in Tucson, unknown to local authorities, for Bill's arrival.

When Bill reached Tucson that evening, he discovered his father at home sitting in the brick-walled patio sipping brandy, a benign expression on his face. As Bill got closer, his father stood, kissed him gently on both cheeks. Then the elder Bonanno shook his head slowly and began to laugh. The whole idea of the meeting was so stupid, so carelessly arranged, he said, that it was comical, hilarious. The sight of grown men running frantically in all directions from the barbecue pit as the police closed in was a scene out of burlesque. But, he continued, the consequences of the gathering would not be so funny. There would be the endless public hearings, the herd of photographers charging through the corridors each day, the rhetoric of judges and investigators, the call for reform by politicians, the legal fees and theatrics of lawyers, the defamation of the defendants, who served as society's scapegoats—this spectacle, he said, he wanted to avoid at all cost. And so he planned to leave Tucson for an undisclosed spot in California, and he would keep on the move, one step ahead of the subpoena servers if possible, until the public clamor had subsided and he knew what was ahead.

Bill could sense without having to be told what this meant for him. He would have to look after his father's interests during his absence. He would have to look after his mother and the homes and property in Arizona and would also take a more active role in his father's affairs outside the state. He would do this because he had to and because, in a strange way, he wanted to. It was an interesting discovery, his awareness that he wanted to do it, wanted to become deeply involved in what he knew was precarious. It meant giving up the life in Flagstaff, the respectable conventional life that most Americans led and that he thought he could lead, wanted to lead. But now he was not so sure, doubting that he truly belonged even though he gave the appearance of belonging. He probably did not belong anywhere except at his father's side or in his father's shadow because, in spite of his education, he was not really qualified to do anything important in the so-called legitimate world.

He had not studied hard in school, had not concentrated on any one subject, had not passed the courses necessary for a degree. His attention span had been too short, his ego had perhaps been too large, his father's existence perhaps too distracting for him to progress normally through the educational system—he did not know or care. He did not know to what degree the system had failed him, or he it. He did not know which of his failings were attributable to his background and which to his inability or desire to rise above that background.

If he did not have his father's resources to fall back on, he might be better off, or worse off, depending on one's point of view. He was confident that he could earn a living on his own, although he suspected that in the legitimate world he was at a tremendous disadvantage. With his name, with his incomplete education, he would probably have to start off at the bottom without influential family friends pulling him upward. He would be restricted to mental tasks in an office, which would bore him, or he would work as a traveling salesman or would punch a time clock in a factory. Or perhaps with his pilot's experience he could become a crop duster, but the money was not all that good and the work was probably as dangerous as any in his father's world—crop dusters had to fly so slowly and so low that when their planes stalled, which was often, they usually hit the ground before regaining power.

But all this reasoning was not the major factor in Bill Bonanno's decision to commit himself to his father. The main reason was that he loved his father, was part of him, and could not, would not, disassociate himself from him during this difficult period. This was a time when he was needed. It was the first time in his life that his father really needed him, and Bill found this both flattering and challenging. Also, he did not feel that his father's activities, or the activities of any of the men at Apalachin, were of a grave criminal nature. Most of the men were primarily involved in gambling which, although illegal, was part of human nature. The numbers racket, off-track betting, prostitution, and their other illegal endeavors would go on whether or not there was a Mafia. The mafiosi were really servants in a hypocritical society, they were the middlemen who provided those illegal commodities of pleasure and escape that the public demanded and the law forbade.

If people would obey the law, there would be no Mafia. If the police could resist graft, if the judges and politicians were incorruptible, there would be no Mafia because the Mafia could not exist without the cooperation of the others. Before there was a Mafia in the United States catering to the crime market, thriving first as bootleggers during Prohibition, there were other ethnic gangs supplying illegal demands and gradually buying their own way out of slums. When the Mafia dies out in a generation or two, by which time the grandsons of mafiosi will have learned the art of tax dodging and legal subterfuge in large American corporations, the key jobs in organized crime, which is a kind of lower-caste civil service, will be occupied by Latin American gangsters or blacks, the element that has already gained control of the lowest rung in the criminal pecking order, the narcotics trade.

But all the sociological speculating by Bill Bonanno in 1947 did not improve his situation—he was a member of a generation caught in the middle; he had followed his father's course, and now, after Apalachin, he felt as trapped as any of the men cited by the police. Nevertheless he accepted his fate, and after his father left for California, he disposed of the house in Flagstaff and returned with Rosalie to Tucson.

As he had anticipated, the life there was suddenly difficult, not only for himself but also for his wife, his mother, and anyone else who chose to remain friendly. The Tucson newspapers, following the trend of the national press after Apalachin, expanded its coverage of organized crime, focusing particular attention on the Bonannos, and began a campaign to get them out of town. Bill Bonanno's presence in Tucson and his appearances at the local airport before or after trips to New York were watched by the FBI and reported in the newspapers. The tax agents began to investigate his income from the wholesale grocery business he owned in Tucson and also from the property that he held in his own name or in partnership with his father or other men. The Catholic parish to which the Bonannos had made large contributions in the past asked Bill if it could buy back the mausoleum he had bought near a statue of Christ in the Holy Hope Cemetery; angrily, Bill agreed, refusing repayment.

His mother continued to attend Mass, but she went only to the early-morning service in order to minimize the embarrassment to herself and other parishioners who might wish to avoid her. Rosalie despised Tucson, and she became resentful toward Bill because of his insistence on remaining there. She had no friends, and, except for visits to her mother-in-law, there were few places that she could go and feel at ease. In her own home Rosalie had to be careful of her conversation on the telephone, could not speak freely in front of the cleaning lady who came occasionally. She could not open charge accounts in stores, because her record of spending might be used against her husband by tax investigators; she had to pay cash for everything, making it more difficult to return purchases if she wished and requiring that she constantly go to Bill for money.

She was also disillusioned by the direction her marriage had taken. She thought that when she moved West after the wedding that she was escaping forever the routine of secrecy that encircled her elders in Brooklyn. But now she could see how naïve she had been, and she felt cheated, deceived. With Bill traveling

so often, she became increasingly lonely and even envious of
the strong bond that existed between her husband and his father.
Then in October 1958 she sank deeper into depression and despair when her first child, a daughter, died shortly after birth.

When she could not become pregnant again during the next
year Rosalie began to doubt her capability for bearing other
children, and Bill decided they should adopt one. He felt, however, that he could not apply to a regular agency, not with the
publicity he was receiving and with his reluctance to respond to
the extensive questioning; so, without consulting Rosalie, he
contacted various men he knew in California and Arizona and
asked that they call him if they should hear of the availability of
a child. Soon he was told that a young woman in Phoenix, who
had left her home in Virginia, was about to have a child that she
wished to place with a family that would cherish and support
him. Bill arranged for her to enter the University of Colorado
Medical Center at Denver; there, within a week, her infant son
was born, with green eyes and of Scotch-Irish ancestry, and Bill
returned with him to Tucson, exhilarated and proud, arriving
home at night after Rosalie had gone to bed. He woke her up
and, without a word of explanation, he placed the baby by her
side.

They named him Charles, honoring Bill's grandfather Charles
Labruzzo, and although Rosalie would soon become pregnant
with a son and would have two more children during the following two years, she would always be in certain ways closer to
Charles than to the others. But in spite of the presence of children, which relieved her of much of her loneliness and feeling
of unfulfillment, her relationship with Bill remained in a state
of tension during their time in Tucson. She felt incapable of
escaping this small town which alienated her and she missed her
mother and relatives in Brooklyn. She could not understand Bill's
attachment to a town that seemed to reject and disown him.
What she did not know was that not everyone in Tucson had
turned on Bill. There were a few of his friends who, undeterred
by the publicity after Apalachin, continued to treat him with
courtesy and did not shun his companionship. There was also a
blonde hostess in a Tucson cocktail lounge who was attracted to
Bill, and she had a blithe carefree attitude that he particularly
welcomed now, a pleasant contrast to the dispiriting atmosphere
that prevailed at home with Rosalie.

She was in her mid-twenties, was tall and graceful. She was born in Germany, had met and married an American soldier there, but was now divorced. Not long after she began dating Bill, the manager of the lounge told her that the FBI was investigating her, and she was warned that if she did not break up with Bill she would lose her job. She lost her job, found another one, and continued to see Bill. She also brought him to her Tucson apartment to meet her two young sons, who soon accepted him as part of the family and called him Daddy.

Bill was infatuated with her. She was undemanding yet seemed totally involved with him. She was resigned to his marriage and, unlike Rosalie, she was not embarrassed by the publicity that associated him with the underworld. If anything she was intrigued by it, was fascinated by Bill's description of his father and the other men. She confided in Bill, telling him about her marriage and her parents in Germany, how their town was destroyed by bombing raids and they lived in damp cellars, how her father was taken prisoner by the Allies and was later reported dead. After the war, after her mother had married again and was widowed again, her father reappeared one day in front of the house, walking slowly up the path carrying a cane, wearing a long white beard, and his daughter thought that he was Jesus.

In 1961, Bill Bonanno conceded to himself that Tucson was too small a place in which to live under present circumstances; so he moved to Phoenix, finding a home for Rosalie and their two sons on the east side of town and a home for his girl friend and her two sons on the west side of town. He supplied each woman with a 1961 Falcon, and he divided his free evenings between the two places. Although he continued to oversee the businesses in Tucson and traveled often to New York, he also became actively engaged in managing a Phoenix supper club that he partly owned. The club was called Romulus, and he employed his girl friend as an assistant manager. When the Phoenix police began to park outside the Romulus each night questioning the customers on their way out, sometimes testing their alcoholic consumption, Bill's business quickly declined. He filed a $100,000 lawsuit against the Phoenix police contending that his constitutional rights were being violated, but the suit was dismissed. The decision angered him and he was determined in a desperate way to fight those who wanted to drive him out of town. Yet the strain of the life he was leading, his getting little sleep and supporting two households and traveling constantly, began to take its toll. One day, mixing up bank accounts, he bounced a $1,930 check; though he made restitution, he was taken to court, received newspaper publicity, and was placed on probation for three years. Later he was charged with income tax evasion, the government agents claiming that he owed more than $60,000 in back taxes for the years 1959–1960–1961. Then his girl friend informed him that she had received a telephone call from one of Rosalie's brothers in New York, pleading with her to leave Bill, offering her money and an airplane ticket back to Germany. She refused, but she and Bill were becoming a bit uneasy. One night a few weeks later, Bill called her home and heard her say, "Your wife is here."

He slammed down the phone, drove quickly to the house. He discovered Rosalie and the other woman seated quietly across from one another in the living room with their children nearby. Rosalie shouted as he walked in, demanding that he immediately choose between them, but he ignored her. He led her firmly out to the car and drove her and the children home without discussing the subject. Later he confessed to Rosalie that he was emotionally involved with the other woman, although he did not admit that she was pregnant with his child and was insisting on having it. Bill was incapable at this time of choosing between the women—his whole life was in such a turbulent state that he needed them both, one complemented the other. Each gave him something the other did not; he respected and loved Rosalie, he said, but the other woman made him feel alive, free, confident. All his life he had done what was expected of him; now he had finally done as he pleased—his affair represented his first blatantly rebellious act against the Sicilian family strictures that had shaped him and sometimes sickened him. When Rosalie proposed that they separate, he said firmly that he would not let her go.

The next day he was again with his girl friend, although he noticed a change in her attitude. She had been more upset by the encounter with Rosalie than he had imagined she would be, and now she agreed with Rosalie that it would be better for all of them, including the children, if he made a choice—either leave Rosalie or leave her. But Bill continued to procrastinate. A week later, on arriving at her home, he was told by a baby-sitter that she had gone out for the evening. Abruptly discharging the baby-sitter, Bill waited for her return. He shut the lights in the living room and sat in the dark facing the door.

Shortly before midnight, hearing a car stop, he saw her with another man. Then she walked alone up the path. When she flipped on the light switch she saw Bill glaring at her. She was wearing a black off-the-shoulder evening dress, his favorite, a dress he had recently bought her before a weekend trip they had taken to Las Vegas. Seeing that dress now seemed to drive him berserk. He grabbed the dress by the top, ripped it off, and began to tear it into several pieces. As she screamed he charged into her bedroom closet and began to rip other dresses. When she fought to stop him, he hit her, knocking her across the room. After the floor was littered with shredded clothing, he left.

Still, the couple continued to see one another. They both lacked whatever it took to end the relationship, even though both agreed that it must stop. Bill in particular recognized the potential danger in continuing; he had heard that word of his affair had gone beyond the Profaci family and had been mentioned by some important figures in the underworld. Although the Profaci organization was not as powerful as it once was, it was still part of the national network, and Rosalie had relatives who had married into formidable families around the nation. Two of her cousins, daughters of Joseph Profaci, had married into the Zerilli and Tocco families of Detroit, and the Profacis were also kin to a family in California. While infidelity was no more uncommon in the underworld than anywhere else, great effort was always taken to protect a wife from embarrassment, and Bill's behavior was considered scandalous. His father appeared one night and appealed to his sense of family honor. "Don't be the first to dirty our name," Joseph Bonanno said. "Our name has been clean so long, for so many generations, don't be the first . . ."

But even his father's visit did not immediately influence him, and Bill was surprised by his own resistance, his independence, wondering if it was not a good sign. Then Rosalie was again pregnant; and after the birth of a son, their third, in March 1963, she took an overdose of sleeping pills and was ill for several days. When a doctor described it as possibly a suicide attempt, it made newspaper headlines, and when Bill returned home he was surprised to be greeted at the front door by his sister Catherine, who had flown in from San Mateo, and he was even more surprised when she told him that his mother-in-law was in the bedroom with Rosalie.

"She is sleeping," Mrs. Profaci said as Bill walked in, feeling very much the intruder in his own bedroom. He stood silently for a moment. Mrs. Profaci sat next to the bed. A large woman with dark hair, an angelic face, and a kindly disposition under normal circumstances, she was at this moment cold and distant. He removed his jacket, loosened his tie. He turned toward the closet for something more comfortable to wear, wondering if his mother-in-law would leave the room long enough for him to change. He slipped out of his shoes, took off his shirt. Mrs. Profaci abruptly stood and left. "I'll be out in a minute," he called after her. "We'll have coffee."

Mrs. Profaci and Catherine remained for days, both wanting to help. But Bill felt the tension every moment, particularly between him and his mother-in-law. She clearly resented his treatment of her daughter, and every time he walked into the bedroom she seemed to bristle; she was like a mother lion protecting her cub. Even though Catherine was critical of her brother, she felt that Rosalie should also share in the blame. She remembered at the convent her impressions of Rosalie as a spoiled and sheltered young girl, and she remembered her reservations about Rosalie before the marriage, thinking that Rosalie lacked the strength to help her brother through the inevitably difficult life—and she recalled how angry the elder Bonanno had become when she expressed this opinion. But Catherine was certain that her brother would not have sought the companionship of another woman during the last two years if Rosalie had fulfilled her role as a wife, and when this viewpoint was subtly conveyed at various times during conversations at dinner Mrs. Profaci was not pleased.

At one point Mrs. Profaci became so upset during an exchange with Bill that she left the table in tears and ran to Rosalie in the bedroom, locking the door behind her. Bill quickly followed, banging on the door. Rosalie woke up screaming, her mother cried out, and Catherine tried to pull Bill away from the door. When he yelled at her, Catherine answered sharply, "Don't talk to *me* that way! I'm not your wife, I'm not your mother . . ."

She continued to pull against him, a tall girl very much in control of her emotions, and when she noticed her brother's anger rising and thought that he might slap her, she said, "Go ahead, do it! I dare you."

Bill felt his sister's breath upon him, heard the wailing and weeping from the bedroom, felt suffocated by the encircling closeness, and in a fit of exasperation he clenched his fist and smashed it through the wall. The house seemed to shake, blood gushed from his knuckles, pain jolted through him. He felt piercing, throbbing sensations and chills, he thought he was close to madness. His whole life seemed to be crumbling with the falling plaster, and he was disgusted with everyone around him, hated them, thought he could kill them, and understood for the first time crimes of passion. Most murders were committed by relatives or friends of the victim, and he remembered all the headlines he had read in tabloids, MAN KILLS WIFE, CHILDREN, SELF, and now he understood why.

He bent in pain, clutching his wounded hand that would be scarred for life, felt Catherine's arms around him leading him toward a chair. She kissed him on the cheek and held him close as he lowered his head and tears came into his eyes. The room was still, there were no sounds from the bedroom. Catherine sat next to her brother in silence, closer than she had ever felt before. She knew his misery and thought about her father's part in all this. Her father had ruined him, she believed. Bill did not belong in that world, was not hard enough, cold enough, although he tried to be; he was by nature easygoing, she thought, a kind and giving man who wanted to be loved, desperately needed love. He was more like his mother or his uncle Frank; he was by nature a Labruzzo. His father had made him into a Bonanno, and now Catherine wondered and worried about what would happen to him.

Two days later, emotionally spent, Bill consented to his mother-in-law's fervent request that Rosalie return to Brooklyn and recuperate under her care. Bill would join Rosalie later. Their being apart for a while might be helpful to him as well, allowing him time to think things over and perhaps arrive at a decision. He knew that his days with two women were over, and he was relieved.

He drove them to the airport—Rosalie, Mrs. Profaci, and the three children, Charles, five, Joseph, two, and the baby Salvatore, two months. After they had gone, he returned home and spent the rest of the day and evening by himself. He welcomed the quietude, not having to speak or listen to anyone. His right hand was bandaged and painful but not broken. Within himself he felt empty, queasy, filled with remorse for Rosalie.

On the following evening he had dinner with his girl friend, and she also was distracted by a feeling of guilt and hopelessness. She sensed that Bill would never leave his wife, nor would his wife leave him, because neither was fully in control of their lives—other people had a hand in every move, and she believed that the only sensible thing to do was to return with her children to Germany. She could account for her third child, Bill's child, by explaining to her relatives in Europe that she had married again but that her husband had died—she could use the surname of a bookmaker friend of Bill's, a bachelor they both had liked and who had recently died in Tucson. And so she made up her mind, she would return to Germany, and when she suggested this to Bill he did not discourage her.

A week later, in early June, Bill called New York and told Rosalie that he wanted to see her. She did not sound enthusiastic, but he found comfort in the fact that Rosalie had not sounded enthusiastic about anything in years. He left for New York and stayed at Frank Labruzzo's home. The next day he asked two of his aunts in Brooklyn to go to the Profaci home to get Rosalie and the children; he did not know what sort of reception he might get from her family, and he thought this way might be easier on his mother-in-law and himself. But later his aunts called to say that Rosalie refused to come.

The next morning Bill and Frank Labruzzo, armed with guns, drove to the Profaci home. Both men realized that the situation was almost farcical, almost like an opera—an impassioned husband battles his in-laws to reclaim his wife. It was absurd and anachronistic, but it was also real, and Bill did not know how else to deal with a situation that was potentially dangerous. For all he knew, half the Profaci organization might be waiting for him, eager to avenge the insult he had brought upon Rosalie and her family, and even Labruzzo had recommended that they be armed.

Pulling up in front of Mrs. Profaci's home, which was next to the home of Rosalie's late uncle Joseph Profaci, Bill looked along the sidewalk for signs of waiting men or for parked cars that he might recognize. Then he walked up the stone steps and rang the bell.

The door opened slowly, and Bill saw Rosalie's older brother, a man in his thirties, sitting in the living room. He also saw Mrs. Profaci walking quickly toward him, heard whispering in the background, but before he had a chance to look around, Mrs. Profaci grabbed him by the lapel, began to shake him and warn that her daughter was not going with him. When Bill demanded to know where Rosalie was, he was told that she was not there. Mrs. Profaci's eyes were moist, her face red with emotion, and she continued to clutch his lapels and pound his chest and repeat that Rosalie would not be going with him.

Bill did not know what to do. He looked at Rosalie's brother sitting calmly in the chair, making no effort to get involved, and Bill hated him for it. If he had stood, Bill could have become aggressive with him, challenged him, done more than he could do with his mother-in-law. Then Bill saw his son Charles coming down the steps. Bill broke away from Mrs. Profaci, grabbed Charles and held him in his arms. The little boy did not protest, seemed only confused.

"I'm leaving, but I'll be back," Bill said. "And when I come back, I want Rosalie to be here and ready to leave."

They said nothing as he left. He drove with the boy back to Labruzzo's home, and from there telephoned Joseph Magliocco in East Islip. Magliocco had been in charge of the Profaci organization since the death of his brother-in-law in June 1962, exactly one year ago. While Bill had found Joseph Profaci a bit remote and difficult to talk to, Magliocco had always been approachable and informal, and after Bill called, Magliocco invited him to come at once.

Magliocco's twelve-acre estate in East Islip was protected by high stone walls, and when Bill drove past the gate with Labruzzo several dogs began to bark. Magliocco greeted them in front of the large house. He was wearing riding breeches and boots and a white polo shirt that stretched across his enormous stomach. He rode every day on his powerful white horse, and he was just walking in from the stable when Bonanno and Labruzzo arrived. At sixty-two he was a virile figure, his shoulders strong, his arms thick and muscular.

"Uncle Joe," Bill began, "I have a problem."

"Yes, I know about it," Magliocco said, in his thick accent, leading them into the house.

"In that case it makes it easier for me," Bill said. "Since you know about it and since I respect your intelligence, I'll wait to see what you can do about it."

"I already called them," Magliocco said. He sat down heavily in a chair, continuing, "I told them to be here this afternoon. Whatever is going on, I know only one thing—Rosalie's your wife, and you're entitled to her."

Bill was pleased by Magliocco's attitude. Magliocco was an old-style Sicilian. He believed that a man's wife was his property. But Sicilians also greatly respected wives, regarded them as objects of honor, and any husband in Sicily who had been as indiscreet as Bill would undoubtedly have been shot to death long ago. Bill also did not know how much Rosalie's mother had told Magliocco. Perhaps thinking it too indelicate or repulsive to reveal the fact of Bill's girl friend and illegitimate child, Mrs. Profaci had merely explained to Magliocco that Rosalie was unhappy in Arizona, became ill, and wanted to return East. Bill decided to say nothing more and see what happened.

During lunch, at which they were joined by Mrs. Magliocco, Joseph Magliocco was a gracious host. There was a great variety of food, much wine and cheese, and from the amount that Magliocco consumed Bill could readily see why Magliocco weighed so much. Magliocco and his wife were childless, and they were the only regular occupants of the fourteen-room house, although there were servants and a caretaker and other men doing odd jobs around the estate.

After coffee, they waited. Hours passed, and Magliocco finally walked impatiently into his office and called the Profaci home. A moment later, embarrassed and angry, he exclaimed, "My crazy relatives—they left for Jersey!" Then turning to Bill, he said, "Look, give me a day. Come back tomorrow. I promise you they'll all be here."

The next day, true to his word, Magliocco was standing in front of the house with the Profaci family as Bill drove in. Rosalie stepped forward; she was wearing a yellow dress, her hair was nicely done, and there was a glow about her that he had not seen in a long time. She kissed him modestly, then walked with him toward the others.

"Are you pregnant?" he asked softly, somehow certain that

she was. During all the problems of recent years she had never ceased to attract him, and though they had a three-month-old child he knew that it was possible that she was again pregnant. Rosalie blushed but did not reply to his question.

Inside the house, there was an atmosphere of formality. Mrs. Profaci had nodded toward Bill but had not spoken. Everyone took seats in the large room. After the children were ushered out, coffee was served. Magliocco smiled, tried to make small talk. He passed a tray of Italian sweets around the room. The awkwardness continued. Finally Bill spoke up.

"Let's get to the main question," he said. "Is my wife coming with me or not?"

"Of course she's coming with you," Magliocco replied, as Mrs. Profaci frowned.

Bill continued, "Because if she's not . . ."

Magliocco cut him off, shouting, "What are you talking so silly for?"

"Because that's the way I feel. If I don't have a right to my wife, I want to know it."

"Nobody says you don't have a right," Magliocco continued.

But then Mrs. Profaci spoke up. "I am sure," she said, "there must have been a reason why Rosalie tried to commit suicide . . ."

She waited as the silence set in, and Bill wondered if she was going to mention the fact of the other woman and the child. He looked at Magliocco to see how he was reacting, but Magliocco did not seem surprised by the mention of the possible suicide attempt and perhaps he knew the whole story. Mrs. Profaci asked her daughter to leave the room. Rosalie turned toward Bill for concurrence. Bill nodded for her to leave.

Then Mrs. Profaci suddenly became very emotional, almost shaking as she focused on Bill. Her eyes were soft but there was a determination about her, a strength of character that surprised and impressed him. She really loved her daughter and would do anything for her.

"*I am warning you,*" she said slowly, solemnly, emphasizing each word, "*that if anything happens to my daughter . . .*" This was clearly a serious threat, and Bill did not doubt her intent.

"*Stop!*" Magliocco interrupted. "What are you talking about?"

"*He* knows what I'm talking about." Mrs. Profaci quickly

pointed toward Bill. Magliocco moved toward her, put his big
arms around her, began to make sibilant sounds as he tried to
calm her. But she continued to glower at Bill until he looked
away. Magliocco then called in Rosalie, her brother, and the
children. More coffee was served and things became more relaxed.

When it was time to leave, Bill suggested what he felt would
further ease the situation. He asked Rosalie to spend another
night at her mother's home, saying he would stop on the following day with their son Charles to get her and the other children.
Mrs. Profaci nodded her approval.

When Bill arrived, Rosalie was already packed; her suitcase
at the bottom of the stairs was the first thing he saw as he walked
in. He was very happy. He had gotten his way, thanks largely
to Magliocco, and now he wanted to make a fresh start with his
wife and to make peace with his mother-in-law. He knew it
would take time and patience, but he also knew he wanted Rosalie back and to accomplish this his mother-in-law's support
would be helpful. He did not hastily leave with Rosalie from the
Profaci's home; he spent the afternoon there and remained for
dinner. The conversation was cordial and calm, even friendly,
between Bill and his in-laws, and when Mrs. Profaci suggested
that they leave the baby for the night, Bill and Rosalie agreed to
it. They would stop for the child on the following day.

Bill had reserved a suite for his wife and the two sons at the
International Hotel at the airport in Idlewild, Queens. He did
not want to drive to Manhattan, and it was too late for a trip out
of the city, and he did not want to stay with relatives. He had
always liked the atmosphere of airports, the movement and bus-
tle, and thought the children would also respond to it.

They arrived at the airport shortly after ten o'clock, obtained
the very best suite, and Bill sent down for hors d'oeuvres and
champagne. After the children had gone to sleep in their room,
Bill ordered more champagne, and he and Rosalie sat together
on a sofa in the soundproof suite overlooking the runway, watching the planes come and go in the night.

They had dinner at Magliocco's on the following evening, and
it was then suggested that the couple and their children live
temporarily in the big house until they decided on their next
move. Rosalie was opposed to returning to Arizona and Bill

agreed, against his better judgment, to look for a house in New York. Spending the summer at Magliocco's would be pleasant in the meantime—they would have their own apartment in the house, there were horses to ride, a boat for fishing, servants, it would be like a resort; so Bill agreed to give it a try. And he was glad that he did. Rosalie seemed much happier, the children became acquainted with their young cousins who came to visit, and Bill was free to come and go as he wished. It was also advantageous for him to be in New York during the summer of 1963—his father was still living an elusive existence, and the dissension within the organization was increasing.

Ever since the unfortunate gathering at Apalachin, the elder Bonanno avoided meeting in groups with other dons, and they became offended by his attitude. While Joseph Bonanno had always been individualistic in his thinking, insisting for example that the "families" were autonomous and that the nine-man commission, of which he was a part, could arbitrate disputes but could not dictate policy to the individual heads of "families," he now gave the impression that he was drifting even further from his fellow dons. On the occasions when his organization was represented at meetings with other organizations, it was never Bonanno himself who attended but rather one of his captains—John Morale, Labruzzo, or sometimes Notaro. But never Gaspar Di Gregorio. A distance had developed in 1963 between Di Gregorio and Bonanno, due in part to the presence of Bonanno's son in New York, whose rise Di Gregorio saw as inevitable, and due also to the elder Bonanno's haughty attitude toward the commission, whose senior member, Stefano Magaddino, boss of the Mafia in western New York and the Ohio Valley, was Di Gregorio's brother-in-law.

Stefano Magaddino, who had little tolerance for individuality and had for years been suspicious of Joseph Bonanno's ambition, encouraged Di Gregorio to boycott the Bonanno family meetings and to spread the word that Joseph Bonanno was due to be suspended and that his followers would either have to switch their allegiance or suffer the consequences.

When Bonanno learned of this, he seemed unconcerned. He believed that the commission was now composed of confused men and he did not intend to follow their dictates, having lost faith in their collective judgment. When they should have had the foresight to maintain ultrasecrecy, such as immediately fol-

lowing Albert Anastasia's death in 1957, they had foolishly
scheduled the Apalachin meeting. And when they should have
demonstrated unified strength, such as ordering the rout of the
Gallo brothers for leading a revolt against their boss, Joseph
Profaci, in 1960, the commission had—despite Profaci's and
Bonanno's protests—voted to do nothing, to let Profaci handle
his own internal problems. Profaci, a member of the commission, became disillusioned and resentful. And while the Gallo
revolt was eventually crushed by Profaci's loyal followers, it was
nonetheless achieved at a considerable loss in bloodshed and
money, and in prestige for Joseph Profaci. At one point in the
dispute, the Gallo men had succeeded in kidnaping Profaci's
chief aide, Joseph Magliocco, and three other Profaci men, and
in forcing Profaci himself to flee to Florida until concessions
were promised. Profaci's organization never fully recovered from
the internal difficulties, and while the Gallo faction claimed that
the trouble had begun because Profaci had not adequately
shared the profits with the underlings in the family, Profaci himself believed that the revolt was inspired by two of his fellow
dons on the commission—Carlo Gambino and Thomas Lucchese. Profaci was sure that these two dons had plotted the Gallo
uprising, had encouraged the Gallo men with the assurance that
the rebellion would be unopposed from the outside.

Profaci went to his grave despising Gambino and Lucchese,
whose two organizations in New York—closely related through
the marriage of Lucchese's son to Gambino's daughter—became
stronger as Profaci's became weaker; and Profaci's successor,
Magliocco, whose sister was Profaci's wife, carried on the
grudge against Gambino and Lucchese.

If Joseph Bonanno had not been on the run during the time
of the Gallo revolt, he might have openly supported Profaci's
cause with additional men, but it would not have helped because
what was really needed was a united front against the Gallos by
the commission; and Bonanno's intervention could possibly have
led to a nationwide war within the underworld, and none of the
dons, including Bonanno, wanted that.

After Profaci's death from cancer in 1962, Bonanno had no
close ally on the commission; and with the sixty-seven-year-old
Vito Genovese serving a fifteen-year jail term, the commission
was coming increasingly under the influence of Gambino,
Lucchese, and Stefano Magaddino. None of the other mem-

bers—Giancana of Chicago, Zerilli of Detroit, Bruno of Philadelphia—had the power or desire to counterbalance the first three, nor did any of them have a particular fondness for Joseph Bonanno. They, like Magaddino, were wary of his remoteness, and they were willing to accept Magaddino's view that Bonanno craved inordinate power and was waiting in semiexile for them to wither in the heat of crime hearings or to die in jail—then, at an opportune moment, Bonanno would return to New York, would consolidate the disunited forces and emerge as the boss of bosses.

This theory gained substance in the summer of 1963 with word that Bonanno's son had moved to New York and was living with Profaci's successor, Magliocco, in East Islip, Long Island, where the younger Bonanno was perhaps working on a plan to unify the Profaci-Bonanno organizations. Even if this last point was not accepted as true by a majority of dons around the nation, they waited with caution and watched the movements of the younger Bonanno. At thirty-one Bill Bonanno was considered too young to lead, and from the way that Stefano Magaddino and Gaspar Di Gregorio had described him, many dons had reservations about him and felt that he was destined to cause trouble. His treatment of Rosalie was known to the commission, and it was given wide circulation by those men who sought to discredit Bill Bonanno.

Then in late July, Bonanno became involved quite inadvertently in an incident that caused even greater damage to his image, as well as to that of his father. It happened on an early Saturday afternoon when Joseph Magliocco, whose driver had taken the weekend off, asked Bill to drive him to the railroad terminal so that he could meet someone arriving by train. Magliocco told Bill to bring a gun, and Magliocco entered the car carrying a shotgun.

Bill was apprehensive but he did not ask questions, thinking that Magliocco would explain everything in the car. But Magliocco, sitting in the back with the shotgun in his lap, said nothing as Bill drove to the Brentwood station. He parked and remained in the car as the train pulled in. He saw a man, a stranger, step from the train and head directly for Magliocco's car. The man smiled when he saw Bill Bonanno behind the wheel, said, "Hello, Bill," then turned toward Magliocco.

"Everything all right?" Magliocco asked.

"Yes," the man said, "everything is being taken care of."

"OK," Magliocco said. "Go ahead."

The man quickly turned and reboarded the New York-bound train. Magliocco asked Bill to return home, still explaining nothing, which was fine with Bill. He was not sure that he wanted to know what Magliocco was up to, being bothered enough by the sound of it. He was also concerned by the manner in which the man had greeted him at the station—the man had seemed surprised and delighted to find Bill with Magliocco, concluding perhaps that Bill and the Bonanno organization were part of whatever was about to take place.

Within a week or two, Bill began to notice Magliocco's increasing nervousness around the house, his pacing at night. Then one day in September, Magliocco revealed what had happened. He had been summoned by the commission, he said; he was fined $40,000 and was lucky to be alive. Magliocco's scheme to dispose of Gambino and Lucchese had failed. Someone had leaked word to Gambino and Lucchese in advance, and now Magliocco was panicked by the possibility of a vendetta.

Suddenly Bill became infuriated. He blamed Magliocco for getting him involved. But Magliocco assured him that he had nothing to fear, insisting that he had taken full responsibility before the commission and had made it clear that the Bonannos played no part. Bill was unconvinced. Even if Magliocco had done as he had claimed, Bill could not count on the commission's giving him the benefit of any doubt. He was sure that he and his father were in deep trouble, and the first thing that he wanted to do was to move out of Magliocco's house, which was a likely target area.

But the home that Bill had found in East Meadow was not yet ready for occupancy; so he was forced to keep Rosalie and the children at Magliocco's for three more months. It was a frenzied fall, grim and ominous as the leaves began to cover the estate and winter moved in and Magliocco rarely ventured outdoors.

Then in mid-December, Magliocco's nerves were further frayed when Bill's two-year-old son, Joseph, accidentally fired rifle bullets into the ceiling. Two weeks later, on December 28, 1963, Joseph Magliocco died of what the police called natural causes.

Suspense and uncertainty continued through the next year. Bill moved his wife and children—now including a fourth child, a daughter—into the home in East Meadow, but he kept the shrubbery trimmed low and installed bright lights in front of the house hoping to discourage gunmen from hiding there at night.

The rumors of the Gambino and Lucchese plot spread quickly through the underworld, and soon there were references to it in the newspapers. The reports, most likely the result of government wiretapping, identified the late Joseph Magliocco and the elder Bonanno as the suspects. It was also reported in the press that the Profaci organization was now under the command of Joseph Colombo, a man the government identified as one of Magliocco's lieutenants who had probably tipped off Gambino or Lucchese.

Bill Bonanno received several messages during the summer and fall of 1964 that the commission wanted to reach his father; but Joseph Bonanno was constantly on the move, traveling with bodyguards between California and Arizona, Wisconsin and New York and Canada. It was not only the anticipation of being "hit" that kept him going; he was also trying to avoid the limelight of government investigators conducting a national anti-Mafia campaign in the wake of Joseph Valachi's testimony before the Senate. Valachi had given special prominence to Bonanno during the televised hearings in 1963, claiming that it was Bonanno who initiated him into the Mafia, pricking fingers and exchanging blood to symbolize their unity. This ceremony had supposedly occurred decades ago, and Bonanno since then had been no more aware of Valachi than an army general would be of a private; but Valachi's revelations about the secret society and Bonanno's link to the traitor were embarrassing to Bonanno.

After being expelled from Canada in late July, Bonanno returned briefly to Tucson, then reappeared in New York. He held secret meetings with his officers, and he also conferred unofficially with emissaries from the commission—among them Sam De Cavalcante of New Jersey—expressing willingness to meet with the commission; but there was never an agreement on a time and place, and there was suspicion and fear of an ambush on both sides. Bonanno also made an attempt during the fall of 1964 to meet with Di Gregorio. Once he reached him by telephone, but his old friend broke down in tears, confessing that he could not meet with Bonanno because of instructions he had received from the commission.

A few of Bonanno's men wanted to dispose of Di Gregorio because of his disloyalty, but Bonanno emphatically rejected the suggestion. It would accomplish nothing, he said, and he was more saddened than angered by Di Gregorio's response. They had known one another nearly all their lives, had been born in the same year within a few miles of one another in western Sicily, had fought together as young men during the Brooklyn feuds. Bonanno blamed Stefano Magaddino for corrupting the friendship; Magaddino's jealousy, the sickness of so many Sicilians, had slowly infected Di Gregorio in later years, Bonanno felt, and while there was no logic to this there was also no cure.

Bonanno's ruling against those who wished to harm Di Gregorio was one of the last decisions that he made in 1964. It was a few nights later that Joseph Bonanno dined with Maloney.

5

Aᴆᴛᴇʀ Bɪʟʟ Bᴏɴᴀɴɴᴏ's lonely Christmas Eve in Times Square and his impulsive decision to escape the grim holiday week in New York, he spent nearly three days and nights on the road to Arizona; then at noon on December 28, 1964, a clear and balmy day, he arrived on the outskirts of Tucson and checked into the Spanish Trail Motel. He was accompanied by his dog and by the young man who had helped with the driving, a relative of Vito De Filippo, whom the government had identified as a Bonanno lieutenant operating a gambling casino for the elder Bonanno in Port-au-Prince, Haiti.

Bill was not tired after the 2,600-mile ride; he was in fact charged with energy and exhilaration, was delighted to be out of New York and back in Tucson, and the first thing he wanted to do upon arrival was to head straight into the center of town to revisit certain places and people, to bask in the familiarity of this small city where he had once felt so much at home. Even now, despite all that had happened, he was confident that he could walk through the main streets of Tucson, could wave and talk to the people he had known for years, and, unless the police stopped him, he could continue in freedom. He did not think that the average citizens of the city were against him, even those few quoted in local newspapers advocating that the Bonannos be ejected; they had been prompted into saying those things by the reporters, he felt sure, certain that it had been largely the newspaper publishers, together with the politicians and a publicity-seeking police chief, who had inspired the whole campaign against his family in recent years. They were hypocrites, he thought, particularly the politicians and a few priests, remembering how often they had come in the past to the Bonanno home, had been dined and wined, and had never once questioned the source of the money that they had quickly pocketed.

Thinking about this embittered him, and he was aware of how personally he had taken each slight in Tucson. What had been said or written about the Bonannos in Phoenix or in Flagstaff or in New York or anywhere else in America did not greatly concern him. But his acceptance in Tucson seemed fundamental to his pride; it was his only home, he had come to it as a boy and had remained for twenty years, had gone to school there, made friends there, and wanted to believe that those friends would not blow the whistle on him now should he walk through the streets of the city. But he had no intention of testing his popularity at the moment.

After settling himself in the motel, he made plans to look up his brother, to drive during the evening past his property, to contact his father's associates. One of the first people he reached was Charles Battaglia, whom the government listed as Joseph Bonanno's top aide in Tucson. Battaglia quietly visited Bill at the motel, and they spent several hours together. Afterward Bill was fatigued, too tired to go out; so he went to bed.

He slept late the next morning, had breakfast with his companion, then went outside to walk the dog. It was another fine day, and he enjoyed the clear air and seeing the great spaciousness of this desert city. He continued to walk for a few minutes with the dog, wondering how difficult it would be to reach his brother; he had not seen him in a very long time but, according to what he had heard, Joe Jr. was as outlandish as ever. His brother was said to be traveling with assorted odd characters between Phoenix and Tucson—long-haired musicians, bronco riders, drag racers, television actors. Anyone who was a bit offbeat would appeal to his teen-age brother, and his brother appealed to them, too, because he was funny and handsome and willing to do anything crazy on a moment's notice, anything to gain attention. Bill remembered how his kid brother had cavorted as a child on the edge of Niagara Falls during a family visit and had nearly fallen; how he had once hidden in an ice truck at the age of three and would have frozen to death if the driver had not discovered him; how he used to shock his mother by bringing home stray animals, once a hamster, once a bobcat, and worms to put in the holy water. Joe Jr. was sent to military school, but had quit, had been to several schools since then, and

now was presumably in college, although Bill had heard that his
brother was training horses and was appearing as a cowboy actor
on television. One of the scheduled shows was NBC's "High
Chaparral," which was to be filmed about fifteen miles west of
Tucson, and Bill smiled at the thought of network executives in
New York sitting in a screening room watching dusty gun scenes
that included, unknown to them, the youngest son of Joseph
Bonanno.

Bill walked the dog farther along the road, his mind wandering pleasantly, and then suddenly he stopped and quickly turned
around. He expected to find someone standing behind him or
someone observing him through binoculars from the roof of the
motel. But he saw no one. There was no sign of movement along
the road, nobody was seated in the car parked in the lot, and yet
he was sure he was being watched, trusting his instinct for sensing such things. Without waiting for further confirmation, he
headed back to the motel.

His room was as he had left it, the television set was on.
In the adjoining room his companion sat reading the morning
newspaper. Bill related his suspicions; then he decided to test
his instincts immediately—he would hang around in front of the
motel for a while, would make himself obvious, and if he was
being followed or sought he would soon know it.

It was an odd decision, and it surprised him at first, causing
him to wonder if being back in Arizona had made him more lax
or careless. But he finally concluded that after so many months
of hiding, there was no longer any advantage in it. In New York,
hiding had been necessary, especially after the disappearance of
his father more than two months ago; it had then been his duty
to remain free for the morale of the men and for whatever con-
tribution he could make during his father's absence. Now, however, that situation had changed. His father was said to be alive,
and there was nothing for him to do until his father's return. If
the FBI or the Tucson police had just spotted him, it was no
tragedy because they could not prove he had committed a crime.
The worst that they might prove was that he had been hiding,
and if forced to explain why, he could say he had become apprehensive over the threats to his safety that he read about in the
newspapers.

He walked casually from his room in the rear of the large
motel to the front of the place, standing near the office along the

road. His friend accompanied him, and they stood talking for a few minutes in the sun. Then Bill noticed a barbershop nearby, and, deciding he could use a light trim, he walked in, his friend following. It was a three-chair shop, was not very busy, and a white-haired barber stood smiling and said, "You're next."

Bill did not recognize anyone in the shop. He picked up a magazine and sat in the chair. His friend took a seat near the door.

"You visiting?" the barber asked, cheerfully, tossing a sheet around his shoulders. Bill nodded.

"You planning to stay long?"

"Yes, if I like the place, I'd like to stay," Bill said.

A manicurist approached him, but Bill shook his head, continued to flip through the magazine, looking up every few moments into the large mirror reflecting the road. He saw a car pull up, then another, then a police car. Two more more police cars arrived, also press cars with photographers.

"Hey, what's all the commotion outside?" one of the barbers asked.

Bill's barber turned toward the window, whistled softly as he continued to snap the scissors over Bill's head. Bill said nothing. Then he spotted a local FBI agent that he had known from the past, Kermit Johnson, walking into the barbershop, followed by other men. Bill forced a smile, waved, and called out:

"Hi, Kermit."

Kermit Johnson seemed embarrassed by the sign of familiarity, but then he softened and replied, "Hello, Bill, how are you?" Johnson stood awkwardly in front of the chair for a moment, and the barber looked at him and said, "Won't be long, sir. You'll be next."

Johnson, looking straight at Bill, asked, "You know why I'm here?"

"Yes, I know," Bill said. "Can I finish my haircut? Or are you going to make a scene?"

"No, I'm not going to make a scene," Johnson said. "Are you armed?"

Bill replied, in a tone of mock innocence, "Kermit, don't be silly."

The barber was becoming nervous.

"Excuse me," the barber finally interrupted, pointing toward the crowd of policemen and photographers gathered along the sidewalk, "what are all those gentlemen doing outside?"

"Those *gentlemen*," Bill said, "are waiting for *me*."

The barber said nothing for a moment, the words setting in; then his hands began to shake, and he could barely hold onto the scissors.

Bill was taken to the sheriff's office of Pima County, was arrested on a material-witness warrant issued by a federal judge in New York. He received a subpoena to appear before the grand jury in Manhattan that was investigating organized crime and his father's disappearance, was held on $25,000 bail pending that appearance, and was forced to relinquish the $215 he carried in his pocket, and also his 1964 Cadillac, toward the tax lien on his Arizona property. Before entering the jail cell, where he would spend two days, he shook hands with the police, waved and smiled at the photographers. Like his father, he was determined not to give them the grim, guilt-ridden picture that he felt sure they wanted.

6

O**N THE MORNING OF** January 6, 1965, Bill Bonanno climbed the stone steps of the massive gray federal courthouse in lower Manhattan to appear before the grand jury. He was carefully dressed in a dark suit, white shirt, and striped silk tie under his blue cashmere overcoat and new gray hat; and he was clean-shaven, having discarded the disguise. He was neither tense nor worried as he entered the building, was actually quite calm, relieved that things were finally becoming resolved and confident that he could handle himself well in court. He had spent the weekend reviewing his case, guessing which questions he would be asked, deciding which questions he would answer and which he would not, and he was prepared for the consequences if his limited cooperation displeased the jury.

He was accompanied by his attorney, Albert J. Krieger, one of the best young criminal lawyers in New York. Krieger was a broad-shouldered man in his early forties, who wore horn-rimmed glasses and had shaved every hair off the top of his head in the style of actor Yul Brynner; but there was nothing theatrical about Krieger in a courtroom. He avoided dramatic gestures, lengthy oratory, or tactics that merely delayed the proceedings, which was one reason why he was popular with judges, and he was always well prepared and alert for every legal advantage, which had contributed to his high standing among his colleagues in the profession. Bill Bonanno considered himself fortunate to have Krieger on his side.

As they stepped toward the elevator on the fourteenth floor, photographers rushed toward them with flashbulbs popping, and reporters asked:

"Is your father alive?"

"Where do you think he's hiding?"

"Who's behind the kidnaping?"

Bill Bonanno continued to walk in absolute silence, impassive, while Krieger shook his head, saying, "Neither I nor my client has anything to say at this time. We will make no comment whatsoever."

In the grand jury room on the fourteenth floor, which was barred to the press, it was quickly apparent to the younger Bonanno that the government had invested considerable time and money in its investigation of him, and he could not help but be impressed by the depth of its research. It was not the government's probing into his illegal activities that surprised him or its evidence that revealed he was part of his father's organization or its knowledge of his hideaway in Queens (the exact location was not yet known); it was rather the government's close scrutiny of his private life that impressed him; irritated him. From the questions he was asked he could deduce that the government was aware of his extramarital affair, his illegitimate child, his problems with Rosalie; it knew about his own problems as a young man and college student, his business ventures in Flagstaff and Phoenix, his pilot training in Tucson, which had led some government attorneys to suspect that he had been flying his father back and forth between various secret places in recent months.

While he issued a denial, he was intrigued by the possibilities of such methods of escape and reminded himself that he should keep up with his flying. In nearly all of his testimony, he was as candid as he could be, admitting for example that he was acquainted with Sam Giancana, having met him at the Desert Inn in Las Vegas, and that he knew Stefano Magaddino, describing him as a "distant cousin." He would not state if he had ever met Carlo Gambino or Thomas Lucchese and said he had never met Vito Genovese. He said that his business interests in New York were in real estate investing, and in his pocket he carried business cards listing himself as an executive vice-president of the Republic Financial Corporation of 140 Cedar Street. Regarding his personal life, he admitted being the father of his mistress's child, adding that he felt a moral and financial responsibility to them both but that Rosalie and his four children came first. He had no idea where his father was, he said, or if his father was indeed alive; beyond that, he would not comment on his father's disappearance, including the fact that it was he who had telephoned Maloney on December 18 with word that his father was alive.

It was Bill Bonanno's contention that the conversation with Maloney was privileged information protected by the rights of a client-attorney relationship—he felt that Maloney at the time of the call was not merely the elder Bonanno's lawyer but also the legal representative for Bill and his sister, Catherine, who had also been summoned to testify before the grand jury. In her instance, Maloney's role was not contested; he in fact submitted reports from West Coast physicians that Catherine's small children were suffering from tonsilitis, that she herself was undergoing treatment for an intestinal ailment and sinusitis, and therefore could not serve as a witness. (The judge countered by appointing another physician in California to examine Catherine and verify her incapability of appearing in New York.) But the legal argument over Bill's relationship with Maloney went on for days, during which several other developments were reported to be occurring on the outside.

There was the announcement in Rome by the news agency Italia that Joseph Bonanno was believed to be hiding out in Sicily; attributing its information to unidentified sources within the police department, the agency stated that FBI agents were now searching the island and it suggested that the elder Bonanno had sailed from the United States on a Panamanian merchant ship under an assumed name and went ashore on a fishing boat.

There were also news reports about an underworld meeting in a Long Island restaurant that had been held to discuss the Bonanno situation; among those present were Sam Giancana of Chicago, Thomas Eboli, reputed leader of the Vito Genovese organization during Genovese's imprisonment, and Carmine Tramunti, an officer in the Lucchese organization. The restaurant in Cedarhurst was closed to regular patrons on the night of the meeting, and as a result the proprietor was subpoenaed along with the others to testify before the grand jury.

Although nothing of great significance seemed to emerge from their testimony, the exposure of that gathering and similar ones in 1965 kept organized crime in the headlines and focused constant attention on such men as Sam Giancana, who had once been able to travel freely between fashionable gambling casinos and night spots in the United States and overseas without interruptions and questioning from agents. But as the media accel-

erated its coverage of the Mafia, a trend concurrent with the
intensified anti-Mafia campaign begun initially at the Justice
Department under Attorney General Robert F. Kennedy and
gradually endorsed by J. Edgar Hoover, there was no longer
much privacy for Giancana and other reputed dons; almost everything they did was observed and made available to the press,
and the publicity not only affected them but anyone with whom
they were seen in public. Giancana's travels with singer Phyllis
McGuire were widely reported, as was his acquaintance with
Frank Sinatra. Giancana's relationship with Sinatra, specifically
his presence at Sinatra's Cal-Neva lodge at Lake Tahoe and his
inclusion elsewhere in Sinatra's entourage, caused a dispute between Sinatra and the Nevada gambling authorities and was believed to have been instrumental in Sinatra's decision to sell his
interest in the Cal-Neva lodge and in The Sands motel in Las
Vegas. But the pursuit of the slim, dapper Giancana continued,
haunting him even on the golf course as agents trailed him from
tee to green, causing him finally to file charges against the agents
in a Chicago court. The judge ordered the agents to stay at least
one foursome behind Giancana, but a United States appeals
court later overruled the judge's surveillance restrictions.

The Supreme Court meanwhile had rejected an appeal by the
family of the late Al Capone on their invasion of privacy complaint against the CBS television series "The Untouchables,"
which dramatized Capone's activities during the heyday of Chicago gangsterism. However, Capone's forty-eight-year-old son,
Albert Francis Capone, Jr., of Fort Lauderdale, Florida, did
succeed in having his name legally changed to Albert Francis,
claiming that his father's reputation "pushes me into the glare
of publicity for even minor violations of the law."

Bill's brother also changed his name, though never legally or
consistently, when he was concerned about getting part-time
work on television Westerns or in rodeos or was trying to arrange bookings for the teen-age musical groups he sometimes
managed. Nevertheless he, too, was subpoenaed in January 1965
by the grand jury to testify about his father's disappearance, and
his photograph was printed in *The New York Times* and other
publications. Joseph Bonanno, Jr., remained in New York for
one day, during which he had no comment to make to the jury
or the press, and he did not smile as the camera lights flashed
into his face while he stood waiting outside the courtroom door.

After he was released from further questioning, he returned quietly to Phoenix College.

Bill Bonanno appeared twenty-one times before the grand jury during January and February, contending throughout that what he had said on the telephone to Maloney was privileged information that should be legally withheld from the jury. But the government attorneys disagreed, and the Assistant United States Attorney, Gerald Walpin, insisted that "the unanswered questions are of vital importance in our efforts to learn what happened to and the whereabouts of Joseph Bonanno."

Bill remained adamant. He had already made one big mistake in calling Maloney, disregarding the warning *don't make waves, don't do anything*, and he feared that his father's life might be in greater jeopardy if he again ignored the advice and discussed the substance of the call he had received at the phone booth and the call he had made to Maloney afterward. So he persisted in his silence as the government interrogators became increasingly irritated, and finally the question of what to do next was placed before Judge Charles H. Tenney.

On March 1 the judge announced his ruling—a client-attorney relationship had not existed between Maloney and the younger Bonanno at the time of the call in December, and the judge therefore ordered Bonanno to reveal the substance of the conversation. Bonanno, facing the judge, replied, "With all due deference and respect to the court, I decline to answer on the grounds of attorney-client relationship." Judge Tenney, suddenly impatient, cited Bonanno for contempt of court. He sentenced him to jail immediately for an indefinite term, and denied bail pending appeal.

Bill Bonanno displayed no sign of emotion as he was led by court authorities out of the room to the elevator, then down to the basement where, in a large dimly lit room, several handcuffed prisoners sat waiting to be driven across town to jail. Bill was searched and relieved of his wristwatch, ring, pocket handkerchief and other personal possessions by a guard who noted the contents on a document that Bill signed. Then he was handcuffed to a large black man with facial scars and a vague expression about the eyes. The black man did not speak, did not even look at Bill as their wrists were linked.

Soon they were lined up with the other prisoners and marched through a corridor up a ramp into a faded green bus. The cross-town ride over the narrow cobblestone streets of downtown Manhattan was slow and bumpy. Bill looked out the window at the crowds of people going home from work, jamming themselves into subway kiosks, waving at cabs. The other prisoners paid no attention to the street; they sat looking at the floor or straight ahead and Bill guessed that they had taken this ride before.

Many of the prisoners were black, a few were Puerto Rican, a few were white and had hard aging faces and hollow eyes common on the Bowery, except these men did not have the shakes and their hands were strong and steady, hands of safe-crackers. Most of the men were probably small-time thieves and dope pushers, pimps and numbers runners, rapists and maybe even killers, but Bill did not sense any great strength of character about them; they were doubtless part of the anonymous mass of criminals who dominate the national statistics but never make a name. Bill was the only one in the bus who was well dressed; the rest wore shirts without ties, tattered coats or leather jackets over rumpled trousers and scuffed shoes, and they sat slumped in the bus looking tired and hopeless, a team of losers after the game.

The bus turned into West Street near the waterfront along the Hudson River, a neighborhood of warehouses, loading ramps, and trailer trucks parked for the night under the elevated road-way still busy with commuter traffic. The bus stopped in front of one sturdy-looking stone building that looked like a ware-house but was in fact the jail, although it was too dark for Bill to see the building clearly from the outside. He heard a guard yelling in front of the bus, heard the clicking sound of handcuffs as the prisoners filed out in twos, then walked with his companion past large steel doors that clanged quickly behind them after they entered the Federal House of Detention.

They passed through small rooms with barred windows; then, in a large room, they were halted, uncuffed, lined against the wall. They waited in line for at least an hour as guards and an orderly inspected each newly arrived prisoner, forcing each prisoner to remove his clothes and stand naked for inspection. While certain guards examined the shoes, particularly the heels where hollow portions might contain drugs, other guards probed between the prisoners' toes, teeth, into the ears, anus, under the testicles. The shoes were returned to the prisoners, although the clothing was confiscated for the term of confinement; cotton robes were issued, and the men, wearing their shoes without socks, were led into the record room. There they were interrogated by desk clerks who collected personal data for the files, then they were fingerprinted and given medical examinations, finally they were led past stock clerks who issued each prisoner a pillowcase and a single sheet for a cell bunk.

Bill noticed that several uniformed prisoners were assisting the jail staff in processing the incoming men—the clerk typists were prisoners, the medical orderlies were prisoners, so were the men in the stock room. These prisoners were more lively and alert than the group Bill had come with, and he also assumed that the holders of these positions held a certain power over the other inmates. But what impressed him most at this point was the deferential manner in which these men were treating him. They had been noticeably attentive as he moved through the lines, a few had smiled at him, and one prisoner—confined to a cell near the corridor—had called out his name, saying, "Hi, Bill, we heard you were coming." The man looked vaguely familiar. He was a white man in his fifties who seemed healthy and relaxed, possessing an air of innocence.

Bill returned the greeting and moved on, following in line up to the second floor, to the captain's office, where cell assignments were announced. Bill was given a cell in the maximum-security section. He was escorted to it by a guard who was formal but not abrupt and who, after Bill had entered the cell, closed the steel door gently. The cell was more heavily fortified with steel than the others he had seen, and it was located in an isolated corner near a staircase. It was small, damp, and depressing, with a bunk in one corner and a toilet and tiny sink in the other. The cell next to it was unoccupied. The place was intensely quiet.

He stood for a few moments, but his feet without socks felt clammy in his shoes. He sat on the edge of the bunk. It was cold and he thought of covering himself with the bunk blanket but decided for no particular reason that he had better wait. It was probably 8:00 P.M. He had not eaten since lunch and was hungry. Now he heard voices echoing in distant corridors along with the clanging metallic sounds of heavy doors opening and closing. He sat for what seemed like an hour thinking about where he was, almost doubting it, and wondering how Rosalie had taken the news that he was in jail. When he left the house in East Meadow in the morning, it was assumed that he would return by evening, a routine he had followed since he had begun appearing in court two months ago. Neither he nor Krieger had ever anticipated that he would be sent to jail without being able to post bond and to remain free pending appeal. Bill knew now that he could remain in prison until the expiration date of the grand jury in April 1966, more than a year away, unless he agreed to answer the question about the phone calls. Although Krieger planned to file papers immediately with the United States Circuit Court of Appeals asking that bail be set, Bill was not optimistic. He felt that the government intended to press him hard now, and he expected no favors from the court.

After hearing the sound of approaching footsteps, Bill saw a guard peeking into his cell holding up a few magazines, newspapers, and a chocolate candy bar.

"Bill," he said, "Harold would like you to have these."

Bill did not reply. Harold? He was confused but did not want to show it. He also did not want to indicate that he knew who Harold was.

"Harold," the guard went on, "you know—the one you saw when you came in."

Bill recalled seeing one effeminate creature among the medical orderlies who had smiled at him, and he remembered the other uniformed prisoners, too, including the gregarious one in the corner cell who had seemed familiar. Then he suddenly remembered that this man *was* named Harold—Harold (Kayo) Konigsberg, the so-called king of the loan sharks. Bill had met him briefly a few years ago in New Jersey, and he also remembered reading in newspapers about Konigsberg as a privileged inmate in a Jersey prison in which guards were accused of allowing women into the cells for brief sexual interludes. Bill was amused and impressed that Konigsberg apparently still knew how to make the best of things behind bars, but he did not reveal any sign of recognition to the guard. He thanked him and accepted the magazines, newspapers, and candy, and he was relieved when the guard walked away.

Bill was now extremely suspicious of the special treatment he was receiving, and he certainly had no intention of eating the candy, although he craved it. If his father's enemies wished to dispose of him in jail there was no easier method than poison. For all he knew, Konigsberg and the others who had been friendly, including the guards, might be involved in a contract with the commission. He remembered reading once how Gaspare Pisciotta, the alleged betrayer and assassin of Giuliano, died of poison in a Palermo jail in spite of the extraordinary precautions Pisciotta had taken. Pisciotta's mother was permitted to bring him food, Pisciotta was allowed to make his own coffee in jail, and he also fed bits of everything to his pet sparrow before consuming it himself. Then one day Pisciotta complained to a prison doctor of chest trouble; vitamin concentrate was prescribed, and Pisciotta added a teaspoon of it to his coffee. Two minutes later he was on the ground writhing in pain, and within a half hour Pisciotta was dead.

Bill put the candy aside and sat reading the newspapers. There was no mention of him in these editions, the grand jury ceasing to be news at this point, although he was sure there would be a story in tomorrow's editions about his imprisonment. Perhaps word of his refusal to talk would make points with his father's captors, would perhaps contribute to his father's well-being. Bill was anxious to see what effect, if any, his going to jail would have on the outside. If nothing positive resulted after a month or two, if he saw no reason for remaining behind bars and thought he could be useful back in circulation, despite having to spend most of each weekday in court, he could inform the warden that he wanted to resume testifying before the grand jury. Judge Tenney had guaranteed his immediate release under these conditions.

In court Bill could tell the jury all about the phone calls, explaining the coinbox system his father had devised, relating the call from the stranger, the substance of his own call to Maloney—things he now considered too risky to discuss. If his father was still missing months from now he might decide that he had nothing to lose by talking. The whole telephone episode, after all, revealed nothing about his father's whereabouts or the men who took him there. The government thought the calls were significant, but Bill knew they were not—in any case his decision about discussing them was something he could consider in the months ahead. Meanwhile he would remain in jail. He thought that jail was perhaps not such a bad place for him at this time. It offered him the luxury of not hiding, not running; he could relax for a while and think about his future. The only thing he had to worry about in jail was staying alive.

Bill Bonanno heard hissing sounds through the bars and looked up. He saw a skinny, nervous dark-eyed prisoner motioning toward him.

"You got any clothes?" the man asked in a whisper.

Bill shook his head, saying he had only the robe that he wore.

"Let me see what I can do," the prisoner said, adding that his name was Joe and that he was a friend of one of the Bonanno organization's bookmakers on the Lower East Side. Joe then disappeared quietly up the steps to the third floor.

Within a half hour, Joe returned carrying a freshly laundered T-shirt and pair of shorts, a blue denim shirt and trousers, and a pair of woolen socks. After Bill thanked him, Joe again disappeared upstairs.

Although the trousers and shirt were small, Bill managed to squeeze into them. He was curious not only about Joe but about the whole way of life in prison. There was obviously a small society and special pecking order within this thick-walled world and he wanted to learn more about it, but he had to be careful, he reminded himself. He began to feel warmer and more comfortable in the clothes. Later he wrapped himself in the blanket and went easily to sleep.

A guard banging on the bars woke him up early the next morning. While other prisoners were escorted to a mess hall, he was confined to his cell where a breakfast tray was soon shoved through a slot in the door. It consisted of oatmeal, toast, and coffee. After he finished, he stood waiting, thinking that soon he would be led out for a shower and shave. He waited for a few hours but no one came. He had noticed that his toilet did not flush, the sink did not work, and he planned to mention this to the guard, but then he decided he had better wait until he understood more about the place before making complaints.

Most of the afternoon passed before a guard appeared. Under his arm the guard carried a folded sheet of paper, and, peeking into the cell, he said to Bill, almost confidentially, "Look, this is not a very good cell. I don't think you're too comfortable here. Why don't you fill out this sheet—it's called a 'cop-out sheet'—and tell the warden you'd like something better . . ."

Bill looked at the guard, astonished. But the guard seemed
sincere. Bill took the sheet, thanked him, and returned to his
bunk, not even reading the paper. If he signed it he was sure it
would somehow be used as evidence against him, would mark
him as a chronic complainer on his first full day in jail, might
even justify some special punishment they had in store for him.
If he got out of this cell, he might be given something worse, if
that were possible, might be placed in some special room designed to break him down or otherwise subject him to incriminating temptations. His imagination raced with dire possibilities.
He waited until the guard had turned away and was gone, then
he placed the ''cop-out sheet'' on a ledge next to the newspapers
and the unopened candy bar.

The dinner tray that night contained food barely edible, although he admitted to himself that nothing would seem palatable
while he was in his current state of mind. Later Joe reappeared
outside the cell holding three hard-boiled eggs in a paper napkin.
He handed them quickly to Bill, explaining that they had been
smuggled from the commissary, then he was gone. Bill was
sorry he had taken the eggs. If he ate them, he might die; if he
did not, he might get caught with them by a guard and be charged
with smuggling, or at least have to explain where he got them.
Quickly he crushed the eggs into tiny pieces which he deposited
into the toilet. He waited, but the guard did not come. He suspected that Joe might be a prison spy, having heard that such
men are commonly found in jails, lessening their own term as
they reported on fellow inmates. Bill also thought it possible
that his cell was bugged, that some hidden camera might be
focused on him, but he was almost accustomed to that feeling,
and it did not bother him.

On the following day the guard returned with another ''cop-
out sheet.'' Again Bill took it but did not sign it, and the same
thing happened on the third day. There was no exchange of
words or emotions between them, it was all impersonal, automatic—the guard shoved the form through the bars, Bill took it,
said thank you, then placed it on the ledge with the other un-
signed forms. But he was becoming increasingly uncomfortable
now without having had a shower or a shave since his arrival,
and he could not escape the odor of his own excrement and the
smell of the eggs.

During the next morning, his fourth day in the cell, he was

escorted to an outside bathroom and told to shave—his lawyer,
Krieger, was waiting to speak to him in the warden's outer office.
Krieger had come to say that the legal papers were filed with the
court of appeals but that the process would be slow. Krieger
noticed that Bill seemed rumpled, unkempt, and he was shocked
to hear that Bill had not been permitted to shower in four days
and that the toilet was not functioning. Krieger wanted to report
this immediately to Judge Tenney, but Bill begged him not to,
saying it would only cause more trouble for him in jail. If Krieger insisted on doing something, Bill suggested that he might
drop a hint to the warden but that under no circumstances was
Krieger to convey the impression that Bill was complaining.

Three days later a guard came for Bill, led him out of the
maximum-security cell and escorted him through a long corridor into a large cell in which there were a dozen or more bunks
on each side and a number of prisoners standing around and
talking. The place was brighter and obviously less restrictive; in
the parlance of prison life, Bill Bonanno was now "in population." Harold Konigsberg and Joe were not there but he recognized a few faces from the first day, and after the guard had
gone the men introduced themselves and a few seemed very
intelligent. At dinner time Bill accompanied them in line to the
mess hall, sitting at one of the long tables and noticing that there
were spoons and forks on the tables, but no knives. He also
noticed that the salt and pepper was sprinkled on tiny pieces of
paper in front of each plate; one prisoner explained to Bill that
there had once been salt and pepper shakers but all had been
stolen.

When the prisoners were not eating or sleeping, they were
kept busy at various tasks; and as Bill had suspected, the prison
was in many ways run by the inmates. The chefs were prisoners,
as were the bankers, plumbers, launderers, carpenters. The blue
denim uniforms worn by the men—Bill had finally received
clothes that fit him properly—were made by female prisoners in
a women's penitentiary. The library was staffed by prisoners,
whose taste was dominated by escape literature—science fiction,
mysteries, but sex novels were prohibited. Prisoners also were
in charge of the movie projector—on evenings when films were
allowed. Bill was often bored by the films that could be shown—
light comedy, Doris Day, Lassie, Tarzan; no gangster films, no

violent Westerns, nothing sexually suggestive. The magazines included *The Reader's Digest*, trade publications dealing with automobiles and sports, comic books but not *Playboy*. It was apparently prison policy to try to curb masturbation by denying access to photographs of naked women, but Bill noticed that several advertisements evidently featuring young women had been torn out of the available magazines, possibly by guards, most likely by inmates. Homosexuals were obvious around the prison, but they tended to keep to themselves, being available if desired outside their circle although fearing the brutality that often accompanied the risk.

Bill's first job, that of a painter in a crew assigned to wainscot the walls of several rooms and corridors, permitted him to move widely through the maze of prison life and to observe and over-hear much of what was said and done. Although the guards were always nearby—sitting in the visitors' room, standing with car-bines on the rooftop enclosure when prisoners were permitted outdoors—Bill realized that the prisoners were nonetheless able, through skill and imagination, through begging, borrowing, stealing, and bartering, to achieve a degree of independence and to obtain certain commodities that were officially forbidden. For example, while it was against regulations to drink coffee in the cells or to drink whiskey anywhere in prison, certain inmates managed to do both by fashioning their own heating apparatus for instant coffee and by making their own whiskey from ingre-dients they smuggled in from the kitchen.

The coffee-making process was relatively simple: they cut off a piece of cord from the electric floor polisher that was kept in the hall closet, and after attaching wire from the cord to the metal handles of two broken spoons and lowering the spoons into a cup of water, the men inserted the plug into an outlet in the cell to heat the water. Then they added the stolen coffee, sugar, and milk.

The whiskey making, however, required more planning and patience. The prisoners began by stealing a jar or vase and put-ting into it pieces of apples, cucumber, potato, and also raisins that they had picked out of the raisin bread at breakfast. They added yeast, which they obtained from the prison baker in ex-change for packs of cigarettes. (From the size of the bread on the breakfast table each morning, Bill could tell whether or not the yeast content was low; if it was, he assumed that somewhere

in the prison whiskey was being processed.) The yeast and the
other ingredients were kept in a jar half-filled with water for
nearly a week, hidden behind brooms and mops in closets that
had air vents that permitted the smell of fermentation to escape.
When the brewing process was considered complete, a prisoner
would pour the liquid through a towel into another jar, and the
men would drink it. Bill had tried it only once, and his stomach
burned for days.

The drink was consumed mostly by black and indigent white
prisoners, not inmates who had money or influence on the outside. These men could often bribe the guards into smuggling in
name-brand whiskey in the tiny bottles served on airplanes.
Equality among men, Bill quickly learned, was as varied in jail
as it was outside; money signified power on either side of the
wall—prisoners with money could have favors done for guards
on the outside in return for privileges within; and these prisoners
could also have money deposited with the commissary each
month in the name of indigent prisoners who would kick back
part of the amount in items purchased, such as cigarettes, or
would repay the debt by relieving their benefactors of prison
chores, such as cleaning the cell or stealing extra clothing from
the stockroom. While the amount of money was small—no prisoner was allowed to exceed fifteen dollars a month credit in the
commissary—there were several prisoners whose family or
friends on the outside could not afford to send even fifteen dollars, and it was these prisoners who became the servants of the
more affluent.

There were social levels within a society of imprisoned men,
and while Bill Bonanno tried to avoid becoming part of any
clique, he tended to associate more with the affluent white-collar
criminals—the stock swindlers, the crooked lawyers, the business executives who had misappropriated company funds. These
men were more articulate and interesting than the others, and
during leisure time in the evenings Bill learned many things,
including how to play chess. But he also sensed about them a
quality of deceit and hypocrisy that went beyond any he had felt
in his father's world—these men knew crime on its most genteel
level, perpetrating their corporate vices on carpeted floors in
paneled offices, and even their presence in jail did not seem to
tarnish their veneer of respectability. They suggested what they
were underneath, however, by their interest in him, their ex-

pressed desire to see him when they all were again free. They said they had propositions that might interest him, and he could imagine what these propositions were, consisting no doubt of intimidating one of their business competitors or subtly threatening a stubborn labor leader or harassing a landlord who refused to sell out to a big land developer or avenging a personal insult or a social snub or beating up a wife's lover.

The newspapers usually described these men as "respectable" executives who had been corrupted by mobsters, but Bill thought that just as often it was the executives who lured others into doing the dirty work. In any case, Bill Bonanno was not interested in any of their propositions. He enjoyed their company while in confinement, was curious about how their minds worked, but once he was released from jail he did not care if he saw any of them again.

Rosalie visited the prison every week, bringing a different son each time. The boys were growing up and already having problems of their own. The eldest, Charles, was doing poorly in school. The second boy, Joseph, was very competitive with Charles; he seemed extremely intelligent and alert but was frequently ill with asthmatic bronchitis and often bedridden. The youngest son, Salvatore, who reminded Bill of his own childhood photographs, was a determined boy with a hot temper and Rosalie found it difficult to control him. The only glowing reports that Bill received in jail concerned his one-year-old daughter, Felippa, who was beginning to walk and had dark hair, bangs, and whose ears were pierced to hold tiny diamond earrings.

Seeing Rosalie in the visitors' room, her reddish hair stylishly arranged, her large brown eyes very expressive, her trim figure attired in her most becoming clothes, reminded Bill of how pretty she was and made him wonder why he had strayed as he had in Arizona. Of course it was difficult in jail for him to feel what he had felt during his final years in Tucson and Phoenix, to remember exactly how maddening his life had been and how necessary his affair had then seemed. Now Rosalie seemed more understanding and aware of his commitments to his father, although she still was reserved and remote, having undoubtedly not forgiven him for what he had done to her. Her visits seemed more an act of duty than anything else, and yet he reminded

himself that he should expect no more from her in this place—
the visitors' room was strange and inhibiting, with Rosalie and
Bill forced to sit facing one another separated by a glass wall
and to speak through telephones. The boys were completely
confused by the surroundings, could not understand why their
father was living there. During one visit Rosalie repeated to Bill
what their younger sons had replied when asked by a neighborhood child where their father was. He was living in a phone
booth, they said, a very large glass booth where they talked to
him through a telephone without paying a dime.

7

On this day, as on so many others, Rosalie Bonanno felt a sense of loneliness without a sense of privacy; she believed that her telephone was tapped, suspected that her home was being watched sometimes by men with binoculars, that even the sound of her footsteps was being recorded by tiny hidden gadgets and if she ventured beyond her door she might become exposed still further to strangers and to herself, for what she was and was not, by the lights of the cameramen who occasionally cruised by.

Her past had not prepared her for the present. As a girl the reality of her family's world was kept from her; the first of three daughters, she was protected like a precious jewel, closely observed, polished, admired, displayed on special occasions. She was sent at seven to a convent school on a gentle hill in upstate New York to dwell in a state of grace and innocence, to learn about God and man from the Dominican nuns. She was awed by the beauty of the place, its atmosphere of obedience and its identity with virtue, and she was saddened when her parents reclaimed her during her twelfth year so that her approaching womanhood could be attained under her mother's guidance.

At home in Brooklyn she continued to live a sheltered existence, attending school during the day within the walls of Visitation Academy, taught by cloistered nuns, and never going out at night except in the company of a member of her family. It was one of the ironies of her life that she had never slept alone until after she was married. At the convent upstate, there was either a nun or classmate sharing the bedroom, and when she returned to live in Brooklyn there was always one of her sisters. After her marriage to Bill, however, she experienced nocturnal solitude for the first time, and she began to dread the night as she never had as a child, and she remained awake pondering the uncertainties of her adult life—the fact that when her husband left the house in the morning she never knew what time he would return or *if* he would return; the unexplained origin of her first son, Charles; the mysterious disappearance of her father-in-law. She did not know why the monthly payments on the home in East Meadow were made in the name of a stranger or why the mailman frequently left letters addressed to people she did not know or whether the various men she had seen across the street observing the house were detectives or reporters or gangsters or merely neighbors whose curiosity had been aroused by photographs of the house in the Long Island press.

On the exterior, the house was not unlike the other modern ranch-type structures along Tyler Avenue, except that the shrubbery was trimmed lower and at night the lighting outside was brighter. There was a patio in the rear and a swimming pool which was boarded over because Rosalie feared that one of the younger children might fall in. The house had eight newly furnished rooms, an enormous basement, and a two-car garage cluttered with bicycles, and cardboard cartons that Rosalie had not yet unpacked. What distinguished the home on the interior from ordinary suburban dwellings was not immediately obvious, although there were items here and there that suggested a preparedness for danger and confinement. There were rifles among the paraphernalia in the garage, and also a rifle in the guest room behind a bureau on which was a statue of the Christ child. A storage room in the basement was lined with shelves packed with canned goods, boxes of pasta, tins of coffee, bottles of wine—there was enough food and drink there to make it unnecessary to shop for months. There was an unloaded pistol on top of Bill's bureau in the master bedroom along with a plastic tube of quarters. There was the debugging device in one of the lower drawers. Rosalie knew that her husband kept other tubes of coins and private possessions and papers in his bureau, too, but she did not pry. His bureau was off limits to her and the children—whatever was on the bureau could be touched by none but himself, and Rosalie always placed his freshly laundered shirts, underwear, and socks at the foot of the bed for him to put away himself. If the children were squabbling over a toy, he threatened to "put it on the bureau," which meant they could not again touch it until he returned it.

He was a good father, strict but also attentive and warm-hearted, and, except for the privacy of his bureau, he did not believe in obscuring any part of his life from them, be it a pistol or a newspaper featuring his picture. He had disagreed with the way Rosalie had been reared, and he told her that as soon as the children were old enough to understand, he would attempt to explain his life to them. Rosalie knew that one of the boys had already asked him why he carried a pistol, and Bill had replied that there were certain people who might wish to harm him, or to harm people he knew, and that a pistol was one way to dis-courage them. The two older boys now accepted the fact of his carrying a gun as readily as they accepted Hop-along Cassidy or the other cowboys, detectives, or soldiers they watched each day on television. Someday they would demand a fuller expla-nation, but Rosalie did not want to worry about that now any more than she wanted to explore her own bewilderment. She sometimes felt that her sanity and security depended on her not knowing and not wanting to know: she did not want to know where her father-in-law was, what her husband did when he was not home, where her son Charles had come from. She was only too thankful to have Charles, and if she had any regrets about him it was in not having had him sooner, in not having been able to send out birth announcements, although she had done the next best thing—with the birth of her son Joseph in January 1961, she had sent cards to friends and relatives announcing with pleasure "the birth of a brother for Charles."

Rosalie was surprised by her emotional attachment to her children because for years she had not contemplated marriage or a family, considering that her vocation was to become a nun. She felt she was incapable of close human relationships, wanting love on an ethereal level, not a physical one. It was not an escape from reality that made the nunnery seem desirable but rather a longing to remain within the walled-in world that she recognized as reality. She felt safe within the walls, felt comfortable with rules, obedience; she would not have to make any more deci-sions as a nun than she had as a young woman—the questions were all answered, the path was defined, the rewards guaran-teed. She was accustomed to restrictions and denial.

As a teen-age girl she was not permitted to date boys. The only boys she saw aside from her brothers were the cadets that her older brother sometimes brought home from military school.

She remembered one she found attractive in manner and appearance, a wealthy South American boy whose parents lived in Acapulco. She liked talking with him, overcoming her natural shyness, and when he wrote her a letter a correspondence had begun. Because of him she learned Spanish in school, thinking that some day they might wish to express things in letters that her parents should not read, but their acquaintanceship never got that far, and during the summer of 1953 she became aware of the presence of Bill Bonanno.

Her parents had been friendly with the Bonannos for years, and Rosalie had always sensed that there was something special about the Bonannos by the extra effort that was made whenever they came to visit the Profaci home. Mrs. Profaci would spend most of the day in the kitchen preparing an elaborate meal, and the table would be set with the best china and silver, and the finest wine would be served. Her father seemed honored whenever the elder Bonanno was in his home, and Rosalie felt the need to respond to these occasions in a certain way, but unable to decide which way was appropriate, she usually became more shy and hesitant than before. Mr. Bonanno was so different from her father, even different from her rich uncle, to whom she compared many older men.

Her father, who was not poor, seemed poor. Though he had interests in real estate, a clothing factory, and a shoe business, he was endlessly frugal and humble, allowing himself one luxury, a modest-sized cabin cruiser, on which he lived during the hay fever season. He dressed in a casual haphazard way that Rosalie knew was embarrassing at times to her older brother in military school, particularly when her father would arrive at the academy to bring her brother home for the holidays in a battered car, wearing a shirt without a tie under a faded Eisenhower jacket and needing a shave. Her father had once bought a farm in upstate New York not far from the convent to which she returned after three years at Visitation, but Rosalie remembered the farm house as a ramshackle place on a hill with a lopsided porch and an even more lopsided picnic table across which wine that was spilled would flow from one end to the other.

By way of contrast, her uncle Joseph Profaci, then the largest single importer of olive oil and tomato paste in the nation, displayed his wealth with ostentation. He adorned his family and himself with jewelry and expensive clothes, and in addition to his comfortable home in Brooklyn, he had a winter place in Miami and a gigantic hunting lodge on a 328-acre estate in New Jersey that was once the summer retreat of President Theodore Roosevelt. Rosalie remembered summers there as a girl with dozens of her cousins, uncles, aunts, and friends of the family, remembered the tremendous feasts and the many children frolicking through the thirty-room house, and how shocked she was when a few young boys sneaked into Joseph Profaci's private chapel and drew moustaches and nipples on the statues of saints.

Joseph Bonanno had somewhat the same aura of opulence as her uncle, but in a more quiet and discreet way. Rosalie could see that Mr. Bonanno liked carefully tailored suits and fine automobiles, but there was a cosmopolitan quality about him and his family that was not so evident in the Profacis. She knew from attending the convent with Catherine Bonanno that the Bonannos frequently took family trips all over the country, read books, went to the theater, were interested in world affairs. Mr. Bonanno spoke French, having lived briefly in France where one of his cousins was a successful painter, and he had also traveled extensively throughout Latin America. Rosalie knew that the Bonannos' eldest son was attending school in Arizona, which she thought of as some exotic place in another world, and when she saw Bill during the summer of 1953 in New York she found it hard to believe that he was, like her, of Sicilian origin— he seemed so American in a lanky casual way, so tall in his Western clothes, he looked like a cowboy, a rancher, there was an inexplicable manner about him that she found different and exciting.

The couple saw a lot of one another that summer, but always in the company of relatives. One day her parents arranged for her to take a motor trip with the Bonannos to Albany and Syracuse, and during the Christmas holidays Rosalie and her older brother were flown to Arizona to visit the Bonannos. In June 1954 she graduated from the convent, but later that summer her father was killed in an accidental explosion of his boat, and she did not go directly into college in the fall. The guardian of her family became Joseph Profaci who removed the wall dividing the backyards of their neighboring houses in Brooklyn, and Rosalie was then answerable to her uncle, finding him as strict and puritanical as her father had been. When Bill was in town to take her out to a movie or show, it was expected that one of her sisters or cousins should also go along; Bill had to buy tickets not in pairs, but in threes.

Bill gradually began to resent this custom, and one night he spoke privately to her uncle about it. Although Rosalie never knew what was said, the next night she went out with Bill alone. She was proud of him, impressed by his ability to deal with her uncle, and she was never more happy than on the summer evening in 1955 when, before an assembled gathering of Profacis, in the center of which sat Joseph Profaci in a high-backed red chair, Bill spoke in Sicilian of his ''intentions'' toward her. Their engagement was formally announced on January 1, 1956, and Rosalie left Finch College during her freshman year to prepare for the wedding in August. She designed her wedding gown and those of the bridesmaids and accompanied Bill to various hotels to meet with banquet managers to select a ballroom large enough to accommodate the 3,000 reception guests.

Rosalie remembered going from the Plaza to the Pierre, from the Sherry-Netherland to the Waldorf-Astoria, standing in the palatial splendor of empty ballrooms hearing her comments echoing from above. She was impressed with the grand ballroom of the Waldorf, but she and Bill agreed that the gilded boxes of the balcony were too remote from the main floor and that guests occupying them would undoubtedly feel isolated. Rosalie rejected the St. George Hotel without inspecting it because it was in Brooklyn. *I no longer want to be a girl from Brooklyn,* she thought to herself, and she was opposed to the Commodore Hotel's ballroom because that was where Joseph Profaci's two daughters had held their receptions, a reaction she revealed somewhat shamefully to Bill, who seemed to understand. Through most of her lifetime she had been aware of how her father and his other brothers had been overshadowed by her uncle Joseph, and how his branch of the family seemed always to be the first in the Profaci clan with anything new—the first with a new seasonal wardrobe, the first with a television set when such things were not common in homes; and Rosalie was determined that on her wedding day she would not follow her cousins to a ''Profaci hotel,'' which is how she described the Commodore to Bill. Her wedding would be unique and her own: the priest would be flown in from Arizona, thousands of daisies would be sent from California, and she would marry a tall thin man whom she liked to think of as an American cowboy.

When they finally saw the ballroom of the Astor, noting how intimate the large room seemed, its low balcony close to the main floor, they both decided that it would be ideal. And it was. The wedding and the reception were everything that Rosalie had hoped for, as was the honeymoon in Europe and their first year together in Arizona. Even when things began to change, when Bill began to spend more time away from home and Rosalie knew that she had not married a cowboy, it took a while for her to recognize the deterioration of her dream because at first his frequent absences merely added to his mystique, accentuated his separateness from the simplicity of her past.

But after the government began its campaign following Apalachin and after the Arizona press focused on her husband and father-in-law, Rosalie suddenly felt exposed and vulnerable. In the vast open spaces of Arizona there was no place to hide, there was no large family within which to lose herself, and she began to yearn for the protectiveness she once had. When Bill was away she felt not only lost but resentful, and when Bill was home she complained incessantly. The arrival of her son Charles was her salvation for a while, but then after they moved from Tucson to Phoenix she slowly began to suspect that Bill had another woman. She sensed this initially by certain small remarks he made: once he said that her body, which she had always pridefully maintained, was getting soft; and on another occasion he observed that she was rather short, a remark that she let pass, but she felt sure that she was being compared with some tall, lean woman.

One day while visiting her husband's supper club, the Romulus, Rosalie noticed the German girl behind the cash register, and from the way the girl looked at her, awkwardly, nervously, Rosalie decided that she was the one Bill was seeing. Rosalie's suspicions were later confirmed when she impulsively visited the girl's apartment, noticed Bill's clothing in the closet, heard the phone ring and the girl whisper, "Your wife is here."

Rosalie learned much about her husband on that day but she learned more about herself. She became aware of her aggressiveness in pursuing the girl—it was so out of character for her to find out where the girl lived, to boldly appear at her door, and to walk directly into the living room expecting to find Bill. She knew that she must have been driven by sheer desperation—her marriage was breaking up, another woman was replacing her, she saw herself abandoned and humiliated, but instead of accepting these grim circumstances, submitting like the stoical convent creature she imagined she was, she had angrily fought back to reclaim her husband. For one who had no experience in the maneuvers of love, she had been remarkably decisive and deft; and after she won her husband back, after he admitted that he did not want to lose her, she surprised herself still further by her coolness and aloofness, deciding that she did not want him after all, at least not immediately. She wanted him to pay for his indiscretion, to linger in doubt for a while. She had suffered too much, had become ill from an overdose of sleeping pills, and after her recovery she awoke in a state of alienation, and it was in that state that she left him and returned to Brooklyn with her children and mother, vowing *the only way I am going back to Arizona is in a box.*

Now, nearly two years later, Rosalie knew that the bitterness was still with her, and she made no secret of her dissatisfaction with Bill in the letters she wrote to Catherine in California during 1963 and 1964, and frequently referring to him as "your brother," as if she wished to disclaim any relationship with him. Catherine did not reply in her own letters to Rosalie's ill temper; Catherine's replies were warm and friendly, stressing the need for love and loyalty particularly now, reminding Rosalie of the burdens that Bill had borne from boyhood because of his name and his ties to his father.

There were times when Rosalie agreed with Catherine's reasoning and conceded the possibility that she had perhaps failed him in ways as a wife in Arizona and that the additional trouble he was involved in since his return to the East was in part related to her. While the newspapers, the FBI, and the Mafia perhaps all believed that Bill had returned to live in New York solely because of the activities of the Bonanno organization, Rosalie knew that one compelling reason for his return to a city he disliked and his willingness to move into the house of Magliocco was that he wanted to win her back, a fact that his Sicilian pride would probably not allow him to admit. If he had not moved East in 1963, he might not be where he was now, in jail, although Rosalie sometimes thought that jail was the best place for him. At least she knew where he was at night, and as she thought about this she was amused—for the first time in seven years of marriage, she knew where her husband was each and every night of the week.

She also thought that her husband looked very well in jail—during her recent visits she had noticed that he had lost weight and seemed quite relaxed, calm, and self-assured. She sensed a pride in his manner, he was doing his duty, was doing *not what he wanted to do but what he had to do*—one of his favorite phrases—and Rosalie came away from each visit thinking that her husband was becoming increasingly like his father, proud, philosophical, preoccupied with and strengthened by values of another world and another time. And yet she responded to this, as much as one could respond through the glass wall in the visitors' room, and she found herself physically attracted to him in a way she had not been in years. His hair was longer and he had lost so much weight that he now looked like the man she had married. He weighed 245 pounds when he was arrested in the barbershop in Tucson last January; by March, partly as the result of an attack of mononucleosis, his weight had fallen to 218, and now after two months in jail it was 203.

He said that his weight had dropped because he was getting plenty of rest in jail, but Rosalie thought that perhaps the opposite was true—in jail he was not allowed to rest, he had to walk a lot, lift things, burn up energy; he did not have people like herself waiting on him constantly, getting him a sandwich, turning off the television set, bringing him a glass of water. He had to get his own water in jail, which meant getting up and walking to a distant fountain, and on the assumption that he was too proud and lazy to do this, even though he normally drank enormous amounts of water, he had cut down on his water consumption in jail, thus losing weight.

Rosalie kept this little theory mainly to herself, however, not because her husband lacked the humor to appreciate it but because it was yet another example of her carping, a habit she had fallen into that she hoped to correct. She did not like herself when she was this way, even when she repressed it, nor was she tolerant of this trait in others. And yet there had been times when her unrelieved frustration turned her into a chronic complainer, but she felt justified because, unlike most chronic complainers, she really had something to complain about. Of all the tearful heroines in the television dramas she had watched to help escape the loneliness, none could match the misery and tension of the life she had led in recent years and was still leading now in East Meadow, snugly trapped on a tidy block of ranch houses that resembled her own except that they were not bugged, not tapped, not ambush-trimmed, not equipped with arsenals, did not have a private grocery store in the basement, plastic tubes of quarters in the bedroom, did not have a jailed husband, a vanished father-in-law, and strange men scrutinizing the property from across the street. It was weird, incredible, she was a marked woman in her own home, she acted like a houseguest, always properly dressed when not in the bedroom, never in her bathrobe or with curlers in her hair because she could never be sure who was watching her or who might intrude at any moment of the day or night.

Although the press had reported that her husband and father-in-law were millionaires, no one could prove it by her. She was forced to borrow from her mother this year and she was constantly unnerved by the uncertainty of money. She wondered who would provide for her and the children if something happened to her husband, and she thought often about Anastasia's young widow, whom she had met years ago through her family. Rosalie sometimes thought of herself as a young widow, devoting herself to her children, living with the memory of a husband that in many ways she did not know. If only she could go out and get a job, she would be more financially independent. At twenty-nine she felt sufficiently young and qualified and even eager to go out into the world and earn money, but she could not have live-in help at this time; she had not had anyone since the birth of Felippa. Rosalie remembered with fondness the last mother's-helper she had, a Puerto Rican girl named Elisa, a very gentle and capable person with whom she had been so compatible. Since Elisa did not understand English, Rosalie spoke in Spanish, making use of the language she had studied years ago to communicate with the cadet that her brother had brought home. But after the disappearance of Joseph Bonanno, the agents began to approach Elisa as she waited for the bus at the corner, using Puerto Rican detectives to interrogate her. Elisa knew nothing about the elder Bonanno or his son, and she presumably told the agents little of interest, but not long afterward Elisa left Rosalie for another job.

Now whenever Rosalie had to go out, taking one of the children to the doctor or visiting Bill, she relied on the baby-sitting of a teen-age daughter of a family friend who lived a few miles away. But during the winter of 1965 Rosalie had rarely gone out. With four young children to care for, with a new house that was not yet organized, she was kept constantly busy indoors. She had begun to unpack the cardboard cartons in the garage that had been sent from Arizona, containing such things as the holiday china her mother had given her and the dolls from the many weddings at which she had been the maid-of-honor and other mementos from happier days. She needed a carpenter to build shelves in the children's rooms, and she wanted a new dining room table—the old one belonging to Mrs. Bonanno was in the basement, too large and sturdy for the dining area that adjoined the sunken living room with its modern furniture and gold-colored draperies. The living room, which had wall-to-wall carpeting and an impressive polished driftwood sculpture done by an artist Bill knew in California, also contained a large Sylvania stereophonic high-fidelity record player that her husband had brought home within the last year despite her protests. She thought it was absurd of him to spend close to $1,500 on a stereo when so many more important things were needed for the house, such as a dining room table, and even now her anger was renewed every time she looked at the stereo.

It was typical of him to spend large sums of money on non-essentials, she thought, reminding herself of the life-sized toy bear on wheels that he had brought home one day from F. A. O. Schwarz. As he later explained it, he had been walking along Fifth Avenue when he noticed in the toy store's window a huge giraffe and wondered how much it was. The clerk inside told him it was $300 and spoke in a manner that Bill took to imply the price was beyond his means. Bill then spotted the bear, which seemed smaller than the giraffe and was presumably cheaper—and was told that it, too, was $300. Whether it was the clerk's manner or Bill's hypersensitivity that made him react, Rosalie never knew; she just remembered him opening the front door one day for delivery men rolling in an enormous toy bear on wheels. The bear was now in the basement next to the three-horse merry-go-round that took up nearly half the floor space and had been given to the children by Bill's father.

Rosalie endured the winter. She nursed her children through three rounds of colds each. She resigned herself to the fact that her son Charles would not be promoted at the end of the school term to the second grade. Charles was marvelous with his hands, creative in the way he constructed huts in the yard out of broken branches and built igloos out of hardened snow blocks collected in the neighborhood and loaded on his sleigh; but he was failing in reading and spelling.

Hoping to break the monotony of her depression, Rosalie dyed her hair blonde, having heard on television commercials that blondes had more fun. But her life did not change. It was still governed by the needs of her children, the ritual of her visits to Bill, and the endless cycle of birthdays, anniversaries, feast days, name days, and reminders of death that she had noted on the calendar that hung on the kitchen wall. With so many aunts and uncles, cousins and nephews and nieces around the nation, to say nothing of her married sister, brothers, and in-laws, there seemed hardly a day that was not in some way associated with a person she knew. Although she had not seen most of these kin and *compare* in years, they kept in touch through the mail, exchanging snapshots of their children, mourning the passing of their old folks, commenting on the commonplace happenings of their lives, but revealing little that would be of interest—or use— to outsiders.

8

BILL BONANNO WAS released from prison on June 5, 1965, after he decided to tell the federal grand jury what he had told Maloney on the telephone during the previous December. Bill had been in jail for three months, and he saw no reason why he should remain longer. There was no further word about his father during that time, he received no sign indicating that his secrecy and imprisonment was acknowledged or appreciated by anyone, and he no longer considered it a risk or violation of confidence to reveal to the jury that on a Thursday night in December he had received a call from a stranger at a coinbox in Long Island reporting that Joseph Bonanno was alive and that he had relayed this information to Maloney on the following day. Bill had made a second call a day later to Maloney, after the lawyer's ill-advised news conference, urging him to say nothing more to the press until the elder Bonanno's safety was assured.

This was the substance of the whole telephone episode, Bill Bonanno told the grand jury during the first week in June, and after the questioning was over—even though the whereabouts of the elder Bonanno remained as much a mystery as before—Judge Tenney ruled that the younger Bonanno had purged himself of contempt, and Krieger asked that his client be released from prison. The judge agreed to do so, overruling objections by legal representatives of the United States Attorney, and Bill Bonanno walked out of the courtroom a free man. He was still subject to recall, however, and the judge reminded him that he could face contempt charges again if he refused to answer grand jury questions.

Bill telephoned Rosalie from Krieger's office, and although the tone of her voice was unchanged after hearing that he was free, he was confident that she was pleased. She promised to convey the news to certain relatives and friends, and on the following evening, a Saturday, a dozen people were invited to the Bonanno home in East Meadow for a celebration dinner.

Bill Bonanno stood in the living room greeting people as they walked in and embraced him, kissed him, and told him how well he looked. One of his aunts, his mother's oldest sister, had cried when she saw him, but now she was drying her tears with her handkerchief, standing in the kitchen with Bill's other aunts and his mother-in-law, who were preparing the large dinner. The women, gray-haired and with matronly figures, were making soup and pasta, roasting a variety of meats, and cooking stuffed peppers and mushrooms with side dishes of string beans and other vegetables. Rosalie moved between the kitchen and dining room, setting the table, having put a heavy linen cloth over two sizable folding aluminum tables that had been placed end to end. She wore a bright yellow dress, had a flower in her hair, and she seemed sprightly and in concert with the excitement around her.

She heard her husband in the living room recounting his jail experiences to the other men, and she knew that he was enjoying the attention he was receiving, the laughter he was provoking by his comic descriptions of the characters he had met. She was privately elated that he was home, had liked waking up in the morning and finding him beside her, and when one of the men in the living room called to her, "How you feeling, Rosalie?" she smiled and replied, "Like a bride."

As the aroma from the kitchen carried through the house, the children ran freely from room to room, pushing wagons, waving plastic guns, riding the giant bear, competing for their father's attention. The color television set in the den was loudly tuned to the "Lawrence Welk Show," which no one was watching, and in one corner of the dining room sat an elderly white-haired uncle, a tailor, sewing up the seams of Bill's trousers that had been taken in. The only young person among the guests was Rosalie's teen-age sister, Josephine, who was being sent in the fall to college in Santa Clara, California, a Jesuit school about which Josephine already had some doubts.

Josephine was a serene brown-eyed girl who wore her long dark hair in a ponytail, and she possessed, but managed to conceal in front of her elders, an inquiring mind. She was beginning to question certain edicts of the Catholic church and certain values and goals that her two older sisters and brothers and her other relatives had accepted unquestioningly—namely, the quest for financial security and middle-class respectability. Josephine, who was eleven years younger than Rosalie, was only seven when her father had died, and she had not been subjected to insularity and strictness as had Rosalie and her other sister, Ann, who was now married to a young man of Sicilian origin and living near Santa Clara. Josephine was beginning to identify with the style of a new generation. She was reading books and thinking thoughts that she was sure her family would neither understand nor appreciate; she could not accept the submissive role of women and all the prerogatives of men in the Italo-American society she had observed at close range, and she did not wish to condone the hardship and suffering that had been experienced by her mother and her sister Rosalie.

Josephine had been acutely aware of the marital difficulties between Rosalie and Bill, and she remembered how frightened she was two years ago on the night that Bill and Labruzzo came to the Profaci home to reclaim Rosalie. Hearing the shouting and commotion after Bill was told by her mother that Rosalie was not at home and would not be going with him, Josephine locked herself in the upstairs bathroom with Bill's two-year-old son, Joseph; when she heard Bill climbing the steps, she quickly turned on the bathtub tap, answering his angry pounding against the door with cries that she was bathing, begging him to leave her alone, and praying meanwhile that the little boy would remain silent. Josephine did not again breathe easily until long after Bill had left the house.

Josephine's opinion of Bill was far from flattering even now, but she veiled her emotions as she helped Rosalie set the table, and she was as friendly to Bill as she was capable of being. She knew how much her mother wanted to end the family friction, to stand behind Rosalie and Bill and forget the past. Watching her mother in the kitchen, a large smiling woman of great generosity and warmth, Josephine was again impressed by her mother's capacity to withstand a lifetime of ordeals; she had been an orphan as a young girl after both parents had died in an accident, a widow before she was forty, a woman who had moved through life without bitterness with a controversial name that one of her sons would change and that another of her sons would keep in public circulation by being charged with gambling in Brooklyn. Her daughters had also been a source of suffering—Rosalie, the model child, nearly dying from an overdose of pills, and Ann, the second girl, rebelling as a teen-ager after the death of her father, keeping her own hours until her mother in a rare moment of frustration threw a plate of spaghetti at her—an incident that the family now considered amusing, one of the few amusing incidents that Josephine could recall from her childhood.

After the table was set for dinner and Bill had opened the wine and the women had come in from the kitchen carrying steaming plates, everyone sat down, and one of the aunts looked at Bill adoringly, and said, "Oh, Bill, you look wonderful," to which he smiled and said, "In jail the food was terrible."

"Did you have any Italian cooks in there?" one of the men asked.

"We had one," Bill said. "He was an illegal entry from Naples. For the few weeks he was there, the food was better, but then they shipped him back and it suddenly got worse. It was so bad that there was a hunger strike for two and a half days, and then it got better, but not much better. There was one dish in jail called Baked Manzanetti, which was macaroni and wasn't bad—years ago there was a cook named Manzanetti who used to make it, and he put his name on the menu and it's still there. But the conditions were so bad, the filth, the rats, that sometimes you just couldn't eat no matter what they were serving."

"Rats!" one of the women exclaimed.

"Yes, rats," Bill repeated. "They were all over. I had one rat that used to come into my cell at night, and I'd tie a piece of food on a string and play with him, and . . ."

"Bill," Rosalie interrupted, wanting to change the subject.

"Some of the men really got depressed in that place," Bill continued, "especially the junkies, and we had plenty of them. We also had a few suicides when I was there—one night this Puerto Rican fellow climbed up on a stool, tied his belt around his neck and hooked it to the ceiling, and told his cellmate—who was playing solitaire—that he didn't want him to call anybody or do anything. The cellmate looked up from his game and said, 'Don't worry.' The guy on the stool tightened the belt, waited for a few moments, then again looked at his cellmate and said, 'Now don't cut me down.' The guy playing solitaire became irritated, and he said, 'Look, you want to talk or you want to jump?' The guy jumped. After he was dead, the cell-mate called the guards.''

"Oh, how terrible," one of the women said, "how could he do such a horrible thing?''

"In jail," Bill said, "you do things. And you don't care.''

As they continued to eat, Bill felt something poking him in the back. Turning, he saw his son Salvatore, smiling, wearing a cowboy hat, pointing a toy gun at him.

"Hey, cut that out!" Bill shouted, laughing, and the little boy ran giggling into the kitchen. Bill then resumed talking, telling his guests that there were many interesting aspects to his jail experience, such as how naturally the prisoners seemed to divide themselves into social classes that were roughly equivalent to the level of social acceptability that they had enjoyed in the outside world: the crooked lawyers in jail associated with other crooked lawyers or stock swindlers; the pimps associated with other pimps or smalltime pushers; and the same was true of the truck hijackers and other thieves.

"Birds of a feather stick together," somebody said, and one of the men asked, smiling, "And where did you fit in, Bill?''

Bill lifted his wine glass in a mock toast and said, "I enjoyed great social mobility." He then added, "Shortly after I arrived in prison, an interviewer who was responsible for assigning us jobs asked me what I did on the outside, and I said, 'Nothing that would be of any use in here.' But I did tell him I could type, thinking he might put me in the records room, but that didn't work. Later on, after I'd worked as a painter, I got to work in the library, which I enjoyed, although there was not much to read in there. They had books by Mark Twain and Thomas Hardy that I'd read in school, but the reading level was very low. I did reread Barry Goldwater's *Conscience of a Conservative*, and I agree with a lot of points he makes—especially his point that the federal government today has entirely too much power, and the individual citizen's rights are being ignored . . .''

There were nods of agreement from around the table, although none from Josephine who had listened quietly throughout dinner but had not offered a comment or revealed in any way what she was thinking. Mrs. Profaci smiled often at Bill during the evening, and no one would have guessed that their relationship had been strained in the recent past. Rosalie also continued to be in good spirits, listening attentively and keeping her husband's water glass filled and the food within his reach.

Although they sat for nearly two hours and discussed many subjects, there was never a mention of Bill's father during the entire evening. It was as if the subject was too delicate, too private to be raised in front of so many people, too awkward or implicating. Perhaps they were also aware that the house might be bugged. Bill's mother, who had been reported missing immediately after the incident and was later speculated to be living with friends or relatives in Arizona or California, was now at her home in Tucson with her son Joseph. Bill said that his mother was ill and rarely left the house. He had no idea what his brother was doing these days; he had not received a letter from him in jail, and although Bill had written Catherine inquiring about Joseph he had received no word of him in her reply, and he was worried. Bill also felt a certain guilt with regard to his younger brother. Shortly before his father had disappeared, the subject of Joseph came up and Bill sensed that his father held him partially responsible for Joseph's drifting existence and the long-haired youths Joseph often associated with in Arizona, an element that neither the elder Bonanno nor Bill could relate to. Bill had been too busy with his own problems in the last few years to worry about Joseph, and still he did worry about him and wonder about him; but on this evening Bill did not seek information from his aunts about his brother—he was in a festive mood and wanted to remain so, and he preferred to divert his guests and himself with general conversation related to his experiences in prison. He described for them his caution after receiving the gift candy bar from Kayo Konigsberg, he repeated words that were part of prison parlance, and he told of his acquaintanceships with such varied prisoners as Lowell M. Birrell, the stock swindler; with an oil executive from Long Island accused of selling secrets to the Russians; with three black militants suspected of plotting to blow up the Statue of Liberty; and with a movie producer who had recently fled Mexico, where he was sought for questioning in the murder of a cast member with an underwater fishing spear. It was this producer, Bill said, who had taught him how to play chess.

Bill also told how the inmates made coffee and whiskey in jail and described the night when an explosion was caused because the whiskey makers neglected to let sufficient air into the jar during fermentation.

"It sounded like muffled gun shots," Bill recalled, "and suddenly the red telephones lit up, the guards started yelling through the intercom, and all the steel doors slammed shut. The prison-break warning was sounded and any prisoner caught outside his cell was in real trouble. We all waited to see what would happen. Soon we saw about nine guards with billy clubs dragging some Negroes away with their buckets and broken jars."

"Oh how awful," one of the aunts said.

"It's so terrible," another said, "that they would risk their lives just to make liquor."

"What's the difference?" Rosalie asked. "Bill smuggled in provolone and . . ."

There was silence around the table. Everyone looked toward Bill, who looked at his plate, neither laughing off her remark nor elaborating upon it. Finally one of the aunts spoke up.

"That was *food*," she said. "That was different."

"Yes," another woman agreed, "that was different."

Rosalie shrugged, got up to get more coffee. Bill then continued to talk, changing the subject to religion in jail, remarking on how surprised he was by the great variety of Bibles that were available to the inmates—there were dozens of different Bibles, he said, Jewish Bibles, Christian Bibles, even the Koran. Every week or so, members from Bible societies would arrive in prison to preach to those inmates willing to listen. Bill said he always attended these lectures, welcoming the opportunity of seeing new faces behind bars, and he was about to say something more when his four-year-old son, Joseph, came running into the room crying, complaining of something that his older brother, Charles, had done to him. But Bill quickly cut him off, demanding, "You want to grow up and become a stool pigeon?"

The little boy stopped whimpering.

"No," he said, "no!"

"All right then," Bill said, "so don't go telling on your brother that way."

9

ALTHOUGH JOSEPH BONANNO continued to elude the hunt of the FBI and the police during 1965 and was still missing as winter turned to spring in 1966, the government claimed it was making progress in its national campaign against organized crime. It had greatly increased its knowledge of the secret society, had intensified public awareness through the cooperation of the press, and it had succeeded in harassing and arresting, if not always convicting, many mafiosi and other gang members of varying ethnic and religious backgrounds who were either employed by the Mafia or were working with it.

In New York City alone in 1965, more than 400 arrests were made in organized crime, and throughout the nation there were continuous raids against bookmakers and loan sharks, operators of illegal gambling casinos and other enterprises that the government called "mob-controlled." Fourteen bolita operators were arrested in Tampa, Florida, by the Internal Revenue Service; thirty-four pimps, prostitutes, and gamblers were arrested in Columbus, Ohio, by the local police; sixty-eight persons were arrested for illegal gambling in Chester, West Virginia, by the state police. Sixty gamblers were convicted in Nashville, thirty-four gamblers were arrested in St. Paul, thirty-one in Denver, twenty-four in St. Louis. The FBI relayed 180,000 items of criminal information to various investigative units on the federal, state, or municipal level, and there was also cooperation between law enforcement officials in the United States and overseas. The police in Sicily interrogated many Mafia suspects in Castellammare about the Bonanno case, and in Germany, agents from Interpol, the international police organization, looked up Bill Bonanno's former girl friend to ask if she knew anything about the elder Bonanno's disappearance. She said she did not, never having met Joseph Bonanno, although she did admit having seen him once a few years ago sitting with another man in the cocktail lounge in Arizona where she had worked. She guessed that he had come to see for himself the woman who had attracted his son, and after he had finished his drink he left the lounge without comment and with a generous tip.

Although the government contended that organized crime was the most lucrative business in America, experts quoted in newspapers and magazines were unable to agree on how many billions of dollars were derived each year from illegal enterprises run by gangs. Their estimates ranged from $10 billion to $40 billion annually; and even the more conservative reports conceded that organized crime probably netted more profit each year than the combined earnings of United States Steel, AT&T, General Motors, Standard Oil of New Jersey, General Electric, Ford, IBM, Chrysler, and RCA.

About three-quarters of the crime revenue was contributed by citizens who bet on horse races and other sports events with bookmakers, or played the numbers. While the typical numbers bettor might be a Harlem housewife on welfare who deposits twenty-five cents each morning with a neighborhood "runner," hoping to overcome 1,000-to-1 odds and "hit" the daily number, which by prior agreement might be the last three digits of the total money bet at the local track that day, and while the typical patron of a bookmaker might be an auto mechanic or a porter who invests two dollars on a horse each day, there are enough of these gambling citizens in America—millions to whom a small bet is a daily tonic and who cannot afford to go in person to a track—to support the fabulous industry of illegal gambling, an industry that has been flourishing for many decades despite the tactics of crime busters and the will of puritanical lawmakers.

The numbers game is the national pastime of city slums, is a source of hope, however small, for the urban poor crowded into blocks of 10,000 people, living in teeming tenements each with its "runner," each with its corner store that may be a "drop" for numbers slips that are later picked up by "collectors" and delivered to "controllers" who record the data and later pay the winners. The controllers, who usually work with their aides in private apartments that are protected by alarm systems and lookouts, are answerable to the neighborhood "banker," who represents the mob that oversees the whole network and covers the bets. If a "runner" or other employee is caught by the police, it is the controller's responsibility to pay for the bail and legal fees out of his profit; but the bribery of the police, whose co-operation is essential for numbers racketeering to function, is handled by a representative of a Mafia "family" or whatever ethnic gang is backing the "bank" in a particular section of the city.

While police graft is expensive, with gangsters complaining that the police sometimes take almost half of the profit (and more when there is pressure from headquarters to "clean up" crime), there nevertheless is enough money after the payoffs and other operational costs to keep hundreds of numbers couriers running each day and the "banks" booming with business. It was estimated in *The New York Times* that the number of lotteries in Harlem alone earned $1 billion a month in profits and that the Vito Genovese "family," which was heavily involved in several Harlem banks, had twenty-seven millionaires among its "soldiers."

The Lucchese "family" was also active in the Harlem numbers, and so was a Puerto Rican syndicate under the leadership of Raymond Marquez, known in the newspapers as "Spanish Raymond." Marquez's father many years ago was a runner for Genovese's men, but Marquez is his own boss, has his own gang, and reportedly earns more than $3 million a year from his banks, although a few are believed to be affiliated with mafiosi and sharing the profits. The numbers kings in the South Bronx are Jewish—Samuel and Moishe Schlitten, whose banks are said to be even more profitable than Raymond Marquez's, but the Schlitten brothers, too, are reportedly in partnership in certain areas with members of the Genovese and Lucchese organizations.

There is probably not a densely populated lower- or middle-income neighborhood in New York that does not support numbers racketeering; and the bookmakers are everywhere. Some of the more respectable business firms in the city have a bookmaker or two among its employees, men who do their jobs and book bets on the side—and it has long been possible to bet through bookies even in courthouses, law offices, and the New York Times Building, where the editorial writers denounced racketeering in print while certain staff members and editors supported it with their betting.

Many bookies in midtown Manhattan, particularly on the West Side and in the garment center, were linked to the Lucchese and Bonanno organizations, and the Bonanno men also worked with Jewish and Puerto Rican racketeers in bookmaking and numbers on the Lower East Side. All the "families," including the Bonannos and the Profacis, had well-coordinated numbers networks in Brooklyn and parts of Queens, and their most persistent bettors were not only the blacks but also Italians and Latin Americans, many of whom had begun playing numbers in their native countries where lotteries were usually legal. While many black Americans worked in organized crime as runners, and a few became controllers, it was largely in the wake of the civil rights movement that black gangsters finally began to demand and achieve equal opportunities. By the early 1960s, the police were able to conclude that a few banks in the black ghettos of Brooklyn were being run by black men, some with Mafia ties, some not.

A second source of revenue for organized crime was loan-sharking, which most crime spokesmen estimate earns more than $1 billion in annual profits. Though the interest rates might be twenty percent, customers are always available because several thousand Americans, many of them black, cannot borrow from legitimate sources, since they have poor credit ratings. Some of these people are on welfare, some are gamblers down on their luck, others are small businessmen struggling because of mismanagement or other personal failings. To such people the loan shark represents the primary source of quick relief.

If they do not repay the debt, however, they will undoubtedly receive threatening phone calls, and they might then seek expiation by going to work in the crime industry. If they have a business, they might accept a gang member for a partner, under whom the business most likely would go bankrupt because the assets were drained. Occasionally a victim of loan-sharking, rather than try to pay or become more deeply involved, will go to the police and become an informer, but such men sometimes pay with their lives.

Another source of money for organized crime in the 1960s was narcotics, which while said to be less than half as profitable as loan-sharking and more risky in every way, nonetheless attracted many members of the criminal establishment in spite of the disapproval of most Mafia dons. The dons could not govern the behavior of each underling any more than a general could control the acts of every soldier, and if the underlings managed to smuggle in a large heroin shipment without getting caught and if they shared the profit with their superiors, questions might not be asked. But a permissive policy toward narcotics by a Mafia boss sometimes backfired when the smugglers were caught, and in 1959 the federal agents were able to link Vito Genovese with a narcotics case and he was sentenced to fifteen years in prison. Joseph Bonanno had a strong policy against narcotics trafficking, once vowing that if any of his men were caught they would be put in one of the ovens of a bakery he owned; however, during one of his extended absences from New York a key officer in his organization, Carmine Galante, was charged with involvement in a narcotics ring, and Galante was convicted and given a twenty-year sentence.

The marijuana market, according to federal agents, had not enticed the Mafia or their associates because marijuana was too easily gotten through the Mexican border and because the trade was overrun with free-lance gangsters and youthful adventurers. But if government agents succeeded in limiting the supply, if tougher laws inhibited and lessened the number of importers and drove up the price, the expert smugglers in organized crime might flock to marijuana as they had to bootlegging during Prohibition. Meanwhile, they had all they could handle in their present endeavors, reportedly making so much money that their main problem was hiding the money or investing it in places that would return a profit but would not expose them to charges of tax evasion. One favorite outlet for such investments was in real estate, where it was not uncommon for the owners of property to function behind "fronts." It was long suspected by the government, for example, that Frank Costello was the secret owner or part owner of the Lucayan Beach Club in the Bahamas as well as the Copacabana nightclub and the Pompeii Restaurant in New York; and there was hardly a name in crime that was not listed in government files as owning either a bowling alley or bar, a trucking company or food-packing concern, a laundry or stretches of undeveloped land.

Carlos Marcello, the New Orleans don, was said to own tracts of land in the path of a federal highway soon to be constructed; and Carlo Gambino, the New York don, was allegedly the owner of several million dollars' worth of real estate in New York City.

Newspaper reporters in 1965 were told privately by the United States Attorney, Robert M. Morgenthau, that his office had information indicating that Mafia groups owned the downtown property in which *The Wall Street Journal* was published, owned the midtown building in which *Vogue* was published, owned the building on East Sixty-ninth Street where the FBI had its headquarters, and owned the Chrysler Building. Although an extensive job of research by *New York Times* reporters failed to produce the evidence to support the disclosures, the *Times* did quote in one article a federal investigator who said: "If the black flag of the underworld were to unfurl atop one of the tallest skyscrapers in New York, it would be a fit symbol of how the Mafia has gained control of that building and many other real estate holdings."

Morgenthau had three grand juries probing into organized crime during 1965 and 1966. One jury focused on the overall picture of the syndicate, the relationships between "families," a second jury delved exclusively into the affairs of the Lucchese family, and a third jury concentrated on the Bonanno family and its missing leader. Hundreds of witnesses were subpoenaed, most of them uncooperative, but the government nevertheless amassed enormous amounts of information that gave new insight into the life-style of the men who dominate the crime charts of the McClellan committee and other investigative units. The government files noted certain gangsters' mannerisms, their styles in dress, their favorite hangouts and restaurants, their hobbies, the great efforts that some took with their lawns and in being good neighbors, and the efforts that such men as Thomas Lucchese made in keeping agents and other interlopers from invading the privacy of his home in Lido Beach, Long Island. All windows of his residence were wired by the Supreme Burglar Alarm System. There was a large two-way mirror in the front door, and a large mirror on a pole in front of the house which allowed anyone looking through the two-way mirror at the mirror on the pole to observe all vehicles entering or leaving Royatt Street from Lido Boulevard. There was a photoelectric eye in the windows and anyone walking by the windows could set off an alarm. There was a large bell alarm system on one side of the house under the eaves. There were spotlights on all sides of the residence.

* * *

The government's special probe into the Bonanno organization was becoming increasingly irritating to many of the members; while they proclaimed their innocence or ignorance of
organized crime in their testimony, they were constantly being
recalled to answer more questions every time the government
produced a morsel of new information or conjecture about increasing dissension within the Bonanno "family." Since the
government did not always know which gang members were
Bonanno loyalists and which had joined the Di Gregorio faction—indeed, many of the men themselves did not know, since
there was so much fence-straddling, suspected disloyalty, and
confusion—the government agents paid particular attention to
the mannerisms of the men gathered in the courtroom corridor
waiting to testify, looking for hints that might reveal which were
friendly and which were hostile. Aware of this, the gang members tried to conceal their feelings, and a few proved to be good
actors, although many were not.

The government also gained further evidence about the dissension, which the tabloids liked to refer to as the Banana Split,
through the use of a hidden camera focused on the wedding
reception of Di Gregorio's daughter at the Huntington Town-
house in Long Island on November 14, 1965. Among those
identified as attending the wedding was the Buffalo don, Stefano
Magaddino, senior member of the commission and Di Gregorio's most powerful ally. Magaddino was quickly subpoenaed,
but his lawyer said he would be unable to appear because he
was confined to his home with a heart ailment. As the government prepared to appoint a doctor to determine Magaddino's
condition, several other subpoenas were issued to men who had
attended the reception, and subpoenas were also served to men
who had been friendly with Di Gregorio in the past but had not
gone to the wedding, or perhaps had not been invited.

A week before Christmas there was a rumor that certain members of Di Gregorio's faction were trying to promote a truce
with the Bonanno men, because they felt that the bitterness and
mutual distrust had lessened the effectiveness of both groups
and made them more vulnerable to police surveillance and intrigue: the police were in a position to play one group off against
the other, to attribute schemes to one group and leak the word
to the press, and the other group had no way of knowing whether
or not it was being deceived. It was also rumored that Di Gre-

gorio was not happy with the responsibilities of leadership, was unnerved by the publicity he was receiving and by being followed by detectives whenever he left his home in West Babylon, Long Island. At sixty-three years old, he had already had three heart attacks, and his men believed that he would soon retire to be replaced by a subordinate officer, Paul Sciacca, who was acceptable to Magaddino and the other members of the commission.

Frank Labruzzo heard about Di Gregorio's situation and the rumored desire for a truce from an informant in the Di Gregorio camp. In January Labruzzo received a message that Di Gregorio's men wanted to have a "sit down" with Bonanno representatives in hopes of reaching some agreement, and Labruzzo relayed the word to Bill Bonanno. Bill was skeptical. He saw no reason why Di Gregorio should be more conciliatory now than he had been during the past two years, and he also sensed the possibility that he was being "set up" to be shot or captured, which he had assumed was part of the opposition's plan since he had gotten out of jail in June. As a precaution since then, Bill had never traveled alone, had avoided predictable routines, had never arranged a meeting in a place that had not been surveyed in advance by his men, who then, hidden, stood guard. He had been wary of sniper's bullets even as he drove from Long Island with his lawyer each morning to appear in court in Manhattan, never following the same route two days in a row. He had mapped out approximately thirty different ways of traveling between East Meadow and lower Manhattan, some direct, some circuitous.

Labruzzo agreed that Bill was wise to do this, and he shared Bill's skepticism about the peace meeting. There was no explanation for a change in attitude from Di Gregorio or Magaddino unless they had reached some private agreement with Joseph Bonanno, and if this were true the elder Bonanno would have somehow communicated this to his own people.

A few days later, Labruzzo received another message, assuring him that the proposed meeting was a sincere attempt to make life more livable for both groups, even agreeing to meet in a place appointed by the Bonanno loyalists. Labruzzo was swayed by the last point. He discussed it with Bill, and within the week Labruzzo sent back word—they would meet at the home of one of Bill's relatives on Troutman Street in Brooklyn, a block which both Labruzzo and Bill Bonanno were intimately familiar with, since it was in the neighborhood where Labruzzo had been reared as a boy and where Bill used to come to visit his grandfather. The German bar where Bill bought containers of beer for his one-legged grandfather was near Troutman Street, and Bill had returned to the neighborhood regularly in recent years to visit relatives and friends who still lived in the area, which was almost exclusively Italian. Along here, forty years ago, Joseph Bonanno had built up his organization, recruiting young men from the crowded tenements occupied by immigrants from Castellammare and neighboring Sicilian villages—men like Gaspar Di Gregorio—and it seemed appropriate now, in 1966 on this bitterly cold Friday night of January 28, that Bill Bonanno and his companions would return to the scene of past unity to meet with other members of the quarreling family.

Bill and his men arrived shortly before eleven o'clock, parking a few blocks away from the appointed place and walking cautiously along the sidewalks of the narrow streets lined with rows of brick buildings. It was very quiet and bleak; few lights were burning in the apartments and houses, and Bill assumed that the elderly Italian residents were already asleep, unlike the residents of the Negro and Puerto Rican neighborhoods that Bill had driven through about five minutes ago. There the bars were crowded, the jukeboxes blared in the clamor of Friday night, the people were younger, livelier, newer to New York. But here in the Italian quarter where there had not been an influx of new people in years, it was as quiet and still as a square in western Sicily late at night, and the old people slept in houses that they had probably moved into not long after landing in Brooklyn's Ridgewood district early in the century, replacing the Germans who had moved out. Bill remembered many of these houses and stores from his boyhood visits, and he was sure that they had looked the same during his parents' childhood days along these blocks. The nearby church where his parents were married in 1931 was unchanged, although the parish had become smaller and poorer; and the grade school that Joseph Bonanno attended as a boy in knee pants was still there, although the elder Bonanno had only vague recollections of his education there since it was hastily interrupted in 1911 by *his* father's decision to return to Castellammare, where there was "trouble" in the hills.

Bill and his companions continued to walk slowly toward the

Troutman Street address, passing certain buildings that had been "drops" many years ago for numbers runners, and he noticed a birdbath on the tiny front lawn of a house that he had played around as a boy, a birdbath that was covered with ice on this evening. He guessed that the temperature was below twenty degrees, too cold to talk as he hunched his shoulders and walked with his ungloved hands in the pockets of his overcoat, his right hand clutching the cold metal of a gun.

Suddenly Bill felt a companion's arm shove him abruptly to one side, and he heard the frantic yell: "Bill, *Bill*, watch out!"

A shotgun was being extended through the slowly opening front door of one of the houses, and as Bill leaped toward the sidewalk, falling beside a parked car, he heard gun blasts and sharp-sounding bullets pierce the icy street, striking the stone walls of buildings around him. He and his men fired back at the sniper, who quickly retreated into the building, but bullets continued to come from another direction, perhaps from an upper floor of one of the buildings across the street, hitting where Bill had been standing a few seconds before.

He crouched lower against the fender of the car while the other men, including Labruzzo and Notaro, dashed ahead for cover, firing as they ran, twisting and turning in frantic formation as they sought to escape the ambush. Bill, separated from his companions, knew that if he followed them he would be in the line of fire; so he remained where he was, tense and angry, swearing silently at Di Gregorio. He turned to see if the sniper had reappeared in the doorway; then he turned back toward the street, rising slightly on his toes as he peeked through the windshield of the car, over the dashboard statue of a plastic saint, trying to see from which building the other snipers were firing. He could not tell. He did not see anyone on the roof ledges, and the only figures in the windows were those people who had just turned on their lights and lifted their shades in response to the noise below.

Bill remained absolutely still for a few moments, breathing into his overcoat so that the visibility of his exhalation on this freezing night would not mark him. Then, pistol in hand, he jumped up from his crouched position and began to run, head down, close to the line of parked cars, running faster than he knew he could, concentrating so intently on his escape that he no longer heard the shooting, did not know whether or not

he was being observed and shot at. He headed south along
Troutman Street toward Knickerbocker Avenue, and at the corner of Knickerbocker he leaped to the right and, without looking
back, ran past Jefferson Street, where his grandfather's house
had been, then past Melrose Street, up George Street to Central
Avenue, right on Central, left on Flushing Avenue, where he
quickly turned around; but no one was following him. He slowed
down to catch his breath, leaning against a wall in the shadows.
He saw a diner on Flushing Avenue and headed toward it, intending to use the phone, but as he was about to enter he spotted
a policeman at the counter drinking coffee. Bill turned around
and walked quickly to Bushwick Avenue, where there was a
tavern on the corner with a coinbox inside; there he called one
of his men, Sam Perrone, who supervised some of the bookmaking operations on the Lower East Side and was at this moment sitting in a Bonanno organization hangout on Second
Avenue and Nineteenth Street, in lower Manhattan, called the
Posh Place. Perrone said he would come immediately.

As Bill waited in the bar for Perrone he heard the sirens of
police cars, saw them speeding through the intersection, red
lights twirling. He looked at his watch and knew that Perrone
could drive across the Williamsburg Bridge and reach Bushwick
Avenue in twelve or fifteen minutes if there were no delays. Bill
ordered a beer and stood at the bar, not far from where a few
middle-aged couples sat watching television, oblivious to the
distant sound of sirens. He felt his heart pounding, his body
exhausted from the run. He wiped his face with his handkerchief
and blew his nose, still feeling the frost in his nostrils, and he
wanted to sit but remained standing so that he could get a full
view of the street. He sipped the beer and watched television
for a while, and then he saw Perrone's car pulling up at the curb,
and he quickly ran out and got in.

On the way to East Meadow, Bill told Perrone what had happened, and Perrone listened gravely. Labruzzo and the others
appeared to have escaped, Bill said, but he was not sure about
injuries. He also did not know which of Di Gregorio's men had
tried to kill him but he vowed he would find out. The whole
thing had been a fiasco, and he conceded to Perrone that he had
been very naïve in thinking that Di Gregorio and his men could
be trusted. But Di Gregorio was in deep trouble now for bun-

gling the job, and an explanation to the commission was perhaps the least of Di Gregorio's problems. He had set off a shooting war; it might be costly and brutal, and the inevitable headlines arising out of tonight's escapade would undoubtedly result in tremendous pressure from the police, tougher decisions from the courts, and longer jail terms for those convicted. Bill was not so angry as he was disgusted and depressed.

Approaching East Meadow, Perrone stopped the car so that Bill could use a pay phone and tell Rosalie to turn on the outside lights of the house. Five minutes later, Perrone's car pulled into the brightly lit driveway. Both men smiled forcibly as they entered the house and greeted Rosalie. She made coffee and they sat around the kitchen table for a while speaking in a general way, keeping their voices low so as not to disturb the children. Rosalie had no idea where Bill had been during the evening, nor would she ask, nor would he tell her. From his easy unconcerned manner, she could have assumed that he had spent Friday night playing pinochle with the boys or had gone bowling.

10

THE NEXT DAY Bill heard from Labruzzo that everyone had gotten home safely but that the police might have found some discarded weapons along Troutman Street and perhaps also the car that Bill had left parked in the neighborhood. The car was parked legally, however, and there was a chance that one of the men could retrieve it before it was ticketed and towed away on Monday, if the area was not surrounded all weekend by the police. Labruzzo, speaking from a telephone booth in Queens to Bill in a booth in Long Island, with Perrone standing guard outside, said he had no idea what the police were now doing or what conclusions they had come to—there was nothing in the morning newspapers or on the radio about the shooting, but Labruzzo felt sure that a police statement would be issued later in the day, and after that the Bonanno men would be in a better position to decide on their next move.

Bill left the booth quickly and returned home with Perrone. They spent the rest of the afternoon listening to the radio, watching television, and playing with the children. Bill was not overly concerned that Di Gregorio's men would make another attempt on his life right away, not with so many people on the alert; and the presence of Perrone in the house through the day and night did not strike Rosalie as being particularly unusual. Her husband's friends often spent the night, sometimes several nights in East Meadow, using the room that Elisa had used or sleeping on cots in the basement, and Rosalie found Perrone far more acceptable as a houseguest than most of the other men. He was neater, more cheerful, and he amused the children. A few years older than Bill, with whom he was in partnership in a trucking business in Brooklyn, Perrone was a short, stocky, pleasant-looking man with dark hair and a wide smile. Like most of Bill's friends, Sam Perrone chain-smoked; unlike them, he was attentive and tender toward Rosalie, to a degree that made her slightly uncomfortable at times. He had a habit, when arriving at the house to pick up Bill, of greeting her with a kiss—not on the cheek but on the mouth. Though she knew it was an innocent gesture, it nonetheless unsettled her. It was too trivial to mention to Bill, who had witnessed it anyway and seemed unabashed, but the fact remained that whenever Rosalie opened the front door for Perrone she instinctively leaned to one side as he entered; but she never seemed out of range for Sam Perrone.

Bill and Perrone spent the rest of the evening indoors; they were visited by other men and listened to each hourly news broadcast. There were no references to the shooting. On the following day, Sunday, when there was still nothing in the press, Bill began to wonder. It was as if the explosive experience on Friday night had been merely a nightmare, a grade-B gangster movie conceived in his own mind. He could not understand how the newspapers, which had been so aggressive in recent years in their coverage of the Mafia, devoting unlimited space to the most infinitesimal facts and unconfirmed rumors about underworld characters, publishing sneak pictures of alleged mafiosi eating in restaurants or attending weddings, printing complete transcripts of tapped telephone talks between reputed dons discussing the weather, he could not understand how the press could miss this story, which was one of the few legitimate gangland stories in several years. Two rival factions did indeed wake up a Brooklyn neighborhood with bullets flying in every direction; yet now, two nights later, not a line had been published about it in any newspaper and not a word about it on any radio station in New York, the communications capital of the nation.

The only conclusion that Bill could come to was that on weekends the media were lazy. Or that newsmen were totally dependent on government spokesmen for news leads and these spokesmen had taken the weekend off. Or—and this possibility bothered Bill—it might be that the police were deliberately keeping everything quiet until Di Gregorio's men could get another shot at him. As improbable as it seemed at first, Bill decided that Di Gregorio or someone higher up could very likely have bought off the desk sergeant or a lieutenant in the precinct that covered Troutman Street, assuring laxity from the police. And yet Bill himself had heard the sirens on Friday night, knew that the police had arrived promptly, and he assumed that there must have been witnesses in the neighborhood who might have called a newspaper or radio station during the weekend. Bill was mystified.

When Monday morning came and went with nothing reported, Bill decided to leak the news to the press himself. It was to his own advantage to do this. He wanted word of Di Gregorio's blunder to be known to every don in the nation, and he also wanted to force the police to stop playing games and to patrol the streets and inhibit Di Gregorio's gang from arranging another ambush.

Bill had become acquainted with several New York newspapermen during his court appearances since 1964, individuals who had often tried to interview him about his father. One of the more persistent ones had worked for *The New York Times*, and it was this man that Bill contacted, and he in turn relayed the information to the *Times*'s metropolitan editor. On the following day, Tuesday, February 1, after the *Times* had confirmed only part of Bill Bonanno's story with the police in Brooklyn, an article was published under the headline GUN FIGHT LEAVES POLICE PUZZLED.

A gang shot up a Brooklyn street Friday night, leaving behind seven guns of various kinds, bullets imbedded in buildings, and a mystery that had police still puzzled yesterday after questioning more than a hundred persons in the neighborhood.

Although residents of Troutman Street, between Knickerbocker Avenue and Irving Avenue, heard more than twenty shots around 11:00 P.M., detectives and patrolmen who rushed to the scene from the Wilson Avenue station house, six blocks away, found no victim and not a single bloodstain. Nor has any complaint appeared.

Detective Lieutenant John W. Norris discounted rumors yesterday that the shoot-up may have been a skirmish between Mafia factions seeking to take over the underworld ''family'' of Joseph (Joe Bananas) Bonanno . . .

''If this was meant to be a professional job, they need a refresher course in shooting,'' Lieutenant Norris said. ''It doesn't have the earmarks of organized activity. It doesn't make sense the way they abandoned all those guns. In all my twenty-three years in the police I've never seen such an erratic action.''

Bill was amused on reading this in the *Times*, and he was also interested in the fact that none of the residents in the neighborhood would admit to the police that they had heard guns blasting in the street. Some said they had been sleeping. Others, like Joseph Taranto, who identified himself as a demolition worker, said he thought the noise was from firecrackers. Another resident of Troutman Street, John Bosco, a handyman, was quoted in the *Times* as explaining, ''We go to bed early on this street. We're working people who have to get up early.''

The only person among the more than one hundred interviewed who would admit to an unusual occurrence on Troutman Street was Mrs. Joseph Cipponeri. It was she who had telephoned the police on Friday night, saying that a man had just broken her door and had run through her living room and kitchen and out into the backyard, smashing the glass of a storm door. When the first of five carloads of police had arrived, they found two revolvers in Mrs. Cipponeri's hallway and another gun at the kitchen door. Mrs. Cipponeri could not describe the interloper because her rooms were dark; all she saw from her bed was a blurred figure of a man racing wildly through her apartment.

The article in the *Times* quickly led to several follow-up stories in all the newspapers and networks, and this put pressure on the police to unravel the mystery and to supply more information to the press, to the public, and of course to Bonanno's men. Within a few days it was fairly well established by the newspapers that Bill Bonanno had been the primary target and that Di Gregorio's men were involved, although the police preferred to hedge a bit because the weapons they found had not been registered in the New York area and they were not listed in FBI files as stolen.

Soon the district attorney in Brooklyn began a wide investigation of the case, and among those sought for questioning was Gaspar Di Gregorio. When the police arrived at Di Gregorio's home in West Babylon, his relatives insisted that he was not there. The police waited, however, and within an hour an ambulance arrived with a doctor, and Di Gregorio was wheeled out of the house on a stretcher. He was said to be suffering from a heart attack. The police served him with a subpoena.

The police also visited the Bonanno residence, but Bill, after recovering the car one morning before daybreak, had disappeared. Having taken the heat off himself by leaking the news of the gun battle to the *Times*, he decided to vanish until he could learn more about the fate of his adversary, Gaspar Di Gregorio.

Within a few weeks Bill heard that the commission was infuriated at Di Gregorio for the Troutman Street failure and the unwanted publicity that had followed, and the next thing that Bill heard was that Di Gregorio was stepping down as the leader of the dissident faction and was being replaced by Paul Sciacca.

During the winter and spring of 1966, as dozens of reluctant witnesses appeared before a Brooklyn grand jury to answer questions about the shooting, Joseph Bonanno was reported to be living in Tunis, the North African birthplace of his wife and a traditional hiding place for Sicilian fugitives. For many generations there had been a large Sicilian colony in Tunis, a city accessible across the sea, and sources in Palermo were quoted in *The New York Times* as saying that the elder Bonanno was residing in North Africa under the aegis of the Sicilian Mafia. One of his visitors there was identified as Frank Garofalo, an elderly distinguished-looking man from Castellammare who was once an officer in the Bonanno organization in the United States. Garofalo had left the United States on a visit to Sicily before the Apalachin exposure of 1957 and had decided to remain there.

Before the agents could verify that Bonanno was really in Tunis, there were other reports claiming that he was elsewhere. During the year various newspaper accounts placed him in Canada, Mexico, Haiti, and other countries. On May 11, United States government spokesmen said in *The New York Times* that Bonanno was definitely hiding in Europe, although declining to specify where.

A week later, on Tuesday morning, May 17, as Bill Bonanno was driving across the Williamsburg Bridge into Manhattan planning to meet one of his men at a café, he heard a radio bulletin announcing that Joseph Bonanno was in New York City.

Bill was about to discount this as another fanciful rumor. But then, amazingly, the announcer went on to say that Joseph Bonanno, accompanied by an attorney, had during the previous hour surprised everyone by walking into the courthouse.

11

JOSEPH BONANNO, SUNTANNED and relaxed, wearing a gray silk suit, a dark gray hat, white shirt and dark tie, stepped out of a car on Pearl Street and slipped into a side entrance of the federal courthouse on Foley Square. While one of his lawyers ran ahead to push the elevator button, the other lawyer remained close to Bonanno, anxious that they get into the building and into the courtroom on the third floor before being spotted by the police or the FBI. If the agents got Bonanno before he was in the custody of the courtroom, where procedure was prescribed and the law precise, there was no telling what might happen; at the very least the agents would probably take Bonanno to their uptown headquarters, would hold him as long as they could, would claim credit for his capture, and would attempt to force concessions and make other face-saving gestures to compensate for their inability to find him during their nineteen months of searching.

But none of these things seemed to concern Joseph Bonanno as he walked casually across the marble-floored corridor at 10:30 A.M. toward the elevator, removing his horn-rimmed glasses and tucking them into the breast pocket of his jacket. Soon he would be facing news cameras and he preferred being photographed without his glasses. He was a handsome man, and he knew it; the reasons for his handsomeness were his softly expressive eyes, his arched eyebrows, the strong lines of his face—features he did not wish to have diminished by spectacles, particularly since he believed that they tended to accentuate his broken nose, a present from the police force many years ago. He had often thought of having the nose fixed but had always decided against it, unwilling to concede such a blatant admission of vanity.

Across the corridor he could see one of the lawyers, Albert

Krieger—who had been hired in Maloney's place because of
Maloney's awkward involvement with the case—standing in a
phone booth trying to reach the United States Attorney, Robert
M. Morgenthau. Krieger wanted to inform Morgenthau of Bonanno's presence in the building. But Morgenthau's line was
busy. Before Krieger could get out of the phone booth, the door
of the elevator containing Bonanno slammed shut; so Krieger
dashed up through the back steps to Morgenthau's office on the
fourth floor to inform him that Joseph Bonanno was en route to
the courtroom.

Bonanno removed his hat as he entered room 318, a large
chamber with high ceilings and rows of wooden pews and with
jury boxes on both sides of the highly polished bar of the judge.
The courtroom activity was characteristically quiet and hum-
drum, and in the pews sat a scattering of spectators, a few of
them sleeping. Even the federal judge, Marvin E. Frankel, appeared to be listening almost listlessly to the routine cases being
processed below his bench. When the judge noticed the gray-
haired man in the gray silk suit walking up the center aisle toward him, he did not recognize him, and he was visibly startled
a few moments later when the man, after an appropriate apology
for interrupting, said, "Your Honor, I am Joseph Bonanno. I
understand that the government would like to talk to me."

Judge Frankel slowly pushed his glasses down to the bridge
of his nose and peered over them.

"*You* are Joseph Bonanno?"

Suddenly the stenographer, the clerk, and others in the courtroom, hearing the name, all turned quickly toward Bonanno,
then turned toward the judge, then back to Bonanno, who stood
calmly holding his hat.

"Yes, Your Honor," Bonanno said.

The judge hesitated, looked around the room. Then, pointing
to an unoccupied area in the front row, he said to Bonanno,
"Please be seated." Bonanno, followed by a tall large lawyer
named Robert Kasanof, turned and sat down. Soon Krieger
joined them, and then Robert Morgenthau, in shirt sleeves, appeared in the courtroom to take a hard look at Bonanno. Satisfied that this was indeed the man, Morgenthau turned without
comment and left the courtroom, which now was being entered
by other men as word of Bonanno's presence spread through the
building. Reporters from the pressroom below came rushing up

to claim front-row seats in the courtroom, and detectives and office secretaries and off-duty elevator operators came in too, and within ten minutes the courtroom was packed and everyone was waiting to see what would happen.

Fifteen minutes passed, a half hour passed. Bonanno, his lawyers, and the crowd of onlookers sat through the tedium of the other cases, wondering when the show would begin. Another fifteen minutes passed; soon it would be lunchtime, and still the government had not made its move. It was as if the government, after investing so much time, effort, and money in its worldwide search for Bonanno, did not really know what to do with him now that it had him.

Finally, at 11:40, two federal marshals walked into the courtroom and took a seat behind Bonanno, and one of them whispered to Krieger, "Albert, we have to arrest your client."

"No problem," Krieger said, relieved that something was finally being done. "Do you have a warrant?"

"Yes."

"Fine," Krieger said, "where do you want us to go?"

"Downstairs," the marshal said, meaning the detention pen on the ground floor of the building.

"Fine," said Krieger, and with Bonanno he followed the federal marshals out of the courtroom. The spectators remained seated awaiting Bonanno's return, noticing, too, that Robert Morgenthau, wearing a jacket this time, had now reappeared in the courtroom accompanied by his staff. Morgenthau handed Judge Frankel a sealed envelope that contained the government's case against Joseph Bonanno. Morgenthau waited.

As Bonanno was downstairs being fingerprinted, palm-printed, and completing other paperwork associated with the arrest, two FBI agents walked into the consultation room of the detention pen, and one of them asked Krieger, "Can we talk to your client?"

"Help yourself," Krieger said.

The agents, Robert Anderson and Ed Walsh, sat in chairs across from Bonanno and proceeded to scrutinize him, seemingly searching for some sign in his hair style, his skin coloring, or the cut of his clothes that would indicate where he had been during the last nineteen months. When one of the agents, Anderson, asked Bonanno where he had been, Bonanno did not reply. Then Anderson stood up and circled around Bonanno, picked up Bonanno's hat and looked inside at the label hoping to find out where it had been purchased. Anderson also looked at the label of Bonanno's jacket, the reverse side of his ties, the shoes he wore. Bonanno cooperated fully, seeming neither irritated nor worried. What the FBI agent did not know was that Joseph Bonanno was wearing exactly the same shoes, the same suit, shirt, tie, and socks that he had worn on the night of October 21, 1964, when he had disappeared on Park Avenue.

In the courtroom, after Joseph Bonanno's return, an indictment was read charging him with obstruction of justice for willfully failing to appear before a federal grand jury investigating the five Mafia "families" in the New York area. When Judge Frankel asked how he pled to the charge, Bonanno answered firmly, "Not guilty."

Judge Frankel then nodded toward Morgenthau, a lean soft-spoken bespectacled man who had been the United States Attorney since 1961. Morgenthau wished to read into the record a description of the defendant's criminal past that might justify the high bail that Morgenthau sought against Bonanno.

"Joseph Bonanno was born on January 18, 1905, in Sicily, Italy," Morgenthau began, "and he is married to Fay Bonanno, and they have three children. He has no known legitimate occupation, and . . ." A look of pain creased Bonanno's face, and he turned toward Krieger, who frowned but did not interrupt Morgenthau as he continued: "He has a criminal record, which includes arrests in connection with attending a meeting in Apalachin, New York, together with major criminal figures from throughout the entire United States. He was also arrested in Tucson, Arizona, in 1956 for failing to appear before a grand jury. He was arrested in Brooklyn for two violations of the Wage and Hour Law. He was also arrested and convicted in Canada in 1964 for making a false statement to the immigration authorities in connection with an application for permanent residence in Canada. The government started to look for Joseph Bonanno in the summer of 1963 in order to serve him with a grand jury subpoena. He was not found in Arizona or in New York, and was finally located in Canada after he had filed his application for permanent residence. After his arrest and conviction in Canada he was then deported to the United States, and upon his arrival in Chicago was served with a grand jury subpoena from this District. He did appear before a grand jury in August of 1964 and was directed to reappear on October 21. According to reports from his attorney, he was allegedly kidnaped in the early hours of the morning . . .''

The crowded courtroom was very silent, and Bonanno listened impassively as Morgenthau went on to describe the extensive but futile efforts of the FBI and other law enforcement agencies to uncover him. Even now Morgenthau had no idea where Bonanno had been during the last nineteen months, and Bonanno, who would not have to testify against himself, did not intend to volunteer the information. It would be the government's burden to prove at an upcoming trial that Bonanno had willfully failed to appear before the grand jury and to disprove the defense's story that Bonanno had been kidnaped by unknown abductors.

"We believe," Morgenthau continued, "that he is a man who has shown that he has complete disregard for the processes of the court and for the law. And we believe that at least since December 19, 1964 [the day after Bill Bonanno's call to Maloney], he has been free and able to come into the court at any time that he wished, and he is only coming in now because it suits his own personal convenience. Under all of these circumstances, we ask for bail in the amount of $500,000.''

Bonanno's eyebrows shot upward in a look of astonishment, the courtroom responded with a murmur, and Krieger shook his bald head in objection and removed his glasses.

"If Your Honor please," Krieger said in a loud voice, standing, "I think that first it is incumbent upon me to correct some of the information which has been given to Mr. Morgenthau concerning the so-called criminal record of the defendant Bonanno. In the first instance, Your Honor, he has only been convicted of one crime, and I think I am misusing the word 'crime'—offense would be more appropriate. That dealt with a violation of the Wages and Hours Act in the early forties, dealing with nonpayment of some overtime to some employees in a dress firm in which he had a one-third interest. The principals pleaded guilty and were fined $50. That is the extent of his record insofar as convictions are concerned, so I am informed.

"In regard to the Canadian situation, Your Honor, on his application for permanent residency there was a question, 'Have you ever been convicted of a crime?' His answer was, 'No.'

This was the basis for a rather complicated perjury prosecution up there. The prosecution was terminated by a withdrawal of the action against him, and he was allowed to leave Canada just as any other person could. He was not deported nor was there an order of voluntary deportation entered. He was allowed to go to the airport, purchase his own ticket, and fly to Chicago.

"On his landing in Chicago he was then served with a subpoena to appear before a grand jury sitting in this district. He did appear here in response to that subpoena. As far as his occupation is concerned . . ."

"He did not reappear as directed, did he?" asked Judge Frankel.

"Well, Your Honor," said Krieger, "that is one of the issues which will be litigated in the prosecution of this obstruction of justice indictment. The query immediately is posed as to whether he was under a duty to appear. The grand jury in front of which he had appeared in August had expired and the grand jury was excused. He was requested to appear before a brand-spanking-new grand jury. Query as to whether the government was perhaps remiss in not resubpoenaing him. But that is one of the legal issues which would be at the heart of a defense to this indictment.

"Now, as far as his occupation is concerned, Your Honor, it is almost disingenuous for the government to argue that he has no legitimate sources of income. The government levied against his property in December of 1964 in some astronomical figure. Those levies were promptly removed after application was made by counsel representing him in tax matters, because he has scrupulously filed accurate and detailed income tax returns over many, many, many years. The most painstaking audits conducted by Internal Revenue Service have failed to reveal any discrepancy even for a civil levy.

"He has very substantial real estate holdings in his own name and jointly with his wife in Arizona. His wife has interests in a very successful cheese company, the Bella Cheese Company. He is a man of comparative means. He is a man of legitimate income, which has been proved time and time again at least to the satisfaction of the Internal Revenue Service. Now, Your Honor, as far as bail being requested in the sum of $500,000 is concerned, that is almost a request for no bail. It is a complete disregard for one of the basic considerations which a court must face when fixing bail. Certainly the fact that the defendant has surrendered here to the court is an indication that he has returned or presented himself before the court to face whatever charges the United States Attorney chooses to bring against him.''

Judge Frankel interrupted, asking, ''Mr. Maloney was his lawyer at the time of the press conference to which the United States Attorney referred?''

''That is correct, Your Honor.''

''So there was a public representation a year and a half ago that he would turn up in court.''

''Well, unfortunately, Your Honor, I think that the circumstances surrounding this most unfortunate situation between Mr. Maloney and the press and also between Mr. Maloney and Mr. Morgenthau came about, as I understand it, through misunderstandings,'' Krieger said. ''There is testimony before a grand jury which was adduced from the person who called Mr. Maloney. That was the son of the defendant Joseph Bonanno, Salvatore. He testified, I am informed, that he had received a phone call at a certain phone booth, and the voice was not that of his father, but the voice said, 'Your father is all right,' or words to that effect. Salvatore contacted Mr. Maloney and advised him of this.''

''Let me ask you,'' the judge cut in again, ''is there some question of privilege or other confidential problem that makes it difficult for you to enlighten me about this year and a half of absence in the face of the press conference? Because this is highly relevant on the question of bail and ensuring the appearance of this gentleman, if there was a notorious awareness that he was expected, on request or otherwise, to come here and that his lawyer then representing him announced that he would come here. It leaves a large question in the court's mind. What happened? Why didn't he come?''

''I appreciate that, Your Honor,'' Krieger said, ''and I am glad that you cut right to the heart of it there. There are many questions which you pose in answer to which I would have to invoke the privilege.''

''You mean your pleasure in the question is mitigated by your inability to give me useful answers.''

''Yes, sir.''

''Well, I understand that,'' Judge Frankel said, ''but it seems to me that the government makes out a rather cogent case for its view that one does not have a solid certainty that this gentleman appears when he is expected in court.''

"Why would he be here today, Your Honor?" Krieger replied. "He walked into this courtroom at 10:35, and he sat there waiting and waiting and waiting, until finally the marshals effected an arrest warrant at about twenty minutes to twelve. Why would he be here if he intended to abscond? He certainly would need no permission to abscond.''

"I don't understand that, Mr. Krieger," said the judge. "If we expect him back next month and he comes voluntarily in 1968, that won't be satisfactory.''

"No, that would not be satisfactory, Your Honor," Krieger agreed. "That is why I cannot argue that a bail should be set. I am not asking for his parole. I think that the court does need some assurance in a realistic figure as to his future appearances before the court, but bail must be realistic, and bail must be sufficient to assure the government and the court of the return of the defendant, but not so unrealistic that it amounts to a request for no bail.''

"Are you saying that he can't make $500,000?" the judge asked.

"He cannot, Your Honor. He cannot.''

"With the property you have described, what bail would you recommend?''

"I would recommend this—that is a twofold question, Your Honor. One, you are asking me how much bail could he possibly put up, and the other question is how much bail do I think would be reasonable here.''

"Why don't you answer them both?''

"Well, I think that $25,000 bail, Your Honor, would be reasonable and realistic.''

"And the other part: what would be possible?''

"In all candor, he could make a somewhat larger sum than that, Your Honor.''

"You realize that I am liable to set it somewhat larger and I wanted . . .''

"I realize that possibility, Your Honor.''

"Whatever help you could give me on that," the judge said, turning before he finished toward the United States Attorney and asking, "Mr. Morgenthau, you mentioned a grand jury problem. You are not asking for bail for his appearance, as a witness, I take it?''

"No, we are not, Your Honor."

"What about Mr. Krieger's point that it is questionable whether this witness was under compulsion to appear before that grand jury?''

"I believe that is a problem, Your Honor," Morgenthau said, "but this is the first time that Mr. Krieger has raised that as a reason for his not appearing. Certainly Mr. Krieger has known for many, many months during which he has represented Mr. Bonanno that we have been looking for him. He certainly has not been with his family or at his residence for that period of the last year and a half. And I would like to repeat again that for the years from approximately the summer of 1963 to the summer of 1964 the FBI and the Internal Revenue Service were looking for Mr. Bonanno, and he was not present in his home or in any of the usual places that he frequented.

"When he went to Canada, he went there for the purpose of trying to establish a permanent residence. He applied to the Canadian immigration authorities for permanent residence. He had, I think without doubt, been a fugitive for about a year and a half. He had full knowledge that the processes of the court were seeking him. Why he has come in at this particular time of course we don't know in detail, but I don't think that anybody who is under a grand jury subpoena should be permitted to select the time in which he wants to come in and appear before a grand jury or before the court.''

"Your Honor," Krieger said, "Mr. Morgenthau is in effect arguing his summation after conviction. He is charged with a specific crime. I am not going to argue a defense for that crime here at the time of arraignment. I think Your Honor is faced with a crime the maximum punishment for which is five years. It is not the most serious or heinous of offenses. I can cite to Your Honor instances where defendants have been convicted of much more serious offenses, have been sentenced to fifteen years in jail, and $100,000 was continued as sufficient bail pending appeal. In the present posture of this case, Your Honor, I again request something in the neighborhood of $25,000.''

"I think," Morgenthau said, "you have got to consider the resources of the defendant, Your Honor, and these resources are very, very large.''

"The defendant's wife is ill," Krieger interjected, "he does have children, he has grandchildren—if he has been a fugitive for a year and a half, as indicated, he hasn't seen them for a considerable period of time. He is a human being. Regardless of any charges against him, he is a human being and he is entitled to simple, basic . . ."

"I appreciate that, Mr. Krieger," said the judge, abruptly. "The question is, what amount of bail will ensure the appearance of this human being in the court when he is expected."

"Yes, Your Honor," Krieger said, gently, as if aware that he may have pushed a bit too hard.

"I will set bail in the amount of $150,000," Judge Frankel said. Krieger and Bonanno did not react; only Morgenthau seemed disappointed.

"Judge," Morgenthau said, after a few moments of silence, "may the government ask that he surrender his passport in whatever name he holds it to the clerk of the court? And also that he be directed not to enter any railroad station, pier, dock, or airport and that if he is going to be away from whatever residence that he gives you for a period of more than twenty-four hours, that he so advise the United States Attorney's office that he will be away and the location that he will be at?"

"Your Honor," Krieger said quickly, "I would request this: in the event that he does make bail, that the bail limits be extended to include the Eastern District of New York. My reason for that is that his son has maintained a residence in Nassau County for about two years plus. He probably will be staying there. I would also request, Your Honor, that the bail limits be extended to include the District of Arizona so that he may visit with his wife. She has resided at their home in Tucson for many, many, many years. She is not well. This is known to the government. A trip from Tucson to here could well be injurious to her health. I would have no objection to the last request, of advising the government as to where he is staying."

"And as to surrendering his passport, if any?" the judge added.

"I understand the passport has expired," Krieger said, "but we will surrender the passport."

"He will surrender the expired passport," the judge repeated.

"It has to be renewed after three years, I believe," Krieger said.

"Whatever passport he has will be surrendered," said the judge, with insistence.

"Surely," Krieger said, "no problem."

"And if he has any other passport other than an expired passport," Morgenthau added.

"Any passport he has he will be ordered to surrender," the judge assured.

"Any passport he ever had was in his own name, and that one will be surrendered," Krieger said, pointedly reacting to Morgenthau's inference that Bonanno used false passports.

"Well," the judge replied, trying to conclude the whole exchange, "the government certainly ought to be able to check on that." After a pause, the judge continued, "Now on the other conditions on which you are not together, would the government feel secure, Mr. Morgenthau, if it were provided, as you requested, that he not enter railroad stations and other such places except for the purpose, on notice to the United States Attorney, of going to and from the District of Arizona to visit his wife?"

"Yes, Your Honor."

"Could you gentlemen formulate that in a way that accomplishes the result; that is, that he is not to go to piers, docks, and so forth, but he is permitted, on notice to the government, to travel to the District of Arizona and return, and to give notice on the occasions of such trips as to when and by what means he will be proceeding to and from Arizona?"

"Yes, Your Honor," said Krieger.

"Mr. Morgenthau, is there any objection to extending the bail limits to the Eastern District of New York?"

"No, Your Honor."

"May we use the ordinary consent form, Your Honor, to the Eastern District of New York?"

"No," Morgenthau interrupted, "I would like you to prepare an order on that."

Judge Frankel concurred, and Krieger said, "All right."

"Will you collaborate in preparing such an order? And I will sign it," the judge said to Krieger.

"Yes, Your Honor."

"Is there anything else?" the judge asked.

"No, Your Honor," Morgenthau said.

"Is there any problem of scheduling for motions and so on?"

"Your Honor, I would like about a month for motions, please," Krieger said.

"That is agreeable, Your Honor," Morgenthau said.

"Is June 20 all right?" Judge Frankel asked, lifting his pencil to his pad.

"Fine," said Krieger.

"That is agreeable," said Morgenthau.

"All right, gentlemen," the judge said, standing.

"Thank you, Your Honor," they said, and Krieger led Bonanno to a place in the building where he would wait while the bail was arranged.

Later in the afternoon, a $150,000 bond was posted by the Stuyvesant Insurance Company of the Bronx at a cost of $4,530 premium, using as collateral Frank Labruzzo's home in Queens and two parcels of real estate in Tucson in the name of Bonanno's wife and one of her sisters. But a document filed with the bond in court revealed an interesting disclosure: it showed that Bonanno or one of his representatives had begun to make bail arrangements more than a week ago, on May 9, and that the insurance company had sufficient collateral to authorize a bond up to the amount of $500,000—the very figure that Morgenthau had requested and that Bonanno had responded to in court with a look of pain and astonishment.

After Bonanno had stood before the United States Commissioner and solemnly swore that while on bail he would refrain from entering any embassies or legations of governments other than those of the United States and after he had returned to him those items that the arresting officers had confiscated as possibly lethal—a silver pencil and a comb—he was free to leave the federal courthouse, which he did at 4:20 P.M.

He smiled as he walked through the corridor, flashbulbs popping in front of him, but neither he nor his attorneys would answer questions that the reporters were asking: Where had he been? Was the kidnaping a hoax? Why did he return?

"I have nothing to say," Bonanno said, repeating it several times as he walked and occasionally shook hands with passersby.

"Well, how do you feel?" one reporter asked.

"Under the circumstances," Bonanno said, cautiously, "as well as could be expected."

At the bottom of the steps in front of the courthouse, Bonanno waved good-bye and walked with Krieger half a block to a parking lot. There he climbed into a 1965 white Lincoln and Krieger drove away.

Ten minutes later they pulled into a lot next to a tall building at 401 Broadway, the location of Krieger's firm, and arriving in the office lobby Bonanno saw his son waiting for him. The two men moved quickly toward one another and embraced for several moments. Then other men who had been waiting also embraced the elder Bonanno. Among the men were Labruzzo, Joseph Notaro, and Notaro's cousin Peter Notaro. There were affectionate exchanges in Sicilian, tears in the eyes of Joseph Bonanno, and awkward moments of silence. Then someone suggested that they all go uptown to La Scala Restaurant on Fifty-fourth Street to have a few drinks and perhaps dinner. The elder Bonanno agreed. La Scala had long been one of his favorite restaurants. But first he wanted to go to a barbershop to get his long gray hair trimmed, wanted also to have hot towels on his face and a shoeshine. The men knew of a barbershop on West Forty-eighth Street that was on the second floor, making it easier for them to protect against a rival gang's "hit" man.

The men drove uptown in a three-car tandem. It was after 5:00 P.M. now, and the streets were crowded with office workers returning home; cars were bumper to bumper and horns were honking. Bonanno looked out with fascination at the pedestrians as he was driven slowly uptown; he noticed how fashion had changed during the months he was out of New York, and he told one of the bodyguards in his car that he would have to go to a tailor soon—his trousers had cuffs, and he noted that the prevailing trend was cuffless trousers. He also observed that the lapels of men's jackets were wider, and the shorter skirts that he saw some women wearing along the avenue amazed him.

As Bill sat in the car with his father, he could not help but wonder where he had been all those months, but he doubted that his father would ever discuss it with him. After all, a trial would be coming up sooner or later, although it might take years because of various delays; in any event Bill would surely be summoned to testify, and the less he knew the easier it would be. Still, Bill was intensely curious about whether his father had moved around from place to place—and how he had done it— or whether his father had remained generally in one place, and he wondered how close his father had come to getting caught, and how he had managed to avoid foolish mistakes during the interminable weeks of tension and solitude. His father now had a deep suntan, and he might well have been in North Africa or Haiti as the newspapers suggested, or even in any of a dozen other places beyond the hot sun—knowing his father, it was possible that the elder Bonanno had gotten the tan from a sun-lamp as a ploy to mislead the FBI in court today.

Half of the men got out at the barbershop on Forty-eighth Street, while the others went to park the cars. As Bonanno sat in the barber's chair, a bodyguard sat waiting inside the shop and another man was posted outside the door at the top of the steps. Both men were armed.

Less than an hour later, they assembled at La Scala; they were given a large table, and drinks were quickly ordered and delivered. Most of the waiters seemed to know him and shook his hand, and other people in the restaurant recognized him from his photographs and stretched to get at look at him. He sat at the head of the table, made several toasts in Sicilian, and thanked the men for their loyalty. After a second round of drinks, there was much laughter at the description of how the FBI agent had grabbed Bonanno's hat in the detention pen and had looked without luck for labels or dry cleaner's markings that might serve as a tipoff as to where he had been. There was more laughter with the description of Morgenthau's crestfallen face on being told that Bonanno had just walked into the courthouse, and the stories continued for nearly an hour—then, suddenly, the laughter stopped. Joseph Notaro, one of Bonanno's most trusted captains, an individual who had devoted himself tirelessly to the organization throughout the chaos, sat slumped forward at the table. The men could not revive him. Notaro had just had a heart attack and was dead.

PART TWO

THE WAR

12

Notaro's funeral in the Bronx was attended by dozens of members of the organization and also by several detectives and FBI agents who recorded the license plates of the cars and took photographs of the mourners. Joseph Bonanno swore silently as he passed the agents on his way to the casket but he did not display his feelings openly. He was overcome with grief. His old friend, Notaro, dead at fifty-six, had been suffering from a heart ailment for years and yet his energy and loyalty remained constant throughout the ordeal following Bonanno's disappearance. On ten occasions Notaro had been summoned before the grand jury and asked questions about Bonanno and the organization, and each time Notaro was worried by government agents' hints that if he did not cooperate, his son, a young lawyer, might suffer the consequences, might possibly be disbarred from New York State; but Notaro held out against the pressure, saying nothing for which he would later be ashamed and not weakening as he continued to receive notices from the jury ordering him to reappear and to testify again. Notaro was scheduled to testify on the day following his death.

When the funeral ceremony was completed, Joseph Bonanno returned to his car and was driven to his son's home in East Meadow. The elder Bonanno traveled under heavy protection—armed men sat on each side of him in his car; two cars with other men drove to the front and rear along the highway; and two men also accompanied him inside his son's home, sleeping there at night and remaining on the alert there through the day. The newspapers that had given front-page coverage to his surprise visit to Judge Frankel also reported the omnipresent threat of rival gunmen: *The New York Daily News*'s headline read BA-NANAS BACK, FEARED RIPE FOR KILLING. There was also spec-

ulation in the press that Bonanno had chosen to return at this
time to direct a full-scale battle against the opposition, realizing,
after his son's experience on Troutman Street, that there was no
peaceful way in which to deal with Di Gregorio's faction or the
Mafia commission led by Stefano Magaddino.

Oddly, one of Bonanno's bodyguards in his son's home was
Stefano Magaddino's first cousin, Peter Magaddino, a stocky
gray-haired man who was once close to the Buffalo don, but
after repeated disagreements with his older cousin, whom he
came to regard as overbearing, he moved to New York City and
became reassociated with Joseph Bonanno. It was Peter Magaddino who had concurred in Bonanno's worst suspicions about
Stefano Magaddino during 1963–1964—that is, Stefano's aim to
control the Bonanno organization through the puppet leadership
of his brother-in-law, Gaspar Di Gregorio.

Peter Magaddino met Gaspar Di Gregorio many years ago in
Buffalo after Di Gregorio had married Stefano's sister, and he
concluded then that Di Gregorio was completely dominated by
Stefano and would never be otherwise. Since Peter Magaddino
had little respect for Di Gregorio and was appalled by what he
considered his cousin's avariciousness, it was a simple decision
in 1964 for Peter Magaddino to side with Bonanno—he admired
Bonanno, whom he had grown up with and had known intimately as a young man in Castellammare del Golfo.

They were born in neighboring hillside houses, which overlooked the sea, to families that had intermarried in the past and
had been allies in the feuds with the mafiosi in nearby towns.
The Bonannos and Magaddinos were both large families with
many branches, and for several generations they influenced the
order by which people lived in that section. They subsisted from
their farms, producing grain, olives, tomatoes, and other vegetables, and they raised sheep and cattle for slaughter or trade.
They controlled jobs for which the government appropriated
small funds, and they had influence along the pier and among
the merchants, receiving tribute for their protection. They literally controlled the towns in that area as surely as had the
ancient princes and viceroys before them, taxing their subjects
for services rendered, services that included the arbitration of
neighborly disputes, the recovery of stolen property, personal
assistance in all family problems, personal redress for wrongs
to one's honor or one's wife. They interceded with the judge at

the trials of their countrymen and received favors from the politicians in Palermo in return for solid support in the hills. They often did things illegally, but their law was largely their own. For centuries their region's poverty and pestilence was ignored by the Sicilian government, by the parliament in Rome, by dozens of previous rulers overseas; so finally they took the law into their own hands and bent it to suit themselves, as they had seen the aristocrats do.

They believed that there was no equality under law; the law was written by conquerors. In the tumultuous history of Sicily, going back more than two thousand years, the island had been governed by Greek law, Roman law, Arab law, the laws of Goths, Normans, Angevins, Aragonese—each new fleet of conquerors brought new laws to the land, and no matter whose law it was, it seemed that it favored the rich over the poor, the powerful over the weak. While the law opposed vendettas among villagers, it allowed organized brutality and killing by government guardsmen or king's armies—wars were allowed, feuds were not—and the first to be conscripted into the king's armies were the sons of the soil. The laws regulating food, drink, dress, drugs, literature, or sexual behavior were usually extensions of the life-style of the nobleman in power. They reflected his past, they varied if his background was prudish or permissive, if he was Christian or Moslem, if he was of an Eastern or a Western culture, if he was merciful or mad. The Germanic tyrant King Frederick II decreed that adulterous women should have their noses cut off, whereas other despots, lax and licentious, condoned concubines in court and the pursuit of other men's wives at will. The fact that the law was often inconsistent from generation to generation and was sometimes even contradictory to existing laws seemed of mild concern to the lawmakers, who were mainly interested in controlling the masses and remaining in power.

Under such an unenlightened leadership, feudalism was permitted to exist until the nineteenth century, and illiteracy prevailed in much of Sicily through the mid-twentieth century, particularly in the barren mountain villages of the western region. Here in an atmosphere of neglect and isolation, families became more insular, more suspicious of strangers, held to old habits. The official government was often the enemy, the outlaw often a hero; and family clans such as the Bonannos, the Magaddinos, and numbers of other large families in neighboring seaside villages or interior towns were held in awe by their townsmen. Though certain of these leaders were vengeful and corrupt, they identified with the plight of the poor and often shared what they had stolen from the rich. Their word was nearly always good, and they did not betray a trust. Usually they went about their business quietly, walked arm in arm with the village priest through the square, or sat in the shade of cafés while lesser men stopped to greet them and perhaps seek a favor. While they bore the humble manner of other men in the town, there was nevertheless an easy confidence about them, a certain strength of character. They were more ambitious, shrewder, bolder, perhaps more cynical about life than their resigned *paesani*, who relied largely upon God. They were often spoken of in hushed tones by other men but never called mafiosi. They were usually referred to as the *amici*, friends, or *uomini rispettati*, men of respect.

Since the ancestors of Joseph Bonanno and Peter Magaddino had long been part of the *amici* in Castellammare, the two men had a certain status at birth, and they were courteously treated wherever they went in the town. As a boy, Joseph Bonanno particularly liked to travel through the town on horseback, to swim near the old castle, to sometimes ride beyond the mountain through the wild pastures to his father's farm near the ancient temple of Segesta, a majestic structure with its thirty-six columns still intact though built during the classical period of the Greeks.

He also traveled once to the city of Monreale to see the great cathedral that was constructed in the twelfth century under the Norman ruler William II, a cathedral whose interior was covered with 70,000 square feet of exquisite mosaics and whose tremendous bronze doors were sculptured by Bonanno of Pisa. He read and reread the history of Sicily as a student, and he often wondered, on seeing such grandeur in towns of such poverty, why there had not been more citizens' revolts against the extravagance of the nobility and the church. But he knew how successful the church was in convincing the people that the reward for their suffering would be found in heaven. He was also aware that those who were capable of organizing the masses were often absorbed into the ranks of the *amici*; and the *amici* were not reformers. They did not seek the overthrow of the system, which they doubted they could do even if they wanted to. They had learned to work within the system, to exploit it while it exploited the country. There was only one dramatic example in Sicilian history where the island's impoverished, embittered population was able to organize a successful national revolt against their oppressors, who in this instance were the French. The cause of the revolt occurred on Easter Monday in 1282, when a French soldier raped a Palermo maiden on her wedding day. Suddenly a band of Sicilians retaliated by butchering a French troop, and as word of this reached other Sicilians, more French soldiers were killed in town after town—a frenzied spree of xenophobia quickly spread through the island as gangs of men wildly attacked and murdered every Frenchman in sight. Thousands of Frenchmen were murdered in a few days, and it was claimed by some local historians that the Mafia was begun at this point, taking its name from the anguished cry of the girl's mother running through the streets shouting *ma fia*, *ma fia*, my daughter, my daughter.

This story was told to Joseph Bonanno as a boy in Castellammare by his father, who had heard it from *his* father, and while certain historians consider many aspects of the incident to be highly romanticized or exaggerated, there was no doubting that the massacre abruptly terminated French rule of the island. But the French were soon followed by other rulers like themselves, corrupt, exploiting the land and inhabitants, and giving nothing in return except to the Sicilian aristocracy, who were the most corrupt of all. For hundreds of years Castellammare was a feudal estate, part of a dowry that noble families transferred from generation to generation, and even Sicily's unification with Italy in the mid-1800s did not improve living conditions for the average citizens—most continued to live in stone hovels without water or sanitation facilities, and with so many children they were unable to afford more than two meals a day. The only escape was through immigration, and by the early 1900s more than a million Sicilians had left the land, some going to South America or Canada and many more going to the United States.

Among those to leave was Joseph Bonanno's father, Salvatore Bonanno, a lean six-footer with a handlebar moustache who was one of the few whose departure was not provoked by poverty. Salvatore Bonanno was extremely bored and restless with life in Castellammare. As a young man he had given serious thought to becoming a priest, a career pursued by many ambitious youths in quest of wealth and social prestige (one of Bonanno's grand-uncles had been a bishop); but before Salvatore progressed very far, he became disenchanted with the church, resentful of the great treasury it hoarded, and one day he decided to reduce that treasury a bit by stealing several jeweled chalices, gold sacra-mental plates, and an ornate gold candelabrum. Then he left the monastery with his booty and returned home without guilt.

Soon he was helping to run the family cattle business, which included smuggling animals from North Africa, and he super-vised a family farm and vineyard that produced figs and grapes. At the age of twenty-five, he was cheered by the birth of a son, and he might have resigned himself to life in Castellammare if he had not heard so many enticing tales about America from those immigrants who sent back word. In 1906, at the age of twenty-six, with his twenty-one-year-old wife, Catherine, and his one-year-old son Joseph, Salvatore Bonanno sailed for New York. Upon arriving he was met by numbers of Castellam-marese, who took the couple to the Williamsburg section of Brooklyn where hundreds of Sicilians had settled before the turn of the century. Soon Salvatore obtained an apartment and pur-chased a restaurant and bar on the corner of Roebling Street and North Fifth. The *amici* had already established themselves in small numbers in Brooklyn, operating an Italian lottery, trying to control the cheap labor market that their countrymen were providing American business, and selling their "protection" service wherever they could. But none of the *amici* tried to extort money from Salvatore Bonanno; his family's position in Sicily was well known, and the New York *amici* were hopeful that Salvatore might bring whatever skills and cunning that he pos-sessed to their Brooklyn operation.

But the Sicilian and Italian gangsters were of little significance at this period in New York, and Salvatore Bonanno did not greatly concern himself with their affairs. The big gangs in New York and other eastern cities were predominently Irish or Jew-ish. The same elements were powerful in Chicago, and further to the West and Southwest, the big names in crime were Anglo-Saxon, spiritual descendants of the James boys, the Barkers, and Pretty Boy Floyd. Although some *amici* were receiving kickbacks and other considerations along San Francisco's Fisherman's Wharf, where many of the fishermen were Sicilian immigrants, the only city in which Sicilian or Italian gangs had made headlines was in New Orleans in 1890, and that episode turned out horribly for the gangmen. The headlines concerned two Sicilian factions battling for control of illegal waterfront operations in New Orleans and the efforts of a vigilant police chief to expose the racketeers. After the chief had ignored bribes and the threatening advice that he not probe further, he was shot in the street one night and died shortly after. A grand jury investigation blamed the murder on a "secret organization known as the Mafia," and nineteen Sicilian immigrants were brought to trial as principals or conspirators. When the suspects were not convicted, a group of enraged citizens, including the mayor and the press, voiced their disapproval, and many people suspected that the jury had been bribed. A large group of protesters marched to the jailhouse, and many of these citizens later broke into the prison where, while the guards were occupied elsewhere, they lynched or shot to death eleven of the Sicilians. News of this traveled around the world, and the Italian government severed diplomatic relations with the United States; although relations were later restored when President Harrison apologized and authorized an indemnity of approximately $30,000, it was many years before law-abiding Sicilian and Italian immigrants felt at home in New Orleans.

In New York City, however, Salvatore Bonanno remained aloof from gang activity and concentrated on learning English, traveling around the city, and operating his restaurant. When his son Joseph was old enough, he entered the first grade at the public school on Roebling Street. A year later, in 1911, Salvatore Bonanno was summoned home by his brothers in Castellammare. A dispute had erupted among various gangs in western Sicily, and while the Magaddino and Bonanno factions were still united, other large local families, such as the Buccellatos, were not and were suspected of conspiring with outside *amici* to take over control of the piers and other operations in Castellammare. Salvatore's land and cattle interests were threatened, he was told; so as soon as he and his wife could pack and board a steamer, they began the voyage back to Sicily. Joseph Bonanno was six years old and was speaking Sicilian with a Brooklyn accent.

By the time the family arrived in Castellammare, the threat of a widespread battle and series of vendettas had simmered

down, and it was soon obvious to Salvatore that his trip home
was something of a false alarm. He was initially angry with his
brothers but decided to postpone his return to America for a
while until he was absolutely certain that the disputes and misunderstandings were settled to everyone's satisfaction.

There was obviously great unrest throughout the island, particularly in the western region, and Salvatore Bonanno was more
aware than ever of the divisiveness of the people. Sicily seemed
to be an island of many islands, a mixture of individualists
united only in their poverty, and their lives were so very different
from those immigrants who had settled in Brooklyn and elsewhere in America. Salvatore noticed that no man in western
Sicily ventured along the open road beyond the town without a
shotgun in his saddle or a pistol in his pocket, which had not
been the case in New York, although it might have been in the
cowboy country of western America. Salvatore became increasingly aware, too, of the hostility of western Sicilians toward
eastern Sicilians, especially since the western capital of Palermo
had been overtaken in overseas trade by the eastern port of Ca-
tania, resulting in dwindling profits for the *amici* and everyone
else who had linked their fortunes to Palermo.

The plight of western Sicily continued to be ignored by the
Italian government in Rome, except in instances that were embarrassing to Sicilians—such as the impeachment from the Senate of a popular representative from Trapani, capital of the
western province of which Castellammare was a part, because
he was charged with padding municipal payrolls, installing his
friends and the *amici* in political jobs, misappropriating certain
funds for personal use or patronage, doing things that Sicilians
believed all politicians did, including those in Rome. When the
Italian government would not drop its charges against the Trapani representative, there were protests throughout Sicily, especially in the western region; the Italian king's picture was
publicly burned, a local street was named in honor of the de-
famed politician, and a French flag was flown in the town square,
suggesting that the Roman bureaucrats were no less hypocritical
or despicable than the French had been centuries ago, and a few
Sicilian citizens advocated a bloody revolt similar to the one that
had occurred in 1282.

The Italian government was not surprised by this response
since many of its members had long felt that Sicilians were

incorrigible, impossible to understand, and perhaps even criminal by nature. The Italian criminologist Cesare Lombroso came close to suggesting this in pointing out that while eastern Sicilians had been greatly influenced by Greek colonization, the western Sicilians had been more influenced by the Arabs, many of whom in the thirteenth century were driven into the hills behind Palermo and were forced to survive through their cunning and deception. Other Italian theorists suggested that western Sicilians living in or near Palermo were generally lazy and unambitious because they had been ruled for hundreds of years by the lax administration of the medieval Spanish. And there were other explanations, too, that were equally unflattering to western Sicilians.

Salvatore Bonanno resented the aspersions cast upon his region, particularly since he had seen for himself in America how hard western Sicilians were willing to work if given a chance. Not only did they work hard but they earned extra money to send back to their relatives in Sicily, and this financial bonus was a boon to the sagging Sicilian economy. Another benefit provided by their immigration was in making more jobs available to those who remained at home, and Sicilian landowners were often heard to complain of their inability to find sufficient numbers of farm workers.

But Salvatore Bonanno saw no change with regard to violence in Sicily—hardly a day passed without a few people being shot in the streets because of one vendetta or another, and there was endless cattle stealing and kidnaping for ransom. Among the many murders during the early 1900s in Sicily was the fatal shooting of an American detective who had come to the island to learn what he could about the Mafia. His name was Petrosino. He was born in Italy and had immigrated at thirteen to the United States. Eventually he became a member of the New York City Police Department and then was selected to work with the Italian Squad, a secret unit established in 1904 to help curb the extortion racket that was growing in New York and was believed to be run by the Mafia, or, as it was also called, the Black Hand or the Unione Siciliane. Petrosino thought that he would be better equipped to fight the Mafia in America if he learned more about its origins in Sicily, and gradually he convinced his superiors to send him. He traveled there under an assumed name, and his mission was confidential, but as he strolled through a

piazza in Palermo on the day of his arrival, he was approached
from behind and was shot four times in the head and back.
Petrosino fell dead in the street. His killer or killers disappeared
into the crowd in the square and escaped.

Salvatore Bonanno's presence had a restraining effect on the
mafiosi of Castellammare and neighboring towns and villages
in the province of Trapani. Since he had been in America during
the five years in which there had been much dissension among
the gang leaders, much infiltration of traditional boundaries, and
unauthorized brigandage, he was able to avoid taking sides with
one faction or another; as a result, he could arbitrate disputes
with apparent objectivity. Though he was young, he commanded respect from his elders; and though he was soft-spoken,
he could be vengeful if necessary and more than one corpse was
found along the narrow hilly roads of Castellammare after his
judgments and warnings had been ignored. Tall and formal of
manner, he was a conspicuous figure wherever he went, and the
people of the town were beginning to extend to him the deference that custom required.

But in 1915, in his thirty-seventh year, he became ill with a
respiratory ailment that was not adequately treated, and in November of that year, while he sat at home writing a letter, he
quietly died. He still held the pen in his hand and seemed to be
meditating at his desk when he was discovered in that position
by Peter Magaddino, then thirteen, who had entered the house
looking for his friend Joseph.

The death of Salvatore Bonanno was recognized throughout
the province of Trapani, and several hundred people followed
the horse-drawn casket through the town toward the cemetery
near the base of the mountain. In the procession were all the
important families of the area—the Magaddinos and Buccellatos, the Vitales, the Rimis, the Bonventres (Mrs. Bonanno's
family), and dozens of other clans together with the priests and
politicians. At the head of the cortege walked Joseph Bonanno,
eleven, with his mother, thirty-one, dressed from head to toe in
black, the color she planned to wear for the rest of her life.

Weeks after the death of his father, Joseph Bonanno returned
to school, deeply depressed but finding comfort in his close
companionship with Peter Magaddino. It was to Magaddino that

he confided things that he withheld from his many cousins and uncles, and one recurring dream that possessed Joseph Bonanno as a boy was to run away from home and become a sea captain of a large ocean liner like the one in which he had crossed the Atlantic with his parents. Sometimes he awoke in the middle of the night screaming with visions of himself sinking with his ship, seeing the bow slowly submerging into the sea. Much of his boyhood was preoccupied with death, not only his own but the death of people he did not know in distant places. He overheard people speaking in Castellammare about the many Sicilians killed fighting in Europe for the worthless Italian government in World War I, and he saw many servicemen returning to the town with amputated limbs or with strange ailments due to inhaling gas on the battlefield. He saw pieces of black cloth on the doors of numerous homes, signifying that there had been a death in the family, and it seemed sometimes that every woman he passed on the street was wearing a black dress and every man wore a black band around his sleeve or on his lapel. Death was the obsession of Sicilians, they paraded their mourning colors almost with pride, and even on bright sunny days, Castellammare seemed black. Among the few vivid recollections of gaiety that Joseph Bonanno had as a boy was the ship's voyage from New York on which were many *Americani* in brightly colored clothes laughing among themselves, singing in the bar.

In 1920, when she was thirty-seven, his mother died. Joseph Bonanno was an orphan at fifteen. He was left with the large house and other property in addition to the farm, cattle, and interests in other businesses. In a town where the great majority of the 14,000 population was destitute, Joseph Bonanno was an individual of rare wealth, and his uncles vied to become his official guardian. They argued endlessly among themselves and bitterness ensued; it lasted more than a year as young Joseph Bonanno shifted between their homes, feeling embarrassment and disgust as the squabbling continued. Finally he made up his mind to leave Castellammare. He arranged for his uncles to have enough money sent each month so that he could support himself, and he left them the problem of dividing the property and other valuables to their own satisfaction. He was going to live in Palermo to attend a nautical college, and his friend Peter Magaddino went with him.

The two young men lived for two years in the capital, and it was a time of great excitement and confusion in Sicilian history. Mussolini had risen to power in Italy in 1922, and he had made trips to Sicily where he delivered speeches promising improvements and reform. In the beginning, Mussolini was cheered by most elements of Sicilian society—the aristocrats applauded his call for the restoration of grandeur, the masses responded to his program for a better life, even the mafiosi were impressed with his valorous demeanor and flamboyant oratory. The mafiosi also assumed that he would work with them, as other politicians had done, in return for their assurance of political support. But the Mafia bosses in Sicily greatly underestimated Mussolini's ego. He was not the sort of man who could tolerate secret groups that he could not control, and a few incidents occurred during his visit to Sicily that sharpened his indignation against the Mafia's traditional independence and lawlessness.

On one occasion while Mussolini was attending a meeting someone stole the hat that he had left in an outer room; the police could not recover it, and then someone suggested, to Mussolini's chagrin, that perhaps the Mafia's aid might be sought. On another trip to Sicily, Mussolini was touring a town in the province of Palermo with the mayor who was also the local Mafia chief. When the mayor observed the many policemen in Mussolini's entourage, he expressed surprise, informing Mussolini with obvious pride: "As I have the whole of this district under my orders, Your Excellency has nothing to fear when you are by my side." Then the mayor, turning to some of his men standing nearby, added: "Let no one dare touch a hair of Mussolini's head. He is my friend and the best man in the world." Mussolini could barely contain his fury. When he returned to Rome he initiated plans to arrest the mayor and to begin a campaign to eliminate the Mafia, which he regarded as the scourge of Sicily and a tremendous impediment to the island's progress and control.

The man assigned to confront the Mafia was a ruthlessly efficient Fascist and former police officer named Cesare Mori; and if Mori, as the prefect of Palermo, did not totally destroy the Mafia in the next few years, he most assuredly did drive it underground. Unhindered by the strictures of justice, Mori's police units arrested hundreds of mafiosi or suspected members, tortured them with electric wires, cattle whips, fire, and stretched and squeezed them on the medieval rack. That many innocent people were condemned unjustly did not concern Cesare Mori, who was backed solidly in the campaign by Mussolini. Most of the island's aristocracy were generally pleased by Mori's results, for now they no longer had to worry so much about the plundering of their property.

Joseph Bonanno, however, was appalled by what was happening, and together with Peter Magaddino and other students in Palermo, he joined a young radical organization that circulated anti-Fascist literature, denounced Mussolini in billboard posters, and stole or damaged the photographs of him on display in public buildings. This activity soon came to Mori's attention, and arrest warrants were issued against the students. But Bonanno, Magaddino, and five others with Mafia connections in western Sicily went into hiding, and later in 1924 they were smuggled on a freighter bound for Marseilles.

They remained briefly in Marseilles, went next to Paris. There Joseph Bonanno visited one of his cousins, who was an artist, and he marked time while arrangements were being made in Castellammare by the *amici* for the seven young men to be smuggled into the United States. There was considerable communication between the mafiosi of Sicily and the United States at this time due largely to the fabulous smuggling and bootlegging business created in the United States in 1920 by the passage of the Eighteenth Amendment banning the manufacture and sale of alcoholic drinks. Mafiosi were traveling back and forth between the two countries carrying messages and recruiting men in Sicily to come to America to work in the vast illegal industry generated by Prohibition. Many people from Castellammare were now rising in the ranks of the American underworld as organizers or enforcers, and many others were contributing their services to the bootlegging industry by driving trucks that delivered the product to speakeasies, by working as smugglers along American piers, by manufacturing homemade whiskey and wine in their stills at home, as they had done in the old country, and selling it to central organizations. Among these people were several friends of the Bonannos, and when they heard that the son of Salvatore Bonanno was coming to America they pledged to help him in every way possible.

Leaving France, Bonanno and his young friends sailed first to Cuba, where they were met by *amici* and provided with a small boat and a pilot who took them at night to the western shore of Florida, slipping them in through a private dock in Tampa. Tampa was a smuggler's paradise during Prohibition, with its many inlets offering a variety of entrances and its low-hung tropical foliage and abundant trees providing excellent concealment as swift motorboats arrived to deliver whiskey or people. Waiting to greet Bonanno and the others at the dock was a man named Willie Moretti, the Florida representative of the Jewish gangster who controlled the rackets in New Jersey, Abner (Longy) Zwillman.

It was not uncommon in the twenties for mafiosi to be working in organizations controlled by Jews; the Mafia was not yet the homogeneous syndicate it would become, and mobsters of Irish, Jewish, and other origins were still big names in organized crime. Dutch Schultz controlled the numbers rackets in Harlem and the distribution of beer. Louis Lepke and Jake Shapiro were top labor extortionists, and they had trucks transporting stolen or contraband merchandise around the nation, and their enforcement gangs were under Bugsy Siegel and Meyer Lansky. There were other figures such as Arnold Rothstein in New York, Charles (King) Solomon in Boston, and Frank Erickson in Florida. Erickson worked closely with Frank Costello, who was one of the first Italo-American gangsters to make a fortune during Prohibition. Costello, who had immigrated to the United States from southern Italy at the age of four with his parents, was a prominent rumrunner in 1923 under Bill Dwyer, who commanded a fleet of twelve steel-plated speedboats, armed with machine guns, that carried whiskey from Canada to the eastern seaboard and Chicago.

It was perhaps in Chicago that the mafiosi were making their strongest impact at the time of Joseph Bonanno's arrival in the United States. The gang of Johnny Torrio, composed of several Sicilians like himself, was beginning to overpower the Irish gangs that had been preeminent for years. Torrio's chief assistant was Al Capone, a Neopolitan, and it was said that they were each earning about $50,000 a week during the early period of Prohibition, although it was a risky business with street murders almost daily. After the Torrio-Capone men killed Dion O'Banion in November 1924, O'Banion's backers retaliated and came close to killing Torrio. Although he recovered from gunshot wounds in the hospital, he decided to abdicate the leadership to

Capone. This decision was received unenthusiastically by some Sicilians in the outfit, who would have preferred to work under one of their own, but since there was no Sicilian to match Capone's organizational ability, his political connections throughout Illinois, and his personal acquaintanceship with mobsters around the country, there was no choice. And during the next five years, despite the almost constant warfare with lesser rivals, the Capone gang prospered as had few gangs before it, earning about $50 million a year from bootlegging, according to tax agents, about $25 million from gambling, and close to $10 million each from prostitution and narcotics. Capone's operating expenses were also high; they included an estimated $15 million a year in contributions to the Chicago police and to other city and state officials.

In New York City at this time, the top Mafia figure was a short, squat old-style southern Italian with a moustache named Jose Masseria, who was known as Joe the Boss. Though he did not possess Capone's talent for organization, Masseria was shrewd and fearless, and in his gang were several ambitious young men who would achieve great notoriety in the future. Among them was his chief aide, Lucky Luciano, twenty-seven, who had come to the United States at nine from a town east of Palermo, Lercara Friddi, where his father had labored in the sulfur pits. There was also the twenty-seven-year-old Vito Genovese, another laborer's son, who had immigrated at fifteen from the village of Nola, near Naples.

Joseph Bonanno, who was nineteen when he arrived, did not immediately associate himself with Luciano, Genovese, or other followers of Masseria who gathered in certain hangouts in Greenwich Village and the Lower East Side of Manhattan. Bonanno instead went directly to the Brooklyn neighborhood where he had lived as a boy with his parents more than thirteen years ago, and he was pleased and surprised at how many people from Castellammare were now clustered within the teeming blocks of Roebling and Havemeyer streets, Grand Street and Metropolitan Avenue, North Fourth and Fifth streets. During his first few weeks in Brooklyn, as the entire neighborhood welcomed him, he heard again the familiar accent of western Sicily, recognized the surnames, saw in their faces a resemblance to relatives still in Castellammare. He also had relatives of his own living in Brooklyn at this time, as did his young traveling companions, all of whom found lodging in the neighborhood except for Peter Magaddino, who had made previous arrangements to join his cousin Stefano and the other Magaddinos who had settled in Buffalo.

Joseph Bonanno lived in the home of his mother's oldest brother, Peter Bonventre, who owned a barbershop. Peter Bonventre was a generous and kindly man who was earning an honest if unimpressive livelihood from barbering. Like the majority of immigrants from Sicily and Italy, Bonventre was a law-abiding, humble man to whom the journey to the New World was the highpoint of his life, the fulfillment of a dream, and he was willing to begin at the bottom and work his way slowly upward. He saw his life as a step in a new direction that would hopefully be followed and improved upon by the next generation, but he was not driven by any desire to achieve for himself great wealth, power, or prestige. He had a younger brother who was smitten by these things, and this brother was now a member of the neighborhood mafiosi. Peter Bonventre wondered whether his nephew would also become a member or whether he could work within the law; and after Joseph Bonanno had been in Brooklyn for a while, Bonventre asked him if he would possibly consider a career as a barber, perhaps one day acquiring a shop of his own. Bonanno smiled and thanked his uncle for his concern, saying that he would give it some thought. But privately Bonanno was surprised by his uncle's lack of insight—not in a thousand years would Bonanno become a barber or anything of the sort. He did not sail thousands of miles across the sea, and slip through the dragnet of American security, to devote himself to the trimming of other men's hair. Even at nineteen, though he had no specific goal in mind, Bonanno envisioned himself a leader of men, an individual destined to face great challenges, to assert himself, to prosper and become a man of respect in a new land. While he was quite certain that he could not attain the respect he sought within the legal confines of an American society that was dominated by Anglo-Saxons, that was governed by men whose grandfathers had muscled their way to the top and had rigged the rules to their own advantage and had learned all the loopholes, he did believe that the ruling classes in America as in Sicily had great respect for two things—power and money—and he was determined to get both in one way or another. The perfect time to do so, of course, was right now, when possibly most of the nation's citizens were breaking the law and making the bootleggers rich. So in his first year in Brooklyn, Bonanno affiliated himself with the neighborhood mafiosi, who were obviously doing very well; they were driving new cars and wearing finer clothes than their humble countrymen who got up each day at dawn to toil in factories or work in construction gangs.

The mafiosi, who slept late in the morning, usually met each afternoon in their private store-front club on Roebling Street, and they would sit drinking black coffee or playing cards. A few doors away from their club was a large bakery that was also a front for a bootlegging business, and after dark the bakery trucks would travel through the city delivering pastries and bread, whiskey and wine, to certain speakeasies and restaurants. The trucks sometimes also drove to freight yards or piers with box-loads of machine guns to be shipped to Al Capone to help fight his rivals in Chicago.

Within a remarkably short period of time, Bonanno was re-garded by the other men in Brooklyn as a potential leader. They had initially accepted him because of his name, but soon they recognized his precocious talent for organization and his quick instinct for seizing opportunities. He greatly expanded their whiskey business after having personally visited the owners of speakeasies, and he did this without resorting to threats or pres-sure; his polished manner and pleasant appearance were assets and he extended easy credit to those speakeasies raided by the police. He expanded the Italian lottery to other areas of Brook-lyn, and he invested the money that he earned in several busi-nesses—clothing factories, cheese shops, a funeral parlor—and he covered his total earnings so adroitly that he would never be convicted of tax evasion.

His name and maneuverings soon became known to Joe Mas-seria in Manhattan, who was becoming increasingly suspicious of the growing number of Castellammarese in Brooklyn. Mas-seria sensed that the Castellammarese were gradually disasso-ciating themselves from his overall leadership, and in 1928 he demanded higher tribute as a test of their loyalty. When they did not agree to his terms, Masseria had one of their men shot to death on a Brooklyn street and another captured and held in a hangman's noose until the prisoner's friends raised $10,000 in ransom.

But these incidents did not achieve Masseria's desired results—the Castellammarese became hostile and more clannish—and finally Masseria lost his patience and decided to
annihilate the entire group. His campaign started slowly with
the destruction of alcohol trucks and with sniper's bullets fired
from cars moving fast through the Brooklyn neighborhood, and
by 1930 there were a number of murders committed by both
sides, and the "Castellammarese War" became a national issue
in the underworld as top gangsters in other cities either supported or opposed Masseria's plan to destroy the Castellammarese. Some gang leaders sent money or guns to the faction
they were backing, others sent cars and men. Joe Masseria had,
in addition to Lucky Luciano and Vito Genovese, such underlings and advisers as Joe Adonis and Carlo Gambino, Albert
Anastasia and Frank Costello. Even though Al Capone was having battles of his own in Chicago, he was sympathetic to Masseria's cause; and in 1930 Capone's men were credited with
killing a Chicago boss named Joseph Aiello who had been sending $5,000 a week to the Castellammarese in Brooklyn.

The boss of the Castellammarese during the war was not
Joseph Bonanno, who was twenty-five, but an older man of
forty—Salvatore Maranzano, a lean, tall, pensive Sicilian with
a receding hairline and severe, almost ascetic, features. Maranzano had been a close friend in Sicily of Joseph Bonanno's father; and, like Bonanno *père* and Bonanno *fils*, he was an avid
student of ancient history. Maranzano was particularly interested in the Roman Empire under Julius Caesar, and Maranzano's apartment in Brooklyn contained many volumes about
Caesar's wars and tactics. Maranzano's chief aides in 1930 included Bonanno and Joseph Profaci, Thomas Lucchese, and
Joseph Magliocco. Maranzano also had an important ally in
Gaetano Gagliano, who had been an officer in another gang
whose leader Masseria had eliminated; Gagliano not only shifted
his men to Maranzano's side but Gagliano himself contributed
several thousand dollars to the fight against Masseria. Another
powerful force behind Maranzano were the Castellammarese in
Buffalo, led by Stefano Magaddino, who was sending Maranzano $5,000 a week as well as supplies and vehicles.

It became apparent by 1931 that the momentum had shifted
against Joe Masseria, who had lost approximately fifty men during the first year of the fighting and whose followers were slowly

realizing that their cause was hopeless and unnecessary. The Castellammarese were better organized, more unified than Masseria's people, and they also had a force of approximately 400 men, which was larger than Masseria's group, some of whom were now defecting. Masseria's advisers, Luciano and Genovese, angry because their profitable bootlegging business and other enterprises had declined during the prolonged feud, began to urge Masseria to make peace with Maranzano—or, if not peace, to at least apply more pressure on Maranzano by enlisting the aid of Jewish gangs and other ethnic organizations. But Masseria, a victim of his own pride, stubbornly refused.

As more of Masseria's men were injured or killed during the winter of 1931 and as more alcohol trucks were stolen by Maranzano's hijackers, Luciano and Genovese and three of their colleagues secretly visited Maranzano and made a deal. They would have Masseria murdered if Maranzano would guarantee their safety and status in the underworld after the deed was done. Maranzano agreed. And so on the afternoon of April 15, 1931, at Scarpato's Restaurant on Coney Island, after Lucky Luciano excused himself from the table at which he had lunched with Masseria and walked into the men's room, gunmen entered the restaurant and blasted bullets at Masseria, hitting him in the back and the head. Masseria fell heavily to the floor and died instantly. When the police arrived, Luciano told them that he had seen nothing, having only heard the noise; and the restaurant employees, confirming that Luciano had indeed been in the men's room at the time of the shooting, were unable to identify the killers.

After Masseria's funeral, Maranzano presided at a meeting attended by 500 people in a hired hall in the Bronx and explained that the days of shooting were over and that a period of harmony was about to begin. He then presented them with his plan of reorganization, one loosely based on Caesar's military command—the individual gangs each would be commanded by a *capo*, or boss, under whom would be a *sottocapo*, underboss, and beneath the underboss would be *caporegimi*, lieutenants, who would supervise the squads of soldiers. Each unit would be known as a family and would operate within prescribed territorial areas. Over all the family bosses would be a *capo di tutti capi*, a boss of all bosses, and it was this title that Maranzano bequeathed to himself.

Luciano, Genovese, and other former members of Masseria's gang were unhappy about this last point. They saw boss rule as obsolete, an anathema to the effectiveness of a large organization; they feared that Maranzano had become, like Masseria before him, obsessed with a sense of singular power, and they saw no solution but to plot against him.

They moved with extreme caution, for Maranzano was a formidable figure after Masseria's death, and quite prosperous, too, as gangsters from around the nation made sizable contributions to fund-raising benefits held in Maranzano's honor. At one such banquet in Brooklyn, Maranzano was believed to have received more than $100,000. But Maranzano was not quick to share the profits with his underlings, nor did he return many of the trucks that had been stolen from men like Luciano; he was also said to have shared in merchandise stolen from a man who was on his side, Thomas Lucchese.

And so while Maranzano basked in glory through the summer of 1931, Luciano intrigued against him, slowly succeeding in convincing even such loyalists as Bonanno and Profaci that Maranzano was in reality an old-fashioned tyrant, not much better than Masseria, and certainly ill equipped to unify the diverse groups in organized crime into a large modern syndicate. When Maranzano learned of Luciano's campaign against him, he hired men to kill him. But before Maranzano's mercenaries could do the job, Luciano's own hired assassins—four Jewish gangsters, posing as detectives, who were affiliated with the Siegal–Lansky mob that was friendly with Luciano—walked into the real estate office that was Maranzano's "front" in the Grand Central Building, at Park Avenue and Forty-sixth Street, where they flashed their badges at the men who sat in the outer room, entered Maranzano's suite and, catching him by surprise, shot him four times and stabbed him six times in the abdomen.

There would be several other deaths on that day—September 11, 1931—and also on the following day, most of the victims being old-style gangsters referred to as Moustache Petes or greasers, men considered too stubborn, illiterate, and incapable of fitting into the modern scheme of things.

The modern scheme, as outlined by Luciano at later meetings, would abandon Maranzano's "boss of bosses" position but would preserve most of Maranzano's other ideas on the organization of "families." Luciano urged that mafiosi no longer seek power through threats and vendettas, but instead adopt the more subtly aggressive tactics of large modern corporations, some of which had been founded by robber barons but were quietly committed to profiteering within a free-enterprise code of rules and restrictions. While Luciano hoped that the mafiosi would continue to work with other ethnic gang leaders, particularly with men like Meyer Lansky, who was a genius at finding profitable investments for Mafia money in legal as well as illegal enterprises, Luciano also believed that membership in the Mafia itself should still be limited to men of Sicilian or Italian origin. Despite their many differences and jealousies, the Sicilian–Italian element felt a rapport with one another that they did not feel with outsiders. Though its membership of perhaps 5,000 was a small percentage of the more than 100,000 individuals that law enforcement officials estimated to be involved in organized crime, it was tighter ethnically at this time than were members of the Jewish gangs, Irish gangs, hybrid gangs, or the numerous cliques and free-lancers around the country. If it could remain cohesive, it could dominate the underworld.

Luciano was not alone in advocating less violence—Frank Costello had spoken similarly at a gathering of gangsters at Atlantic City in 1929—but Luciano was now a most persuasive figure. At thirty-four, living up to the nickname that had been inspired by his luck at gambling, he had managed to dispose of both Masseria and Maranzano, and yet, partly because he had resisted the top job himself, he was able to convince the surviving leaders of his sincerity for solidarity and peace. Without tactlessly denigrating the life of Maranzano, Luciano nonetheless deglamorized him in the eyes of most Castellammarese by depicting him as a victim of excessive power, a follower of Caesar in an era of the organization.

Lucky Luciano was a consummate organization man, and while younger men like Bonanno and Profaci remained individualistic in outlook, they had no difficulty in relating to Luciano, a fellow Sicilian whose astuteness and forward-looking approach they quickly respected. Bonanno was in agreement with Luciano that the ''boss of bosses'' title should be eliminated and that no one boss should have the right to dictate to other bosses—the individual bosses would be largely autonomous in their designated areas. Bonanno was somewhat concerned, however, about the future role of the commission and the spe-

cific steps the commission could take in the interest of maintaining peace within the national brotherhood. During the five
months that Maranzano had been the boss of bosses, Bonanno
worked with Maranzano on a concept of the commission, but
neither Maranzano nor Bonanno had been entirely satisfied with
the result. Bonanno still felt that a commission might develop
into a policy-making body that could intrude upon the autonomy
of individual bosses, and Bonanno urged at the meetings that
the commission be clearly designed to serve as a forum for
debate or explanation but not as an agency with power. Other
Mafia leaders, less independently minded, were not opposed to
the prospect of an authoritative commission, although they did
not wish to argue for it. There had been so much disagreement
among the mafiosi in recent years that they now wished to avoid
delving into another controversial issue.

There was rather quick agreement to Luciano's general proposals, and soon the twenty-four separate groups of mafiosi
around the nation each elected their own boss and received the
proper recognition and respect accorded a Mafia "family."
Many of the twenty-four families were widely scattered in cities
through the Far West and the South and had memberships of
only twenty or thirty each, while other families, concentrated
in the industrial centers of the Midwest and the Eastern Seaboard, had memberships of between 300 and 500.

In New York City, the largest market for illegal activity, five
Mafia families were established. Luciano was the head of one
family, the other charter-member dons were Vincent Mangano,
Gaetano Gagliano, Joseph Profaci, and Joseph Bonanno. At
twenty-six, Bonanno was the youngest don in the national syndicate.

On November 15, 1931, two months after Maranzano's death,
Joseph Bonanno was married to Fay Labruzzo. The elaborate
wedding reception was held at the Knights of Columbus Hall at
Prospect Park in Brooklyn and was attended by an impressive
gathering that included all the New York bosses and several from
out of town.

After the party, the bridal couple left in Bonanno's new Chrysler Imperial for a honeymoon in Niagara Falls, and thus began
a period of tranquillity and prosperity that would dominate the
next twenty years. Bonanno's large cash reserve permitted him
to make many profitable real estate investments during the De-

pression; and unlike the other bosses, Bonanno seemed to have a sure instinct for avoiding controversy and trouble.

Al Capone was convicted in 1931 for income tax evasion and served seven years in prison. In 1934, Vito Genovese, an underboss in Luciano's family, became involved in a murder charge and fled the country. Luciano himself was sentenced in 1936 to serve a thirty-to-fifty-year term because of his prostitution business, a conviction obtained largely through the efforts of an aggressive prosecutor named Thomas E. Dewey. Other mafiosi, despite their previous endorsement of a policy against violence, were again shooting at one another as disputes arose over the territorial boundaries of certain bookmaking and numbers rackets, for these two enterprises had replaced bootlegging as the primary source of revenue after the repeal of Prohibition.

The single encounter Joseph Bonanno had with the law during this period occurred when a Brooklyn clothing factory that he partly owned was charged with violating the Federal Wage and Hour Law; he was fined $50. He was in the process then of becoming an American citizen, having left the country in 1938 and reentered it legally at Detroit from Canada. He became naturalized in 1945, by which time he was a multimillionaire.

He owned a home in Long Island, another in Tucson. He was a respected member of both communities, a major contributor to charities and to the church. His organization of slightly more than 300 members was one of the smaller New York families, but it was probably the most unified and coordinated—it had virtually no internal dissension and little harassment from rival gangs or the law. Bonanno's principal officers, all from Castellammare, included Frank Garofalo, a persnickety white-haired bachelor in charge of management details; John Bonventre, an equanimous elder who handled personnel problems bucked up from the captains; and Carmine Galante, a tough cigar-smoking underboss who dealt with representatives of other gangs when there were issues to be resolved or cooperative ventures to be planned. Among the eight captains, each commanding a crew that might consist of thirty or more soldiers, the closest to Bonanno was Gaspar Di Gregorio. Bonanno also had what was unique in the national syndicate—a kind of alumni association comprised of a dozen retired mafiosi in their seventies who had known Bonanno's father or grandfather and who were now invited by Joseph Bonanno to attend meetings and offer advice or even to arbitrate minor differences within the family.

The Bonanno organization's bookmaking and numbers businesses in Brooklyn and on Manhattan's Lower East Side, far from declining during the Depression, actually became more lucrative; people seemed to be gambling more during hard times, and none of the twenty-four families in the syndicate was an economic victim of the thirties. With the coming of World War II, conditions became even better as the Mafia expanded into black-marketing enterprises to meet the public's demand for war-rationed food products, gasoline stamps, and similarly controlled items.

The war also restored to prominence several Sicilian dons whose careers abroad had been diminished by Mussolini and such American dons as Lucky Luciano who had been removed from circulation by law enforcement officials in the United States. As the war began, Luciano was serving what seemed to be a lifetime sentence at the New York State Penitentiary at Dannemora. He was treated regally by the prisoners there and was able to send out messages and orders to his organization through visitors and convicts who were being discharged, but he had no expectation of regaining his own freedom in the immediate future.

Then in 1942, as incidents of German sabotage were believed to be increasing along the New York waterfront and after the huge French liner *Normandie* caught fire and capsized at her West Side berth in Manhattan just prior to becoming an Allied troopship, the Bureau of Naval Intelligence and other federal agencies decided, after much debate and soul-searching, to seek the aid of mob-controlled longshoremen, truckmen, and watchmen in guarding against future sabotage or infiltration by enemy spies. The man the navy contacted was Joseph (Socks) Lanza, a dock leader whose men worked along the East River piers in lower Manhattan and in the Fulton Fish Market. Though Lanza was under indictment for extortion at the time, the investigators for the navy saw him as a patriotic American, and thus he was entrusted to help organize the program.

Within a year, since no other suspicious incidents occurred, the navy concluded that the program was working, and it wished to expand it to include the dock workers on the West Side. But Lanza could not get their cooperation on that side of town—the

West Side was Luciano's territory, and only he could guarantee their compliance. So the naval representatives traveled to Dannemora and visited Luciano in jail. When he promised to cooperate, he was transferred to more comfortable quarters in a prison near Albany. There he soon played host to numbers of visitors, not only naval officers but also individuals from the ranks such as Frank Costello, Meyer Lansky, and Willie Moretti. And, as on the East Side, the navy believed that the West Side waterfront was made more secure by the vigilance of the dock workers.

What specifics were discussed in the many meetings with Luciano, what precise contributions he and other mafiosi made, were never fully revealed and would remain a mystery long after the war had ended. Even Senator Estes Kefauver in 1951 was unable to gain access to the Pentagon's secret files on the subject. The navy was then apparently embarrassed about its dealings with gangsters, although during the uncertain period of the early forties when German submarines were considered capable of slipping through the defense of the port of New York, it had seemed both a practical and wise thing to do.

The United States Army also fostered a relationship with the Mafia during the war, a fact documented years later in several articles and books that cited the names of certain American officers and mobsters; and again a significant role was said to be played by Luciano. He reportedly sent messages through his henchmen to his fellow dons in western Sicily, where bands of mafiosi were organized to serve as underground agents and guides for the arriving Allied armies. After invading the southern shore of Sicily in the summer of 1943, the Allies moved quickly from one village to another, retracing the steps of a thousand conquerors before them, but this time being greeted by cheering crowds particularly in western cities like Castellammare. Although the British and Canadian troops that moved through eastern Sicily did engage in battles with the retreating German and Italian armies, the resistance was short-lived and undermined by incidents of civilian sabotage. The entire island of Sicily was in Allied hands in approximately five weeks; and then, as the Allied officers advanced the war to the Italian mainland, they appointed to key positions in many villages and towns men who were militant anti-Fascists and, in most cases, also members of the Mafia.

As the Allied armies moved into Naples, there was working within their ranks an Italian civilian who served as a translator and liaison official. This man was knowledgeable and helpful, but he refused to accept money from the Americans, a gesture they had rarely encountered. They were further impressed by his awareness of several cases of bribery and black-marketeering among civilian personnel and his willingness to report these to the officers in charge. Three American officers wrote letters of commendation for the man—Vito Genovese—a master in the art of success through shifting, who during the previous year, 1943, had been working with the Fascists.

When Genovese left the United States hurriedly in 1934 after being linked to the murder of a hoodlum named Ferdinand Boccia, he had with him about $750,000 in cash that enabled him to buy favor with Fascist leaders in the region of his birth near Naples. Genovese contributed $250,000 to the construction of a municipal building in that area, bought a power plant, and soon he received from Mussolini the government's highest civilian title of *commendatore*. Genovese was believed to have further ingratiated himself with Mussolini by arranging for the fatal shooting in January 1943, on Fifth Avenue and Fifteenth Street in New York, of Mussolini's most vitriolic critic in the United States, an Italian-language newspaper editor named Carlo Tresca.

But Genovese's charmed life in Italy seemed to be coming to an end in the spring of 1944 when an American agent in the army's Criminal Investigation Division, while gathering information about the black market in the Foggia–Naples area, learned that Genovese was at the center of it, a situation that had somehow escaped the Allied officers Genovese had worked with so closely as a translator and liaison man. Then the agent was further surprised to discover, after urging that Genovese be brought to trial and exposed, that higher authorities were reluctant to do so. Genovese obviously had many friends in important places in the local Allied command, and he was possibly in a position to implicate a few of them as accomplices in black market operations if the investigation deepened. The agent did succeed, however, in arresting Vito Genovese and in informing the FBI of Genovese's situation in Italy; and, to the relief of the Allied military, the FBI responded with little interest in Genovese's black market dealings, preferring to focus attention on Genovese's ties to the unsolved murder in 1934 of Ferdinand Boccia.

Genovese as a result was returned to the United States to stand trial, and the case against him seemed strong—until the chief corroborative witness against Genovese was fatally poisoned in a Brooklyn jail where he was being held in protective custody. The witness, a cigar store salesman with racket connections who had supposedly seen the Boccia murder, died suddenly after drinking a glass of water containing pain-relieving tablets he was accustomed to using for his gallstones—tablets that a New York toxicologist later claimed were sufficient "to kill eight horses."

So the case against Genovese was dropped; he was a free man in America. And inasmuch as Lucky Luciano had just been deported to Italy—Luciano's release from prison being more or less a reward for his war work, though he would never be allowed to reenter the United States—Genovese, as Luciano's number two man, was now in line for the top job in the Luciano family. But securing it would not be easy, for during Genovese's ten years of exile in Italy and Luciano's seven years in jail, the family's acting boss, Frank Costello, had earned the respect of the dons and had developed close relationships with certain captains and crews; he had also, through his own initiative, achieved political influence in New York through contributions to Tammany Hall and friendships with district leaders, judges, and a man who would become mayor of New York, William O'Dwyer.

While Genovese was welcomed back with cordiality by Costello and the other subordinate officers, it was soon apparent to Genovese that the lines of loyalty and the family's management style had changed somewhat during his absence. Costello had ruled gently, had allowed maximum authority to the captains—Genovese wanted tight control under himself. Costello believed that power could be attained without violence, preferring bribes to bullets, while Genovese believed that when it came to gaining compliance, nothing worked faster than fear. Costello opposed members' involvement in drug trafficking; Genovese endorsed this in principle, but he was not averse to sharing in narcotics profits if he felt that his connection was untraceable—indeed Lucky Luciano himself, after his deportation from the United States, had a hand in the international smuggling ring that moved drugs through the Mediterranean from Turkey.

Given these and other differences between Genovese and Costello, it was inevitable that there would be conflict; and soon after Genovese had returned, he began to chip away, slowly and methodically, at the stature of Frank Costello. He began with a whispering campaign among his clique in the family that dwelled on Costello's presumed failings, stressing that Costello, a millionaire, was no longer hungry, no longer eager to take risks in search of new fortunes in which the underlings might share. Genovese questioned Costello's judgment in associating with such sidekicks as Willie Moretti who, while once competent, was now detrimental to the brotherhood. Genovese hinted that Moretti was suffering from brain damage resulting from advanced syphilis, a condition that drove Moretti to excessive verbalizing and boasting that might inadvertently reveal Mafia secrets to outsiders. In October 1951, after Costello had been subjected to the spotlight of the Kefauver hearings—the result of which he would receive an eighteen-month sentence for contempt of the Senate—Willie Moretti was shot to death in a New Jersey restaurant by men close to Genovese.

During the following year, Genovese ordered the murder of a narcotics peddler who was believed to be a federal informer. Nine months later, feeling betrayed by a man with whom he had once been in partnership in nightclubs, Genovese had him strangled to death. Genovese continued his tactics of terror and intrigue through that year and the next, while Costello—named the "number one racketeer in this country" by a Senate committee report in November 1953—remained preoccupied with court cases that threatened him with deportation and charges of income tax evasion.

Costello was convicted of a tax evasion charge in 1954 as investigators dug deeply into his past spending—the $18,000 in cash for his parents' mausoleum, the charge accounts of his wife at Saks Fifth Avenue and Lord & Taylor—and determined that he was living above the $39,000 annual income he reported he earned from real estate investments and partnerships in such businesses as the Beverly Club in Louisiana. Costello was accused of evading $28,000 in taxes during a two-year period, for which he was sentenced to five years in prison. After various appeals had failed he went to jail in May 1956 but was released on $25,000 bail in March 1957 when his lawyers convincingly contended that his conviction was based on illegal wiretap evidence.

One night two months later, as Costello returned in a cab to his apartment building at 115 Central Park West, after having dined at a restaurant, a black limousine pulled up behind him and a large man with a pistol followed him into the lobby, then said, "This is for you, Frank." Turning as the gunman pulled the trigger, the bullet grazed Costello's scalp—there was bleeding but no serious injury. Costello fell back into a leather couch. The gunman turned and rushed toward the street, got into the car and his driver sped away.

Costello later told the police that he had seen nothing and could not imagine why anyone would wish to shoot him, but the doorman on duty that night admitted to having witnessed the scene and, with the aid of police photographs, he identified the gunman as Vincent (The Chin) Gigante, a former prizefighter who was one of Genovese's men. But when the doorman testified in court, he seemed nervous and uncertain, and Gigante's lawyer easily shattered his credibility. Gigante went free, although he was immediately rearrested on scofflaw charges and he pleaded guilty to ten traffic tickets. The doorman, who had received wide publicity in newspapers and whose wife had received threatening phone calls during the trial, returned timidly to his post and often had the smell of liquor on his breath; soon after, he was fired from his job, his wife gained a separation, and he drifted away and was not seen again by the tenants.

Vito Genovese had of course anticipated Costello's revenge; and when Genovese was informed that Costello had been meeting privately with Albert Anastasia, one of the most feared men in the syndicate, and was presumably arranging details for Genovese's murder, Genovese made his move quickly, after first gaining the support of other dons, which in this case was not difficult. Anastasia was a controversial figure in 1957. Volatile and violent, identified with many murders, he lived in a large home in Fort Lee, New Jersey, that overlooked the Hudson River and was protected by walls and vicious dogs. He controlled, among other things, the Brooklyn waterfront, and at this point he was one of the five dons in New York City. He had seized that position after the mysterious disappearance in 1951 of Vincent Mangano, one of the original family leaders selected in 1931 after the Castellammarese War. The persistent rumor in

the underworld was that Anastasia, after much bickering with
Mangano, had had him quietly assassinated and buried in a
concrete foundation of a housing project in Nassau County, Long
Island.

The Mangano murder, as despicable as it may have been to
other leaders in the national syndicate, was nonetheless a family
affair and did not easily justify outside interference. But other
acts by Anastasia since then had clearly violated the jurisdiction
of other families or had ignored national policy, and it was for
these reasons that Anastasia was in a precarious position in 1957.
He had mistakenly assumed that he could move his men into
the gambling casino business and related lucrative enterprises
in Florida, Cuba, and other Caribbean resorts—areas under the
province of Meyer Lansky, Luciano's friend, and Santo Trafficante, Jr., who with his Sicilian father had been for many years
on intimate terms with leading Mafia figures in the United States
and abroad. Anastasia was also charged with ignoring the commission's policy against initiating new members without commission clearance, a policy designed to maintain the balance of
power among the larger families.

So in the summer and fall of 1957, various secret meetings
were held to discuss the Anastasia situation, and the police became aware of some of these through wiretapping and electronic
bugging. Genovese was known to have communicated with one
of Anastasia's lieutenants, Carlo Gambino, and also with
Thomas Lucchese, who became a New York don in place of
Gaetano Gagliano, who died of natural causes in 1953. The
police also became aware of Joseph Bonanno's trip to Sicily in
1957, where, beginning on October 12, there were alleged hotel
conferences in Palermo attended by Lucky Luciano, Bonanno
and such Bonanno associates as Garofalo, Bonventre, and Carmine Galante. Bonanno was also observed during that week in
Castellammare receiving a hero's welcome from his townsmen,
and later conferring with some of the top-ranking *amici* of western Sicily at a hillside café.

On October 25, as Albert Anastasia reclined under hot towels
in the Park-Sheraton Hotel barbershop on Seventh Avenue and
Fifty-sixth Street in Manhattan—his bodyguards were paying
little attention—two gunmen walked in and riddled Anastasia's
body with bullets, which killed him instantly.

Three weeks later on November 14, at Genovese's suggestion, the Apalachin conference was held. Genovese preferred having it in Chicago, but Stefano Magaddino, citing the fact that a secret meeting had been held in Apalachin the year before without interruption, thought it was better to hold it there again. The upstate New York community was also more convenient for the senior commissioner, who at sixty-six did not like to travel great distances, and there was ample room on the large estate of Magaddino's fellow Castellammarese, Joseph Barbara, to accommodate the many visitors.

Most of the delegates represented families in the Northeast, the center of many of the current problems. Twenty-three men were from New York City or New Jersey, nineteen were from other parts of New York State, only eight had come from the Midwest, three from the West, two from the South, and three from overseas—two from Cuba, one from Sicily. Among the major items on the agenda was the reaffirmation of Genovese's position as the head of his family, with the assurance that Costello and his friends had nothing to fear so long as they did not challenge Genovese; the reiteration of the commission's policy against drugs and new memberships; and the clarification of any questions with regard to the Anastasia family, which would now be headed by Carlo Gambino.

But before the sessions could begin, the New York State Police launched their surprise raid that would prove to be disastrous to the national syndicate and would terminate the many years of relative tranquillity enjoyed by such dons as Joseph Bonanno. For Vito Genovese, the Apalachin meeting was merely a precursor of other bad news.

Federal narcotics agents had just arrested a Puerto Rican dope peddler on the West Side of Manhattan who, after being sentenced to a four-to-five-year term and feeling double-crossed because the organization had not fixed the case in court, decided to turn informer. One man that he informed against was Vito Genovese. It did not seem possible at first that the testimony of the informer, Nelson Cantellops, could lead to convictions; but like so many racketeers who have trained themselves to put nothing in writing, Cantellops had almost total recall, and he recited names, places, and incidents that linked the Genovese family with narcotics, and he also described a time when he had personally overheard Genovese discussing a narcotics deal with other men in the Bronx.

In 1958 a federal grand jury in New York returned an indictment against twenty-four individuals who Cantellops swore were involved in narcotics trafficking, and among the names on the list were Carmine Galante of the Bonanno family, John Ormento of the Lucchese family, Joseph Valachi of the Genovese family, and Genovese himself. Genovese and fourteen others were brought to trial in the spring of 1959, and by 1960 he was in the Atlanta Penitentiary beginning a fifteen-year sentence for narcotics smuggling.

Even in jail, where his mere presence instilled fear in the other prisoners who did not address him unless he spoke first, Genovese dictated orders to his captains beyond the walls and fomented tension in the underworld. Suspecting one of his officers, Anthony Strollo, of double-dealing and cheating him of money, Genovese is supposed to have ordered his death in 1962. Genovese at this time also suspected, incorrectly, that his fellow prisoner in Atlanta, Joseph Valachi, a veteran associate, had become a government informer; and when Valachi himself sensed that he was marked for extinction, he wildly bludgeoned to death with a pipe an innocent inmate who he thought was his potential assassin.

Faced with the death penalty for the brutal slaying, Valachi decided to cooperate with the federal government to save his own life, and in so doing he made life miserable for every don in America. What little privacy they had after the endless investigations and publicity in the wake of Apalachin was invaded by Valachi. Testifying before the Senate on nationwide television, and with his words also disseminated through national magazines and a best-selling book by Peter Maas, Valachi described the organizational structure of the Mafia, unmasked many of its leaders, and recalled old feuds and murders. He told how he had been recruited in 1930 to fight on Maranzano's side in the Castellammarese War and how he later was initiated into the brotherhood with Joseph Bonanno performing the ritual. After the death of Maranzano, Valachi was absorbed into the Luciano family, where, even though he never rose higher than the rank of soldier, he managed to prosper and survive for many years until the recent terror tactics of Genovese influenced his fate and that of many other mafiosi.

It was during this period, in the early 1960s, that Joseph Bonanno seriously contemplated his retirement as the head of his family and as a member of the commission. He was disgusted with the way things had gone in the past few years, and he doubted that the situation would or could improve. The decline of the Profaci family was particularly upsetting because he believed that two members of the commission, Lucchese and Gambino, had encouraged the Gallo brothers' revolt against Profaci, violating the commission's own policy against interference in the internal affairs of a family. With the death of Joseph Profaci in 1962, and Joseph Magliocco a year later, Bonanno lost two strong allies.

Bonanno also felt that he had nothing to gain and much to lose by remaining in the chaotic atmosphere of the Northeast in the company of fellow dons that he could no longer trust. He was approaching sixty, and he had been a don for thirty years. He would be happier living in retirement in Arizona or Canada or Wisconsin or California and letting younger men assume the role of leadership over his organization. The only problem was in finding a younger man capable of succeeding him. Unfortunately for Bonanno, he realized too late that the experienced men upon whom he had most relied during the last decade were either his own age or older—such men as Garofalo, Bonventre, Angelo Caruso, the imprisoned Carmine Galante, Gaspar Di Gregorio, and John Tartamella, who had just had a heart attack. And the younger officers in the family were not that much younger: John Morale was in his fifties, as were Frank Labruzzo, Vito De Filippi, Thomas Di Angelo, Paul Sciacca, and the ailing Joseph Notaro. Charles Battaglia was in his forties, but he was in the Arizona branch of the family and Bonanno liked having him there.

Among the ranks of soldiers, there were few who had particularly impressed Bonanno by their leadership potentialities; in fact, Bonanno felt that the average Mafia soldier today, not only in his own family but also throughout the national syndicate, was far less disciplined than were the soldiers he had known thirty years ago in Maranzano's time. The younger men today were for the most part American-born, were not as cool or quick under pressure as the men from the old country had been, not as driven or alienated; and Bonanno believed that just as Italian prizefighters were now declining after years of prominence in

the American ring, so too would the Italian and Sicilian gangsters soon be replaced by a tougher breed of men. Twice during
the past year Bonanno had heard his captains complain that soldiers had asked to be relieved of an assignment because they
had to be with their wives on that particular evening.

The younger members, or the associate members—those men
awaiting a family vacancy or commission approval of their in-
iation—were too often the dregs of the second generation, the
element left behind at the bottom of the barrel. They were not
suited to an executive career in the legitimate world—such as
Notaro's son, who became a lawyer, or Lucchese's son, who
graduated from West Point and helped to run his father's large
garment manufacturing business—nor were they sufficiently authoritative and shrewd and motivated to become Mafia dons.
And so if they gained admission into a Mafia family, perhaps
having had a father or uncle who had been a member, they
usually spent the best years of their lives taking orders from
aging superiors, doing the dirty work as gunmen and hijackers;
or they worked as managers of nightclubs, as second-echelon
labor organizers, or overseers of numbers and bookmaking
rings. In any case they would never acquire the qualities of leadership that Bonanno sought in the younger generation; in fact,
in his whole organization there was perhaps only one individual
he considered bright enough, bold enough—and trustworthy
enough—to someday become a don, and that was the person
about whom he had the most reservations, his son Bill.

Bill Bonanno at this time had just moved East from Arizona
to tidy up his problems with Rosalie and to help look after his
father's interests while his father kept on the move to escape the
notoriety of the Valachi testimony and other rumblings rising
out of rumors linking him to Magliocco's alleged scheme to
murder Lucchese and Gambino for their part in the Gallo brothers' revolt. While Joseph Bonanno was comforted by his son's
presence in New York and was relieved of various responsibilities, he regretted that his son was now becoming more deeply
involved in the management affairs of the secret society at a
time when the elder Bonanno saw grave problems ahead. And
he was even more apprehensive, and yet strangely proud, when
he was informed in Canada in February 1964 that his captains,
following his suggestion, had held a meeting to elect an officer
to take over the number three position vacated by John Tarta-

mella, who had just suffered another stroke that left him partially paralyzed and restricted him to a wheelchair. Tartamella's successor was his son Bill.

The number three job in a Mafia family, often referred to as the *consigliere* or counselor, was an advisory as well as strategy-planning position that coordinated the proposals and tactics emanating from the captains and presented these to the boss and underboss for final approval. While the scope of the *consigliere* varied from family to family, depending largely on the management style of the boss—in some families the *consigliere* was merely an amiable confessor, in others he was a strong buffer between the two top men and the rest of the subordinates—the *consigliere* in the Bonanno family was of real significance, was perhaps more important than even the underboss, because of the closeness between father and son. It meant that the underboss, John Morale—who had recently been appointed by Bonanno to take over for the retired Garofalo—was now almost a supernumerary, since the captains and crews would assume that what Bill Bonanno said or did had the approval of his father. Thus the role of Morale, who would normally be the boss's spokesman in the boss's absence, was diminished.

But if John Morale was upset by this, he gave no hint of it at the secret meeting of the captains; in fact, he, together with Labruzzo and Notaro, strongly supported Bill Bonanno's nomination as *consigliere* after it had been proposed in a loquacious speech delivered in Sicilian by the patriarchal Angelo Caruso, an old intimate of Maranzano. Caruso had used the nomination speech to recall at length the tradition of the Bonannos in Sicily and to recount the three decades of outstanding leadership in New York under Joseph Bonanno, whom he referred to reverentially as Don Peppino; and nothing would be more appropriate, Caruso continued, than to elevate to the rank of leadership the courageous young man who bore the same name and heritage.

The response to Caruso's suggestion was unanimous except for one man, Gaspar Di Gregorio, who could not conceal the look of disappointment on his face. For a moment he seemed stunned, speechless. Then he recovered his composure, stood before his fellow captains and made a motion that the nomination be seconded. And it was.

It was not until many months later that the depth of Di Gre-

gorio's disapproval became known to the membership in the
Bonanno family. Joseph Bonanno learned of it from his friend
Peter Magaddino, who had left Buffalo in 1964 and returned to
live in New York. Bonanno was also in New York in the fall of
1964, having abandoned Canada after a summer of problems
with the immigration authorities. Di Gregorio was embittered;
but besides that, Bonanno heard, Stefano Magaddino was now
using the unhappiness of his brother-in-law as an excuse to force
Joseph Bonanno into coming before the commission to explain
the procedure by which Bill Bonanno had been selected and to
respond to charges that the nomination had been so quickly
contrived that no other member had had a chance. Joseph Bonanno believed that these charges were false, and in any case he
did not intend to appear before his fellow commissioners to
explain a situation that was none of their business.

Another part of Stefano Magaddino's strategy, Bonanno heard,
was the spreading of stories that disparaged the character of Bill
Bonanno and focused upon his controversial past—his Arizona
mistress and the child, Rosalie's alleged suicide attempt, his
being in Magliocco's car when the contract was given for the
murder of Gambino and Lucchese. If these and other issues
were successfully exploited by Magaddino, the commission
might recognize as valid the objection to the younger Bonanno's
elevation to *consigliere*, and then the elder Bonanno might be
pressed to defend his son and to answer other questions as well—
Joseph Bonanno would be on the defensive, which was precisely
where Magaddino wanted him to be.

Joseph Bonanno had much to answer for, in Magaddino's
view: Bonanno had lived safely and elusively for years, skillfully
side-stepping the government and the commission while other
dons had squirmed uncomfortably in the public eye. Magaddino
felt uneasy about Bonanno's presence in Canada, circulating
close to Magaddino's territory that was centered in Toronto, and
Magaddino also suspected, as he had for years, that Joseph Bonanno was slowly angling to take over the entire underworld, to
become the boss of bosses. Having placed his organization under his son, Joseph Bonanno was now free to float around the
country to rally support for his higher ambition. It was a pro-
pitious time for such dreaming, for there was suddenly a power
vacuum in New York. Vito Genovese, sixty-seven, was serving
a fifteen-year term in prison, and the Genovese family was with-

out a strong successor. The Profaci family, not yet disembroiled from its internal difficulties, was reportedly under a new untested leader named Joseph Colombo. Although the plot to eliminate Gambino and Lucchese had failed, there was no guaranteeing that another attempt would not be made. The big bosses in other cities—Giancana of Chicago, Zerilli of Detroit, Bruno of Philadelphia—either were facing jail terms or were inhibited by the close scrutiny of the police. Magaddino himself could not wander far from his front door without attracting patrol cars, which followed his every move.

But with the help of his brother-in-law in New York—the despondent Di Gregorio—Magaddino saw a way of neutralizing Bonanno's position by splintering the family. Magaddino began by sending coded messages to Di Gregorio to boycott Bonanno family meetings, inasmuch as Bonanno had repeatedly ignored the commission's request that he meet with its representatives. Di Gregorio was later informed that Bonanno and the son were due to be suspended from leadership, and Di Gregorio was to organize an anti-Bonanno group among the members which the commission would support and protect from reprisals. A few dozen members responded immediately, and many more men joined Di Gregorio's factions when the commission, working through the labor unions in which it had influence in New York and New Jersey, ordered all of Bonanno's soldiers who were on the payroll as union workers or officials to be deprived of earnings unless they affiliated themselves with Di Gregorio. Despite the economic squeeze, most members continued to be loyal to Bonanno through the fall of 1964; and Bonanno stubbornly refused to meet with the commission, insisting that it had no authority to interfere in his affairs. He was aware that if he agreed to a meeting he might be setting himself up to be "hit."

So he kept on the move through the month of October as rival gangs tried to learn where he was living and as the government sought to bring him before the federal grand jury to testify. But his exact whereabouts remained a mystery until the dramatic announcement of October 22 that he had been kidnaped the night before by two gunmen on Park Avenue and was presumed to be dead.

Then nineteen months later, after an attempt on his son's life had failed and with the underworld as tense as ever, Joseph Bonanno had made his remarkable reappearance. Now, free on

$150,000 bail, he was living at his son's home in East Meadow, Long Island. It was spring and the flowers and trees were in bloom along Tyler Avenue, and Bonanno's four young grandchildren played on the swing in the yard under the watchful eye of bodyguards who squinted through the lace-curtained windows. Occasionally an automobile would pull into the driveway, and men would be admitted into the house to confer briefly with Bonanno in the living room, speaking softly before the sound of the ever-playing stereo. Then the men would leave, and the children would receive Joseph Bonanno's full attention, being bounced on his knee, being held high in his arms. Sometimes neighbors would stop on the front lawn and attempt to get a look at the man who had received so much publicity; but he did not venture outdoors, and, except for visits of various men during the day, there was nothing about the quiet ranch-style house that would mark it as the new headquarters of the Bonanno organization.

13

JOSEPH BONANNO, HIS eyes half-closed, reclined in a soft chair in the living room listening to the soothing sounds of Mantovani on the stereo. He wore a gray zippered cashmere sweater over his tan silk shirt; his feet, shod in doeskin Indian slippers from Arizona, hung limply over a footstool, and within easy reach on a small table was a snifter of brandy. It was nearly three in the afternoon, a mild cloudy day in the middle of June, and Joseph Bonanno was getting a few moments of rest before having to get up, put on a tie, and greet the arriving guests.

Rosalie, after spending the last two hours in the kitchen with her mother preparing dinner for a dozen people, was now moving about the dining room in a sullen mood, rattling the stacks of dishes she carried and the silverware in a way she hoped would distract the burly bodyguard, Carl Simari, who sat smoking a cigar at one end of the table reading a newspaper spread out before him. She wished that Simari would take himself and his smelly cigar into another room or, better yet, would go out to the patio where the children were watching her husband light the charcoal burner. But no subtle hints were getting through to Carl Simari on this afternoon, and Rosalie did not feel that she could complain openly—her father-in-law and his men had been living there less than a month—still, she did not know how much more she could take. Since their arrival in May, it had been a daily routine of endless cooking, of men coming and going at odd hours, sometimes taking naps on her sofa; and she was often awakened in the middle of the night by the sound of heavy snoring soaring up from the basement where the bodyguards slept on cots directly below her own bedroom.

She preferred to believe that the snoring was not coming from Carl Simari, who, despite his cigars and the moments of minor irritation he caused her, she found to be ruggedly handsome, with interesting blue eyes and an engaging manner, a man who was not above looking after the children once in a while, during which time they behaved ideally. The supersnorer, she believed, was probably none other than her father-in-law's old sidekick, Peter Magaddino, a stocky man with a sizable nose and a gravel voice who chain-smoked all day, alternating between Marlboros and Kents, and doubtless had difficulty breathing at night. What made Magaddino's snoring particularly bothersome was not that it was loud, which it was, but rather that it lacked a familiarizing rhythm, a consistent noise pattern that one could eventually adjust to. Sometimes his snoring would be punctuated by abrupt snorts and gasps, at other times it was characterized by elongated flowing sounds under which could be heard elaborate little hisses and whistles. Not surprisingly, her husband was never disturbed by it; nor, she was sure, was her father-in-law, the sole occupant of the guest room down the hall, out of range.

As if by agreement, the men appeared for breakfast each morning at precisely 8:40. This was ten minutes after Rosalie's three sons left for school. During this reprieve, she usually managed, though not always, to clear the children's dishes, to release two-year-old Felippa from the high chair, and to reset the table for the second shift. The men were invariably cheerful in the morning, clear-eyed, smelling of her husband's Aqua Velva, and usually fully dressed in business suits and ties. They looked like commuters, except that they did not commute. Their completeness in dress, which reflected the propriety of her father-in-law, who would never have tolerated his men appearing in front of Rosalie in their bathrobes, meant that she too was influenced by the demands of modesty, and she therefore did not venture beyond her bedroom door in her robe, or display her hair in curlers, or reveal her legs uncovered by hose. The sense of formality and preciseness reminded her of her days in the convent, and she recognized, beneath her irritation, a feeling that was strangely comforting.

Although she had been married to Bill for nearly ten years, she still regarded her father-in-law as a distant, almost occult, figure, one whom she most comfortably referred to not as Dad but as Mister B. Having assumed until recently that he was dead and having prayed for the redemption of his soul, she now could not quite take casually his presence around the house. He moved quietly, spoke softly, was immaculate about his appearance, orderly in every way. She had never known him to lose his composure or to utter a word of profanity. Everything on the top of his bedroom bureau was carefully arranged, as were the clothes in his closet, which she imagined was one of the habits he passed down to her husband. Both men stuffed the shoes they were not wearing with wooden shoe trees, both adorned their pinky fingers with beautiful rings, neither man smoked cigarettes.

By ten thirty each morning, her husband and Carl Simari usually left the house for some unknown destination, possibly to make phone calls, and as Rosalie cleaned up in the kitchen or changed Felippa's diapers, she could overhear the conversation in the living room. Her father-in-law and Peter Magaddino, having read *The New York Times* that was delivered each morning to the door, were often engrossed in discussions about the latest news, about which they were keenly interested but emotionally detached. They sometimes talked about the war in Vietnam, but not in the passionate, contemporary terms that she heard on the television debates. To her father-in-law and Peter Magaddino, Vietnam was just another invasion in many centuries of invasions, a situation in which official governments professing peace at home committed atrocities beyond their borders, and justified it. It was an old story.

Oddly, though the word "Mafia" was in newspaper headlines nearly every day, she never heard mention of it in conversations around the house. If and when the men were dealing with the subject, it was obscured in such a way that she was never sure what they were specifically discussing. They seemed to have a language all their own; it was a mixture of certain English phrases and Sicilian phrases that, though she understood Sicilian, she could not translate, and she assumed that they had turned their vocabulary around in such a way that necessitated being familiar with things other than those expressed in order to achieve understanding.

What she could understand and enjoyed overhearing were the lengthy reminiscences of her father-in-law and Peter Magaddino about their youth in Castellammare, their student days in Palermo, and the elder Bonanno's nautical training and his dreams of piloting a great sinking ship and dying a captain's death. He seemed as preoccupied with death as the eighteenth-century English poets she had read in school, and more than once he expressed the wish that he would live long enough to return once more to Castellammare to visit his parents' grave. He was remarkably unembarrassed at admitting to certain fears and doubts, even in front of her, although she concluded that this was probably his way of trying to convince her that he was as normal as anyone else and was not the mystical creature she might imagine him to be or the murderous monster that was portrayed in the press.

Still, she felt shy and awkward when she was alone with him, confused by so many things about him. He was so unlike her own diffident father, nor was he like her more blusterous uncles, Magliocco and Joseph Profaci, whose notoriety in the newspapers was so carefully clipped and concealed from her innocent eyes. Joseph Bonanno seemed open, proud of what he was, except Rosalie did not know exactly what he was. She would sometimes see his softly smiling photograph in *The New York Times* resting on the breakfast table, a celebrity of sorts given equal space with General de Gaulle and the president of General Motors. Occasionally she heard the Bonanno name referred to on WINS' radio news show that was played continuously through the day, items concerning private wars, midnight shootings on the streets of Brooklyn, missing bodies. Then she would hear her father-in-law's gentle voice coming from the living room, would see him sitting comfortably across from Peter Magaddino and recalling, as might old men in a café, the simple pleasures of the past. And then her children would return from school, would run toward their grandfather, embracing him warmly, freely, feeling none of the restraint and confusion that she felt.

She was neither so naïve nor personally unaware as to fail to admit privately that some of her reservations about him were based on envy, envy of that part of his relationship with her husband that excluded her. She was also deeply resentful of the ruinous effect that that relationship had on Bill, although the degree that she felt this varied from day to day. There were moments when she truly hated her father-in-law for failing to keep his son out of his world. At other times she was not ashamed of his way of life or Bill's—the larger world outside, blind to its own worst ills, used such men as the Bonannos as its scapegoats. Bill had said this, and she believed him. Yet she frequently wished that she and her children were free of the pressure of being a Bonanno. She wished that the children could be spared the embarrassment of going to school and hearing from other students that their father was a gangster, an event that had not occurred but was sure to happen when they were a bit older. She also wished that, at the age of thirty, she did not contemplate and fear the prospect of widowhood, and also see it as a certain escape.

It would be an escape not only from the strange men coming and going in her house but also from her father-in-law who somehow created tension within her by merely speaking to her for a few moments. When he asked her a question she felt the necessity of answering intelligently, wisely, carefully—it was almost as if she were being tested. She remembered hearing her husband speak of his days as a schoolboy and how his father would sometimes help Bill and his sister Catherine with their homework—and then, days later, when they least expected it, their father would suddenly quiz them, demanding the precise answer to the lessons they had studied a few nights before. Rosalie was also conscious, when speaking with her father-in-law, of the possibility that he would detect any sign of insincerity in her words, her private thoughts about him, her mixed emotions. And thus she marveled at the ease with which her eight-year-old son, Charles, responded to Joseph Bonanno's teaching him Italian. Each evening at the dinner table, if there were not other guests, Charles sat next to his grandfather and proudly recited an Italian prayer of thanks which the elder Bonanno had taught him.

All the places at dinner were somehow prearranged, as if there were place cards: Joseph Bonanno and Bill sat at either end of the table; to the elder Bonanno's left was Charles, and next to Charles sat his six-year-old brother, Joseph, and to the left of young Joseph was Rosalie. Between Rosalie and Bill was the baby Felippa, and on Bill's right was Carl Simari. On Simari's left was Bill's third son Salvatore, not quite three and a half, and next to him was Peter Magaddino.

Young Salvatore had insisted from the beginning that he be allowed to sit between the thick-armed bodyguards, whose rugged features attracted him, or so it was interpreted by Bill Bonanno, who believed that Salvatore was by nature a tough, strong-willed little boy, and that if any of his sons would follow in his footsteps, it would be Tory. Charles, the adopted son, seemed too easygoing and unrebellious for a life outside the legitimate system. The six-year-old, Joseph, thin and weak from childhood ailments, was intense, alert, and bright in school—he was Bill's top candidate in the family for a full-time legitimate career. Tory was different in that he was bold and fearless, was unafraid of the dark, was always into some household mischief, and was already trying to give orders to his older brothers.

When Bill looked at Tory, he was reminded of his own childhood photographs—the boy had large brown eyes, broad shoulders, and a round innocent-looking face that belied a quick temper. Bill sometimes admitted, though never to Rosalie, that if Tory became a mafioso in twenty years or so—if there was a Mafia then; Bill had his doubts—he would not be disappointed. Bill would not concede, even to himself, that what he did in life was morally wrong. He was no more wrong than an American combat officer in the jungles of Southeast Asia or at the Berlin Wall—except that his main enemy at the moment was not Ho Chi Minh or the Soviets but the Mafia's national commission. If his son Tory someday believed that there was an issue worth fighting for, and risking his life for, then Bill thought that his son should fight and take his chances.

Bill had high hopes for Tory. So did Simari and Peter Magaddino, who liked to wrestle on the rug with Tory, tease him a bit, and watch his temper flare up. Magaddino could always provoke Tory by referring to him as a little girl, sometimes calling him Josephine. "You have a brother named Joseph, and your name is Josephine," Magaddino would say, as Tory would frown and make threatening gestures with his little fist. One evening before dinner when Magaddino called him Josephine, Tory suddenly dropped his pants to the floor, grabbed his penis, thrust it at Magaddino and said, "*I'm* not a little girl!"

As the guests arrived for Sunday dinner, Joseph Bonanno, wearing a white shirt and gray silk tie, stood greeting them as they entered the living room. Bill was outside on the patio stoking the charcoal fire, and he had not heard the front doorbell ringing because his son Charles was noisily hammering nails, constructing a small shed out of orange crates. Bill was proud of Charles's skill at carpentry. It was the one thing, the only thing, that Charles excelled at, and Bill did not have the heart to complain about the noise, although it was slowly giving him a headache.

Carl Simari, who had opened the door and escorted the people into the living room, was now back at the dining room table, sitting in Joseph Bonanno's place, reading the Sunday *Times* and smoking a cigar. Simari believed in smoking a cigar until the lighted end almost burned his lips, and, having reached that point now, he crushed the butt into an ashtray and was about to light up a fresh cigar when, from the kitchen, Rosalie appeared with two bottles of wine for him to uncork. Simari took the wine but, before removing the corks, he lit the new cigar.

Rosalie stepped down into the living room, smiling, embracing the middle-aged women and men from Brooklyn and Long Island who stood around her father-in-law. Most of them were relatives or friends of the Profaci side of the family, being merely acquainted with Joseph Bonanno, but Rosalie invited them to dinner because she had not seen them in a long time. They had been very considerate of her and her children during the many disruptions of the past two years, and she also had grown tired of seeing only her husband's and father-in-law's friends around the house. On this Sunday, except for Carl Simari, the men were told to stay away until evening, canceling the afternoon card game usually held in the basement.

Seeing the people in the living room, Bill Bonanno came in from the patio, wiped his hands in the kitchen, then came in to shake hands with everyone. The children followed shyly, facing people they did not know, but they were quickly met by delighted shrieks from the women who rushed to embrace them, kiss them, and exclaim on how much they had grown, especially Felippa, who had not even been walking when they had last seen her, before the elder Bonanno's disappearance. Joseph Bonanno, smiling, reached down and grabbed Tory. He tossed him high in the air, and asked in his soft accented voice, "You like-a me?"

"Yes," Tory said, grinning, as his grandfather bounced him in the air.

"You like-a me?" Joseph Bonanno repeated, holding him higher, bouncing him faster.

"Yes," Tory giggled, "*yes*." Bonanno let him drop, caught him again, hugged him, kissed him.

Everyone sat down and drinks were served. As Bill returned
to the patio to put the chicken on the broiler, one of the visiting
men said that he had recently been to California and had seen
Joseph Bonanno's daughter, Catherine. Bonanno suddenly
seemed almost misty-eyed.

"You have *seen* my daughter?" he asked in a voice filled with
wonder, tenderness. He himself had not seen Catherine in nearly
two years, and while he was immediately curious as to how this
man had met her, a man he was now meeting for the first time,
he waited patiently for an explanation.

The man said that they had met through mutual friends in San
Mateo, that they had gone one night to Catherine's house for
cocktails, and that she and her husband had later been among
the crowd that had gone to dinner in a restaurant. Catherine was
a charming, bright and lovely girl, the man continued, as Joseph
Bonanno remained silent. He seemed to be many miles away,
drifting in some private memory; and when the man perceived
the effect he was having on Bonanno, he stopped talking, and
there were moments of awkward silence. Finally one of the
women, pointing to Bill standing in the smoke of the charcoal
burner, added that the elder Bonanno also had a right to be proud
of his son.

Bonanno looked at her, looked at his son, and slowly nodded.
Then in a voice still choked with emotion, he said slowly and
in a special and formal way: "The mother, the mother—she is
responsible for my wonderful family. All credit to the mother.
My wife. Fay. She is to be thanked for these children." He
paused for a moment, and looking at the woman who had spoken, he added: "Also, I appreciate it to hear this about my son.
My son and I, he is my little brother." There were smiles around
the room, the lifting of glasses in a toast. Then Bill came in to
the living room again, and, noticing that his father's brandy
snifter was empty, he poured him another drink.

"Thank you, little brother," said Joseph Bonanno. "Thank
you."

Outside it was becoming suddenly darker, windier, and Bill
returned to the patio to look up at the sky. Clouds were forming,
and the sun was no longer visible.

"It looks like rain," Bill said. "Maybe I'd better move everything inside."

His father appeared on the patio, looked up at the sky, studied the cloud formations for several moments with his navigator's knowledge.

"It will not rain," the elder Bonanno said, still squinting at the sky. "It will not rain," he repeated. And it did not.

14

THE SUMMER PASSED slowly and somberly for Rosalie, as summers for her always had, evoking girlhood memories of stagnant lakes at inland resorts, of hot afternoons at her father's farm in Newburgh with horseflies buzzing around the lopsided picnic table, of weekends spent in the kitchen helping her mother prepare food for the omnipresent guests. Her life had not changed much in twenty years; except now, during the summer of 1966, she barely had an opportunity to get out of the house and had no chance of escaping the rising tension within it.

She did not know precisely what was happening, but the men suddenly seemed more restless, ill-tempered, anxious. They were smoking more, as she could see from the ashtrays filled to the brim each night with cigarette butts of almost every major brand. Sam Perrone seemed to be averaging close to three packs of Chesterfields a day, or so the rumpled wrappers he left behind indicated. Peter Magaddino, who had switched from Marlboros exclusively to Kents, was up to two packs a day. Frank Labruzzo, who had been suffering from emphysema and should not have been smoking at all, was unable to stop. Even when he was admitted to a hospital in late July and was known to have cancer, Labruzzo arranged to have cigarettes smuggled in to him by members of his crew.

Although Bill managed to resist cigarettes, he was eating more, and his weight was now about 230 pounds. The elder Bonanno displayed no signs of physical change and appeared to be as controlled as ever, and yet his customary sense of caution now bordered on obsession. When a tube burned out in the color television set, he would not have it sent out to be repaired—it was as if he feared that it might be returned containing electronic bugging devices, or maybe a time bomb. He temporarily borrowed the portable set from Rosalie's bedroom, returning it after the men had appeared one night with a new color set. Then the malfunctioning set was placed in a corner of the library, remaining there through the summer and fall.

From what Rosalie could gather from the newspaper and radio reports, and from what she overheard around the house, the Bonanno organization was suffering from a series of recent defections by members responding to the economic pressures of the unions. There were also references to gun-fighting—Frank Mari, who was said to have been Di Gregorio's top triggerman in the Troutman Street ambush attempt on Bill Bonanno in January, was himself set up to be "hit." He was trailed and trapped in the crossfire of the Bonanno gunmen in the Bay Ridge section of Brooklyn, was shot in the left shoulder and grazed on the temple, but Mari managed to escape. Another defector from the Bonanno organization, Angelo Presenzano, who was in University Hospital in Manhattan for surgery, was reported in the *Times* to have been discovered by a nurse to be keeping a loaded .38-caliber revolver in his night table—protection he apparently thought he needed in the hospital against uninvited visitors. The gun was removed, but a police guard was stationed outside of Presenzano's room.

In August, the Bonanno household was grieved by the death of Frank Labruzzo. He had been in a Brooklyn hospital for weeks; his cancer was found to be incurable, and he died quickly. He was fifty-five. Among the membership Bill was the most shaken by Labruzzo's death. In many ways nobody had been closer to him than Labruzzo, with whom he had had an intellectual rapport that was uncommon among men in the underworld. Labruzzo was the only individual that Bill had ever known who could pass the idle hours between dangerous assignments reading worthwhile books, fiction by J. D. Salinger, essays by Mark Twain, William Shirer's *The Rise and Fall of the Third Reich*. Labruzzo, like himself, was a kind of misfit, an outsider in a secret society, a man born into a special way of life which he had not chosen to escape but in which he did not entirely belong, particularly in its present condition of deterioration.

Bill felt embittered and betrayed at the time of Labruzzo's passing—many low-echelon men had just gone over to Di Gregorio's side because they no longer wished to be deprived of the money they earned as supervisors or workers in trucking firms, or on the waterfront, or in factories, or in utility trades whose union leaders were abiding by the commission's request to keep the Bonanno loyalists idle. In the old days, Bill was sure, loyalty was based on more than money, and he wondered, as he stood among his men at Labruzzo's funeral, which of the remaining members would be the next to defect. Those who had already defected had not really been starving—true, their illegal operations had declined during the months of unrest, and they were undoubtedly hard-pressed because of the loss of their legitimate income, but Bill was nonetheless depressed and angered by their unwillingness to make sacrifices. *This thing of ours is absolutely going to the dogs*, he thought.

With Labruzzo gone, and with Joseph Notaro having died three months before, the Bonanno organization had lost two officers for which it had no comparable replacements. Its membership was now perhaps less than 200—it was impossible to know the exact figure because many men had recently disappeared from sight, taking prolonged summer vacations rather than remain in New York and face the problem of choosing sides. The six remaining captains were, like Bill, still under John Morale, the number two man, although Morale was rarely reachable at the Brooklyn tavern that he owned, and Bill began to sense a distance between Morale and himself when they were together. Bill wondered if John Morale felt that he had somehow been shelved or had lost some of the respect of the membership since the elder Bonanno had returned to live in East Meadow and was relying more closely on Bill. But Bill could not believe that Morale would be that sensitive to the tight father-son relationship that was part of a temporary emergency arrangement. Bill wanted to believe that Morale had been an intimate part of the Bonanno family for too many years to ever feel left out, or to want to get out; he had joined the organization as a young man in Brooklyn during the Castellammarese War, had lived for long periods in the elder Bonanno's homes in Brooklyn and Long Island, and during much of his boyhood Bill thought of John Morale as his brother. Later, Morale married the daughter of Vito Bonventre, Joseph Bonanno's mother's brother.

After the elder Bonanno's disappearance in 1964, Morale's home in Queens was under constant watch by the police, and in September 1965—after Morale had successfully evaded federal interrogators for twenty-two years—he was caught by the FBI near his home and was held on $50,000 bail. He appeared before the grand jury on several occasions since then and was subjected to close police observation wherever he traveled; and Bill preferred to believe that it was Morale's ultracaution and the continuing tension that were responsible for changes in his manner.

The tension and pressure continued unabated through the summer into the fall. While the feuding factions headed by Bonanno and Di Gregorio felt haunted and hunted by each other, they were pursued indiscriminately by federal agents and the police, as the government's campaign against the Mafia remained a national policy, a political issue, and a subject for headlines. Even the mayor of New York, John V. Lindsay, became involved in Mafia news in 1966 because two of his Youth Board officials had solicited the help of the Gallo brothers' gang in suppressing racial disorders between whites and blacks in a Brooklyn neighborhood. Albert Gallo met with white youths in a predominantly Italian area of South Brooklyn and warned them to ''cool it'' with regard to forays with the neighboring blacks— and it worked. But despite the positive results, the Gallo role was protested by a Brooklyn civic group, by the Brooklyn District Attorney, and by the Patrolmen's Benevolent Association, all of which denounced the impropriety of employing mafiosi as peacemakers. Mayor Lindsay disagreed, saying that when it came to preventing the escalation of rioting in a neighborhood where there had already been one death and considerable hostility, ''you can't always deal with people who are leaders in the Boy Scout movement.'' The Brooklyn District Attorney, Aaron E. Koota, nevertheless insisted that the decision represented a ''deplorable abdication of official responsiblity,'' and he began an investigation of Albert and Larry Gallo's relationship with the Youth Board officials who had approached them.

But before this investigation progressed very far, the headlines shifted suddenly to the Queens District Attorney's office, where it was announced that thirteen Mafia figures were subpoenaed to appear before a special grand jury after being caught in the basement dining room of La Stella Restaurant in Forest Hills. The men were in the middle of lunch when the police arrived to break up what Chief Inspector Sanford D. Garelik called a Little Apalachin Meeting, adding that the raid was part of the police department's campaign "to rid the city of top hood-lums."

The men, though surprised by the intrusion, offered no resis-tance, and a few continued to eat. But they were forced to leave the table, and to enter the police cars outside, neglecting to pay the check. Though they did not carry guns, the police search revealed that they carried considerable cash—the least amount in anyone's pocket being $600, most of it in fifty- and hundred-dollar bills. They were at first charged with consorting with known criminals—that is, themselves—but this was then changed by the Queens District Attorney, Nat H. Hentel, who, fearing that it might permit the men to go free on low bail, decided to hold them each as a material witness in a grand jury investiga-tion, and bail was set at $100,000 each. Among the thirteen diners identified by the police were Santo Trafficante of Miami, Carlos Marcello of New Orleans, and such men from New York as Carlo Gambino, Joseph Colombo, and two ranking officers from the Vito Genovese family, Thomas Eboli and Mike Miranda. They had assembled, according to law enforcement officials, to discuss pressing problems in the underworld—particularly the Bonanno situation, certain dissatisfactions in the Genovese family since their leader went to jail, and the question of the most capable candidate to replace the ailing Thomas Lucchese, who was now in a coma with a brain tumor at the Columbia-Presbyterian Medical Center.

When they appeared before the Queens grand jury, the men refused to testify, pleading the First, Fourth, Fifth, Eighth, and Fourteenth amendments to the Constitution. Outside the jury room, their attorneys complained to the press that their clients' rights to assembly had been violated, that they had been arrested unlawfully without a probable cause, that their bail was exces-sive, and that they had been denied counsel while being detained for thirteen hours. Although their clients' personal possessions seized by the police had been returned, the attorneys said that their money was still in the hands of detectives and that legal action would be forthcoming to determine which detectives took the money so that it might be recovered. The attorneys' com-plaints were supported in several instances by the New York Civil Liberties Union, which accused the Queens District At-torney and the police of flagrant violations of civil liberties and suggested that Hentel, who was up for reelection in November, was using the grand jury hearings for personal publicity. Hentel indignantly denied this.

Eight days after the raid, five of the men returned at lunchtime to La Stella Restaurant to try again. This time they brought two lawyers with them, and they also invited to their table two plainclothesmen who were following them. But the detectives refused, choosing to sit solemnly two tables away. News photographers and three reporters also observed the luncheon, and the mafiosi cooperated by posing for pictures as they consumed linguine with white clam sauce, striped bass, baked clams, fresh fruit, and espresso coffee. The bill for the seven men came to $49.05, and they left a $10.95 tip. When asked by the reporter how long the grand jury hearings would continue, one of the lawyers replied, ''Until the election is over.''

By the time the election was over—Hentel had lost—Bill Bonanno was in jail. He was serving a thirty-day sentence for contempt of court because, during a Brooklyn grand jury session held in July, he had refused to talk about the Troutman Street shooting that occurred on the night of the previous January 28. He began serving this sentence in mid-October; and of all his jailhouse experiences, he was finding this one the most tolerable. The quarters were clean and uncrowded and without the rats and the nonworking toilets and washbasins that had characterized his stay in the Federal House of Detention on West Street during the winter of 1965. Located on West Thirty-seventh Street in Manhattan, this civil jail was largely populated by men refusing to pay alimony. The guards here seemed almost sympathetic to the inmates, and they were also polite to Rosalie when she came to visit. They did not object to her slipping to Bill through the gate a book that he wanted to read—a new book on the Mafia, *The Secret Rulers* by Fred J. Cook. They also did not object when Sam Perrone brought Bill a hero sandwich that Perrone had gotten from Manganaro's Restaurant on Ninth Avenue. Perrone even succeeded in getting a few bottles of wine and chunks of imported cheese to Bill, a violation of prison policy that would never have been condoned had Bill not recently done a favor for one of the resident prison officials.

Bill had overheard, shortly after his arrival, that the official was rudely awakened early each morning by the clanging of garbage cans and the grinding of truck gears by the private collection agency that serviced an all-night diner across from the officer's home in Queens. When Bill informed one of the guards that he might be able to solve the officer's problem and was given permission to try, he telephoned Sam Perrone, who quickly sent a few men to visit the garbage collectors. On the following morning, the cans were handled with incredible delicacy and silence.

A second privilege that Bill obtained through the favor was the acquisition of practically the entire third-floor prison space for himself and seven other members of the organization who were also serving thirty-day sentences for their refusal to testify about the Troutman Street incident. One of these was John Morale. Morale was friendly to Bill, but Bill again felt an undercurrent of resentment on Morale's part. It was not from anything that Morale said—indeed, none of the men said anything in jail about the organization, aware of the possibility of bugging—but there was nonetheless a remoteness about Morale that was disquieting to Bill. Morale seemed more pensive than usual, perplexed, perhaps searching for an explanation to the problems that had suddenly befallen the organization, an organization that had existed for decades without serious problems. Perhaps Morale blamed Bill for what had happened, tracing all trouble from the moment Bill came East from Arizona in 1963, blaming Bill because he could not bring himself to blame Joseph Bonanno, the man who had been his boss for more than thirty years.

On November 10, when Bill was released from jail, he went to his father and said that he was afraid that John Morale had left them. When the elder Bonanno suddenly turned pale, disbelieving, Bill did not pursue the discussion. He and his father would probably know soon enough, and his father meanwhile was informing the United States Attorney's office that he would be leaving New York for a while, would be returning to Tucson to spend the Thanksgiving and Christmas holidays with his wife and younger son, whom he had not seen for a very long time.

A large crowd of people, including federal agents, newsmen, and dozens of curious citizens of Arizona, watched Joseph Bonanno step out of a jet at Tucson International Airport. If he had bodyguards with him, they were keeping their distance, and the impeccably dressed gray-haired Bonanno gave the appearance of a typical corporation executive traveling first-class—except in place of a briefcase he carefully carried in his right hand a white cardboard box containing Italian cookies. Bonanno was amazed by the size of the crowd, which had been alerted to his arrival either by a news report or by the presence of the many policemen and photographers waiting at the gate near the landing field. As the flashbulbs began to pop, Bonanno smiled and waved. When one reporter, trying to start Bonanno talking, asked what he was carrying in the box, there was laughter at Bonanno's almost sheepish reply: "Cookies."

Bonanno declined to comment on the latest speculation that he had spent most of his hiding months in Haiti, and he avoided answering other important questions, saying only that he was happy to be back again in Tucson. Then, spotting a taxicab that awaited him, he slowly made his way through the crowd toward the front of the terminal building, carrying only the box, his luggage evidently coming later with someone else. But before he got into the cab, he overheard a teen-age girl standing several feet away asking her friend, "Say, who was that guy, anyway—a movie star?"

Unable to resist replying, Bonanno turned toward her and said with a smile, "I'm Errol Flynn's younger brother."

The casual return of Joseph Bonanno to Tucson, and the almost friendly greeting that he received at the airport, offended some of the leading citizens of the city. Among the most outraged was the editorial board of the Tucson *Daily Citizen*, which quickly made clear its position on the reappearance of its highly publicized resident. Under the headline BONANNO IS NOT WELCOME HERE, the editorial read:

Reputed Mafia king Joseph Bonanno is in Tucson this week for his first extended visit to his home in more than five years.

His arrival in Tucson International Airport and the later arrival of Mafia associate Pete Magaddino were well attended by the news media and Tucson Police Department intelligence unit officers.

Lest anyone—and especially the shadowy characters Bonanno and Magaddino themselves—be misled that news stories of their arrivals indicate that Tucson is proud to welcome them, let us set the record straight.

Tucson does not want Joe Bonanno. He is not welcome

here. Neither is Magaddino or any other of Bonanno's henchmen.

Nor should anyone be misled by the dapper Bonanno's jovial appearance when he arrived to spend the holidays at his
home at 1847 East Elm Street.

Joe Bonanno is hardly spending a jovial holiday. He is
marking time in the brick home whose Christmas manger
scene in the front yard belies the underworld character who
may look upon it only by peeking out through tightly drawn
curtains. His is a furtive existence at best.

There was only one reason certainly for the *Citizen* and
presumably for the other news media to publicize the return
of the man whom gangland informer Joe Valachi named as
"his godfather or sponsor" in the Cosa Nostra—the Mafia
organization.

That reason is publicity. Be they big shots or not, one thing
the underworld figures do not seek or want is publicity, no
matter how broad their smiling masks may appear in a front-
page news photo.

Bonanno, Magaddino, Pete Licavoli, another underworld
figure who frequently has lived in Tucson, and others of their
ilk fear and shun publicity.

In 1960, the *Citizen* told Licavoli editorially that his presence here, and the presence of other underworld figures in
Tucson, at any time would be news and would continue to be
news. Their arrivals, departures, and activities in Tucson
would be duly reported. The glare of publicity would be kept
on them.

There are those in Tucson who prefer the ostrich approach.
Ignore the Licavolis, Bonannos, Magaddinos, and others and
they will go away, or, at least, pretend there are no underworld characters in Tucson. Fortunately, most Tucsonians are
concerned.

Bonanno was quoted as saying the attention he received by
the press at the airport was all "very confusing."

It shouldn't be.

It's Tucson's way of saying we're watching you, and we're
looking forward to saying farewell with much more enthusiasm than our representatives, the police, said hello.

15

For Rosalie Bonanno, the coming of the new year—1967—promised no relief from the grim reality of life as she had come to know it. Once the holidays were over, the men returned from their families to her home; and with their reappearance came the tension, the chain-smoking, the nocturnal snoring. Sometimes as many as eight men were there, a few sleeping on the floor, and her children tripped over them in the morning on the way out to school. When the children were as disturbed as she by the snoring, they would often come into her bedroom, climb into bed beside her. One night Charles tripped in the darkness, hit his head on a piece of furniture, and in the morning Rosalie found blood all over the rug.

Bill was rarely home except on weekends, and she did not know exactly where he spent the nights, nor would she ask. She had become resigned, because she had little choice, to the fact that something strange and extraordinary was going on. It was a private war that had placed her and the men in the house under a kind of martial law. Fear and confusion dominated her emotions, her will to scream or run was stifled. She could not protest as she saw other people do on the nightly television news, marching through open streets demanding or denouncing; she could only try to endure this secret ordeal that encircled her and these men, although she sought refuge at night in her bedroom and sought a modicum of comfort during the day from the words uttered softly by her father-in-law, who seemed to be reading her mind when he said *pazienza*, patience, *coraggio*, courage. He spoke these words almost in the form of an exhortation, spoke them as a high priest might at benediction; but she could not respond to her father-in-law. At night, in bed, she quietly cried.

She was terrified, fearful for her husband's life. She hated him, loved him, worried, and prayed. She wondered why he and not one of the other men went on these mysterious missions that took several days. She knew that he had recently been in Montreal because there was an article in the paper reporting that he and five other men were spotted by the Canadian police and were held on suspicion of having a conference with Montreal mafiosi. Bill and his men were deported from Canada after receiving a suspended sentence for illegal possession of firearms.

He returned briefly to East Meadow, explaining nothing, and then he was gone again, behaving in a way she had never seen before; he was totally preoccupied, desperate, a man possessed. At unexpected moments she would be notified that he wanted to talk to her, and, leaving the children in care of the men, she would drive to a certain telephone booth at a shopping center in Long Island or to a particular booth in Macy's in Manhattan where at a precise moment he would call. His calls were sometimes for mere conversation, sometimes for arranging a place where they could meet in person; and sometimes, if he wanted to make love, which was often, he would ask her to meet him at a certain motel.

Once she remembered meeting him and, after getting into his car, hearing him request that she get into the back and lie on the floor. He did not want her to see where he was taking her. They drove for fifteen or twenty minutes through the dark streets of Long Island or Queens; then the road seemed suddenly softer, smoother, quiet, and she got the impression, though she did not know why, that they were somewhere close to the World's Fair grounds, perhaps inside the grounds, which would have been vacant and clustered with empty buildings at this time, long after the fair had closed. He stopped the car, told her to cover her eyes with her hands. Then he led her into a building, up steps, through a long corridor, turned left and stopped. She heard a door latch click and, when she opened her eyes, she was standing in a dimly lit room that was sparsely furnished but had a bed.

One night much later, in East Meadow as she slept in her room, she was abruptly awakened in the middle of the night by hands caressing her body. She felt someone kissing her, and was about to scream. Then she realized that it was Bill. He wanted her almost desperately, more than she had ever remembered him wanting her before, and he did not even take the time to remove all of his clothes. In the middle of their lovemaking, she felt against her breast an object that was cold and heavy. After a few seconds, she realized that it was a gun. It must have fallen out of his pocket or holster, and she knew it must be loaded. She waited, holding her breath; she had never been more frightened.

After he left her that night she lay awake until daybreak, her heart pounding, her head throbbing with shock and disbelief.

Winter extended slowly, uncertainly, maddeningly. She never knew what to expect or what was expected of her. There was great excitement one afternoon when a suit that was believed to be Bill's was discovered in the back seat of one of the men's cars, but nobody remembered who put it there or why it was there or if the suit had been placed there by the enemy as a way of announcing that the owner of the suit would no longer be needing it. Rosalie was in her room when she heard the men's frantic conversation, and then her father-in-law hurriedly approached her door and asked her what color suit Bill had been wearing when he last left the house. Rosalie said she did not know. There was shocked silence from the elder Bonanno, and also from the men who stood behind him in the hall. *She did not know!* It was as if she were guilty of some atrocious act of carelessness and neglect, and as she watched their faces register signs of disappointment or disapproval, she wanted to shout at him, *How in God's name am I to know what he was wearing? I hardly see him anymore because of you people!* and she was tempted to tell them to leave her house immediately, she had had enough of their damnable little war and their endless intrigue. But she said nothing. She too was overcome with fear that something had happened to Bill.

Late that night, Bill returned safely with Carl Simari, seeming casual and unconcerned. He spent the following afternoon at home, conversed at length with his father, then he was gone again. Nobody mentioned the suit, and she did not question him about it during the few moments they were alone together in the bedroom. She was determined to avoid becoming a victim of the madness in this house, the manias, the obsessions with tiny details, the things that preoccupied her father-in-law more than anyone else—his mind seemed always in motion, he was always

talking to the men in a strange oracular manner that confused
her, he missed nothing that was going on. He was even aware
that one of her husband's watches was missing from Bill's top
bureau drawer, and he asked her about it. Rosalie had been
carrying the jeweled watch around with her in her purse, explaining to her father-in-law that her own watch was in need of
repair. But she wondered what her father-in-law was doing in
her husband's bureau, in her bedroom; and she also wondered
if he suspected that she intended to hock the watch, which was
one of four expensive ones that Bill owned. And if she had the
nerve to do such a thing, she would have felt justified, for with
Bill away so much she was always short of cash, lacking the
money for personal things that she and the children needed, and
not being able to ask her father-in-law for money because this
would have embarrassed her husband, would have reflected
poorly on his efficiency and capacity as a provider. She also
knew that she could not relay hints to her father-in-law through
Carl Simari because, as she already had discovered, it was a
violation of protocol for Carl to go to the elder Bonanno directly
without first clearing it through Bill. Protocol and male ego were
driving Rosalie Bonanno to a breaking point, and yet only once
during the winter did she lose control and complain openly about
her shortage of spending money.

This occurred early one evening as a friend of Rosalie's, a
woman of about her own age, stopped by the house to accompany Rosalie to a movie. As Rosalie was leaving, she informed
her father-in-law that she would be going in her girl friend's car
because "her car has gas in the tank." When Rosalie returned
home that night, the elder Bonanno was there to meet her, furious. She had humiliated him in front of the other woman, he
said, embarrassed him, and had inadvertently revealed personal
matters that should never have been discussed outside the family. Rosalie began to tremble as she stood facing him—never
before had she been directly criticized by him—and as he perceived the effect he was having on her, he quickly softened his
tone, became conciliatory.

Life had been very difficult for her, he conceded, and he said
he understood her frustrations and grievances. But he reminded
her that these conditions were temporary; things would improve. He pleaded with her to not crack under the pressure,
saying that when she was a young girl he sensed that she had

the character and strength to withstand adversity, and that was why he had been pleased by her marriage to his son. *Pazienza*, he repeated, slowly stressing each syllable. *Coraggio*.

She nodded, forcing a smile. He offered to give her money, but she refused, backing away.

In the spring, there was a front-page article in *The New York Times* with a photograph of Joseph Bonanno and a headline that read BONANNO REGAINS POWER IN MAFIA GANG.

Joseph (Joe Bananas) Bonanno has returned to a position of influence and profit in the Mafia gang from whose leadership he was forced at gunpoint two and a half years ago, according to local and federal law enforcement officers.

They say that the sixty-two-year-old underworld chieftain's comeback was maneuvered by his eldest son and heir apparent, thirty-four-year-old Salvatore, sometimes called Bill . . .

The transition has taken place against a background of shifting allegiances that turned cousin against cousin, godfather against godson; a plague of heart attacks that killed one interregnum caretaker and inactivated several adversaries; international underworld intrigue; financial lures; and vengeful passions in the gang of more than 250 members.

Law enforcement officers say that they have confirmed Bonanno's emergence from exile through underworld informers, around-the-clock surveillance of key mafiosi and the observation of such changes as new "street men" taking bets for bookmakers or handling collections for loan sharks in scattered areas . . .

Precise information is lacking about the new ranking order and on how the income from the rackets is divided. Inspector Louis C. Cottell, the head of the Police Department's Central Investigating Bureau, said in an interview:

"The situation has not jelled fully. We fit together pieces of information and get a general picture, but you must remember that the Mafia does not publish annual reports nor does it announce its personnel promotions and departures in the business-news pages of *The New York Times*."

The elements in the present situation are still volatile, and other changes may follow, according to investigators. They do not rule out the possibility of further gunplay . . .

The elder Bonanno and the men seemed genuinely pleased by the article, and there were four copies of the *Times* around the house that day. But if the situation had indeed improved for the Bonanno organization, Rosalie could see no convincing signs of it at home. There was no less tension, no fewer men, no lessening of security arrangements. Her father-in-law rarely left the house except to make a phone call. Bill also continued to be away most of the time, and Rosalie was forced to borrow money from her mother.

The prolonged pressure and newspaper publicity now also seemed to be having some effect on her children, who came home from school complaining of small fights and the fact that the other children insisted on calling the Bonanno boys "banana." Of her sons, only Tory seemed to adjust completely to the overcrowded conditions at home and to accept as normal the presence of bodyguards such as Carl Simari in the family. One afternoon when Tory, Felippa, and a young cousin were sitting on the floor in the library, having decided to play "house," Tory was overheard to say: "OK, you play the mommy . . . you play the daddy . . . and I'll play Carl."

The prospect of another hot summer spent in the house in East Meadow began to depress Rosalie before the summer had even begun. She did not want the children to be secluded with the men and cigar smoke from June to September, and she did not want to spend hours every day over the sink and stove. She showed symptoms of her growing tendency toward rebellion during May when on two occasions she deliberately returned late from shopping, letting her father-in-law and his aides wait for their dinner. She surprised herself by staying away until eight and nine in the evening, and in June she was again late on two more occasions, forcing the men to cook for themselves. Peter Magaddino had often talked proudly about his career as an army cook in the Pacific during World War II, and Rosalie decided to let Magaddino display his talents in her kitchen. On returning home she would explain that she had been visiting her mother, who was not feeling well, or that she had taken a long ride in the car in an attempt to calm her nerves, which in most instances was the truth; except that Rosalie discovered that she usually ended up in commuter traffic jams when driving, and this made

Joseph Bonanno, 1941

Salvatore Bonanno,
father of
Joseph Bonanno, 1890

Joseph Bonanno,
age 5, 1910

Joseph Bonanno, in Brooklyn, 1926

Charles and Marie-Antoinette Labruzzo,
parents of Fay Bonanno, Joseph's wife

Joseph Bonanno and wife, Fay, (née Labruzzo), 1936

Joseph Bonanno and son Bill (age 4), 1936

Joseph Bonanno, 1936

Fay Bonanno, 1941

Joseph, Fay, and children Bill and Catherine, 1936

Bill Bonanno, age 21, Tucson, Arizona

*Bill and sister,
Catherine*

*Bill Bonanno, age 12,
at ranch school,
Tucson, Arizona*

*Bill, in ROTC
at the University
of Arizona, 1952*

*Joseph Bonanno, Jr.,
at his First
Communion, 1951*

Bill Bonanno and Rosalie (née Profaci), wedding reception at Astor Hotel, New York City, 1956

Rosalie and son Joseph, 1961

Bill and Rosalie, with children (left to right)
Charles, Tory, Felippa, and Joseph, 1970

Joseph Bonanno,
Tucson, Arizona

Joseph and son Bill at Moulin Rouge
Restaurant, Hollywood, California

Bill Bonanno prepares for federal case

Joseph Bonanno and daughter, Catherine, on her wedding day, Tucson, Arizona, 1960

her more nervous. The men seemed sympathetic, and Magaddino evidently proved to be an adequate substitute.

But what happened in July to provoke her to a point of doing the wildly dramatic thing that she did had nothing to do with the men. It had to do with a woman. Rosalie was in the kitchen in the early afternoon when the phone rang, and a woman's voice asked for Bill. Rosalie recognized the German accent immediately, and she felt her right hand shaking as she held the phone, her palm perspiring. It was Bill's former girl friend from Arizona, now back in the United States on a visit from Europe, calling to say hello. Rosalie was stunned by the woman's cool and casual approach, and she felt threatened by the woman's return. As calmly as she could, Rosalie said that Bill was not home and was not expected home at any specific time. Then, not knowing what else to add, Rosalie said good-bye and hung up.

Within an hour of the call, Rosalie saw Bill's car pull up in the driveway. She was surprised that he was home at this time of day, not yet 3:00 P.M., but she did not tell him about the call when he walked in, followed by Carl. She hoped that Bill would not notice how disconcerted she was, but in a way she hoped that he would; at least that would indicate that he was paying attention to her, was aware of her, cared about her, a feeling that at this moment she needed very much. Instead, Bill informed her that a man would be coming in from California later in the evening and would probably be spending the night on the sofa. Rosalie said nothing. She waited until Bill had tended to a few details in the house and then left again in his car with Carl.

Rosalie went into the bedroom and calmly wrote Bill a note, saying that she was leaving him. Then, after putting into her purse the $350 that she miraculously managed to save and borrow during the last year, and after packing a few things in paper shopping bags and a small suitcase and carrying them through the kitchen door to the garage, she gathered the children and told them she was taking them for a ride. None of the men seemed to be paying any attention to her as she walked out with the children, started up her 1964 Comet, and headed for the highway toward Manhattan.

She had no idea where she was going, and she did not care. The children must have sensed something different in her manner, a firmness, a cold-eyed vengeance, for they remained very quiet and did not even ask where she was taking them. It was 4:00 P.M., the roads to New York were relatively uncongested. It was a warm sunny afternoon but there was a fine breeze in the air and she felt free and oddly in control. Felippa sat beside her, with Charles also in the front seat; in the back were Joseph and Tory.

Within an hour Rosalie had driven past the Triborough Bridge in Manhattan and was heading upstate on the thruway. She was in heavy traffic now, had to stop a few times as cars jammed up at intersections or toll gates, but she remained calm, relaxed, listening to the rock 'n' roll music coming from her radio and the radios of other cars moving slowly next to her with their windows open or their convertible tops down. Convertibles were rare in the world that she knew, and the sight of people driving with the tops down, people who did not fling anxious glances into the rearview mirror every few seconds, reminded her of the reality that she had missed. She also noticed that many people were carrying vacation equipment in their cars—inflatable rubber floats, fishing rods, surfboards—and, suddenly, Rosalie wanted to go to a beach, to inhale the salt air of a seashore town, to walk on soft white sand. In her whole lifetime of miserable summers she could recall only one summer at the shore, and that had been about fifteen years ago at a north Jersey resort when her father was alive. She remembered the soothing sound of the ocean at night, the crashing of the waves, the noise of crickets. She remembered going out on her father's boat with her brothers and sister Ann and how her father used to push them into the water to force them to swim; and they all had learned to swim in this manner, except for her. She had been too afraid of the water then, and still was, but this did not make the idea of going to the seashore now seem less enticing. During her years with Bill in East Islip and East Meadow she had noticed the long line of cars on summer weekends heading slowly toward the Hamptons and Montauk, but when she went away for weekends, it seemed always in another direction—away from the ocean toward the interior hills and mountains, possibly because Bill and his friends would have felt trapped on an island resort where the exits and entrances were limited.

Now, as Rosalie continued to drive with her children, it gradually occurred to her that at this very moment she was retracing the familiar route that she had often taken with Bill and her parents: she was headed upstate on the New York Thruway toward Newburgh, where her father's hillside farmhouse had been, where the convent she had attended still was. Unknowingly, as if driving by rote, she had been on the road for nearly two hours moving back to her past, lured perhaps by the sense of security she once felt within convent walls. As soon as she realized where she was heading, she decided to change her direction. Taking the first exit she saw, she circled around to an opposite route and stopped when she spotted a large luxurious motel with a swimming pool in which people were splashing and diving.

After registering for the night and handing the children their bathing suits, Rosalie sat under a poolside umbrella watching her children play in the shallow end. She ordered a gin and tonic and knew that in a few hours' time she had come a very long way.

In the morning she checked out and, after consulting a road map, decided that the most convenient beaches for her were back in Long Island. New Jersey seemed too far, New England too unfamiliar, and while she had no specific place in mind on Long Island, she thought she would merely drive through the towns with beaches and stop when she found a place that she liked and a cottage she could afford.

Reentering the thruway, she spent the morning on the road, crossed the Throgs Neck Bridge and headed for the southern shore of Long Island. She soon realized that she was drifting back in the general direction of East Meadow; but having already made one wrong turn on the Bronx Expressway and another on the Cross Island Parkway, she decided that it was wiser for her to remain on those few roads she was familiar with. There was absolutely no chance of her returning to the chaotic atmosphere of her home, her boarding house, and there was little possibility of Bill's locating her no matter how close she was to him—she doubted that he would even look for her. So she ventured through the beach towns that she knew to be within fifteen to twenty-five miles of her home, stopping at several real estate offices in Atlantic Beach, East Atlantic Beach, and Long Beach. She was astonished at the prices for small houses near the water, rentals of close to $1,000 and more a month, and after a long and discouraging afternoon she considered herself fortunate to have gotten a damp basement apartment for $225 a month in a house within walking distance of the beach.

There were no cooking utensils in the kitchen, no linen or pillows in the bedroom, but Rosalie discovered a few faded bedspreads and soft pillows in the vacant apartment upstairs, and she bought cheap spoons, forks, and plates at a nearby five-and-ten. From the supermarket she purchased several frozen TV dinners for supper that night, planning to use the tins in which they came for pans later on.

The weather during the first week was sunny and warm, without a drop of rain, and Rosalie was getting a suntan and feeling healthier than she had ever remembered feeling. She lost the two or three pounds that she had gained during the winter; and as she looked in a mirror at herself wearing a bathing suit, she was pleased and impressed with her trim figure. She had always been conscious of gaining weight, which was the tendency among women in her family, a tendency that she resisted through careful dieting. Although she would not easily admit it to others, she was vain and secretly proud of her vanity. Beginning with her sheltered Brooklyn girlhood as the protected pearl of the Profaci family, she had been very aware of herself, sensitive to the impression she was making on others, and she carried within her a mental image of each of her movements. She lived in horror of looking foolish—which was why she had never learned to swim—and she resented being taken for granted or feeling abused—which was why she had left her husband twice in the last four years. In each instance she had determinedly felt no guilt, convinced that her husband's brazen behavior or the intolerable conditions he imposed upon her were such an affront that they had forced her to leave.

Still, after her first week at Long Beach, she began to wonder when, or if, he would begin to look for her. From a drugstore she telephoned her mother, the only person who knew of her whereabouts, but learned that Bill had not called. Though not surprised, she was nonetheless disturbed and hurt; and even more so when she contemplated the possibility that the German girl was seeing Bill, perhaps sleeping with him, although Rosalie knew that such philandering would never be allowed in East Meadow as long as Mister B. was in residence—and Mister B., she thought petulantly, might be in residence forever.

During the weeks in the sun, with the children playing freely around her on the beach, she looked back on the life she had been forced to live during most of her marriage and she considered it absolutely incredible. She doubted that there was another woman in her family or among her in-laws or distant relatives who would have survived such a marriage as long as she had, and this included her heralded sister-in-law, Catherine. Rosalie felt that when Catherine was spoken of in exalted terms, she, Rosalie, indirectly suffered by being unfavorably compared, even though she found no basis for comparison: Catherine, while extremely loyal to her father and brother, and unintimidated by the bad publicity, nevertheless had not married a man who was in and out of jail, who was shot at in the street, who allowed strangers to live in his house while he disappeared for weeks at a time. Catherine had married a hard-working, prosperous dentist, a man whose father had come from Castellammare and had known the Bonannos but who had somehow managed to avoid a career of notoriety. Catherine's husband led a normal life, came home at predictable hours, and her children would never fret over the word "banana." Rosalie wondered what Catherine's reaction would be if she learned of this runaway summer, and she was tempted to write to her, but decided against it. She had already written too many letters complaining and justifying herself to Catherine, and now she wanted to keep this time of independence to herself. She felt free now and less concerned with what people thought. And until she felt differently, she decided to enjoy the summer with her children; to share only with them the sun, the hot dogs on the beach, the unclocked hours of the day.

Rosalie was awakened one night by the sounds of men's voices and their footsteps in front of the house. She sat up immediately, tense and apprehensive, pulling the bedspread around her, waiting to hear any second the thumping of heavy knuckles against the flimsy screen door. She feared that men had been sent to bring her back, and for the first time since she had left she was afraid of facing Bill again, confronting his explosive temper.

She listened intently to the voices outside, but none seemed familiar. Then she heard the men climbing the staircase along the side of the building, opening the upstairs door, dropping their luggage heavily. Rosalie breathed more easily. They were

apparently the new tenants in the upper apartment, and from the
noise they made Rosalie guessed that there were four or five of
them. *Men*, she thought, *gangs of men. I cannot escape them.*

In the morning, hearing them coming down the steps, Rosalie
peeked out from behind her drawn window shade and noticed
that these men were not the sort that she was most accustomed
to having under her roof. These were obviously college boys,
husky young men who were barechested and wearing Bermuda
shorts and bathing trunks. Two of them were drinking beer out
of cans.

Later that afternoon, as Rosalie and the children were walking
slowly back from the beach, she noticed them sitting on the
upper porch with their bare feet on the railing, again drinking
beer. One of them said hello to her, and she looked up, smiled,
and returned the greeting. Charles and Joseph, Tory and Felippa
also said hello, and a brief conversation followed in which
the young men asked Rosalie if she would like to come up and
join them for a beer. She politely refused, and taking Felippa's
hand she entered her apartment.

As she quickly rinsed the sand and salt water off Felippa and
instructed the boys to do the same for themselves, she felt pleased
and light-hearted. Later, having showered and put on a cotton
dress, she prepared a dinner from cans and containers that would
hardly have been considered sufficient in her parents' home or
in East Meadow, and she marveled at the joy and simplicity of
the exchange with the new tenants. There was nothing to hide
from them, nothing to fear, which was ironic, considering that
this was the first time in her life that *she* was hiding. She even
reveled, as she never had before, in her shortage of money, her
limited wardrobe, and the transient condition of her existence.
Here she was answerable to no one; and there were no men in
the next room waiting expectantly for her to set the table, cook
their meals, and wash their dishes while they retired to a smoke-
filled living room. Here she did not have to put on stockings
each morning or hear snoring at night. The children also seemed
happier; and although she did not ignore disciplining them, she
was more relaxed, less nagging, permitting them to run barefoot
much of the time and to play louder games than she would have
allowed at home. They also met other young children on the
beach, and the college men upstairs proved to be polite and
friendly with her and the children, treating them to ice cream

from the Good Humor truck and sometimes taking Charles for rides in their car. It was all a new experience for Rosalie and the children—they were indulging in a kind of American childhood that none of them had had before.

Rosalie often wished that it could continue indefinitely, but it ended abruptly in the middle of August, which was when young Joseph and Felippa were stricken with asthma. Wheezing, struggling to breathe, they were unable to sleep at night, and their crying kept the other children awake. What made matters worse was the change in weather—there had been rain this week and a series of cloudy days that accentuated the dampness and darkness of the apartment, creating an atmosphere that was unrelievedly depressing.

Rosalie held out for a while, nursing the children with medicine from the drugstore, but she knew that Joseph in particular required a doctor's care. Not wanting to call her mother, who did not drive anyway, Rosalie thought she had no alternative than to notify Bill. She was nearly out of cash and, as galling as it would be for her, returning home was now in the children's best interest.

She did not telephone Bill in the morning, not wanting to talk to her father-in-law or whoever else might answer; she waited until the afternoon and called the warehouse and trucking company on Leonard Street in Brooklyn that was jointly owned by Bill and Sam Perrone. It was where Bill received messages and was sometimes reachable.

Perrone answered and was as cordial as usual; and after a pause during which he went to get Bill, Perrone returned to say, apologetically, that Bill did not want to talk to her. Rosalie became almost hysterical, pleading, telling Perrone that it was an emergency concerning the children. Perrone left the phone again, and after a few moments Bill was on the other end. He sounded sullen and irritable. She had left him, he stated formally, and added that insofar as he was concerned she could stay away forever. Rosalie began to cry, imploring him to consider the children's condition, and after several minutes of reasoning and beseeching, he finally agreed to come to Long Beach to take the children to a doctor. But she could not return to East Meadow right away, he quickly added; he had had all the locks changed on the house, and he would arrange for her to stay at a motel with the children until he could properly prepare his father for her return.

Rosalie was stunned by the remark, too confused and infuriated to reply. After he had hung up, and as she packed the few belongings she had and awaited his arrival, she sat on the edge of the bed feeling humiliated. His logic was absurd, she thought, it was nauseating—first he turned her homelife into a private hell, and now he wanted her to linger in limbo for a while until she had paid a kind of penance! And his *father* had to be properly prepared for *her* return. What did his father have to do with all of this? And in what manner was he to be prepared? It was as if she, a fallen angel, a sullied soul, had to be decontaminated before regaining her privileged position as the cook and bottle-washer. The Bonannos, she thought, scornfully, are simply unbelievable.

When Bill arrived he looked pale and fatigued, in need of a shave. Though he was kindly with the children he was cool toward her. He handed her $250 and told her that he had made reservations for her and the children at a motel on Hempstead Turnpike, not far from their home, adding that she could take the children to see a doctor and that he would let her know when she could return to the house. He was obviously preoccupied, and Rosalie did not press him, did not argue or ask questions, knowing that to do so at this time would probably make things worse.

The motel, which had a swimming pool, was comfortable and bright, and the children seemed to enjoy staying there. Joseph's condition improved, and within a week Bill came to bring them home. He seemed more relaxed now, and whatever trepidation Rosalie had with regard to the reception of her father-in-law quickly ended when he greeted her at the door as naturally and warmly as if she had never gone away. The other men, taking their cue from him, also expressed pleasure at seeing her, but concentrated their attention mainly on the children, who responded immediately. My children, she thought, are the most adjustable little creatures in the world.

Going into the bedroom, Rosalie found nothing to indicate that other people had slept there or had even entered there during her absence, a condition that pleased her until she reminded herself that, when it came to concealing evidence, her husband

was undoubtedly an artist. Still, she was glad to be home, for
reasons that she was sure were illogical. Home sweet home, she
thought, wryly, listening to Tory tumbling on the rug in the
living room, giggling as Peter Magaddino wrestled with him
and tickled him. She heard that Peter Magaddino had done the
cooking during her time away, which was one of the few subjects
that Bill had discussed at length during a visit to the motel,
adding that Magaddino had a mania about cleanliness, had emp-
tied the garbage pail whenever it was half-full, had never left
potato peelings in the sink or clogged the drain with garlic and
onion skin. Rosalie, getting the hint, had changed the subject,
but now on returning to her kitchen she was impressed with how
spotless it was.

In September the children returned to school, and as the fallen
leaves littered Tyler Avenue and the cooler breezes swept through
the yard and kicked up the ashes in the outside grill, Rosalie felt
that life was again closing in around her. The men seemed once
more on edge, and there were times when tension filled the
rooms as if it were a tangible substance. The feud that the press
referred to as the "Banana War" was being reported in the
newspapers more frequently and in more detail. It had obviously
reached some kind of climax, with men being hunted and fired
upon in the streets.

In late October, Vincent Cassese was shot in the chest and
arms, and Vincent Garofalo was hit by a bullet in his left side,
although both men lived. Two weeks later, in what the police
speculated was perhaps an act of retaliation by a Bonanno loyalist, three men were shot to death while having dinner at the
Cypress Garden Restaurant in Queens by a short, stocky man
who seconds before had entered the restaurant from a rear door
and walked casually through the kitchen down the aisle along
the tables carrying a submachine gun under his black raincoat.
Approximately twenty patrons were in the restaurant at the time,
but no one paid attention to the gunman except the three marked
men, who, apparently recognizing him, jumped up from their
table, upsetting their chairs. The gun was pointed directly at
them, however, and a burst of twenty bullets hit them at close
range. They fell dead to the door.

As the killer turned and headed back toward the kitchen the
other people in the restaurant dove under their tables, cowered

in corners, raced toward the front door. At one empty table a
fork with spaghetti wrapped around it was resting on a plate.

The police later identified the victims as Thomas Di Angelo,
James Di Angelo, and Frank Telleri, once affiliated with the
Bonanno organization but most recently associated with the Di
Gregorio faction. The killer was not immediately identified, but
from the description of a few witnesses who were shown police
photographs, the prime suspect was Peter Magaddino's younger
brother from Castellammare, Gaspare Magaddino, who was also
being sought at this time by Sicilian police in connection with
other activities.

An international hunt was organized by the police, but it would
take them more than a year to find him, and when they did locate
Gaspare Magaddino he was dead—killed by a shotgun blast on
a Brooklyn sidewalk. On his body was found a newly acquired
bricklayers' union card, but a detective said, "His hands were
smooth. This man wasn't a bricklayer."

16

AN UNSETTLING CALM followed the triple murder at the Cypress Garden Restaurant as the men from the feuding factions remained off the street, and the headlines shifted in December to a scandal at City Hall. James L. Marcus, the water commissioner, a personal friend of Mayor Lindsay and son-in-law of former Governor John Davis Lodge of Connecticut, was arrested on FBI evidence that he had received $16,000 of a $40,000 kickback on a city reservoir contract that involved, among other people, two lawyers, a bakery unionist, a bank director, and a mafioso from the Lucchese organization named Antonio Corallo.

The case—which would result in jail terms for Marcus and Corallo and would also implicate onetime Democratic leader Carmine G. De Sapio—provoked pious indignation from certain citizens and editorial writers, but it reminded others of New York's long history of political corruption and of the fact that while politicians usually denounced organized crime in public, they often profited from it privately.

During this period, in which the Mafia's national commission was trying to determine its next move toward dealing with the Bonanno organization, Bill Bonanno quietly left New York for Arizona, where in late February he was scheduled to defend himself in court against a government claim that he and his wife owed $59,894 in back taxes for the years 1959–1960–1961. He was accompanied on the motor trip by Peter Notaro, cousin of the late Joseph Notaro, and by Vincent Di Pasquale, an uncle of Bill's who was married to his mother's eldest sister. The three men left New York in mid-February and took a leisurely journey across the country, traveling through Indiana into Illinois, crossing the Mississippi River at St. Louis, and heading through Joplin into Elk City, Oklahoma, where they were briefly stalled in a snowstorm. A day later they passed through New Mexico into Arizona, arriving in Tucson almost five days after leaving New York, which was twice as long as Bill had taken on some previous occasions. But he was using this trip almost as a pleasure excursion, and for once he did not carry large amounts of cash in his pocket, paying for gas, food, and lodgings with a Diners' Club credit card that Sam Perrone had loaned him.

Perrone had handed the card to Bill in lieu of Bill's share of their monthly income from their trucking business, explaining that he, like Bill, was suddenly short of cash. Perrone's problem stemmed largely from a run of bad luck in his gambling operations—a few big "hits" by numbers players combined with the defection of certain bookmakers to Di Gregorio's side. There was also the ongoing expense of police graft and the general difficulty of trying to earn a dishonest dollar while the underworld was in ferment and members of the brotherhood were shooting at one another. Bill's difficulties, while inevitably related to the problems of Sam Perrone and other income-producing subordinates, were on a much grander scale. He and his father were having trouble financing the Banana War, an expensive campaign that included the subsidizing of soldiers who were kept out of work by the unions, the leasing of apartment hideaways and getaway cars, the expense of bail bondsmen and lawyers for members taken into custody, the payoffs to informers in rival camps.

Some gang members, unable to supplement their income in any other way, resorted to hijacking trucks, a risky and complicated undertaking that involved kickbacks to the company dispatchers who pinpointed the travel routes of trailer trucks carrying cargo worth stealing, the renting of garage space large enough to hide a "hot" trailer, and the contacting of "fences" to dispose of the stolen merchandise. Because of the great haste with which information was often now obtained, a team of hijackers recently captured the wrong truck, discovering that instead of stealing a vanload of television sets they had stolen thousands of boxes of Ping-Pong balls, which they quickly abandoned in embarrassment and disgust. Another revealing sign of the hard times confronting the Bonanno men was the fact that many were economizing on their telephone calls—they made long-distance pay phone calls only when necessary, they limited the length of each call, and they were reduced to using dimes for local calls, which contrasted with their former practice of carrying nothing smaller than quarters.

It was in such a state of austerity that Bill Bonanno found himself in the early fall of 1968, forcing him to go to Perrone and other men in the hope of collecting old debts or loans or of obtaining an advance against anticipated earnings; and it was with gratitude and relief, if not with his customary caution, that Bill accepted the Diners' Club card from Perrone and agreed to sign all charge slips not in the name of Bonanno or Perrone but in the name of the person to whom the card was registered— Don A. Torrillo.

Perrone had introduced Torrillo during the previous year as a friend of his, a young man with whom he had a "few deals" going and for whom he had done a few favors. While Torrillo was not a member of an organization, Bill was given to believe that he was the type of man commonly found on the edges of organized crime, a fringe character who got some peculiar thrill or sense of power through his shady connections. Bill would never trust a Torrillo when situations were particularly dangerous, suspecting that types like Torrillo usually collapsed under pressure and could often be coerced by the police into turning informer, but Bill was nevertheless pleased to have Torrillo's help at this point, as Bill had had twice in the past.

Fifteen months ago, while Bill was serving a thirty-day sentence in Manhattan, Perrone visited him at the West Thirty-seventh Street jail and reported that the mortgage holders of Bill's East Meadow house, disturbed by the newspaper publicity and considering Bill a poor business risk, were threatening to discontinue the financing of the house. Perrone said that his friend Torrillo, who was in the real estate business and had good credentials with the Dime Savings Bank, would take over title to the property and Bill could make future payments through Torrillo, which Bill did. A year later, when Bill and Perrone made a quick trip to California, Bill noticed that Perrone had purchased the plane tickets with Torrillo's credit card. And so in February 1968, when Perrone offered the card to Bill for the Arizona trip, with the stipulation that Bill sign Torrillo's name, Bill did not question the procedure, being in no position to be particular.

Bill had high hopes that after a few weeks or a month in

Arizona, after settling his tax case, he would be able to regain some of his property that the government had confiscated and he would then be able to sell it at a price that would relieve his financial burdens. Bill was an optimist, a quality that he had cultivated long ago, recognizing it as essential to successful leadership; and while he had no reason to be optimistic about anything in 1968, he exuded even more buoyance than usual during his cross-country ride to Arizona, and on arriving in Tucson he charmingly entertained various friends at restaurants and cocktail lounges, often paying the bill with Torrillo's credit card. He signed Torrillo's name after taking five people to dinner at the Pancho Mexican Restaurant in Tucson, and he used the card during a trip to San Diego. He experienced no difficulty until the afternoon of March 11, 1968, when he and his companions walked into the David Bloom & Sons shop in Tucson and submitted the card after purchasing about two hundred dollars' worth of men's wear and a bottle of cologne. While he waited and continued to browse through the store, an assistant manager telephoned the Diners' Club collection office in Los Angeles to check on the credit rating of Don A. Torrillo, and it was learned that certain past bills had not been paid. The Diners' Club spokesman in Los Angeles asked to speak to Mr. Torrillo, and when Bill came to the telephone and replied incorrectly to a few personal questions that were asked about Torrillo, the man suspected that the card was in fraudulent hands, and he ordered the store manager to destroy it. Bill protested, explaining how he had gotten the card and wanted it back; but the manager of the store refused. Bill did receive permission to place a collect call from the store to New York; reaching Perrone at the trucking firm, he loudly complained about the unpaid bills on Torrillo's card.

Perrone apologized, but said that there was nothing to worry about—Don Torrillo would take care of the situation right away. After Bill had hung up and left the store and after he had kept an appointment with a man who was helping him to compile various records and receipts for the tax case, he met with friends at the Tidelands cocktail lounge. There he received a call from his uncle, Vincent Di Pasquale, who was at the elder Bonanno's Tucson home, saying that Carl Simari had just telephoned from East Meadow and wanted Bill to contact him immediately; it was very important.

Bill dialed East Meadow, and Simari picked up on the first ring. He asked Bill for the number of the cocktail lounge so that he could call Bill back from an outside phone. Within five minutes, Simari was back saying that he had bad news. Sam Perrone had just been shot in Brooklyn and he was dead.

Bill stood holding the phone, stunned, silent, as Simari gave additional details. Perrone, accompanied by another man, was walking out of his Brooklyn warehouse, was crossing the street to buy a pack of cigarettes, when two men suddenly jumped out of a car, fired at least eight bullets at Perrone at close range, then sped away in the car. Bill leaned against the wall for support, still saying nothing. He looked at his watch. It was 5:31 in Tucson. Less than five hours ago, he had spoken to Perrone.

Bill's father later sent word from East Meadow that Bill was to remain in Tucson and under no conditions was he to return to New York. The rumor circulating was that Bill was the next target. The Di Gregorio gang's top triggerman, Frank Mari—the one who had led the Troutman Street ambush—had been spotted a few days ago sitting in a parked car with two other men, all three carrying guns; and it was believed that Mari had had the contract to dispose of Perrone.

The newspapers, quoting the police, said that Perrone's murder was partly in reprisal for the shooting earlier in the month of an officer in Di Gregorio's group, Peter Crociata, who survived even though he had been hit by six bullets as he parked his car near his Brooklyn home.

The death of Perrone was extremely painful for Bill. The newspapers described Perrone as his bodyguard and chauffeur, but Perrone had been much more than that. Since the death of Frank Labruzzo, Perrone had been his closest friend and companion, a man his own age with whom he had communicated easily, whose humor he had enjoyed, and whom he had trusted absolutely. It was Perrone who had driven to Bill's rescue on the night of the Troutman Street shooting, and now that Perrone had been murdered Bill felt personally responsible for avenging the death. He was strongly tempted to disobey his father and return to New York. He stayed up all night in his father's home, pacing the room like a wild creature in a cage, swearing, vowing, sobbing softly.

He was still visibly distraught on the following day, as his

uncle and Peter Notaro tried to calm him down, saying at
1:30 P.M. that the FBI was at the door wishing to speak with
him. Bill yelled to Notaro to tell the agents to go around to the
back door. Then, rising from his chair in the living room, Bill
walked through the house to the yard, where, after opening the
back door gate, he saw two men wearing suits and ties, seeming
very officious. Bill invited them into the patio and asked them
to be seated. The taller agent, who introduced himself as David
Hale, began abruptly, "Well, I see your friend got it."

Bill glared at him. "Are you gentlemen here on official business," he asked, sarcastically, "or is this a social call?"

"You know damned well we're here on official business,"
Hale said.

"Look you son of a bitch," Bill said, standing up, pointing
a finger down at Hale. "Either you're going to conduct yourself
properly, or you're going to get the hell out of here right now!"

Hale looked hard at Bonanno, turned to the other agent, who
said nothing, then looked back toward Bonanno. Hale then
asked, more softly, "Well, are you going to be rushing back to
New York?"

"I'm going back to New York when I feel like it," Bill said
sharply, and after that he refused to say much of anything, professing ignorance to the questions or saying he would have to
consult with his attorney before replying. The agents remained
for another moment, then stood and left.

Bill Bonanno was back in New York within two weeks; and
on Monday, April 1, accompanied by an attorney, he answered
a subpoena to appear at the Supreme Court in Brooklyn with
several other gang members and defectors who were again being
questioned, as they had been on many previous occasions, about
the Troutman Street incident, which was now more than two
years old but still an unsolved mystery insofar as the government
was concerned.

Most of the mafiosi who appeared in court this day had already served terms in jail for previous unresponsiveness on the
Troutman Street issue, and they now were again threatened by
contempt of court citations. But if they were concerned about
this, or were worried about anything at all on this day, they did
not show it as they entered the Supreme Court Building and
waited in the corridor to testify. They were aware that their every

gesture was being observed by detectives and federal agents, who were attempting to assess the relative strength and relationships between members of the feuding factions. What the law enforcement men did not know was that the mafiosi were now as confused as everybody else with regard to which men were on which side.

For example, when Bill saw John Morale in court, whom he greeted in a manner that was polite but unrevealing, he was quite sure that Morale had left the Bonanno organization, but he was not sure whether Morale had become part of a third force that was rumored to have splintered off from sections of the Di Gregorio and Bonanno units. At the same time Bill was very cordial to Michael Consolo, a sixty-four-year-old veteran of the Bonanno organization who Bill knew had recently joined Di Gregorio's men. It was only when Bill learned later that night that Consolo had just been found in the street, lying next to his car, with two bullets in his head and four in his back, that he realized how confused everyone had become. Consolo must have been murdered by his own men, possibly through misinterpretation of orders or possibly because he was seen conversing so amiably with Bill during the day in court, and this must have misled some people into thinking that Consolo had gone back to the Bonanno side. Or maybe Michael Consolo was killed by the third group for some other reason; Bill did not know. But both he and his father agreed on the following day that the war had now reached a level of insanity—nobody could tell from which direction the next volley of bullets would be coming, and Bill was concerned about the safety of Rosalie and the children in a way that he had not been before.

If a man was just murdered because he was observed speaking in a friendly manner with Bill, then Bill Bonanno had seriously underestimated how intensely some people hated him, and it was not inconceivable that his East Meadow home could become a target, that a bullet or bomb would soon penetrate the thin-walled residence that was located close to the street.

Bill wanted to move to another house. Safety was not the only reason to relocate, for there was a possibility that he would soon be evicted from the East Meadow house. According to Perrone's plan of more than a year ago, Bill's monthly payments were made through Don Torrillo, whose credit card Bill had been forced to surrender; and since Perrone's death, Bill had been unable to reach Torrillo. Bill could not sell the East Meadow house, in which he had already invested $15,000, without making the necessary arrangements with Torrillo, and Torrillo now seemed to be ignoring the efforts of Bill's attorneys to communicate with him through the mail, telephone, or telegrams.

Then one of Bill's attorneys learned through a courthouse source that Torrillo had been conferring with detectives and was believed to be in some deep legal difficulty, perhaps because of gambling or other crimes; and what most worried Bill now was that Don Torrillo, in return for the lessening of whatever criminal charges were being brought against him, was going to serve as the government's key witness in establishing a case against Bill Bonanno in the credit card situation. Torrillo might claim that Bonanno and Perrone had stolen the card from him or had forced him to relinquish it. As optimistic as Bill was about most things, he knew that he would probably have a tough time in court disputing Torrillo. Without Perrone to testify, it would be Bill's word against Torrillo's, and Bill suspected that a jury's sympathies would be with Torrillo, an unknown figure, rather than with a highly publicized Mafia leader.

Still his main concern at the moment was not reaching Torrillo but the immediate problem of remaining alive and moving his wife and children to a safer place. Bill discussed the situation with Rosalie, and he was surprised by her quick reply, suggesting that she had given thought to the subject. She wanted to move to northern California, she said, preferring to settle near her married sister, Ann, who was in San Jose; her sister Josephine, a college student who had transferred from Santa Clara to Berkeley; and also Bill's sister, Catherine, who lived in the community of Atherton, south of San Francisco.

After reviewing it with his father, Bill decided that Rosalie's going to California was a sound idea and that the sooner it was done the better. His father concurred, saying that it was foolish for any of them to remain in the East much longer. The organization was in a quandary, as was the opposition. Nobody was sure anymore who the enemy was. As a result, most of the soldiers were in hiding, although there were a number of Bonanno loyalists who were determined to fight until the end, settling old scores.

The elder Bonanno nevertheless felt that the hostility and confusion would subside if he and Bill left town for a while, since it was they who were the main sources of controversy. Joseph Bonanno planned to take some of his men with him to Tucson, in time to spend Easter with his wife, and he suggested that Bill should leave immediately with Rosalie and the children for California. After they were settled there, Bill could come alone to Arizona. Bill agreed; and on April 10, packing the car with only the most essential household equipment, and leaving the furniture behind to be collected later, he left with his family for California, planning to go first to Catherine's.

Along the way he kept in touch by telephone with events in New York, and, contrary to his father's expectations, the shooting did not stop. One of Perrone's warehouse employees was injured, though not fatally, by one of five bullets fired into his Cadillac; and then one of the Di Gregorio men was shot three times as he sat in a Democratic club in Brooklyn, but he too survived. Also in April, in a Brooklyn luncheonette, there was the fatal shooting of Charles LoCicero, who was not affiliated with the Bonanno or the Di Gregorio faction but with the Joseph Colombo family, a fact that puzzled the police at first. But later, on the basis of a report by an underworld informant, the killing was said to have been done by one of Bonanno's men in response to the elder Bonanno's alleged remark, following his famliy's most recent casualty: ''The next time they hit one of my men, they lose one of their *capos* (captains), first in one family, then in another.''

17

NOT LONG AFTER his arrival in Tucson, Joseph Bonanno complained of pains in his chest, neck, and left arm. After consulting a physician, he was sent to St. Joseph's Hospital for treatment of what was diagnosed as a mild heart attack. But word of Bonanno's ailment was received skeptically in New York by agents and the police, who suspected that Bonanno was merely making excuses to avoid appearing before a Brooklyn grand jury investigating the Banana War, and a physician was appointed by the court to examine Bonanno in Tucson. This examination, however, apparently confirmed the illness because Bonanno was not forced to fly to New York. He remained in the hospital for a week, leaving after a switchboard operator reported receiving a call at 5:40 P.M. from a man who refused to give his name but who said, slowly and precisely: "I am calling from Sky Harbor Airport in Phoenix. We are going to assassinate Mr. Bonanno."

Accompanied by bodyguards, Bonanno was moved slowly by wheelchair on the following morning to an awaiting Cadillac driven by his son Bill, who had left Rosalie and the children in an apartment in San Jose, California. The elder Bonanno's companions also included Peter Magaddino, Peter Notaro, and a few men who were strangers to Tucson, although the police later identified one of them as a Mafia "muscle man" from New York named Angelo Sparaco, whose last arrest was on charges of assault with brass knuckles. Carl Simari was not seen in Tuscon and it was assumed that he was still in New York, where a few dozen Bonanno loyalists were engaged in guerrilla tactics with the Di Gregorio followers led by Paul Sciacca.

Tight security arrangements existed at the elder Bonanno's home on East Elm Street, with guards posted through the day and night behind the high brick wall in the rear of the house and

with additional men stationed near the front of the house between bushes and trees and equipped with walkie-talkies so they
could alert the men in the house if anything suspicious happened. Bill Bonanno, who was in charge of security, was concerned not only about the telephone threat but also by some
letters that he had recently received, letters that predicted his
father's death and his own and seemed to have been written by
someone who had an insider's knowledge of the organization.
There were references to men who had worked under the late
Joseph Notaro in the Bronx, hints about some of Sam Perrone's
activities that had not appeared in the press. The letters were
not the typical hysterical illiterate notes that self-appointed vigilantes frequently sent to mafiosi whose addresses were published in newspapers, and for this reason Bill took them seriously
and arranged for around-the-clock protection of his father's
home.

The men slept in shifts through June and July, constantly on
the alert for any intrusion, but nothing happened. The monotony, Bill thought, the monotony is maddening, and he was
tempted at times to leave again for California; but each time he
resisted, fearful that a disaster would strike moments after his
departure. Then on Sunday night, July 21, he heard on the radio
that two explosions had shattered a shed and damaged four vehicles on the ranch of Peter Licavoli, a part-time Tucson resident
who was a Mafia leader in Detroit. Licavoli and the elder Bonanno had been friends for years, and yet after the explosions the
newspapers reported the police suspected that trouble might be
simmering between some of Licavoli's men and Bonanno's.

This made little sense to anyone in the Bonanno household,
but on the following evening, Bill Bonanno decided to stand
guard himself at the rear of the house, since this was where his
parents' bedrooms were located and since he was considered
the most accurate marksmen among the men. After loading his
shotgun, he climbed the makeshift stone steps that had been
piled against a large tree in the backyard from which he could
observe the motor traffic and pedestrians coming and going along
Chauncey Lane, which bordered the back of the property.

Bill remained in the tree for more than an hour; it was a warm
night with a bright sky, and the faint noises that he heard were
coming from a television set in the living room, where his father
and another man were sitting, and from the German shepherd

watchdog, Rebel, who paced about in the patio, digging in the
dirt, shaking off flies. Bill's mother, who had been ill with a
nervous condition for months, was already asleep. Having seen
so little of her in recent years, he was appalled on returning to
Arizona this summer to discover how quickly she had aged,
although it was understandable. In fact, it was remarkable that
she had endured as well as she had during the years of uncertainty and solitude, remaining loyal to her husband and sons
despite a multitude of accusations against them, never running
away, rarely complaining. Bill thought that his mother had been
well prepared for life's difficulties by her stern and demanding
father, Charles Labruzzo, a man who seemed to have spent so
much of his energy warring with the wind. Once in the early
1930s, Joseph Bonanno brought Labruzzo to an organizational
meeting, thinking that he might wish to become affiliated; but
on entering a crowded clubroom, and after spotting a man he
intensely disliked, Labruzzo shouted an insult and left the room,
declaring that any group that tolerated such a creature was un-
worthy of consideration. Another man would have been shot for
such behavior. But not Charles Labruzzo. His alienation was so
total that the mafiosi felt no special disrespect.

Shortly after 9:00 P.M., hot and thirsty, Bill climbed down
from the tree to go into the house for a drink of water. But before
he entered, he heard a car passing through Chauncey Lane, and
so he waited, his right hand on the doorknob, his left holding
the shotgun. He looked at his watchdog standing at his side,
growling softly; then suddenly Rebel's fur bristled, he leaped
forward and charged toward the gate, barking, and Bill followed
with his shotgun ready—but he quickly stopped as he saw flying
through the air a black object that landed heavily in the barbecue
pit.

Bill heard a sizzling sound, smelled burning tar. Running up
the steps to the high branch of the tree, he saw a man running
away from the gate. Bill took aim, fired. The man staggered and
fell. But then Bill felt the explosive impact of a bomb knocking
him loose from the tree, flinging him to the ground. He had
fallen about fifteen feet, but was not hurt, although bits of glass
and parts of the garage roof were crashing to the ground around
him.

As he got to his feet, a second explosion knocked him off
balance again, the force of the blast turning him around, tossing

him against a lemon tree near the wall. He was stunned, yet conscious of everything around him, hearing the house windows crack, the bricks bouncing and breaking, and he saw a portable grill skidding at great speed across the patio floor, banging into a wall. His father came running out of the house yelling, "Are you OK? Are you OK?"

"Yes," Bill said, finally sitting on the ground, looking at the large hole in the brick wall. The hole was wide enough to drive a truck through, and the rear door of the house and the garage door were knocked loose and splintered. "But I think I hit somebody," Bill said, getting up. "I'd better get out of here quick." The other men and his mother were now all around him, asking him how he felt, wiping off the dirt and dust that covered him. But he insisted that he had probably hit and killed a man and that he had to leave; if the police arrived, he might be held for homicide, might be confined for months. So he ran through the house out the front door, across the gravel yard toward Martin Avenue where there were many large oleander bushes. He hid behind them for a few moments, watching lights turn on in neighboring houses, but he was confident that no one in those houses had seen him leave. He was excited, very tense, but miraculously unharmed by the explosions. He crouched behind the bushes for a few moments, then made his way carefully to Warren Avenue, then Maple Street. He was wearing dark slacks and a black polo shirt, his tree outfit, but he had of course left his shotgun at home, knowing that the men would clean it and hide it.

He ran across Speedway Boulevard and soon entered the central campus grounds of the University of Arizona, which was not far from his home and which he had attended less than fifteen years ago. He knew that at this hour, close to 10:00 P.M., there would be many summer students strolling around the grounds, some couples walking arm in arm, some students returning home from the library.

Soon he was among them, and he stopped running. He could not see anyone clearly in the semidarkness, and nobody seemed to be paying any attention to him as he walked along familiar paths, past familiar buildings. He wiped the perspiration from his forehead, breathing more easily as he walked, feeling again some of the peace and security that had been his when he belonged here. The students who now sat talking on the stone steps where he had once sat were as casually dressed as he was at this moment, and it was suddenly strange for him to be back—in a matter of minutes he had been blown out of a tree and had been swept back into the 1950s.

He was also aware that his reason for returning tonight was to be among strangers, to lose himself by moving with people in open spaces. A distinguished alumnus returns, he thought, savoring the absurdity, and then he paused briefly as he came to the Student Union Building, where he had once spent the hours between classes; and then he walked past the ROTC Building, from which he had led squads of Pershing riflemen wearing silver helmets and spit-polished boots. In those days, he remembered, he had been conditioned to shoot at Communists in Korea, and he had been able to display his rifle proudly before thousands of people as he and the other cadets marched into the football stadium to hang the flag before the game.

He continued on, seeing the Agriculture Building, where he had taken courses in agricultural engineering to prepare himself to run the family cotton farm that the government now controlled; and he also saw the tri-Delt sorority house, where he had dated a girl whose name he could not remember.

Then slowly but determinedly, he made his way to the Standard Oil Gas Station on University Street, where he knew there was a telephone booth, and there he called a man who would soon pick him up.

Bill hid for nearly a week, reading the newspapers and listening to the radio, but there was nothing about the death or injury of the bomber. Even if the police were deliberately keeping this fact secret, the Bonanno men had sources in hospitals who would probably have overheard talk of a death from shotgun wounds; but so far there were only discussions about the bombings. And while no one in the Bonanno house had any idea who was behind the destruction, the police seemed certain that the Banana War had extended to Tucson. The Tucson *Daily Citizen*, which in the past had published editorials urging Bonanno and his friends to leave town, was indignant over the bombs in its latest editorial.

Has gangland warfare come to Tucson?
We join all the decent residents of this area in hoping that it has not. But the blasts which rocked Pete Licavoli's Grace

Ranch and Joe Bonanno's patio on successive nights this week make us wonder.

Sheriff's officers hinted that at least the Grace Ranch explosions may be related to infighting among gang leaders.

Licavoli, a Detroit leader of the Mafia, is a part-time Tucson resident who has legitimate business interests here and in Phoenix. His record reveals several arrests in the Detroit area and a two-year sentence to federal prison.

Tucson's biggest underworld figure is Joe Bonanno, whose patio was bombed Monday night. Last spring he brought several bodyguards to Tucson to protect him and his son Bill from a rival faction headed by Paul Sciacca, his former lieutenant.

In so doing he may have moved the Mafia war to Tucson from New York, where several of his followers were gunned down last winter.

There may be no connection between the bombings and fighting within the Mafia. One wonders, though, whether Tucson is not beginning to reap the bitter harvest which may follow having notorious underworld figures as part-time Tucsonians.

A little more than two weeks after the publication of the editorial, there were two explosions in the rear of Peter Notaro's home, splintering a patio gate and breaking two windows, but no one was injured. Neighbors told the police that two men had fled from the scene in a blue or green getaway car shortly before 10:15 P.M., but it was then too dark to see them clearly. When Notaro returned home, finding his wife and daughter frightened but unharmed, he assured the police that he had no idea who might be directing the bombings, although the police and local politicians continued to attribute the damage to a gangland war.

Tucson's mayor, James R. Corbett, Jr., announced publicly that he would be "happy if underworld figures chose to live elsewhere." The Democratic congressman, Morris K. Udall, appealed to J. Edgar Hoover to send more FBI agents to Tucson to deal with the Mafia, and Hoover promised that he would cooperate in every way possible. Former Senator Barry Goldwater, in a speech delivered to members of the Prima County Republican Club, criticized the Lyndon Johnson administration in general, and Attorney General Ramsey Clark in particular, for failing to deal adequately with organized crime in America, and Goldwater demanded that the "reign of the princes of the Cosa Nostra must end."

In September 1968 there were four more bombings in Tucson: one was at an automobile company said to be patronized by hoodlums; a second was at a women's wig salon that employed Mrs. Charles Battaglia; a third was at the home of a man associated with a mob-connected vending machine distributor; a fourth was at the home of an individual who had been one of Joseph Bonanno's character witnesses in Bonanno's citizenship case in 1954.

By October, as the anti-Mafia campaign continued and a citizen's crime commission was formed, it was estimated that at least one-fourth of Tucson's 250,000 residents had heard at least one blast. Among the many speeches by politicians expressing alarm, only one man publicly doubted that the Mafia was involved in the bombings: he was G. Alfred McGinnis, a Republican candidate for Congress from the Second District, who postulated that youths might be responsible, using the situation for the bizarre kick of playing cops and robbers. McGinnis explained that he had lived in New York and Chicago during periods of Mafia warfare, "and I can tell you this—those guys are pros and when they bomb a home or a neighborhood, it does not result in a few broken windows or a damaged patio."

None of Bonanno's men or Licavoli's offered any comment on McGinnis's theory, although they did know at this time that the bombing missions were being directed not by mafiosi or thrill-seeking youths but rather by a private agency of some sort whose personnel included a dark-haired woman. It was Bill Bonanno who discovered this toward the end of the summer after one of his men, equipped with a walkie-talkie and hiding behind a bush one night, saw a slow-moving car with its lights off heading up East Elm Street. On receiving the warning, Bill ran out of the house with his shotgun, crouched in the shadows, and waited as a cream-colored 1967 Chevrolet sedan came closer. The car almost slowed to a stop in front of the Bonanno home, and, after the window opened on the passenger's side, Bill saw the woman toss out a package that rolled under one of the cars that was parked at the curb.

Because it was a woman, Bill did not shoot; but he did get a look at the car's license number and a quick glimpse of the woman and man as they drove away. He waited, flat against the ground, expecting the package to explode at any second. When it did not, he jumped to his feet and dashed into the house. He waited with the other men for several minutes, but it still did not go off.

Later one of the neighbors on East Elm Street saw the package, picked it up, and, without looking inside to examine its contents, brought it to the Bonannos' front door and presented it to Mrs. Bonanno. She accepted it with thanks, saying that she had probably dropped it out of her shopping bag as she returned from the market earlier. Inside, bound with tape, were six sticks of dynamite. The fuse, apparently lit in great haste, had burned out too early to cause detonation. One of the men disposed of the dynamite outside the house, and no report was made to the police.

But on the following day, after checking the license number with a Bonanno source in the motor vehicle bureau in Phoenix, it was determined that license number JBW-110 registered a 1967 Chevrolet sedan owned by the Deluxe Importing Company of 5001 North 40th Street in Phoenix. Bill sent his brother, Joseph, to Phoenix to learn what he could about the company, but his brother returned late that afternoon from the 260-mile trip complaining that there was no such address in Phoenix. All that he could find in the approximate area was a vacant lot.

This was when Bill began to suspect that a private agency was behind the bombings; and he became even more strongly convinced of this a week later when Peter Notaro called to say that, while having a beer at Gus & Andy's Bar, he overheard two strangers knowledgeably discussing the bombings, and he noticed that the car they were driving was a cream-colored 1967 Chevrolet. However, the license number was JBW-109, one number lower than the one Bill had seen.

After checking this number with the source in Phoenix, Bill was told that it, too, was registered to the Deluxe Importing Company, but the address was given as 4008 North 48th Street. Bill again sent his brother to Phoenix to see what was at that address, and when Joseph returned he reported that the only thing he saw near the address was Camelback Mountain.

Still later, Bill learned from his friend in the license bureau that there were a series of license numbers registered to the Deluxe Importing Company, and Bill no longer had any doubts that he was facing formidable opposition. He suspected that the

Deluxe Importing Company was a front for the CIA or FBI. But both he and his father agreed that they should do nothing with the information at this time; they should remain calm, alert, and try not to overreact, although that was admittedly difficult under the circumstances.

A few weeks before, in late September, Bill, apprehensive and suspicious, had pointed a gun at a man who sat in a car parked outside Peter Notaro's home. The man was a policeman in an unmarked car. Bill was arrested. Freed on $300 bond, Bill returned home, furious at what he regarded as police harassment; and then a week later he was arrested again, this time for speeding. Bill emphatically denied the charge, telling the policeman that he had been driving cautiously because he was aware that the policeman had been following him for several miles. But when the case came up in city court in late November, Bill Bonanno was found guilty by Magistrate Hyman Copins, who fined him fifteen dollars and said that Bonanno had been so intent on being "tailed" that he had failed to pay attention to the traffic signs and to a second police vehicle that was following him and clocking his speed.

Bill's problems with the law became exceedingly worse in December when he learned that he was being charged in a federal indictment with having stolen Don A. Torrillo's Diners' Club card to finance the trip that Bill had made to the West during the previous February with his uncle Di Pasquale and Peter Notaro. The indictment accused Bill Bonanno and Notaro of conspiracy, perjury, and fifty counts of mail fraud. The multiple charges of mail fraud had been compiled because each charge slip bearing Torrillo's name, forged by Bonanno or Notaro, traveled by mail between the locale of the business transaction and the Diners' Club office that paid the bills. A government spokesman was quoted in the newspapers as saying that if Bonanno were found guilty of each count, he could get up to 220 years in prison and fines of $65,000; and Notaro could receive 215 years and fines of $63,000. The late Sam Perrone, who had obtained the card from Don Torrillo and had assured Bill that Torrillo had willingly agreed to its use, was cited in the indictment as a co-conspirator.

Bill was depressed but not surprised by the news. When his lawyers had been unable to reach Torrillo after Perrone's murder and when Bill had learned that Torrillo was conferring with detectives, Bill sensed that his legal position was precarious. All in all, 1968 had been a very bad year. He had lost his Arizona tax case and owed the government about $60,000; he had almost no chance of regaining his Arizona property or his home in East Meadow; he was involved in a war in New York, bombings in Arizona, and was facing a federal case in which the newspapers claimed he could get 220 years. It was so preposterous it was laughable, except it was not very funny to him.

Among other developments in 1968 was the report from New York that Frank Mari, Di Gregorio's triggerman, the man who had allegedly led the fusillade on Troutman Street and had accomplished the murder of Sam Perrone, had suddenly vanished in mid-September with his bodyguard and another man, and now all three were presumed to be dead.

PART THREE

THE FAMILY

18

THE RED RANCH-STYLE house that Rosalie Bonanno rented in San Jose was not unlike the one that she had left in East Meadow, but her new neighbors in California seemed to be more friendly and open-minded, not the type that would ostracize her and the children because of the notoriety attached to the Bonanno name. At first she suspected that they did not associate her with the name in the headlines; but then, shortly after she had settled in San Jose, the local newspapers reported, prominently, that Bill Bonanno, who with his wife and children was renting a house at 1419 Lamore Drive, had been charged with stealing and illegally using a Diners' Club card, and was believed to be engaged in gangland activities in the East and West. Rosalie was initially worried by the publicity, fearing that the short-term lease on the house might be canceled, that her children's new friends might turn on them, and that the teen-age girl who lived a few doors away, and had been baby-sitting, might be prohibited by her parents from returning.

But none of these things happened, and it was not because the people in San Jose were unaware of who she was; in fact on the evening after the newspaper articles had appeared, Rosalie attended a class in computer programming that she had just joined, and the students asked her questions about it, displaying not disapproval, as she would have expected, but curiosity and friendship toward her. She was surprised and pleased.

She enjoyed the computer class, which she was attending on Tuesday and Thursday evenings, not only because she had long felt the need to get out of the house and meet new people, but because she was now finally preparing herself for a career. If her husband was to be convicted in the credit card case, a case that would surely come to trial within the year, she might have

to help support herself and the children after Bill had gone to
jail. Computer programmers were in demand in the San Jose
area, a busy center of modern corporations—IBM, Ford, General Electric's atomic power department, Lockheed's Polaris
missile project, and several other companies with defense contracts and ties to the Pentagon. It was an ultra-new, almost fu-
turistic community that had been built over what had once been
a Spanish pueblo, later a dried-fruit-packing center at the foot
of the San Francisco peninsula; but now it was populated by
electronics technicians, nuclear physicists, engineers, aircraft
workers; and at night, as Rosalie drove along the highway between San Jose and San Francisco, she could see large glass-
walled factories with bright lights glowing in rooms without
people, and she could imagine the soft clicking sounds of busy
computers.

The wide highways that she used were newly paved and without the cracks and potholes that had characterized the roads in
New York; the commuter traffic in the late afternoon seemed to
consist entirely of new cars, and the ranch-style houses that
lined the quiet streets back from the highways were freshly
painted and equipped with the latest modern gadgets, fixtures,
and appliances. Rosalie wanted to own such a house, and recently she had visited sample houses in a new development and
had been awed by the freshness and glow of everything she had
seen—the polished brass doorknobs, the aluminum sash windows, the sliding glass doors to the patio and pool, the elegant
modern furniture with colorful cushions that had filled her with
a sense of opulence and comfort. She had also been amazed,
while walking from house to house along the sample block, that
no guards were standing by to prevent visitors from damaging
or stealing the transportable furniture, the silverware, china, and
delicately shaped wine glasses that she had seen on a dining
room table set for a dinner party of eight—she remembered
leaning over and picking up one of the glasses, half expecting it
to be attached by wire or otherwise linked to the table; but it
was not. The linen napkins, the brass ashtrays, the pans and
pots in the kitchen also were free to be handled, as were the
lamps on the tables in the living room and everything else in
the house. This would not have been the case in New York, she
knew, recalling a visit she had made years ago to a sample house
in Long Island and discovering that the lamps were bolted to

the floors, that every movable object was somehow secured to the floors or tables, and that the rugs and furnishings were covered with transparent plastic.

The people that Rosalie had seen in this computerized community in California, those she had observed in shopping centers or at the McDonald's and Kentucky Fried Chicken stands that she visited with the children on Saturday afternoons, also seemed to radiate a special freshness and health; they smiled often, displaying good teeth, and there was never a whiff of garlic on their breath. Rosalie had finally arrived in a portion of America that seemed right out of the television commercials— it was Reynolds-wrapped, polished with Johnson's Wax, filmed in Kodacolor; it all seemed tidy and tradition free. And although no one seemed very rich or ambitious, they gave the appearance of contentment as they lived peacefully in their new houses, greeted their new neighbors, and drove their new cars each morning to work in industries that were geared for the preservation of big business, the conquest of outer space, and the logistics of international war. It was a rather odd place for Rosalie to be awaiting her husband's return from the feudal world of his father.

Bill left Arizona after the bombings had subsided and returned to San Jose in time for Christmas, 1968; and he remained there through the next few months. It rained during most of February, but the California experience continued to please Rosalie, and for the first time in many years she saw her husband drive a car without bodyguards, a sure sign of change.

He seemed moody and restless, however, and he had a calendar of court appearances confronting him in 1969, meaning that he had to remain close to home in anticipation of his attorney's call notifying him of the time and place. Since the courts in New York and Arizona never gave Bill much advance warning and since he was usually given a maximum of forty-eight hours in which to get there if he did not wish to forfeit bail, he was kept constantly on edge and could never make plans.

Among other things, he would have to stand trial in Arizona for having pointed a gun at the police officer who was parked outside Notaro's house, and he would probably also be summoned to testify about the bombings when and if the investigators ever discovered who was responsible. So far he was displeased with the progress made in the bombing inquiry; the FBI's customary vigilance in prosecuting crime seemed a bit slow in this instance, since the agency had possibly discovered what he already knew—the Mafia was not involved. But aside from the fact that he had traced the license plates to the mysterious Deluxe Importing Company and had seen the woman toss the dynamite in front of his father's house, Bill had been unable to learn anything more about the Arizona bombings in the last two months.

In New York, Bill was due to make further appearances before the grand jury that was still delving into the Troutman Street shootings, the Banana War, and organized crime in general; and he also knew that sooner or later he would have to go to trial on the credit card case, a subject that he preferred not to think about. From his daily reading of *The New York Times*, which he purchased at a newsstand not far from his sister's home in Atherton, and from the clippings that someone in New York mailed him occasionally from *The Daily News* and *Newsday*, he could see that the editorial writers were still depicting the Mafia as the main corrupter of society, that the federal government was appropriating large sums of money for the fight on organized crime, and that the small-time mafiosi were struggling as usual, shooting at one another in the street and attempting to scratch out a living.

The FBI announced the arrest of three alleged Bonanno soldiers in connection with the armed hijacking of two trailer trucks loaded with $120,000 worth of cigarettes and other merchandise, and a later search of the suspects' homes uncovered a high explosive bomb and 2,000 rounds of ammunition for rifles, pistols, and shotguns. The death from natural causes of seventy-seven-year-old Matteo Di Gregorio, brother of the ailing Gaspar Di Gregorio, was also given wide coverage in the press, and among the 800 mourners in Lindenhurst, Long Island, were several plainclothesmen and agents who claimed to recognize more than twenty major Mafia figures. The most prominent among them was Carlo Gambino, whose family of more than 700 members was now said to be the largest in New York and in the nation; and the police also spotted men they believed to be affiliated with the Colombo family, the Stefano Magaddino family, and—Bill was not surprised to read—John Morale.

The latest casualty in the continuing Banana War was identified as one of Di Gregorio's men—Thomas Zummo, twenty-nine, who the police said died in a blast of gunfire on February 6, at about 5:00 A.M. as he entered the lobby of his girl friend's apartment house in Queens. His friend, a model, notified the police moments after she heard the shooting, but Zummo apparently died instantly, having been hit by four bullets with five others stuck in the lobby walls. A week later, Bill read that Vito Genovese, seventy-one, had just died of a heart ailment at the Medical Center for Federal Prisoners in Springfield, Missouri.

Genovese, who had begun a fifteen-year sentence in 1960 for narcotics smuggling, would have been eligible for parole in March 1970. He had been transferred to the medical center from the federal prison at Leavenworth two weeks ago, and there was now considerable speculation in the press as to Genovese's successor, the three most likely candidates being Jerry Catena, sixty-seven, the alleged acting boss during Genovese's imprisonment; Michele Miranda, seventy-two, the family's *consiglieri*; and Thomas Eboli, fifty-eight, a onetime prizefight manager who in 1952, after his fighter Rocky Costellani had been ruled knocked out, had jumped into the ring and hit the referee. This triumvirate was said to be directing the Genovese family at present, but there was a fourth contender who might seize control, according to a Mafia expert named Ralph Salerno, a former New York City policeman and currently a consultant to the National Council on Crime and Delinquency. This fourth individual, whom Salerno described as "young and ambitious," was Salvatore (Bill) Bonanno.

Reading this in the San Jose *Mercury*, which had gotten it from the New York wire services, Bill was almost flattered but at the same time irritated: he knew that Salerno's naïveté could cause him additional trouble once he arrived in New York. He knew, as Salerno should have known, that he had absolutely no influence with Genovese's men; and, indeed, Bill had reason to wonder at this time if he had any influence with his *own* men. Nevertheless, Salerno's statement might be believed by a few of Genovese's unhappy triggermen in New York—in this current state of confusion in the underworld, *anything* might seem plausible and the last thing that Bill wanted to do was to arouse more envy and resentment among the men in the street.

Still he could not help but be affected by the status accorded him by the Mafia expert Salerno; it was something that Bill might even be able to trade on in this secret society where status, power, and the illusion of power were intertwined, flaunted, fought over. During the last year Bill had become sensitive to newspaper reports emphasizing the deterioration of the Bonanno organization and his own decline, and it had occurred to him recently that in the past two years he had not been asked by any relative or friend to serve as their children's godfather. This meant nothing and everything to him, for it symbolized the esteem in which he had once been held by other people, deservedly or undeservedly, and was no longer. And yet he knew that in this shifting, unstable little society of which he was a part, his status could rise overnight, could change on the basis of such public comments by men like Ralph Salerno.

Already Bill had sensed the influence of Salerno's words on the men who visited the house earlier in the day to say hello and to ask if there was anything that they could do for him. These men had known the elder Bonanno and had been helpful to Rosalie after she had moved to San Jose with the children, but they had not stopped by in several weeks. Now they had returned, interrupting his breakfast on this Saturday with their good cheer and supplicant manner and the affection they showed the children in the living room. As they waited for Bill to finish breakfast, they sat watching the children playing with plastic airplanes and rockets, and Bill heard his daughter Felippa telling them that when she became older she was going to work as an airline stewardess. Tory, Bill's six-year-old son, announced to the men that he planned to become an astronaut—or a dentist.

"A dentist?" one of the men repeated.

"Yes," said Tory. "My uncle Greg's a dentist, and he knows a lot."

"Well, your father knows a lot too," the man said.

"Yes," Tory agreed, "but he doesn't know the square root of ten."

"Yes he does," said Charles, the eldest son, as Felippa quickly agreed.

"Well," Tory said, "he isn't a dentist."

"What is your father then?" the man asked. In the breakfast room, Bill stopped eating, listened carefully.

"He's a driver," Tory said.

"A *driver*?"

"Yes, he drives a car."

"He does more than that," the man said, egging Tory on.

"He watches television and he drives," Tory said with final-
ity, as the men laughed. Bill was also amused, but not entirely.
He thought it very coincidental that the subject of his occupation
should be discussed by his children at a time when he, too, had
been giving considerable thought as to how he would or could
explain his life to them. Sooner or later, particularly if he went
to jail for a long term, he would attempt to explain himself to
his children, which was something that his own father had never
done with him. Bill recalled that he had been in his teens before
he had understood why his father had been treated with such
formality and respect. Before he understood this Bill had thought
of his father as merely a successful businessman, the owner of
a cheese factory in Wisconsin, a laundry in New York, a dairy
farm upstate, land in Arizona. Would it have made any difference if he had known the "truth" about his father earlier than
he did? Bill doubted it. He had been magnetized by his father,
would have followed him through hell, and when he finally had
perceived the full range of his father's power he had been even
more impressed and proud. But Bill did not expect to be that
persuasive with his own children—he would never be the towering figure to them that his father had been to him; times had
changed, the dynasty was disintegrating, the insularity of Italian
family life would most likely not survive the third generation,
which was probably a good thing for his children. Bill remembered how angry he had become the other night when, while
Rosalie was in computer class, he had returned home to be told
by the baby-sitter that the children had behaved badly; and he
had immediately announced that they would be punished—no
toys or television watching for two days. But later, after they had
gone to sleep, he wondered what right he really had to tell them
anything. He thought that perhaps the less they listened to him,
the better off they would be. He was not sure that he really
believed this, but the thought had occurred to him, briefly, an
infrequent acknowledgment of disquieting self-doubt; and now
again, as he overheard the conversation in the living room, he
wondered about his children and was curious to know their
thoughts about him, what they suspected, what they knew, what
they would admit to knowing.

Later in the day, after the men had left and while Rosalie was
shopping, Bill decided to find out. Opening the patio door, he

called to his eleven-year-old son Charles, who was building a
new rabbit cage out of orange crates and chicken wire. Charles
was constantly improving his skills as a carpenter and maintenance man; he was the one who fixed the flat tires on the bicycles, tightened the loose wheels on Felippa's toy baby carriage,
mowed the lawn and uprooted the weeds. With the Blue Chip
trading stamps that he received from his mother and his aunt
Catherine, he was saving toward an electric lawnmower, planning to earn extra money by tending to neighbors' lawns. Although Charles was a year older than his classmates in the fourth
grade, having been left back once in Long Island, he seemed
neither embarrassed nor contrite when he brought home his latest unimpressive report card for Rosalie to sign. He possessed
almost no competitive spirit as a student, caring mainly about
things for which he would not be tested or graded. He was
interested in animals, birds, and the insects that he was endlessly catching. He was always polite and patient; and though
he was the adopted child and aware of it, he was the one who
seemed most at home in the Bonanno household.

When he heard his father calling him, Charles did not frown
or fret as his brothers might have done; he came immediately,
followed his father into the television room and remained standing as his father closed the door. Tall and thin, with green eyes
and a lighter complexion than his brothers, Charles's gentle good
looks were not marred by the fact that his upper left eyelid
drooped slightly, a congenital defect that did not impair his vision and that a doctor said could easily be corrected with minor
surgery when the boy grew older.

Bill sat down in a black Barcalounger against the wall, looked
at Charles, whom he called Chuckie, and asked: ''Chuckie, do
you know what I do for a living?''

''No,'' the boy said, seeming slightly confused but not upset.

''Does your teacher ever ask you what I do for a living?''

''No,'' said Charles.

''Do you ever wonder yourself?''

''No,'' Charles said, casually.

''You don't give a darn, do you?'' Bill asked lightly.

Charles paused, then said, ''Well, in New York you used to
work in a hardware store.''

''A *hardware* store!'' Bill repeated.

''Well, didn't you?''

"Don't you mean a *warehouse*?" Bill asked.

"Oh, yes, that's what I mean, a warehouse."

"Suppose one of your teachers or someone you know at Cub Scouts asks, 'What does your father do all day?' What would you answer?"

"I'd say that he sits around and watches TV."

Bill smiled. Then he asked, "Do you remember Uncle Hank?" referring to the late Sam (Hank) Perrone.

Charles nodded, and Bill asked, "What did he do for a living?"

"I forget."

"You're not a very cooperative witness," Bill said, raising an eyebrow in mock disapproval. Then Bill continued, "Suppose your scoutmaster asks you a direct question, Chuckie, wanting to know what I do—what would you tell him?"

"I wouldn't tell him anything."

"Why?"

"Because I don't know what you do."

"Why don't you know?"

"You never told me."

"What about money—if you had none, wouldn't you be worried?"

"Yes, kind of."

"But you think I have money, don't you?"

"Yes."

"How do you know?"

"Because lots of times, when I go in your room with Mommy, I see a lot of money."

"You do?" Bill asked, surprised. "Where?"

"On your bureau."

"A lot of money?"

"Sure. Quarters, dimes, I've even seen a jar full of coins."

"You think that's a lot of money?"

"Sure," Charles said, adding, "and you said you were going to buy me some big cages for more rabbits. . . ."

"Next witness," Bill interrupted, telling Charles to send in Joseph.

Joseph was thin and frail, had large brown eyes and long lashes. He was competitive by nature and there would have probably been continuous discord between Joseph and his older brother if Charles were less conciliatory. The fact that Joseph was so often ill with asthma and unable to exert himself physically influenced their relationship, and much of Joseph's discontent was no doubt attributable to the frustration of having to gasp for each breath.

But despite Joseph's condition and his frequent absences from school, he seemed to have no difficulty in keeping up with his class. He read constantly when confined to bed, and he spent hours working on crossword puzzles. He was curious and aware and had already expressed confusion about Bill's unusual business hours and unpredictable routine. Joseph had not yet asked direct questions about it, but Bill suspected that when the time came for him to explain his way of life, Joseph would have already figured it out; and Bill wondered at this moment whether it was desirable to pursue this little game with his most sensitive son, who now stood before him, unsmiling. Bill decided to proceed with caution.

"What grade are you in, Joey?" Bill asked.

"Third."

"Do your teachers ever ask what I do?"

"Yes," he said.

Bill hesitated for a moment; but then he went on, "What do you tell them?"

"Mom once told me you were in the trucking business," Joseph said. "That's what I tell them."

"What do you mean by trucking business—do you know what I do?"

"You drive around, I guess."

"Did you ever see me in a truck driving around?"

"No," Joseph answered, "but Tory said once you gave him a ride in a truck."

"Yes, that's true," Bill said. "We went to the warehouse one day. But what do I do now?"

"I don't know," Joseph said, slowly, seeming suddenly tense. "But I know you're not in the trucking business."

Bill looked at Joseph standing uncomfortably in the middle of the room. Bill stopped the questioning. He was sorry he had indulged his curiosity in this manner, but decided to finish what he had started with his children as hastily as he could. Abruptly thanking Joseph, he asked that Tory be sent in.

Tory, six years old, had a round angelic face and bright brown eyes, and of the four Bonanno children he was clearly the most personable and entertaining. He was also clever, and he could worm his way out of punishment he deserved by offering ridiculous, funny excuses. One recent evening after supper, Tory asked his mother if he could go outside and play, to which Rosalie replied, sharply, "It's seven o'clock!" Later, after Rosalie caught a glimpse of Tory playing on the sidewalk with other boys and rushed out to grab him and scold him for disobeying her, he pleaded innocently, "But you didn't say I couldn't go out—you just told me what time it was!"

Tory was also skillful at finding loopholes in the family rules that were an attempt to regulate his rough behavior toward Felippa, who was one year younger and was constantly provoking him, secure in her knowledge that her father had warned Tory against ever laying a hand on her. Invariably, on leaving the house for an overnight trip, Bill would remind Tory: "Now remember, I don't want you to be hitting your sister while I'm away," and Tory would usually to nod in agreement. But a few weeks ago, shortly after Bill returned from a weekend out of town, he saw Tory swatting Felippa on the head because she had deliberately scribbled across his coloring book. Bill grabbed Tory, but before Bill could say anything, Tory blurted out his explanation: "You said I couldn't hit her when you were away—well, *now* you're home."

As Tory walked into the room wearing a football helmet, with dirt on his face, Bill was reminded of the comic strip character Sluggo. Bill smiled and asked: "Tory, did anybody ever ask you what I do for a living?"

"No," Tory said.

"Did you ever think about what kind of work I do?"

"No."

"Do you remember Uncle Hank?"

"Yes."

"What kind of work did he do?"

"I don't know."

"Don't you remember the warehouse?"

"Oh, yeah."

Tory started to pick his nose, and Bill told him to stop it, to stand up straight.

"You remember the trucks, don't you?"

"Yes," Tory said.

"Remember when we took a ride?"

Tory nodded.

"Well, where do you think Daddy gets his money from?"

"People give it to you."

"Do people give you money?"

"No."

"Why not?"

Tory shrugged, nonchalantly.

"Suppose your teacher asked you what your daddy did—what would you answer?"

"I'd say I didn't know."

"Right," Bill said. "Now send in your sister."

Felippa, who was called Gigi around the house, walked in carrying a doll. Her reddish brown hair was cut in bangs, she wore small gold earrings, and she was very self-assured. She seemed to know, even at the age of five, that there was nothing her father would not do for her. If she was spoiled, and there was little evidence to refute it, Bill held himself completely responsible, and he would have it no other way. He was totally enchanted with her and he knew that what he would most miss about home—if he had to face a long stretch in jail—would be the uncritical acclaim he always received from his daughter.

"Gigi," he began, "do you know what Daddy does for work?"

"Yes," she said, smiling.

"What?"

"I don't know," she said, starting to giggle.

"Where do I get my money from?"

"From a man."

"Which man?"

"I don't know." She giggled again.

"Remember Uncle Hank?"

"Yes."

"What kind of work did he do?"

"I don't know," she said, and when Bill laughed, she laughed too, running into his arms, and as he hugged her he announced, "Court is adjourned."

19

A FEW DAYS later, Rosalie's mother flew to San Francisco from New York carrying among her luggage a box of live snails that she had personally selected at a Brooklyn fish market, live lobsters from Maine, special Italian sausages stuffed with cheese, and other delicacies that were rare in California and that she intended to serve at a large family gathering on the following day, the first Sunday in March.

The dinner, to be attended by a dozen people, would be held at the home of her daughter Ann, who was in her seventh month of pregnancy, and with whom Mrs. Profaci would be staying in San Jose until after the birth; she would help with the cooking, would look after Ann's two young children, and would also be available for whatever assistance she might provide her eldest daughter, Rosalie, and her youngest daughter, Josephine, who was twenty-one and would be getting married in June, shortly after her graduation from Berkeley.

Josephine would be married in the chapel on the Stanford campus to a non-Catholic, non-Italian, hazel-eyed young man with long blond hair named Tim Stanton, the son of an upper-middle-class family in Westchester County, New York. Josephine had met Tim Stanton at a college barbecue exchange in the spring of 1966 when she was a student at Santa Clara, and during that summer in New York she went with him to the suburbs to meet his parents, an encounter she had dreaded in advance even though, early in their dating, she made it clear to him who her relatives were, learning to her surprise and relief that this precaution was unnecessary; he already knew. The meeting with his parents turned out to be unexpectedly pleasant, because the Stantons succeeded in making her feel welcome and comfortable.

During the next two years, after Josephine had transferred to
Berkeley and as her relationship with Tim Stanton became closer
and there were plans for marriage, it was not Tim's family, but
Josephine's, that seemed the more concerned. That it was to be
a non-Catholic wedding ceremony was most disappointing to
Josephine's mother and older brother; but when they sensed how
determined Josephine was and how inseparable the young couple obviously were, they accepted the inevitable and Josephine's
brother agreed to escort her up the aisle on her wedding day.

The extended family, however, which included Bill Bonanno
and his friends in addition to other in-laws and relatives of the
Profaci's, still expressed doubts about the wisdom of such a
marriage; and by the time of the large family dinner, Tim Stanton had been the subject of several conversations and debates in
Brooklyn and San Jose. They had all met him by now, inasmuch
as Josephine had introduced him at various times during the last
year; and since he was so different from anyone who had ever
approached the family threshold before, he was a subject of both
fascination and confusion.

Some of Bill's friends, reacting to Stanton's long hair and his
casual style of dress, and having heard him denounce the war
in Vietnam and hint at his own refusal to fight if drafted, regarded him quickly if incorrectly as part of a radical new generation that wished to overthrow the system; and in any
showdown with the new generation, Bill's men would be curiously on the side of the system—the government, the police, and
"law and order." These men did not want the system to col-
lapse, for if it collapsed they would topple with it. While they
recognized the government as flawed, hypocritical, and un-
democratic, with most politicians and the police corrupt to a
degree, corruption was at least something that could be understood and dealt with. What they were most wary of and what
centuries of Sicilian history had taught them to mistrust were
reformers and crusaders.

Bill Bonanno's view of the younger generation, however, was
less rigid, and he agreed with Tim Stanton on many issues—
except when he learned that Stanton was thinking of registering
as a conscientious objector or of joining the Peace Corps and
serving in Malaysia with Josephine after the marriage. Bill believed that joining the Peace Corps was "copping out" since it
was subsidized by the same government leaders who were fo-

menting war in Vietnam. If Stanton did not wish to engage in an immoral war, then, according to Bill, he should be willing to pay the price and should go to jail. Jail was the place for many honorable men these days, Bill believed, including himself in such company.

Rosalie was not upset by any of Stanton's political views, but she was distressed that Josephine was marrying outside the church; she preferred that her youngest sister agree to "go along" with the Catholic wedding and the religious beliefs that she had grown up with and ostensibly had accepted until recently. But in this instance, Bill supported Josephine's decision not to give the appearance of believing what she did not; and yet Bill was bothered by Josephine for other reasons, vaguely definable ones that were inspired by his suspicion that Josephine privately detested him. He was perceptive enough to sense that Josephine remembered well certain raging scenes between himself and the Profaci family after Rosalie had left him in Arizona in 1963 and had returned to New York. Josephine had since then seemed quiet in his presence, occasionally suggesting her disapproval by certain gestures and remarks; and Rosalie herself recently said that Josephine had probably decided on a different course with regard to marriage and religion because Josephine had seen how Rosalie had suffered by following the ways of the past. Bill knew of course that he could count on Rosalie not to miss an opportunity to portray herself as some sort of martyr; but he also knew and took pride in the fact that Rosalie's sister Ann had never held a grudge against him—Bill and Ann always got along splendidly, and he had often said in jest at family gatherings that he had married the wrong Profaci.

Ann, though a bit heavy like her mother, had a beautiful face, expressive eyes, and, uncharacteristic for a Profaci, a sense of humor. Ann was an efficient homemaker, a wonderful mother, and, while she was intelligent, she deferred to her husband's judgment; her husband was clearly in charge. But Josephine, Bill was sure, would lead a different life, she was the product of another time. She was the first daughter to finish college, and, without being a feminist, she undoubtedly identified with the cause of modern women seeking greater liberation, which was probably one reason, Bill thought, why she disliked him, for he typified everything that she as a modern young woman undoubtedly rejected—he was the dominant Sicilian male who did as he pleased, came and went as he wished, unquestioned, the inheritor of the rights of a one-sided patriarchal system that the Bonannos and Profacis had lived under for generations.

But at this point, in March 1969, with his mother-in-law visiting San Jose, Bill Bonanno was not eager for any further friction with the Profacis; and at the Sunday dinner that Mrs. Profaci was preparing, and at which Josephine would be present and perhaps also Tim, Bill decided that he would be on his best behavior.

In the morning, however, Bill woke up with a mild headache, and as he went out to the patio with the Sunday newspapers and a book under his arm he noticed that two of Charles's rabbits had broken out of their pens, had dug into the flower garden, and were now chasing one another wildly around the backyard. The yard was also littered with toys and pieces of wood.

"Rosalie!" Bill yelled to his wife in the kitchen. "Is Chuckie getting out of bed today?"

"He's not feeling well, and I thought I'd let him sleep for a while."

"I want him to clean up this mess out here and catch these rabbits!"

"He's not feeling too well," she repeated, her voice rising. "What do you want me to do?"

"I told him three times this week I wanted this place fixed up," Bill said, sitting down on a patio chair in the midmorning sun and putting on his dark glasses. He had stayed up half the night reading the book that he held in his hands, a new novel about the Mafia called *The Godfather*. He was half-finished, and so far he liked it very much, and he thought that the author, Mario Puzo, had insight into the secret society. Bill found the central figure in the novel, Don Vito Corleone, a believable character, and he wondered if that name had been partly inspired by "Don Vito" Genovese and by the town of Corleone, which was in the interior of western Sicily southeast of Castellammare. Bill believed that his own father possessed many of the quietly sophisticated qualities that the writer had attributed to Don Vito Corleone, and yet there were also elements in the character that reminded Bill of the late Thomas Lucchese. Lucchese in real life, like Don Vito Corleone in the novel, had influential friends in Democratic political circles in New York during the 1950s, men who reportedly performed special favors for generous political contributions; and in 1960, Lucchese went to Los Angeles to mingle with some of these friends who were attending the Democratic National Convention. Lucchese favored the nomination of John F. Kennedy, but other dons such as Joseph Profaci, influenced partly by an immigrant Sicilian's traditional suspicion of the Irish, were against Kennedy. Most Irish politicians, like Irish priests and cops, would do no favors for the Italians, whom, in Profaci's view, they privately abhorred—a view that Lucchese did not share, nor did Frank Costello, who had been on intimate terms with William O'Dwyer. But after Kennedy became president and after the Irish Mafia rose to power, and when only Valachi among Italians achieved fame in Washington, many mafiosi asserted that Profaci had been right.

The Sicilians described in *The Godfather*—not only Don Vito Corleone and his college-educated son Michael (with whom Bill identified) but other characters as well—were endowed with impressive amounts of courage and honor, traits that Bill was convinced were fast deteriorating in the brotherhood. The novel was set in the years following World War II, and in those days the Mafia was probably as the novelist described it; and, as Bill continued to read the book, he became nostalgic for a period that he had never personally known. He read on the patio for nearly an hour, then was interrupted by the sound of Rosalie's impatient voice coming from the kitchen.

"Joseph," she yelled, "stop blowing that balloon—I don't want you exerting yourself today!"

Bill resumed his reading, but was interrupted again by Rosalie who stood at the patio door saying that she was going with the children to Ann's house to help prepare dinner. Bill, who had an appointment with a man at noon, would join her there later.

"Now don't be late," she called, as she turned to leave.

"I won't," he said, waving at the children, and saying nothing to Charles about the condition of the yard or the fact that the rabbits were running loose somewhere behind the small bushes and plants. Bill would deal with that tomorrow.

He read for another half hour, then got up to shave and get ready for his appointment. He was dressed casually on this Sunday, looking as if he were headed for the golf course. He wore light blue slacks and brown loafers, and glaring from under his gray sweater was a Day-Glo orange shirt. In the kitchen, after pouring himself a cup of coffee, he decided to telephone Brooklyn and say hello to his aunt Marion and his uncle Vincent Di Pasquale, with whom he would again be staying when he reappeared before the Kings County grand jury in a few weeks. That the phone was tapped was of no concern to him now, since he would be saying nothing of importance on this call; but after his aunt Marion had picked up the receiver, Bill heard a series of clicking sounds and various extensions being picked up, and he called out, "Hey, how many people are on this phone?"

"Hello," his aunt said in a voice he could barely hear, and he also heard his cousin Linda on the bedroom extension in the Brooklyn house, with a child crying in the background.

"Is that you, son?" his aunt Marion asked, a childless woman who had always called him son. "Is that you?"

"Yes," Bill said, "it's me and the FBI on my end, and on your end it's you and Linda and the baby and probably Aunt Jeanne upstairs and the New York detectives, right?"

"Hello," said Linda, "how's everybody there?"

"Fine," Bill said. But before he could say much to Linda, his aunt Marion, a woman in her late sixties who kept abreast of nearly every trivial detail concerning the several relatives of the Bonannos, the Labruzzos, the Bonventres, and other kin and *compare* at home and overseas, had several things to say; among them was that her back ailment was improving, that Bill's uncle's cold was no better, that her nephew was doing well in art class, that the weather was chilly, that the television set needed a new tube, and other bits of vital information that Bill knew would fascinate the federal eavesdropper who was recording this conversation for posterity.

Mrs. Profaci stood at the stove cooking the snails, the lobsters, and preparing the ravioli, while Rosalie and Ann helped her, and Josephine sat in the living room with the men. Ann's husband, Lou, was serving drinks, and the six children were running through the house, which was handsomely furnished and had a guitar near the fireplace that Lou used to play, along with the bass, when he sang professionally in small clubs where he was thought of as a second Russ Colombo. A relaxed, genial man approaching forty, Lou was now in business and sang only in the shower. But he appeared to have no regrets, was happily

married and on good terms with his mother-in-law, delighted
that another child was expected, and seemed to be unaware of
the noise the children were now making as they scampered
through the room out toward the patio. Lou noticed that his little
son Lawrence was waving a toy pistol that Bill had given him;
and while Lou knew that his wife did not like even toy guns in
the house, he said nothing.

Bill was not yet at the house, nor was Tim Stanton. Tim would
probably be late and they would not wait for him before starting
dinner; but there was no question of going ahead without Bill.
Until he arrived and greeted the assemblage, all would wait and
talk among themselves, never thinking of sitting around the table
without him, for in many subtle ways Bill was regarded as the
head of the family.

He walked in shortly before 2:00 P.M., followed by another
man and also by Catherine's husband. Catherine was in Tucson
with her children visiting the elder Bonannos; she would be
returning by plane later in the evening. Bill greeted his mother-
in-law and Ann cordially in the kitchen, nodded toward Rosalie,
then continued into the living room, where Lou got up to pat
him on the back and mix him a drink. Josephine, who sat wearing bell-bottomed trousers, a white sweater, and the round-toed
shoes that were the latest fashion, focused her dark eyes on Bill
momentarily, then announced with just the slightest edge,
"Well, the man has arrived, and now we can eat."

Bill forced a smile, ignoring a reply, and then Rosalie, removing her apron, came in and sat down, and Lou fixed her a
drink. From the kitchen could be heard the rattling sound of
snail shells cooking in the pot, reminding Rosalie of the large
family feasts from her girlhood days when her uncles Joseph
Profaci and Magliocco had been alive, and she remembered that
when the live snails were left in the sink and ignored while other
food was being prepared, they would sometimes slowly crawl
up from the sink and would begin to climb the walls. Bill rem-
inisced about those days too, about Magliocco's voracious ap-
petite, and the extraordinary sight of Magliocco, who weighed
about 300 pounds and was not very tall, gracefully mounting a
horse each morning and galloping around the estate at East Islip.
When Mrs. Profaci stood smiling in the doorway, indicating

that dinner was ready, everyone was seated, and steaming plates were passed around the table. Bill inhaled the aroma of the food spread before him, and after tasting the snails, he complimented Mrs. Profaci and lifted his wine glass in a toast. Then he proceeded to tell everyone about the new book that he was reading, *The Godfather*, which none of the others had heard of; and after describing a few dramatic passages, Ann said, "Boy, that sounds like a wonderful organization—I'd like to join it as a gun moll."

"You should," Bill said, "you've got good recommendations."

Everybody laughed except Josephine, who did not look up from her plate.

Mrs. Profaci said that she had recently seen *The Brotherhood* at Radio City, starring Kirk Douglas, but before she could offer her opinion of it, Bill interrupted to say that it was one of the most stupid films ever made.

"There's this ridiculous scene in the end where two brothers kiss, and then one brother takes a gun and shoots the other," Bill said. "It's real Hollywood crap."

Mrs. Profaci, without refuting him, said nonetheless that she had been moved to tears during one scene when a character was identified as Turiddu, which was what her late husband had been called. Even as she repeated the name now, at the table, her voice became soft, and she said, "May his soul rest in peace."

Her husband had been a kind and loving man, Mrs. Profaci continued, after a pause, although she did admit that he had been extremely strict and that his rules had been especially hard on Rosalie, the first-born daughter. Mrs. Profaci remembered one evening many years ago when, because her husband was expected to be out of town for a few days, she permitted Rosalie to accept a date to attend a dance with a West Point cadet. But just as Rosalie was about to leave the house, dressed in a beautiful gown, her father unexpectedly appeared, and he immediately demanded to know where she was going. Mrs. Profaci, trying to seem casual, had explained that Rosalie was joining other young girls at a dance, adding that she would be home early; but Mr. Profaci, furious, insisted that his daughter return to her room and change her clothes—she would be going nowhere on this evening.

As Mrs. Profaci recounted the incident now, more than fifteen years later, there was silence at the table. Then Rosalie stood and turned toward the sink, carrying a few dishes.

The next course was ravioli, and Lou poured red wine in the glasses as Bill tasted the ravioli. His expression changed slightly, and he said to Lou, who sat next to him, "I think it's not cooked enough. Mine is a little hard."

Lou tasted the ravioli from his plate, and agreed that it was hard. Mrs. Profaci, who did not seem at all perturbed, offered to cook the ravioli a bit longer, but Josephine from the opposite side of the table disagreed, saying after she had sampled it, "It's very good, Mom. I like it hard."

Bill looked at Josephine, measuring her for a moment, and then he said with a grin, "Oh, you like it *hard*, do you?"

Josephine looked directly at Bill, having caught the double entendre immediately, and she replied, "Yes, Bill, I like it hard."

Ann laughed and then changed the subject by focusing on Bill's Day-Glo orange shirt: "That's some shirt you're wearing, Bill, that's quite a color."

"It's designed for men who stand on aircraft carriers, and flag down planes," he said. "It makes a wonderful target, which is why I don't wear it in New York."

This got a laugh around the table, and then Bill asked one of the men if he had heard any news from New York. When the man said he had not, Bill frowned and said, "I'm going to make a call."

Ann again addressed Bill, asking in a good-humored chiding way, "Why do you people spend so much money on phone calls? Why don't you write a letter once in a while?"

"*What*," Bill exclaimed, laughing, "and put it in writing!"

They continued to eat the ravioli, which Bill had not permitted his mother-in-law to cook longer, preferring to drop the subject. And then Mrs. Profaci noticed a car pulling up in the driveway—Tim had arrived, and Josephine stood to greet him at the door. While the others continued to eat and Bill told a joke, the young couple spoke between themselves for a few moments in the vestibule; then Josephine, followed by Tim, returned to the table. Lou and Bill and the other men stood to shake hands, and Tim greeted them by name. He had met Bill and Lou many times before and he seemed poised and particularly pleased to see Mrs. Profaci, who had already met his parents and was on friendly terms with them. A chair was obtained for Tim, and he squeezed in next to Josephine. He was wearing chinos and boots, and a button-down shirt under his sweater, and his blond hair was long but neatly barbered. As Bill looked across the table at Tim, he was reminded of the fact that Tim resembled the photographs of Robert F. Kennedy years ago when Kennedy had been the attorney general.

As Mrs. Profaci got Tim a plate of food, and Lou poured him a glass of wine, the conversation became more general; but Josephine, who was holding Tim's hand underneath the table, turned to him and soon they were speaking softly to one another, ignoring the other conversations. They were a typical young couple about to be married, completely absorbed in themselves and only remotely aware of the rest of the family around them. Occasionally Mrs. Profaci or Rosalie or Ann would pass a serving dish of food toward Tim but they tried not to interrupt the private conversation. They were very happy that Josephine seemed happy, were pleased about the coming marriage despite whatever reservations they had once expressed. Josephine Profaci was going off in a new direction, was breaking with many traditions and customs of her family, but her older sisters and her mother were secure in their belief that the love they shared with Josephine would keep them close no matter how far she moved in the future from the familiarity of their past.

After coffee was served, Josephine and Tim stood and said that they had to be getting back to their respective campuses. Both had schoolwork to do that night, they said, and Tim, an English major, further explained his hasty departure to the Bonannos and Profacis: "I've got a paper due on Lear."

20

DESPITE THE FACT that he owed the government a small fortune in back taxes and claimed to be bankrupt because all his property and other assets had been confiscated by Internal Revenue agents, Bill Bonanno walked into the Brooklyn Supreme Court Building on Monday morning, April 14, wearing an expensive pair of alligator shoes, a new green suit that had cost $250, and displaying a broad smile and a deep suntan. Should anyone remark on his tan, he would reply that he had been playing golf every afternoon at Pebble Beach in California; but this explanation would be as false as the front he was presenting at this moment as he strolled jauntily out of the elevator on the sixth floor and headed toward the courtroom, seeing ahead of him at the end of the corridor the pale, grim face of John Morale and other dour-looking men from the Di Gregorio camp who reportedly had spent a miserable winter hiding indoors in New York. Bill hoped that he would make them more miserable by presenting to them today his own sunny portrait of good health and prosperity.

There was little else that could be accomplished during this visit to Brooklyn, for he had known even before leaving California that his attorney, Albert Krieger, would be occupied for weeks with a trial in Staten Island, which would result in the rescheduling of Bill Bonanno's appearance until sometime in May; but even so, he was ordered by the court to come in person to Brooklyn to deliver the affidavit that Krieger had signed. While Bill had no choice in the matter, he decided that he would at least make an impressive entrance in Brooklyn, and he had begun during the previous week by sunning himself in his backyard in San Jose, by selecting his most flamboyant wardrobe to wear in court, and by planning to exhibit in the corridor a carefree spirit that might perturb those codefendants who had defected but who, according to the latest rumors, were now unhappy with the shortage of money and weak leadership that they were experiencing under Di Gregorio's successor, Paul Sciacca. The sidewalk shooting in the Bonanno feud had stopped, the cold war phase had now begun.

When Bill was almost to within speaking distance of Morale and the others huddled in the corner, he heard a girl's voice calling out his name. Turning, he saw Krieger's pretty young secretary carrying the legal papers that Bill was to take in to the clerk or the judge. Bill greeted her warmly, putting an arm around her. Then he asked in a voice loud enough to be heard across the corridor, "Jane, how long do you think this'll take?"

"It shouldn't take more than a few minutes," she said.

"Good," he said, "because I really want to get out of here."

"What's your hurry?" she asked, lightly. And it was the question he had hoped for.

"I have this golf date tomorrow at Pebble Beach," he said, casually, "and I'd like to keep it." He perceived through the corner of his eye that the men were listening and were pretending that they were not.

"Well, Bill, you really look great," Jane went on, looking at his new suit and his silk tie and the white shirt that accentuated his tan.

"Why shouldn't I?" he asked, shrugging his shoulders. "I don't have a care in the world out there. No responsibilities, no worries. The biggest problem I have, really, is getting to the course on time."

She laughed, and stood waiting for another moment. Then, looking at her watch, she said that she had better be getting back to the office.

"Listen," he said quickly, "why not wait for me for a minute? I've got to go to the city anyway, and I'll drop you off."

"I can't be late, Bill," she said. "Al will be calling in, and I have a thousand things to do."

"Don't worry about Al," he insisted. "I'll be quick." He turned and headed toward the courtroom, the papers in hand, and with a smile he called over to the men, pleasantly, "Good morning, gentlemen."

They looked up, startled, and two of them replied, less pleasantly, "Good morning."

Bill was not detained for more than five minutes at the clerk's counter, and after he left the courtroom he put his arm around Jane and escorted her down the corridor toward the elevator, pausing only to say, "Good-bye, gentlemen." There was no reply. The trip from California had been worth it.

A man was waiting for Bill at the elevator, and another sat waiting in a car outside the court building. They drove over the bridge to Manhattan and left Jane at Krieger's office on lower Broadway; then they drove uptown.

Bill had little fear of being followed and fired upon by his enemies in New York on this sunny spring day because he and they knew that they were undoubtedly being closely observed by government agents and detectives. Dozens of investigators were now assigned to the Banana War in an attempt to solve the murders and shootings of the past three years; and because of this tight police surveillance, the men knew it was unwise to carry guns, and they recently had recognized a temporary unofficial truce.

One of the vexations of membership in a declining and divided Mafia family was that the FBI and police maximized their efforts on it as they minimized the pressure on the stronger organizations—the weaker ones offered greater opportunities for infiltration, arrests, ultimate convictions. A declining organization had many unhappy, disillusioned members who felt betrayed and frantic, and such men might be converted into informers if the right deal was offered by law enforcement authorities.

Bill Bonanno did not know how many men could be trusted among the Bonanno loyalists in New York at this point, a group of indeterminate size under an old friend of his father's named Natale Evola, who had been an usher at the elder Bonanno's wedding in 1931. The Di Gregorio–Sciacca faction and a third group said to be under Philip Rastelli were also of uncertain size and were equally determined to remain out of sight and out of the headlines during this period that they regarded as a government inquisition. And so Bill felt very secure after leaving the courthouse in Brooklyn and crossing the bridge into Manhattan, believing that he was undoubtedly being followed by an unmarked government car that he would not try to avoid. Since he had no intention of meeting with any of his father's men on this trip and since the few friends and relatives that he would be seeing in New York could not be linked to the Mafia, he had nothing to hide and little to fear if he remained cautious and alert.

Parking the car in a garage near Thirty-fourth Street and Fifth Avenue, Bill Bonanno walked into Altman's department store, where he had promised to buy a dress that Rosalie saw advertised in Sunday's *New York Times*. He had in his pocket the advertisement that Rosalie had clipped, and also her attached note that read: "Size 12-M, blue-orange print, V-neck, long sleeves. Sixth floor at Altman's in Misses Dress Dept."

On the sixth floor, Bill Bonanno was greeted by a perfumed atmosphere and dim blue light and the sight of mini-skirted salesgirls standing among the racks of clothes. The decor resembled a discotheque, with multicolored lights racing along one wall and rock 'n' roll music blaring from a large stereo jukebox in the corner. Bill paused momentarily, then walked slowly toward the jukebox. He studied it for a second, bent down, and looked along the sides to see if it bore a label that would mark it as one of Thomas Eboli's machines. Eboli had jukeboxes in Greenwich Village bars and in several places uptown, but apparently, he had not yet made it with the Misses Dress Department at Altman's.

As Bill turned around, he saw a middle-aged woman standing behind him, glaring at him through her rhinestone harlequin-framed glasses, and she said to him curtly, "May I help you, young man?" It's just my luck, he thought—in a store filled with sexy young salesgirls, I attract the one old battle-ax who has been at Altman's since the First World War.

"My wife wants this dress," he said, handing the woman the advertisement. "She wants it in a size 12-M and blue-orange print." The woman took the advertisement, and within a few moments she returned with a flimsy garment draped over her arm.

"This is it," she said, holding it up for Bill to see. It was really a dress with pants, which Bill had not realized, and he did not think that Rosalie would look well in it. It was an imitation Pucci print, and the whole outfit looked to Bill like a pair of pajamas; but he told the woman to wrap it, and he was mildly offended by the direct manner in which the woman replied: "Would you pay me first, young man?"

"You don't trust me?"

"Store policy," she said.

He reached into his pocket and handed her two twenty-dollar bills and watched her disappear with the money and the dress. As he stood waiting he thought it odd that he was supposed to trust her when she obviously did not trust him; she had now gone off with his money and the merchandise presumably to record the sale and wrap the garment, leaving him with no proof that he had paid her, and while he realized that he was stretching a point, he was nonetheless irritated by the woman's attitude. If he were dealing in *his* world, he knew that he would never have parted with the money until he had the merchandise in hand; it would have been a simultaneous exchange. But as he thought more about it, he suspected that he was exaggerating the saleswoman's suspicion of him. Or perhaps he was reacting automatically to salespeople, remembering his unhappy experience with Torrillo's credit card at Bloom's store in Tucson. He stopped his brooding when he saw the woman returning with the package; and as he left Altman's he decided that the next time Rosalie wanted a dress, she would buy it herself.

It was mild and sunny along the sidewalk, and since Bill had little to do for the next hour he decided to leave the car in the garage and to take a leisurely stroll through midtown Manhattan, which he had not done in years, and which if he had tried to do a year ago would surely have been suicidal. Although it was not quite noon, he could see that the early-lunch crowd was moving toward luncheonettes and restaurants, and there were people standing at the curb waving and whistling at cabs. There was a pace and pressure about New York that did not exist in San Francisco, Los Angeles, or any other city, and although he had always hated New York, he was at this moment pleased to be back, briefly, knowing that tomorrow he would be gone. He was now a tourist, and as he walked up Fifth Avenue he recited the tourists' favorite cliché, hoping that he would never have to live here again, not as a resident nor as an inmate in a prison.

Everything about New York was more difficult, more expensive, more exhausting. The town was tougher on everyone—cabbies and truckmen, businessmen and waiters, secretaries, and cops and gangsters. People came to New York looking for big money and big deals, but they usually died early as a result—it was a killer town, no less lethal to cops than robbers. Bill guessed that the life expectancy of the mafiosi in New York was less than in other places; those men lucky enough to escape the bullets usually died prematurely of heart ailments. Bill had recently read that Thomas Eboli, fifty-eight, reputed aspirant to Vito Genovese's title, had collapsed at a crime hearing and had been taken by stretcher to a hospital, and Bill was almost willing to bet that there was not a don or underboss approaching sixty in New York who was not suffering from a heart condition or from high blood pressure. Whenever the police searched Mafia officers for concealed weapons, they usually discovered instead small bottles of heart-stimulant pills. Carlo Gambino had a chronic cardiac ailment, and Bill had just heard that Paul Sciacca, fifty-nine, was also suffering from heart trouble, which was one reason why Sciacca was a poor replacement for the ailing Di Gregorio. In the final analysis, it was not only the government that was bothering the Mafia—it was more the day-to-day pressure of living in New York, a pressure unknown to seventy-seven-year-old Stefano Magaddino in Buffalo, or seventy-two-year-old Zerilli in Detroit, or seventy-one-year-old Paul De Lucia in Chicago.

On Forty-second Street Bill headed west toward Times Square, and he was soon surprised to discover how many familiar buildings had been demolished or refaced in this ever-changing city. The Paramount theater, which he remembered as a boy, was gone, and he also regretted that a new building was replacing the once-elegant Astor where his wedding reception had been held.

Turning east again along Forty-second Street, heading back toward the garage, Bill noticed an upper-story sign that identified a travel agency that was partly owned by an old friend, and he decided to go up and say hello. In past years his friend had often tried to interest Bill in certain propositions in the Caribbean and elsewhere, but Bill had always been too busy. But now he was curious whether the offers were still open—in fact, he was more curious about the offers than about specific proposals, realizing that because of the court restrictions on his travel he was really in no position to accept anything; and yet he still wanted to hear what his friend had to say, to know whether or not he was still a friend.

But after he had approached the receptionist, he was told that his friend was out of the city and would not return until the following week. Bill was disappointed but did not show it.

"Is there any message?" she asked.

"Tell him that Bill from California was here, and I'll get in touch with him later."

"Any last name, sir?" she asked, writing on a pad.

"It's not necessary," he said. "Just say that Bill stopped by. From California. He'll know."

The receptionist smiled at him, seemed to be impressed by his suntan, his suit, his manner, the mystery of his name. Bill from California. He smiled back and left.

Less than an hour later, he was in Brooklyn, in another world. The buildings were lower, the sky larger, there was no glamour or mystique about the place—it was a has-been borough of old whites and young blacks, of brownstones gone to seed, and of women sitting in rooms with the shades down, watching television in the middle of the afternoon.

Bill stopped the car in front of a corner brick house on DeKalb Avenue where his uncle and aunt Di Pasquale lived, and he walked up the path to knock on a double-locked door. His aunt Marion, after peeking from behind a curtain, let him into the living room, where his uncle, a slim and distinguished-looking man of about seventy, sat in a soft chair watching television. The uncle stood, quickly put on his jacket, and left with Bill, pleased to be getting out of the house on this sunny afternoon; he was grateful to his nephew for having called and suggested a ride out to Long Island.

Bill wanted to get a look at the East Meadow property, to scrutinize its condition and see if anyone was occupying it. Whether the house was still his was a complex issue not yet resolved by the courts, but Bill did not much care at this point one way or the other, knowing that he would never reoccupy it and knowing that if he were permitted to sell it the government could claim every penny. His trip to Long Island was more in the nature of a personal sight-seeing trip, a pleasant way to pass the afternoon. Although he was committed to spend the evening with the Di Pasquales, where he would be joined for dinner by Frank Labruzzo's widow, he would be leaving tomorrow morning for California, and after that he might not be seeing much of his Brooklyn relatives. It was possible that on his next visit to New York he would be preoccupied with the credit card trial, and he would then be staying in a hotel with his codefendant, Peter Notaro, and would spend most of the time that he was not in court with his attorneys. So he wanted to share what was left of this trip with those few close relatives he had in New York and to revisit certain places where he had once lived and where he had once nearly died. He was no less romantic than many soldiers about the battlefields of the past—except that his were made of concrete and were entrenched with tenements—and a few minutes after he pulled away from the curb at the Di Pasquale house, he approached the block that evoked for him the most haunting memory of his life.

"Remember this place?" his uncle asked, facetiously, as Bill paused at a stop sign, then moved slowly and cautiously forward. It was Troutman Street. At this time of day, in the early afternoon, it seemed abandoned, not a pedestrian in sight or even a car parked at the curb; and because the street was narrow and the tight row of brick and frame houses had no trees in front or much vegetation of any sort, there was something artificial and lifeless about the street—it looked almost like an old movie set. But when Bill reached the end of the block and looked to his right at a store on the corner, he was suddenly aware of the grim reality of Troutman Street. There, along a side wall covered with metal sheeting, were holes made by bullets that had been aimed at him on that freezing January night more than three years ago. He saw other traces of bullets along the sidewalk he remembered running over, running for his life, dashing south toward Knickerbocker, several bullets pounding into the pavement, ricocheting wildly, and as he looked at the street now he was reminded of how narrow it was, and he was amazed that the snipers had missed him from such close range. He felt his palms moist on the steering wheel, and, turning off Troutman Street, he continued to drive through other streets, following no particular direction while he carried on a conversation that he was paying little attention to.

He cruised past the Cypress Garden Restaurant, scene of the triple murder in 1967, and as he paused in front of it now he could see more bullet holes on the sidewalk, and also a sign in the window announcing that the restaurant was closed because its liquor license had been revoked. Continuing on to Roebling Street, Bill saw the spot where his grandfather, Salvatore Bonanno, had opened a bar shortly after arriving from Sicily in 1906, and he saw the public school that his father attended for one year, in 1911, at the age of six. On nearby Havemeyer Street and Metropolitan Avenue were the store-front clubs in which Joseph Bonanno had hung out as a young man in the 1920s, ready to join forces behind Maranzano in the Castellammarese War; and on Suydam Street, Bill drove past the church where his parents were married in 1931; and on Union and Havemeyer was the church where he himself was baptized in 1932, at four months of age. It was remarkable, Bill thought, how it was all here, clustered within so few blocks, the landmarks in the lives of three generations of Bonannos. These were the blocks to which thousands of Sicilian and Italian immigrants had come at the turn of the century to fulfill whatever fantasy they had about the American dream, and Bill remembered from his early boyhood in Brooklyn how noisy and crowded these blocks had been, remembered the pushcarts and games in the street and the mothers calling from tenement windows to their children below; but now, in 1969, the Italian neighborhoods in this area of Brooklyn were no longer characterized by noisy young people in the street but rather by the elderly who remained indoors, securing with locks what was left of their lives. There were still a few mafiosi here, but they too were old, and their children had moved to Queens or to the suburbs to avoid the encroaching blacks and Puerto Ricans and other newcomers who would perhaps find hope and opportunities along these streets that to Bill Bonanno seemed dated and dead.

As he drove, his uncle pointed to a building where he had once been in a partnership in a coat factory, explaining that that was where he met Marion Labruzzo, a seamstress, whom he had married in 1922. They later opened a factory of their own on Jefferson Street, he continued, eventually employing about forty people; he added that this building still existed in its original form and was flanked by what had been Charles Labruzzo's butcher shop and the home that the Labruzzos occupied when Joseph Bonanno began courting Bill's mother, Fay. In those days, the uncle recalled, his eyes lighting up, Joseph Bonanno was driving a new Graham-Paige car. Bill remembered snapshots of that car, and he also remembered very well the Labruzzo house from his boyhood visits to his grandparents'; and, though he was now headed in the opposite direction, he turned around and headed back toward Jefferson Street.

Soon Bill was parked in front of the red-brick house where he used to sit on summer days with his one-legged grandfather, and he remembered how the old man basked in the sun sipping beer, speaking Sicilian to the people who passed, and how when he hobbled up the street on crutches he would be followed by a pet chicken. On the opposite side of the street, where there was once a row of houses—in one of which snipers waited for several weeks in 1929 hoping to get a shot at Bill's father—there was now only a high wall that blocked from view what appeared to be a commercial trucking firm or brewery or warehouse of some sort. To the right of the old Labruzzo house was the onetime coat factory, as his uncle had said, and next to the factory was the building in which Labruzzo's butcher shop was located. Both buildings were now obviously vacant, with the windows of the shop painted black; but the six-bedroom Labruzzo house, which the family sold in 1947 for not much more than the $5,000 that Charles Labruzzo had paid for it in 1923, had curtains on the windows and seemed to be occupied.

Bill got out of the car and walked to the door. Near the bell he saw the name Malendez. He rang the bell, which did not work, and so he knocked on the door. Within a few moments a thin dark man opened the door, looked at Bill, then at the car, his face crinkling with confusion.

"We used to live here," Bill began, awkwardly, trying to smile in a reassuring way.

"Yes?" the man said.

"Many years ago," Bill said, "and we're just visiting New York. I wondered," he continued, "if we could take a look inside."

The man hesitated for just a fraction of a second before saying, "Yes," and then he stepped aside. Bill, who was surprised by the man's lack of skepticism, introduced himself, extending his hand. The man shook it, saying his name was Malendez. Speaking almost perfect English, Malendez explained that the house was now divided into apartments, and since he was the only person at home now, Bill would only be able to see one apartment. Bill thanked him and took only a quick look into Malendez's apartment, failing to find anything familiar about the room. Bill walked through the dark outside hallway, where he noticed the familiar staircase and the smooth banister that he used to slide down as a boy; and looking through a window at the rear of the hallway, he saw the yard where his grandfather kept a goat and several chickens. The yard, littered now with old tires and pieces of scrap metal, seemed smaller than Bill remembered it from his boyhood, and so did the house; but then he guessed that the memories from one's youth magnified everything.

Bill turned and, thanking Malendez again, he departed. When he stepped onto the sidewalk he saw his uncle peering through the windows of the dark empty factory. They both walked to the corner, trying to peek through the blackened windows of what had been the butcher shop, but they could see nothing inside. They were about to turn around and head back to the car, when Bill saw two young Puerto Rican boys walking up Jefferson Street. They were in their early teens, lean and graceful.

"Do you live around here?" Bill asked.

One of them nodded.

"Do you know what's inside this place?"

"I think they make records," one of the boys said.

"What kind of records?"

"You know, music, man. Rock."

"But the place is closed," Bill said. "Nobody's there."

One of the youths regarded Bill suspiciously, looked at the way he was dressed, and then asked, "Hey, man, you a cop?"

Bill said that he was not, and then as they kept walking, he turned toward the car. It was nearly 3:00 P.M. now and Bill knew that he had better start toward Long Island if he intended to be back in Brooklyn before darkness. He did not want to press his luck at night. He drove without delay through several blocks in Brooklyn, crossing quite unintentionally the corner of Leonard and Scholes streets near the spot where Perrone was shot. It has already been more than a year, Bill thought—March 11, 1968, three days after Perrone's thirty-ninth birthday. Perrone's birthday was the same as that of Bill's daughter, Felippa, and Bill knew that from now on he would never be able to look at his daughter's birthday cake without also remembering Hank Perrone.

Within a half hour Bill was in Garden City, moving through the familiar streets that he had so often used in recent years to shake the police or FBI; and then he was in Hempstead, paused in front of the Tudor-style house at 61 Clairmont Street that his father had owned between the years 1936 and 1949. This house, which had obviously been kept in good repair by its present occupants, still had the vacant lot next door where Bill and Catherine had played, and also the birdbath that his father had bought, as well as the row of Christmas trees that his father had planted, uprooting one each December as he replanted another—trees that now were forty feet high.

"That house on the other side, the white one with the shutters, was where my scoutmaster used to live," Bill said, pointing it out to his uncle. And then he inquired with a smile, "You didn't know that *I* was once an honorable Cub Scout, did you?" He continued to reminisce for a moment, the motor idling. Then he stopped talking as his attention was drawn to his rearview mirror, and the car that was coming up the street with two men. It was a tan Chevrolet, and Bill and the others in his car were suddenly alert and waiting silently. But then the other car cruised past, its passengers paying no attention, and so Bill made a U-turn and proceeded on toward East Meadow.

Soon he reentered the quiet residential community that had been his official residence between 1963 and 1968, and moments later as he made a left turn on Tyler Avenue he saw his house. It had been ignored since he left it; the lawn was sprouting weeds and high grass, the bushes grown wild. The lawn had not been cut since Chuckie cut it more than a year ago, Bill thought, and the windows had not been washed in at least that length of time. He was half-tempted to get out and peek in, but when he saw a few neighborhood women walking with their children in his direction, he decided against it. He did not want it known that he had returned; and he was now not as curious about the house as he had been earlier in the day. He guessed that he had already seen too much of his past for one day; and as he looked at it he realized for the first time that he hated this house on Tyler Avenue. It had never been a happy home; in fact, of all the houses he had owned, this had been the center of the most tension and trouble, and it was possible that his troubles with it were not yet over. Bill had heard that the government might try to indict him for tax evasion on this property, inasmuch as he had arranged through Perrone to have the house payments made in Don Torillo's name, which could be defined as a fraudulent transferal of ownership. What he least needed now was another court case, and because of this house he might have one.

Without regret he left East Meadow, heading back to Brooklyn in silence as his uncle slept in one corner of the back seat.

Bill was also tired, emotionally weary. He felt almost as if he had spent the afternoon roving through a graveyard, stepping between withered flowers and headstones bearing the names of his family, his friends, and himself.

At dinner he continued in a quiet mood, despite his best efforts to appear cheerful in front of Frank Labruzzo's widow, and finally his aunt Marion commented on it, saying, "Son, you're so serious—what's the matter with you tonight?" He made a feeble excuse, but she continued to berate him in a way she felt was jovial and not offensive, unaware that she was bothering him, particularly when she said, tossing up her hands, "Oh, you used to be such fun when you came to town. You used to tell jokes and cut up and be the life of the party. What happened?" He continued to deny that he had changed, and after standing up to fill everyone's glass with more wine, he tried to switch the subject. He commented on his aunt's cut-glass wine goblets, saying that they were nicely designed and that his mother in Arizona had a set of glasses similar to these.

His aunt said that she was aware of that, recalling that they had bought the wine glasses from the same place many years ago. But his aunt added that his mother no longer had her set, having written in a recent letter that the glasses were destroyed when the home in Tucson was bombed.

After a late breakfast on the following morning, Bill was driven to the airport to catch the TWA noon flight for San Francisco. Included in his luggage was the dress he had bought for Rosalie at Altman's. As usual, he traveled in the first-class compartment; while he might be able to save between thirty dollars and forty dollars by traveling tourist-class, a saving that he might apply to the overdue milk bill or some other household expense, it would not occur to him to travel in any other way. Until he was down to his last dime, he would not economize in small ways, or live in the style of ordinary people. He was not an ordinary person. He might be many things both good and bad, but he assured himself that he was not ordinary, and he would not even allow himself to *appear* before a planeload of strangers as a man who might be interested in saving thirty dollars or forty dollars. On his epitaph he wanted no ordinary inscription, no hint that he had been a member in good standing with the anonymous multitudes during the mid-twentieth century or that he had saved pennies for a rainy day. He saved coins only for long-distance calls, and it occurred to him at this moment that an appropriate headstone for his grave would be a granite replica of a telephone booth.

Entering the 707 jet, he removed his jacket and handed it to the stewardess; then he sat back in a soft seat in the front row where there was maximum leg room and loosened his tie. After buckling his seat belt, he looked at his watch—it was exactly noon; 9:00 A.M. in California, and Rosalie and the children were up and about, and he was sure that Chuckie's rabbits were still running wild in the yard. Bill was looking forward to getting home, cognizant of the fact that "home" now was a place that he did not know well, San Jose; and he also reminded himself that during his thirty-seven years he had never been in one house for very long. As a child he had moved from place to place like an "army brat"—an infancy in Brooklyn, an early boyhood in Hempstead, then at the age of ten to Tucson where he lived alone in motels, later in the winter homes that his father had rented or bought there at various times, homes that were abandoned during the summers as Bill returned with his family to New York. Perhaps the only home with which he had identified personally was the one in Flagstaff that he and Rosalie had moved into on returning from their honeymoon in 1956. That was the one year in his adult life when he had tried to blend in with what he regarded as conventional society, joining Kiwanis, investing in a small radio station, associating with people who worked nine-to-five. During that period he had gone weeks, sometimes months, without being reminded of his father's activities or his own dark secret. But then the scandal of Apalachin the following year abruptly terminated his masquerading in middle-class America; and since that year, with all his traveling and shifting from one address to another, he began to identify his "home" not in the strict terms of a particular house but rather with the airport in the town in which he was residing. After leaving Flagstaff he was "home" every time his plane landed at the airport in Tucson or Phoenix; or, after 1963, at La Guardia or Kennedy; and now it was the terminal in San Francisco or San Jose.

But at this moment he was obviously going nowhere; his plane was immobile on the runway at JFK, and the stewardess had just announced that there would be a delay due to excessive air traffic. Bill looked out the window and counted at least a dozen planes lined up ahead of the one he was on, flight 41, and he

knew that it might be another hour before takeoff. He thought
again of his aunt Marion's remark at the dinner table last night,
and he was still bothered by it. *Oh, you used to be such fun
when you came to town. What happened?* He knew the time she
was referring to—it was before East Meadow, a period in the
late fifties and early sixties when the Bonanno organization was
thriving, when he had more cash than he knew what to do with,
and more problems than he recognized. He would fly into New
York from Phoenix every few weeks on one pretense or another,
and would take his aunt and other relatives to the Copacabana,
to Broadway shows, to expensive restaurants. He recalled one
night when his bill at the Copacabana was approximately $900,
which he casually paid out of a thick wad in his pocket, loving
the feeling at that moment. It was not a sense of opulence,
power, egotism, or a satisfaction in having so much cash; it was
almost a contempt of money that he had felt, a wanton disregard
for the thing that others craved, an easy-come-easy-go attitude
that mocked the miser in mankind and demonstrated a reck-
lessness about life and a fearlessness about the future—all this
and more had contributed to the private joy that Bill felt on that
night when he had placed nine hundred-dollar bills and a
hundred-dollar tip on a silver tray at the Copacabana, not caring
that the lights were dim and that nobody was watching except
the waiter. Fun. His father had undoubtedly felt the same thing
a thousand times during his lush years, and Bill remembered
hearing of an occasion when, after another man had beaten his
father to a check in a restaurant, a rare instance, his father nonchalantly took the hundred-dollar bill that he held, ripped it up,
and left it in an ashtray.

What piqued Bill about his aunt's remark was the inference
that without his pockets full of money he had lost something of
his character, his humor, his impulsiveness, or whatever it had
been that had made him different from the ordinary people that
were most of his relatives and friends. He thought that his aunt
was wrong—he had not lost his humor, and the fact that he was
officially bankrupt did not bother him. It merely required that
he be extremely careful in how he spent whatever income he
still received from private sources; it meant that he had to borrow money for his air fare, being always prepared to identify
the relatives or friends who lent it to him; and it meant that he
could leave no trace of his other expenses, could not even pa-

tronize the same gas station too often lest the attendant become
a witness to the amount that Bill spent on his car. Without a
sense of humor Bill knew that he could never have slept peacefully at night with the absurd knowledge that at the end of every
day the government added $168 in interest and penalties to the
nearly $100,000 it claimed he owed in various tax suits in Ari-
zona and New York.

After nearly a two-hour delay, the plane was in the air; and
as it rose higher Bill watched the city fading below the clouds,
and one of the last things he saw was a section of Queens that
was once considered Bonanno territory. But now, like so many
neighborhoods in Queens and Brooklyn, it was splintered into
blocks of confusion. He could not remember a time in New
York when there seemed to be so few mafiosi in sight, when
hundreds of men had apparently been driven underground, which
had made it possible for him to do such sight-seeing as he had
done yesterday. If he had done that even a few months before,
he reminded himself that it would probably have been fatal.

The plane ride was smooth and pleasant, and Bill sat reading
Time and *Newsweek* and sipping Chivas Regal Scotch. He also
flipped through a glossy magazine distributed by the airlines and
was amused by one item in a column of jokes and oddities.

> The earth is degenerating these days. There are signs civi-
> lization is coming to an end. Bribery and corruption abound.
> Violence is everywhere. Children no longer respect and obey
> their parents.
>
> —*From an Assyrian tablet, circa 3000* B.C.

After a lunch of filet mignon, he watched the film *Bullitt*,
starring Steve McQueen, in which McQueen played a detective
in a murder mystery that also featured a few Mafia types, one
of whom reminded Bill very much of Sonny Franzese. Unlike
such films as *The Brotherhood*, this film captured certain scenes
of violence that Bill found to be impressively realistic, such as
when a mob informer is riddled with machine-gun bullets in a
hotel room. The most awesome scene in the movie featured a
wild car chase up and down the hilly streets of San Francisco,
with bullets flying and tires screeching, and Bill was aware
throughout the picture of how intently the other passengers were

engrossed in the film. This is what these business executives really like, he thought—bullets in the air, murder at high speed.

Bill was met at the airport, and on the way back to San Jose he stopped at his sister Catherine's house in Atherton. He wanted to know what Catherine thought of their father's recently expressed deliberations about leaving Tucson and buying a house in Atherton, a move prompted by Mrs. Bonanno's anxiety over the prospects of more bombings in Arizona in the future. Even if his father could obtain court permission to leave Arizona, Bill knew that his moving to the exclusive community of Atherton would undoubtedly provoke controversy among certain citizens in Atherton, and it could seriously influence Catherine's social position there, as well as the continued acceptance of her children and husband.

Catherine's husband had through hard work built up a large, prosperous dental practice in suburban San Francisco, and because of his success he had recently gained entrance into social organizations, friendships with the more affluent elements in town, and he had been able to purchase an impressive home surrounded by acres of verdant land and trees. But because of his marriage and his friendship with Bill and the elder Bonanno, his income tax returns were regularly audited, his home and office telephones were believed to be tapped—a supposition more or less confirmed by a friend claiming to be in a position to know—and he and his wife had received considerable unwanted publicity in the press. Both had been subpoenaed by federal investigators after the elder Bonanno's disappearance in 1964, with Catherine being referred to in headlines as the "gangster's daughter"; and both were somewhat concerned about the effect this sort of publicity, if it continued, would have on their three young children.

Still their concern up to now had not prompted either of them to shy away from Bill or any other publicized family member or friend. Since Bill had moved to San Jose, he had been in almost daily contact with Catherine on the telephone or in person, and if a few days passed without her hearing from him she usually took the initiative to find out why. Bill enjoyed a compatibility with her that he had with no other woman. She understood him as Rosalie could not, and she understood his relationship with his father from a position that was curiously both loving and detached. She was a perceptive and wise young woman.

When Bill arrived at her home, passing through two white stone posts and rows of flowers along the driveway, he rang the bell a few times, and after a short delay he heard her voice through the outside intercom. After he identified himself, she came to the door, expressed delight on seeing him, and kissed him on the cheek. Tall, lean, her dark reddish hair teased and coiffed, her dark eyes alert and alive, she explained apologetically that she had been playing the piano as he rang, adding that she had been surprised to discover earlier in the piano bench certain pieces of old sheet music that she and Bill had played at school concerts in Long Island back in 1940 and 1941. Bill was nine years old at the time, and Catherine seven, and as she now led her brother into the large step-down living room he noticed that the piano on which she had been playing was the one from the Hempstead house on which he had taken lessons for five years. He had stopped after leaving for boarding school in Arizona in 1942, but his sister had continued with her music through most of her school years, and she played very well.

"Do you remember these?" she asked, handing him two programs from children's concerts at which they had played a duet.

"How could I forget?" he said, smiling, recognizing them immediately. "It was the highpoint of my career." He scanned through the programs, noting that on the back page among the list of sponsors were the names Mr. and Mrs. Joseph Bonanno. "I remember walking into the Garden City Hotel wearing my navy blue jacket, white flannel pants, white shoes, and you were wearing a long white dress. I remember the applause after we finished, how nervous and excited we were, and how proud Mom and Dad seemed afterward. I never wanted to take piano lessons, really hated it at first, but he made me do it; and I wish that he hadn't stopped."

Bill bent over the keyboard, pressing a few chords; but failing to get the desired results, he stopped and backed away.

"Rusty," he announced, "rusty and too old for a comeback."

As Catherine went into the kitchen to get coffee, he was greeted by two of his nephews who had been in the den watching television. Bill grabbed them one at a time, tossed them in the air as they shrieked with pleasure. Then, after he put them down, they hurried back to their television show, and Bill stood in the large room pacing slowly across the thick soft carpet, looking around. Through the sliding glass doors he could see the sprawl-ing lawn and trees that the gardeners were now trimming and clipping, as another workman was skimming the pool. The maintenance and taxes on this property must be tremendous, he thought, which was probably why his brother-in-law, Greg, was working this weekend, drilling teeth at his clinic while the slow-moving gardeners were soaking up the California sunshine and earning twenty dollars an hour. Bill wished that his brother-in-law would relax and enjoy himself more, and he had often thought of urging him to change his routine, but Bill had finally decided against giving advice to the one member of the family who was obviously doing well. Bill remembered from his col-lege days at Arizona that Greg had always been hard-working and industrious in his studies, never so popular with the girls as Bill had been but always with an eye to the future. Through their fathers' acquaintanceship that went back to Sicily, Bill and Greg had become quick friends years before Catherine had taken an interest in Greg; in fact, she had deliberately avoided him during the period when they attended classes concurrently on the Ari-zona campus, not because she found the thin, dark-haired man unattractive but because she regarded him merely as a friend of Bill's. Later Catherine had nearly become engaged to another man whose Italian family was known to Joseph Bonanno, and Bill thought that the wedding plans had met with everyone's approval, underestimating the private power of his mother, Fay. Fay Bonanno waited until her husband had gone out of town on a trip, which was one month before Catherine was to announce her engagement formally, when she boldly told Catherine that she did not want to see the young man in the Bonanno home again. She offered no explanation but hinted that she knew something about him that was too distasteful to mention. Cath-erine, confused and hysterical, demanded to know why her mother had not spoken up sooner, why her father had not been informed before his trip; but Mrs. Bonanno remained adamant, almost tyranical in her sudden control over her daughter. Cath-erine became silent, and angrily determined that she would wait for her father's return.

Catherine's relationship with her mother had always been re-mote when compared with the demonstrative affection she ex-changed with her father, and Bill wondered if there might not have been a subconscious mother-daughter rivalry. While his mother had always put her husband ahead of the children, she had permitted Bill and his younger brother almost total freedom during their adolescence, while Catherine as the only daughter had been bound by a strict code of behavior, not allowed to date boys unchaperoned until after she had entered college. Bill remembered that Catherine was a tomboy during her girlhood, playing with the neighborhood boys in Hempstead and resenting her exclusion from her father's male companions who had come to the house and had invariably included Bill in their circle of conversation. These men used to wrestle and play with Bill in those days as Bill's men played with Tory now; and Bill remembered one Christmas Eve in 1940 when his father's men arrived carrying an enormous train set, and as he sat waiting with wild anticipation the heavyset men crawled uncomfortably along the floor for hours, hooking pieces of track together, linking various pieces that formed the station platform and the cantilever bridge.

Catherine had felt abandoned when she was forced to remain in the convent in upstate New York while her parents spent the winters with Bill in Arizona, and it was during this time that she regularly wrote her father letters that he had saved to this day. Catherine's girlhood in the convent was not unlike Rosalie's, except that Rosalie submitted to it and was comforted by it, while Catherine had rebelled, and she was never to lose her spirit of individuality and independence. The fact that she did not marry the man to whom she was to become engaged was not due to her mother's objection, but rather to her own disappointment with him in not having stood up to her mother during the weeks that her father was away. Catherine could never have married a man who could be intimidated by her mother, and so she broke the engagement of her own will, and when her father returned she did not even mention the conflict. Since that time Mrs. Bonanno respected Catherine's independence and never again challenged it. She often visited her daughter in Atherton, as she had after the bombings, but both women took great care to avoid another confrontation.

Catherine returned with the coffee and after she and Bill discussed at length the possibility of her parents' moving to Atherton, Bill was pleased and not surprised to learn that Catherine favored the move, and she suggested that they live with her until they found a home of their own in Atherton or in a nearby community. As for the adverse publicity or the potential loss of her friends in the town, Catherine was unconcerned, saying that if her friends dropped her because she opened her home to her parents, then good riddance to the friends.

Bill and Catherine talked for a while longer, then he stood to leave. He had called Rosalie from the airport more than an hour ago, and she was expecting him for dinner. He walked into the den to say good-bye to his nephews, and Catherine told them to get up and turn off the television set, and to get washed and ready for dinner. One of her boys protested, saying, "But I want to see the FBI!"

"Turn it off," she insisted, "you'll be seeing the FBI soon enough."

21

On the Tuesday morning after Bill's return, Rosalie reminded him that they were expected to take the two older boys to a music school that afternoon where several local youths were to receive an aptitude test in guitar playing. Bill had been vaguely aware of Rosalie's driving Charles and Joseph to the school several times during the past month, having been invited to do so by a woman who had come to the door and announced that the school, anxious to promote music appreciation among young Californians, was willing to loan them guitars for a few dollars and to give them free lessons in the hope of discovering and encouraging musical talent. Now, Rosalie explained, their two sons were among a group to be examined by instructors, and all parents had been requested to observe the test and to witness the awarding of trophies to those students who made a passing grade.

While Bill was not particularly anxious to spend the afternoon in the company of a noisy pack of guitar-strumming pupils, he had nothing better to do, and he also felt obligated to attend because he had been away from the children so often this month and because on the following Thursday he would again be leaving home to visit his father in Tucson. Bill also sensed how excited his sons had seemed today about the test, and as soon as they returned home from their regular school they proceeded to drill one another on the material from which the examination would be drawn. Bill thought it odd that the instructors would give the students the answers in advance, but when he was assured by Charles and Joseph that they were not reading from a stolen test and that all the students had been issued the same preexamination sheets, he said nothing more.

Now in the car, driving toward the school, Bill could detect increased anticipation in the back seat, where Charles and Joseph were jumping up and down as they recited their answers to the questions, arguing, singing, and chanting.

> *One banana*
> *Two banana*
> *Three banana*
> *Four . . .*
> *Five banana*
> *Six banana*
> *Seven banana*
> *More . . .*

"OK, OK," Bill called back to them, after Tory and Felippa began to join in, "calm down. I'm trying to drive."

They remained quiet for a few moments as Bill continued slowly through a crowded business district that was congested with the first waves of homeward-bound commuter traffic. Rosalie sat next to him, her head bent forward as she read from a textbook in preparation for her computer class later this evening. The children soon began to bounce on the seats again, whistling, pushing, and then Charles and Joseph burst into a song that they had obviously rehearsed together.

> *Write me a letter*
> *Send it by mail*
> *Send it in care of*
> *Birmingham jail*
> *Oh Birmingham jail . . .*

"Stop it, will you please!" Bill shouted, as Rosalie also turned, frowning at the children.

"It's one of the songs we play in class," Charles said.

"I don't care," Bill replied. "I'm trying to drive, and you're giving me a headache. I don't want any more noise back there or I'm turning around and we're going home."

The boys maintained their silence for the few remaining miles until they had arrived at the place where they were to be tested. The building was actually a large music store, with wide display windows in the front showing photographs of Glen Campbell, Elvis Presley, and other television personalities, in addition to a number of glittering and colorful electric guitars. As Bill entered the store, following Rosalie and the children, who knew the way to the audition rooms in the rear, he saw many long-haired teenagers standing around, and from the ceiling dangling from thin strands of wire were electric guitars and instruments of every variety.

At the end of a corridor, seated along a row of folding chairs against the wall, were a dozen children with their parents, and in one corner behind a desk a middle-aged blonde was writing down the names and addresses of the people as they arrived. Above her head was a sign THE RICHEST CHILD IS POOR WITHOUT MUSIC and to her right was a large bulletin board on which were at least fifty individual photographs of smiling young people holding guitars or displaying their trophies. There was also a sign on the bulletin board LESSONS MUST BE PAID FOR IN ADVANCE.

As Rosalie and the children sat waiting and Bill wandered through the store looking at the instruments, the doors of the audition rooms in the rear were opening and closing, while pupils came and went with their parents and the instructors waved good-bye or said hello to the participants in this musical crash course. None of the children who had completed their test seemed unhappy; on the contrary, they left the room smiling, receiving a pat on the head from the instructor, and their parents followed carrying guitar cases and amplification boxes.

Within ten minutes, the woman behind the desk called out: "Will Mr. and Mrs. Bonanno come in, please, with Joseph." Charles waited outside with Felippa and Tory, as Joseph and his parents entered one of the small rooms, where they were greeted effusively by a short man of about forty-five who had a southern accent and wore his reddish hair in a crew cut on top but long and slicked back on the sides. The man shook hands with Bill and Rosalie, waved them into the chairs next to his desk, and then, turning to Joseph, said, "Young man, it's been a pleasure having you here these past weeks, and I'd like Mother and Dad to know that you're one of our best students, and we think you have what it takes to go on with your music. Music is a rare and good quality to develop among young folks like yourself, and if we had more music among our youths today there would not be so much rioting, not be so much anger, there would be more respect for one another in the streets and campuses. It is through music that many young men have gone on to bigger and better things, to television and to movies, and they all began, Joseph, as you have, by taking lessons. Elvis Presley had to take lessons at one time just as you did this month, and now, Joseph, I'm going to give you a little oral test to see how well you can reply to the basic questions.''

Joseph stood in front of the man's desk, his hands at his side, not looking at his parents as the man asked, ''Now, Joseph, which finger picks the first string?''

''The second finger or middle finger,'' Joseph replied.

''Good,'' the man said, and continued, ''which finger picks the second string?''

''First finger or index finger.''

''Fine, and which do you use on the three, four, five, and sixth strings?''

''The thumb,'' Joseph said.

''Good, and what is the rule for tuning your guitar?''

''Playing the taps.''

''Good, and how do we stop the rattle of the strings?''

''By putting the fingers down on the strings behind the bar.''

''Bright boy,'' the man said, turning to the Bonannos and shaking his head with a look of mild amazement. ''And when the thumb is pushed across the strings, it's called what?''

''A strum,'' Joseph said.

''Yes, and where is the proper place to pick or strum the guitar?''

''Around the sound hole.''

''*Yes,*'' the man said quickly, his blue eyes flashing, ''and what do we call this sign?''

''A treble clef sign.''

''*Yes*, Joseph, very good, Joseph,'' the man said, turning to the Bonannos for confirmation. Rosalie seemed to be blushing with pleasure, while Bill sat watching his eight-year-old son standing in front of the instructor's desk, appearing to be enjoying this moment. There had been no wheezing or coughing from Joseph, and this pleased Bill most of all.

The instructor asked Joseph to be seated next to Rosalie while Charles was brought in. Charles tried without success to keep Tory from entering, too, and after an exchange of pushing and shoving at the door, the instructor invited both Tory and Felippa to come in and be seated, asking only that they sit quietly. Then the instructor smiled at Charles and delivered the same introductory speech that Joseph had heard, and soon Charles was being asked the same questions. While Charles's replies were not as precisely accurate as Joseph's had been, the instructor seemed no less ecstatic, and at the conclusion of the questioning he turned to Bill and Rosalie and said, "In all sincerity, Mr. and Mrs. Bonanno, I think your boys here are truly gifted, truly gifted. Does either of you have a musical background?"

"I played the piano," Bill said.

"Ah, *yes*," the man said, nodding, "that's it, *that's* where it must come from."

The man then stood up, reaching into the drawer of his desk, and held up two small gold-colored plastic trophies.

"Boys," he said, almost solemnly, "I now want to formally present a token of congratulations to you both. You have demonstrated not only an ability with rhythm in your previous instruction, but now you have shown an understanding of the fundamentals, and I'd like to give you these trophies which mean that you've both made 100 in your examination, the highest mark." The boys, smiling, accepted the trophies and stood silently.

"And now, Mr. and Mrs. Bonanno," the instructor said, "the next step is up to you. We have determined that your sons have what it takes to go on with their music, and we wonder if you can see your way clear to allow them to continue."

"What can we do?" Bill asked, sensing the sales pitch coming, the whole reason for today's production.

"We will give your boys advanced lessons in guitar once a week for three years, including the sheet music free, with the purchase of an electric guitar for each boy. They are now ready to expand their talents with an electric guitar, which we will provide for a special low price of $495, and the boys will also be allowed to join our junior band. Our first band meeting is tonight at seven o'clock, and so you're just in time to start. With a down payment, we'll extend the credit to pay for the guitars and amplifiers. All you have to do is look over this application form here and list the banks and stores where you keep an account, and we'll get your boys started without delay."

The man handed Bill the application blank. Bill took it but did not look at it, and he certainly had no intention of signing it. And yet, while he recognized this whole program as a gim-

mick to sell guitars, he did not necessarily think that an invest-
ment of $495 for each boy's instrument, plus three years of
weekly lessons, was unreasonable. Bill assumed that his father
had spent at least that much money on his piano lessons, and
Bill had often wished, while listening in nightclubs to skilled
musicians, that he had mastered an instrument. Although Bill
did not now have the thousand dollars to spare on two electric
guitars, this did not mean that he could not somehow raise the
money. He hated to find himself in a position where a shortage
of money prevented him from following his instincts, which at
this moment urged him to enroll both sons in the guitar class,
but he knew that he needed more time to figure out where the
money might come from. He looked at Charles, skeptically, and
asked, "Are you sure you'll practice every day if I decide to
buy these guitars?"

"Yes," Charles said. Joseph also nodded. Bill then turned to
Rosalie, who was busily buttoning Felippa's coat and adjusting
Tory's hat, avoiding his glance. Bill looked at his watch, and
then said quickly to the man, "Look, my wife has to get to
computer class right now, and I have to drive her. Let me get
her there, and I'll bring the boys back at seven o'clock and we
can handle this then." Bill knew he would not return at seven,
for he had a meeting with a few men, and the older boys were
going to Cub Scouts while Rosalie went to computer class; but
he wanted to get out of the music store as quickly as possible,
finding the situation suddenly awkward and embarrassing.

"Fine," the man said, smiling. Bill turned to leave with the
children but before he was halfway to the door, he heard the
man calling after him, "One moment, sir, take these with you."
The man was carrying two silver cases containing new electric
guitars, and also the amplifiers. Bill hesitated, but the man insisted that he take them, explaining, "Let the boys see how they
like them. They can practice at least a half hour before you come
back, and they'll be better prepared for the band."

Charles and Joseph exclaimed their approval, and Bill accepted the instruments with thanks; he carried them out to the
car and carefully placed them in the trunk.

"Bill," Rosalie said softly, urgently, "we can't afford to do
this."

"We'll talk about it later," he said, sharply, not wanting to
discuss it in front of the children. As Bill got into the car, he

waved at the man who stood watching from the store window, and headed for home.

The children talked excitedly, and Rosalie sat quietly next to Bill, feeling frustration and guilt. She wished that she had found out ahead of time the main reason why both parents had been invited; if she had, she might have protected Bill from that which made him most vulnerable, his ego. Rosalie did not doubt that if Bill had had a thousand dollars in his pocket five minutes ago, he would have handed it to the man in the music store, and at this moment he would be as happy as the children seemed to be, riding home with two electric guitars that soon would be vibrating noisily through the house and the neighborhood.

Bill pulled into the driveway and, after carrying amplifiers and guitars into the living room, he inserted the plugs into the electric sockets and flicked his fingers over the strings, hearing the twang and piercing echo. He strummed the strings a number of times, turning the knobs and admiring the sleek design of the red and silver instrument. Then he handed the guitars to the boys, who had been waiting impatiently, and walked into the kitchen, where Rosalie was preparing the children's dinner. It was after 6:00 P.M., and the baby-sitter would be arriving soon.

"Bill, I'm sorry," Rosalie said, standing in front of the stove. "It was a mistake. It's an impossible situation."

"Don't worry," Bill said, in a jocular way, "the difficult I do immediately, the impossible takes me a little longer."

"Let's be serious," she said. "We can't afford it."

"We can't afford *anything* if you look at it that way," he said. "I can't afford to fly to New York, I can't afford to drive to Arizona, I can't afford or justify any of the things I do. And if I can't justify what I do, what right do I have in not letting them have music lessons."

"Yes," Rosalie said, "but we have so many other things to do. We have the house to worry about."

"Don't worry about the house. I'll get the money for the house."

"Where?"

"Don't worry."

"I *am* worried. We're talking here about a thousand dollars' worth of equipment. Before I put the money toward that, I'd rather put it toward the house."

"Look," he said, "where there's a will there's a way. When

you want something badly enough, you always find a way to get it, right? Just like you somehow managed to find the money for your computer class.''

He was touching on a sensitive subject now, and Rosalie said nothing. He had never encouraged her to go to computer school, had tried to avoid the subject whenever she mentioned it during the previous summer. But in the fall, with no financial help from him, she came up with the $1,250. He could only assume that she had gotten it from her mother, not knowing who else could have given it to her, and not really wanting to know.

''Look,'' he said finally, more softly, ''I'm not saying you did anything wrong in taking these computer classes. I'm just saying that when you want to do something, you do it. You find a way. You wanted a career, and now you're getting one, right?''

''I'm doing it because I need the money,'' she said.

''You're going to be spending more money than you'll ever make out of this career,'' he said, ''when you consider the cost of the baby-sitter every day, the cost of your clothes, and the transportation, and all the extras—it'd be cheaper if you didn't work.'' It was an old argument that she had heard before, and she was tired of talking about it.

''Who's going to pay for the things I need?'' she asked. ''I need fifty dollars a week for myself. I want . . .''

''You want . . .'' he interrupted.

''I'm tired of *asking* for everything,'' she cried out.

''And I'm tired of hearing this,'' he said. He paced through the kitchen as Rosalie took dishes from the cabinet and placed them around the kitchen table where the children would eat supper.

''Rosalie,'' Bill said, calmly and authoritatively, ''stop worrying. You don't see me worrying do you? After all I've been through these past few years, you think *this* is worth worrying about? After all I've been through, I'm now supposed to worry about a guitar school? I'll get the money. I'll beg, steal, or borrow it, but I'll get it. I've been living on borrowed time for years, and I've learned to survive in dangerous situations, and I've lived with bullets flying around, with bombs going off, with cars coming at me, and *I have survived*. And you think I'm going to worry now about two lousy electric guitars?''

''Who,'' Rosalie asked, wearily, ''is going to pay?''

''I said I'd get the money.''

"How?"

"Somehow I'll get it. Have I ever failed you before?"

She looked at him with astonishment.

"Sure," he said, sharply, "sure you always can remember the bad times, can't you? You never remember all the times I've come through, but you sure can remember any little failure!"

"All right," she said, after a pause, "but suppose you have to go away to jail, then what? Who will meet the monthly payments for the music school if you're in jail?"

Before he could reply, a child's voice cried out, *"Jail?"*

Bill and Rosalie both turned suddenly toward the door between the kitchen and dining room and saw Joseph standing there. He appeared pale, shaken, and behind him stood Tory, confused. Charles was still in the living room playing the guitar.

"Daddy's only kidding," Rosalie said, trying to smile. "We're just talking, but we're kidding."

"Daddy said there was shooting in the street," Joseph repeated, solemnly.

Bill said nothing. He wanted to say, *Yes, there is shooting in the street, and that's the way it is,* but he could see how upset Rosalie and the boys were now, and he did not interrupt her as she repeated, "Daddy was kidding—there is no shooting in the street."

"There's shooting in the hills on television," Tory said, nodding.

"There is shooting in the street," Joseph said.

"Look," Bill said, finally, "you kids are supposed to be going to Cub Scouts, right? So why aren't you getting dressed? And," he added, looking at Joseph, "before you and Chuckie go out, I want those guitars to be put away in their cases and put in the closet. And you, Tory, I don't want you to touch anything, you understand?"

"Yes," Tory said.

After the children left, Bill said to Rosalie, "Let's end this, OK? I'll get the money for the music lessons somehow and let's just not talk anymore."

"And the house?" she asked. "What about the house?"

Bill was surprised by her persistence. Years ago, he thought, she would not have been talking back to him this way; but years ago, he reminded himself, he had not been home so often.

"What house are you talking about?" he asked.

"The one I asked you to look at, on Forest Ridge Drive, the one with five bedrooms."

"Is that the house with the lot next door to it?"

"What do I know about a lot next door?"

"You don't," he said, "but I do. It has a lot next door and too many bushes all around the place."

"You always think of yourself," she said, "but *I'm* the one that has to live there."

"I'll be living there, too," he said.

"For how long?"

"Rosalie," he said, insistently, "those *bushes*."

"It's a five-bedroom house," she said, "and I've looked around, and it's the best I've seen, and we don't have much time left to look."

"I don't like it," he said.

"Oh, I'd like my *own* house for a change, I'm sick and tired of renting," she said, shaking her head slowly. "I want the security of my own house if you have to go away."

"There is no security in things like a house," he said. "A house is not security. Money is not security. *You* measure security in dollar signs, but it doesn't work that way. If you ever think you've found security in life, you're dying. When you feel secure, you're receding. Security is boring. I've never known security, and so far . . ."

The doorbell rang. It was the baby-sitter. Rosalie and Bill stopped talking. Rosalie called the children to come in to eat, and while the baby-sitter took over in the kitchen, Rosalie went to her room to dress for class. Bill watched the news on television for a while, and then a man came by to pick him up. Without saying good-bye Bill left the house.

On the following day, the telephone rang several times but Rosalie did not answer it. Some of the calls might have been from real estate agents responding to her previous inquiries about homes advertised in the newspaper, but she felt sure that the music store was also calling and she did not want to face the situation. The children were in school, and Bill had taken the car earlier in the morning and, as usual, had not told her when he would return. They had not discussed the guitars at breakfast but she had refused to let the boys play with them before going to school. She did not want the instruments scratched because she knew—and imagined that Bill also knew even though he would not express it in words—that the guitars would be returned to the store. Bill was going to Arizona early tomorrow morning and Rosalie hoped to settle the situation before that, but she preferred waiting until Bill returned today before daring to answer the telephone. She did not want the music store to reach her when she was alone.

Bill returned shortly after 5:00 P.M., and they sat down to an early dinner with the children because he would start the drive to Tucson at dawn, wanting to reach at least Phoenix before nightfall. Dinner was very quiet, and the boys also seemed to sense and to accept the fact that they would not be keeping the guitars, for neither of them had asked for the instruments after they came home from school. Bill was preoccupied at the table and irritable; twice he corrected Tory's manners, and he was unresponsive to most of what Rosalie said about a number of different subjects.

As she was pouring the coffee, the phone rang, and she could not resist saying, "Oh, I'll bet it's the music man."

"Well, answer it," Bill said.

She walked into the kitchen, picked up the phone, and after a few moments of silence Bill could hear her saying, softly, "I'm sorry about that, but I just wasn't able to arrange for the transportation. And I'm going to have to return them." There was another pause before Rosalie said, "Yes, yes—I'll get them there tonight, before nine." She hung up and returned to the table, saying, "Well, that's taken care of." Nobody said anything.

22

SHORTLY AFTER 6:00 A.M., Bill Bonanno drove through the San Joaquin Valley in central California heading southeast toward Bakersfield, planning to turn east near Burbank past the San Bernardino Mountains into the desert at Palm Springs toward Phoenix. It was a beautiful drive over smooth wide roads through green hills and valleys, and as the sun began to rise in a cloudless sky Bill Bonanno felt very remote from the trivial tensions of his home in the town he had left behind. The automobile was his true home, his opiate, and long trips like this filled him with a sense of pleasure and movement in a life that was standing still.

Nothing seemed to be happening now; he had no immediate goals or plans, days passed uneventfully, the hours were long, yet he never felt that his time was his own. Within a day or week or month he would be notified again to appear in court, and as always he had to be free and available, but this time it was the summons he dreaded most, for it would ultimately lead to the moment when he would learn whether or not he was going to prison. He imagined that it was the same now with his father, and Peter Notaro, and dozens of others who had made headlines during the Banana War but were presently inactive, waiting or hiding, pondering an uncertain future.

When the average American citizen thought about the Mafia, he usually contemplated scenes of action and violence, of dramatic intrigue and million-dollar schemes, of big black limousines screeching around corners with machine-gun bullets spraying the sidewalk—this was the Hollywood version and while much of it was based on reality it also wildly exaggerated that reality, totally ignoring the dominant mood of Mafia existence; a routine of endless waiting, tedium, hiding, excessive smoking, overeating, lack of physical exercise, reclining in rooms behind drawn shades being bored to death while trying to stay alive. With so much time and so little to do with it, the Mafia man tended to become self-consumed and self-absorbed, focusing on minutiae and magnifying them, overreacting to each sound, overinterpreting what was said and done around him, losing perspective of the larger world beyond and his very small place in that world, but nonetheless being aware of the exaggerated image that the world had of him. And he responded to that image, believed it, preferred to believe it, for it made him larger than he was, more powerful, more romantic, more respected and feared. He could trade on this and profit from it in neighborhoods where he ran the rackets and in other areas where he hoped his inflated ego would allow him to expand; he could, if he was sufficiently bold and lucky, exploit the fact and fantasy of Mafia mythology as effectively as the FBI director did at budget time, and the politicians before election day, and the press whenever organized crime was topical, and the movie makers whenever they could merchandise the myth for a public that invariably wanted its characters larger than life—tough-talking, big-spending Little Caesars.

No less than anyone else, Bill Bonanno was influenced by the myth and often chose to live the lie. It fed his compulsion to travel first-class on airplanes, to lease a Cadillac when he could barely afford payments on a Volkswagen, to stroll into a courtroom with a suntan that he claimed to have gotten while playing golf at Pebble Beach. It was essential, if one wished to succeed in the secret society, to at least give the appearance of prosperity and power, to exude confidence and a carefree spirit; although in so doing, the Mafia man's life became more difficult for him in the larger world where government agents were watching him, tapping his phone, bugging his home, seeking to determine the source of his illegitimate income so that he might be indicted for income tax evasion. The Mafia man was consequently forced into an almost schizophrenic situation—while he was pleading poverty to Internal Revenue and was attempting to conceal his resources, he was also attempting to impress his friends by picking up checks, driving a new Cadillac or Lincoln, and by otherwise living beyond his means. But he really had no alternative if he wanted to maintain the respect of his colleagues in the underworld, or indeed in the larger world of American capital-

ism, where there has traditionally existed a grudging admiration
for the truly wealthy gangsters, possibly because their success
reaffirms every tycoon's belief in the free-enterprise system or
possibly because the gangster's shrewdness and initiative re-
minds some industrialists, bankers, and statesmen of how their
grandfathers had begun. Thus it was not difficult to understand
why Frank Costello had been on friendly terms with the Wall
Street leaders and merchant princes with whom he took his daily
steam bath at the Biltmore, or why Lucky Luciano had been a
respected resident of the Waldorf, or why such an avowed enemy of the Mafia in Italy as Benito Mussolini would have bestowed the title of commendatore on a fugitive from America,
Vito Genovese, after Genovese had made generous contributions to municipal construction projects near Naples.

But there were undoubtedly other Mafia veterans who had
been portrayed in the press as millionaires but who were relatively impecunious, adroitly concealing this fact behind a pretense of Old World modesty or a convincing aura of effrontery.
He remembered from his boyhood the many well-dressed men
who used to visit his father, men who drove up in big cars and
wore diamond rings on their pinkies, and he wondered if he had
been beguiled as a boy merely by their appearance or if they
had indeed been men of substantial power. He would never
know. But he was aware through his personal knowledge that
the newspapers invariably overestimated the value of the homes
of nearly all reputed Mafia leaders, describing most of the dwellings as "palatial." His father's rather modest brick home in
Tucson, worth in the neighborhood of $40,000, was in no sense
palatial though it was often called that; and the same was true
of the residences of most other prominent dons in the 1960s,
including Genovese. Those who preferred a more ostentatious
hermitage, such as Magliocco and Joseph Profaci, were both
proprietors of several successful legitimate businesses, principally in beverages and foods, and they lived on a scale and style
roughly comparable to that of the New York head of a large
corporation. Bill Bonanno also believed that newspapers had a
fixation about building up all Mafia feuds into "wars," and, in
the case of *The New York Times*, of sometimes giving as much
space to a Mafia "war," which rarely produced two corpses a
week, as to the Vietnamese war that produced thousands. The
Banana War, beginning with the shooting on Troutman Street

in 1966 and extending into 1969, had so far produced only nine deaths; and the Profaci-Gallo rivalry in Brooklyn between 1961 and 1963 accounted for only a dozen murders, which Bill assumed was probably less than the number of murders each month among married American couples. If compared with some of the publicized atrocities by Allied troops on civilians in Southeast Asia or with the intrigues of the CIA or the tactics of Green Berets (who in 1969 disposed of one disloyal spy by weighting him with chains and tire rims and dumping him into a river), the exploits of the Mafia would hardly seem to justify the elaborate news coverage that it received. And it would not be receiving it were it not for the mythology factor, the George Raft reality, the fact that the Mafia in the sixties, like Communism in the fifties, had become part of a national illusory complex shaped by curved mirrors that gave an enlarged and distorted view of everything it reflected, a view that was widely believed because it filled some strange need among average American citizens for grotesque portraits of murderous villains who bore absolutely no resemblance to themselves.

Bill Bonanno's ponderings on this subject during his twelve-hour trip to Phoenix were partly inspired by the radio news reports that he had been listening to, the announcement of President Nixon's message to Congress requesting $61 million to combat the Mafia and other elements in organized crime. Nixon told Congress that the Mafia was now "more secure than ever before," had "deeply penetrated broad segments of American life," and was causing the "moral and legal subversion of our society." The annual "take" from illegal gambling, Nixon said, was between $20 billion to $50 billion—a figure that impressed Bill Bonanno mainly for its lack of preciseness—and it was the president's wish that the federal government be given wider power in law enforcement, extending into jurisdictions now largely run by state and local authorities. The president called for the establishment of twenty federal racketeering field offices, to be known as "strike forces," in major cities, and also the creation of a special federal-state racket squad in the Southern District of New York State to focus on the "heavy concentration of criminal elements in the nation's largest city." In requesting a budgetary increase of $24.7 million over the $36 million that former President Johnson had requested for the fight on organized crime, President Nixon explained that about $9 million of the new money would go mainly for more FBI agents, Justice Department lawyers, and federal marshals; and that approximately $8 million would be added to the Internal Revenue Service to strengthen its attack on tax evasion by criminals.

As Bill Bonanno listened to the various broadcasts, and later read the newspapers at roadside restaurants, he was awed by the government's escalating crusade against an organization whose demigods were a half dozen tired old dons trying to think big, and he could not help but speculate that the main problem of the government was not that the Mafia was alive but that it may well be dying and that perhaps the only thing that might save these rare creatures from extinction would be a government subsidy of some sort. Since great cathedrals could not have been built without devils and since to diminish the size of the antihero was to diminish the size of the hero, it would be in the interest of future crime-busting budgetary increases to preserve the dons and underbosses from the natural forces of attrition; unless of course some other group like the Black Panthers, or societies of radical students, could be magnified into such proportions as to replace the menacing image of the Mafia. But Bill Bonanno doubted that this could be done.

The Panthers were too rootless ever to unify, too small in number to ever amount to much, and its leadership had already exaggerated its power so much that it could not really stand any further stretching or inflating from the government. Most student radicals were too soft to be heavies, and while their membership was potentially large, they were too self-centered to cooperate for long in the kind of national syndicate that Bill believed was necessary to survive outside the system. Their greatest vice, marijuana, which many of them imported and distributed along with hard drugs without Mafia affiliation, would in time become a less punishable crime, perhaps no crime at all. Since so many sons of politicians and prominent citizens had been arrested for its possession, the ruling class in America would undoubtedly use its influence to try to change the law rather than to enforce it. Marijuana use had become a crime of the middle class and upper middle class, and it would not be enforced so strictly as the lower-class crime of betting on the numbers.

So for the present, Bill thought, the government was stuck with the Mafia as a national symbol of sin, and most members of the brotherhood were doing their best to live up to their roles, brandishing their bravado in public and contemplating their private domain in universal terms, as Stefano Magaddino was doing when he complained about the elder Bonanno: ''He's planting flags all over the world!'' Even when talking with one another on the telephone, it seemed that the men conversed in an unnatural way, faking their voices to sound more gruff or affecting a Brooklynese speech that was characterized by double negatives and a coarseness that seemed befitting a grade-B gangster film but which Bill knew was not the way they normally spoke in person to their wives or nonprofessional friends. Their hoodlumlike speech pattern seemed to be a subconscious mannerism, and it had nothing to do with trying to conceal their identity from the wiretappers. When they wished to do that, they were marvels of confusion, mixing Sicilian metaphors and slang with pidgin English and obscure references, and no one was more skilled at this than his father. In fact, one reason why Bill was driving to Arizona now was that his father had been so vague and incomprehensible on the telephone the other night that Bill had no idea what he was talking about, and he therefore decided that a personal visit was in order.

By midafternoon Bill had crossed the California border into Arizona at Ehrenberg, a small town near an Indian reservation on the Colorado River. It had been a smooth journey interrupted only by a brief sandstorm outside Palm Springs, and by 6:00 P.M. he was driving into Phoenix, deciding to spend the night at the Desert Sky Motel. He could have gone on to Tucson, but there was a favorite little restaurant of his in Phoenix where he knew he would meet a few friends, and that was where he went after showering and changing clothes at the motel.

The headwaiter greeted him cordially at the door, patting him on the back, and then the owner joined Bill at the bar and bought him a drink. Three other dapper dark-haired men, accompanied by two blondes, also stopped by to say hello, and one of them expressed regret that Bill was not going to be in town longer because he had something he wanted to discuss. Bill said he would get in touch the next time he was passing through.

After dinner Bill drove to a supper club where the buxom waitresses wore leather shorts and black net stockings. The proprietor smiled as Bill walked in. They talked for a half hour at the bar, which glowed under pale blue light, and in one corner of the room a jazz quintet entertained the customers who sat at small tables and banquettes.

During the intermission the musicians came by to say hello to Bill, and one of them asked to be remembered to a mutual friend in San Francisco. Bill asked the musician how his bookings were going, and when he said that things could be better Bill suggested that if he planned to be in northern California to give him a call.

Bill was the central attraction at the bar, and he was reminded of the days when he had his own club in Phoenix, the Romulus, and he lived in a house on Camelback Mountain that had a swimming pool and six telephones. That was back in 1961, two years before he had left Phoenix in an embittered mood and with the lingering memory of patrol cars parked outside the Romulus and the police interrogating the customers each night as they left. But now he felt good about being back, surrounded by those who accepted him; and, on leaving, the proprietor shook his hand and asked him to stop in again on his return to Phoenix. Bill said he would. It was like old times; the old mystique was still there.

Bill woke up late the next morning, and after breakfast in the coffee shop, he went for a swim in the motel's pool. It was a warm sunny day in Phoenix and he felt refreshed after the swim. Later, as he sat under an umbrella at poolside relaxing with the previous day's edition of *The New York Times*, the cool and pleasant feeling began to leave him as he read the text of President Nixon's anti-Mafia speech. The story of the speech was at the top of page one under the headline NIXON REQUESTS WIDE U.S. POWERS TO COMBAT MAFIA, and it was featured above a story announcing the seizure of the Biafran capital by Nigerian troops, and above the North Korean government's castigation of Nixon for continuing to send American spy planes over North Korean territory and for permitting American forces in South Korea to fire heavy weapons into areas in violation of the Korean armistice agreement. Although Bill Bonanno was familiar with the highpoints of Nixon's speech from yesterday's radio reports and the local press, the thrust of the president's attack seemed somehow more preponderant in the sober gray columns of the *Times*. As Bill read and reread certain paragraphs from the text, he became irritated by its naïveté and somewhat defensive. To the president's statement that "many decent Americans contribute regularly, voluntarily, and unwittingly to the coffers of organized crime," Bill Bonanno objected to the term *unwittingly*, convinced that anyone who dealt with a bookmaker was well aware of what was going on. In fact, the horseplayer or numbers bettor had to take the initiative to place an illegal bet, had to seek out the bookie, an individual who did not advertise and who was wary of customers he did not know personally or had not met through a trustworthy contact.

To the president's statement that the Mafia's victims included such divergent groups as the suburban housewife and the college student, the secretary and the bricklayer, and "the middle-class businessman enticed into paying usurious loan rates," Bonanno again took exception to the term *enticed* and he also wondered if the president knew that most citizens who sought money from loan sharks were individuals who had failed to pay off debts in the past, were wheeler-dealer types and chronic gamblers, were the sort who would accept money and agree to the terms and then, rather than pay it back, would go to the police and inform on the loan shark. If the so-called victims of loan sharks were reliable people, Bill thought, they would undoubtedly have found a banker at Bankers Trust, or a friend at Chase Manhattan, or a benefactor in government, and would not have sought out a loan shark in Harlem or Brooklyn.

The general tone of the president's speech that Bonanno quarreled with was the notion that most of the citizens who contributed to the multibillion-dollar crime industry were mindless individuals who had no will of their own, no responsibility for their own acts, they were innocent and pure and had been corrupted by mobsters. Among those "corrupted" in the president's speech were the police who took bribes, as if the mob had to force money into the pocket of the policeman. There was also the suggestion that illegal gambling flourished because the public was "apathetic," when in fact, Bill felt that the public found nothing immoral in such gambling, it being the one form that they could easily afford; they could wager a few dollars every day of the week and still find it cheaper than the expense of one afternoon at Aqueduct or a night at the trotters. Also if they hit the number or scored heavily with the bookie, they could avoid the taxes, it being one of the few loopholes for the workingman who could not write off winter business trips to Florida that coincided with the opening of Hialeah.

By the middle of the afternoon Bill was on the road to Tucson, driving for two hours over a desert highway at great speed, seeing no cars behind him and nothing around him but cactus plants, distant mesas, and wide stretches of copper-colored sand reflecting in the sun. Though he drove with the windows up and the air-conditioner turned to "super cool," he could feel the intense desert heat from memory, recalling the many afternoons that he had spent as a boy following his father's instructions and sitting with his left ear cocked toward the sun to stop the draining, and he reminded himself now that Arizona no longer offered any cure for his problems—it merely seemed to add to them.

His Tucson visits in recent years had invariably produced confrontations with the police, and during his last extended stay he was arrested twice and was blown out of a tree by bomb blasts. Although there had been no explosions since September 1968, seven months ago, the FBI and the police had failed so far to identify the bombers, not even the woman Bill saw throwing a package of dynamite from a car as it cruised past his father's home last summer. Perhaps his father now had new information, Bill thought, and maybe that was what he was attempting to convey during the incomprehensible telephone talk a few days ago.

As Bill approached the city he could feel his muscles tensing; the long road trip from San Jose had been marvelously relaxing, but now with his destination in sight he felt his freedom constricted, and slowing down below the speed limit he automatically began to dart glances at the rearview mirror. It was not only being in Tucson that alerted him, but approaching his father, returning to live for even a few days in a house where he would become again the son, subjected to another man's rules, even a man whom he deeply loved; his reaction being new, he did not pretend to understand it fully, for he had felt it only occasionally and briefly since his father's reappearance in 1966. It might have evolved out of their sudden and increased interdependence on one another after years of separate solidarity in better times, but Bill was aware that he was now more self-conscious in his father's presence, more on guard.

Nearing his father's house on the corner of East Elm Street,

Bill saw his younger brother Joseph leaning against a car parked at the curb talking with a few girls and young friends. Bill waved as he passed, noticing Joseph's long hair and thinking how characteristic that before leaving San Jose he had had his own hair cut. As he turned the corner to enter the garage, his father came out to greet him, and the watchdog was barking.

The elder Bonanno was deeply tanned, and his bright dark eyes and silver-gray hair accentuated his handsome features. He wore tan linen trousers, Indian moccasins, and a green knit turtleneck shirt through which could be seen the outline of a gold medal and chain around his neck. Bill was pleased and surprised at how well he looked. Bill noticed that the portions of the brick wall that had been destroyed by bombs had now been rebuilt, and he also noticed, after entering the house and kissing his mother, that certain furniture had been rearranged and that his father's office was undergoing a kind of spring cleaning—books were stacked on the floor, drawers were open, and on top of the desk were framed photographs, documents from the filing cabinet, several old photo albums, personal mementos and letters.

"Look," his father said, leading Bill by the arm into the office, "I want to show you something I found." The elder Bonanno flipped through a pile of papers and, smiling, held up a report card form his grammar school days more than a half century ago. Pointing to a grade in arithmetic, he announced, "Ninety-eight," and he added in what was typical of his humor, "not bad for an Italian."

Bill also saw several photographs showing his father posing with politicians, priests, and Tucson businessmen at banquets years ago, and there was one large inscribed photograph of a powerful minister in the Italian government named Bernardo Mattarella, a native of Castellammare and a boyhood friend of Joseph Bonanno. There were photographs, too, of the elder Bonanno's parents, and on the wall a framed map of Castellammare, and a small colored postcard that Bonanno had recently received showing an aerial view of the Sicilian town as it looks today. "Castellammare has not changed at all," Joseph Bonanno said, "and that is what I like about it, and why I wish that before I die I could see it once more. How nice it is to go back to the place where you were young and to see that it has not changed."

Bill excused himself a moment and went into his bedroom to unpack the small suitcase that he carried. The room was now as it had been when he lived in this house twenty years ago, and the window next to his bed was secured by the lock that he had occasionally unhitched in the middle of the night when sneaking out to keep a date with a young woman whom he had never dared to introduce to his father. In such situations Bill behaved so differently than his brother Joseph did, who made no secret of his private life, coming and going as he wished, and if the elder Bonanno objected, Joseph Jr. would express indignation and would argue with his father in ways that Bill never would have done, and would still not do. His twenty-three-year-old brother had essentially grown up without a father, for the elder Bonanno was on the move so much during young Joseph's formative years, although young Joseph did carry the burden of the name. Once, in military school, Joseph took a swing at an instructor who asked while reprimanding him: "Are you going to grow up to become a gangster like your father?" Joseph soon left that school without protest from the faculty, and in recent years, failing to complete college, he divided his time between bronco riding and car racing, managing a rock group and having his own difficulties with the law.

A year ago in Beverly Hills he and the twenty-two-year-old son of Peter Licavoli of Detroit and Tucson were arrested on suspicion of car theft and armed robbery, an incident that made national headlines but was later dismissed for lack of evidence. The car was registered to Sam Perrone, and Joseph Jr. complained after the case that the Los Angeles police had been tailing him constantly, trying to provoke an incident. It would not be difficult for the police to provoke Joseph because, as Bill knew, his brother was very sensitive to caustic remarks or innuendos from the authorities, and with the anti-Mafia campaign so rampant in the nation now, particularly in Tucson, it was inevitable that Joseph Bonanno, Jr., would have problems.

Bill often thought that it would be better if Joseph left Tucson, but he had no idea where he might go to settle down; he had already left home once or twice after disputes with his father, and these had been bitter experiences for the elder Bonanno, who after Joseph's departure would ritualistically remove all pictures of his youngest son from the wall and would turn facedown those that were on bureaus or tables.

While Joseph had many girl friends, one a tobacco heiress from North Carolina, he had so far terminated every relationship that might have led to marriage, which pleased his mother. She liked having him home. Joseph's interest in car racing, which had once kept him traveling, now seemed to have subsided although Joseph still kept his trophies on display in the house. Perhaps one reason that Joseph had stopped, which might also partially explain why he was now living with his parents, was that his driver's license had been suspended after his conviction on eleven traffic violations. Bill remembered hearing that when the motor vehicle inspector came to the Bonanno home looking for Joseph, the inspector was attacked by the German shepherd, who bit him on the leg, thereby producing another summons for the Bonanno family. It was the second such summons for the dog, and Bill thought that the animal was a very compatible pet.

In the living room, Bill joined his parents for a drink. It was close to dinner time now, and Mrs. Bonanno turned on more lights, including those that focused on the painted portraits of herself and her husband that hung on the wall behind the television set. Bill noticed that his father had smiled for the artist in the same serene way that he had for so many newspaper photographers, while his mother's portrait was more formal, her dark eyes and lean face pensive if not melancholy and her hair less gray than it was now. Still, Bill thought, his mother had now regained the poise that she had temporarily lost during the bombing incidents of last summer, and she also was spry and quick as she moved about the room.

The conversation in the living room was general, centered around references to Bill's children in San Jose and the forthcoming wedding in June of Rosalie's sister Josephine—which Mrs. Bonanno, who was Josephine's godmother, planned to attend. Then Bill remembered that he had brought with him a book about the Mafia, called *Theft of the Nation*, that his father had wanted to read; the book was written by a professor of sociology named Donald R. Cressey, who had been a national crime consultant in Washington. The elder Bonanno, like his son, read books about organized crime as avidly as people in show business read *Variety*; and while Joseph Bonanno believed that much of the reporting about the Mafia was fictitious he nonetheless was interested in references to himself, a subject that he did not find unfascinating.

In handing the book to his father, Bill indicated that his father came off perhaps better than most who were mentioned in the book, although Bill knew that there was a reprint of an FBI transcript quoting a Rhode Island don as saying that the elder Bonanno "was the cause of his own downfall because he was so greedy." Joseph Bonanno inspected the book's black jacket momentarily, the red letters of the title on top and below a white drawing of the Capitol dome in Washington smeared with big black fingerprints obviously meant to represent the Mafia. Bonanno smiled softly, shook his head. He flipped through the book, noting that it contained no photographs but that it did contain charts of the five New York "families" that were organized after the Castellammarese War in 1931. Of the five charter-member dons of 1931 in New York—Luciano, Mangano, Gagliano, Joseph Profaci, and Joseph Bonanno—only Bonanno was still alive. Bonanno placed the book gently on the table next to his chair, thanking Bill for bringing it. Bill was almost sorry that he had, for on page 156 there was an insulting reference to himself; the author had reported Bill as being "rather stupid and eccentric," which prompted Bill to conclude that Cressey was rather stupid and eccentric, but Bill did not cite the reference to his father.

A moment later, Joseph Jr. walked into the living room, followed by a tall, handsome young man with long blond hair named David Hill, Jr. He was from San Antonio, was twenty-two, and had been a friend of Joseph's for more than a year. Hill's father was a retired army general, a war hero. But the son was a connoisseur of art who had studied in Paris, was a young man with strong views on politics and hypocrisy in America who shared with the Bonannos a conviction that the family had been much maligned in the press. When Bill Bonanno had first met David Hill during the previous summer he had been skeptical, concerned that his brother Joseph, who in the past had attracted many unusual and interesting friends, had on this occasion possibly attracted an FBI protégé or a spy of some sort. But Bill soon altered his thinking, being guided largely by his father, who took an instant liking to the young Texan, admiring his independence and intelligence and appreciating his friendship at a time when friends were rare. Now David Hill, Jr., stayed at the Bonanno home, and he occasionally drove the elder Bonanno around town on errands, accompanying him and assisting him almost in the manner of an aide-de-camp. He received no financial remuneration for this, being in fact quite wealthy—which young Joseph confirmed after a visit to Texas in Hill's company—but Hill claimed to be gaining something of value from his closeness to Joseph Bonanno, namely an insight into an unusual mind, a broadening awareness of life from another point of view.

When the FBI became aware of Hill's living in the Bonanno home, word was quickly sent to the Hill family in San Antonio, and the young man himself was asked to appear at the FBI office in Tucson. When David Hill arrived, he met with an agent who expressed shock and dismay at Hill's choice of friends, but said that Hill might be able to compensate for his faulty judgment by assisting the federal government in compiling data about the habits of the Bonanno family. When Hill refused, and when he emphatically stated that he would not reconsider the FBI's proposition, the agent proceeded to insult him, calling him a disgrace to the family and to his country, adding that young Hill would never be able to hold a position with the United States government, a threat that Hill accepted without appearing to be distraught.

David Hill, Jr., and Joseph Bonanno, Jr., were sitting in the Bonanno living room, equally at home, listening to the elder Bonanno speaking softly on a wide range of subjects, and the elder Bonanno continued to speak freely about his life and times throughout dinner. Dinner was not served in the dining room that adjoined the living room, but rather at the long table in the sun porch to the rear of the house. Mrs. Bonanno did the serving, assisted by a middle-aged Tucson woman who was a close friend of hers, while Joseph Bonanno, encouraged by David Hill's interest, spoke elaborately about his boyhood background, about the history of Sicily, and about his travels to Paris, his recollections of the United States during the thirties when there was more individual freedom than there was now in the sixties, the era of big government. David Hill interrupted freely to express his own opinions, or to ask for a larger explanation from the elder Bonanno, which Bonanno did with apparent satisfaction.

While Bill had heard all these stories before, he was aware of how animated his father seemed in retelling them now to someone new, an outsider with long blond hair who had a rapport with Bill's father that was not obstructed by their difference in age or the complications of a father-son relationship.

Mrs. Bonanno, standing to unset the table and warm the coffee, seemed pleased that her husband was enjoying the discussion; and young Joseph complimented his friend's ability to put into words what he, Joseph, felt—and Joseph was also privately satisfied with his own role in introducing his father to David Hill, one of the few things that he had done recently that had not resulted in a summons.

After dinner, throughout which Bill had been rather quiet, cheese and fruit were passed around, and also brandy. The elder Bonanno remained seated at the table for another hour, even after the dishes and silverware had been removed. He was in an expansive mood, wanting to talk for hours, and Bill thought how lonely it must have been for his father during the past winter in Tucson. His father had been restricted to the companionship of a few men, and if he left the house he was usually followed by the police. He could not take a short vacation trip out of town, for if he requested it the government might seek to counter the doctor's opinion that Joseph Bonanno's heart ailment and the damage that might arise from additional tension justified Bonanno's failure to appear before juries in New York or elsewhere. He was still free on $150,000 bond on the three-year-old federal charge of obstructing justice, although he was essentially a prisoner in his home, and Bill could appreciate how diverting an evening such as this was for his father.

Still, as the discussion at the table continued and as David Hill remained deeply engrossed in whatever the elder Bonanno was saying, Bill could not conceal his restlessness and fatigue. He was beginning to feel the effect of the long motor trip, and he also complained of a mild toothache. He excused himself briefly and walked into the living room where the television was on; he walked out to the front lawn, looking up at the stars and the promise of a clear day tomorrow. He returned later, and took his seat to the right of his father at the table, listening absently for another half hour. His hand rested on a brandy bottle in front of him; and soon, with the nail of his right thumb, he began to scratch into the red wax seal on the neck of the bottle. He did not seem to be conscious of it, but his nail was picking determinedly at the seal, cutting into it, chiseling it down, and tiny pieces of hard red wax began to fall along the tablecloth.

His father continued to talk, and nobody seemed to notice what Bill's hand was doing, except his mother. She stood in the doorway to the kitchen, holding a tray of glasses, watching him for several moments. She frowned slightly, but said nothing until she finally got his attention. Then she spoke softly, directly, her words intended only for his hearing.

"Do you want a scissors," she asked, "or a knife?"

Bill slept late the next day, and when he woke up and went in for breakfast he discovered that his father had waited to have breakfast with him. His father asked about his toothache, seeming concerned and conciliatory.

Later, with Joseph Jr. and David out for the afternoon, Bill spoke with his father without interruption. They dealt with many of the things they had been unable to discuss during the months they had not seen one another, including Bill's court case over the credit card, which would probably go before the jury in the fall. Bill relayed one of his lawyer's opinions that if convicted on all counts of mail fraud, perjury, and conspiracy, he could expect a minimum sentence of ten years in jail. He thought that that was a heavy price to pay for having spent not much more than $2,000 with Torrillo's credit card; but the lawyer had reminded Bill that the government had a strong case and that things might even be worse if Bill took the witness stand in his own defense. The government prosecutor could then interrogate him about subjects other than the credit card incident, and Bill's reluctance to answer could make him seem even more sinister before the jury. It was Bill's assumption now that his lawyers would probably not put him on the stand.

The elder Bonanno strongly urged his son not to concern himself at this time with such eventualities; things often took care of themselves in time, and the government's case might not really be as strong as it seemed. It would have been unfortunate if the case were before the jury now, with public opinion so strongly aroused about organized crime—it was reminiscent of Mussolini's witch-hunt against alleged mafiosi in the 1920s in Sicily. But in six or eight months, there might be a swing back to more rational thinking, and less flailing of the dead horse that the Mafia had become.

As for the Tucson investigation of who had bombed the Bonanno house, there was not much that the elder Bonanno could say that Bill did not already know or suspect. They both knew that it was not a Mafia job. And yet it was somehow organized and well planned, as had also been the bombing of the Licavoli ranch, Notaro's house, the wig salon where Mrs. Charles Battaglia had worked, and the others. Bill's guess was that a citizens' committee of vigilantes, or some kind of political agency, was sponsoring the destruction; but aside from knowing about the mysterious sedans registered to the Deluxe Importing Company, he had made no further progress—and neither he, his father, nor any of their friends could risk pursuing the bombers. They had to leave it to the FBI and police, for if they became involved it might make matters worse; it was perhaps precisely what their adversaries were seeking—a confrontation with the Mafia or a plot portending a scandal or newspaper publicity charging mafiosi with threatening the lives of innocent citizens.

What the Bonannos wanted least in Tucson now was publicity, which was why Bill chose to remain indoors during the day for the entire weekend. He kept the car locked in the garage, did not even stand near the windows during daylight hours. He was fairly certain that the local police were unaware of his presence; if they had known of it, he was sure that they would have invented an excuse to visit the house and ask questions, and then there would have probably been stories in the press speculating on this visit, implying that within the house a secret conclave, with far-reaching underworld implications, was being held.

There were no stories that weekend, but the publicity that the Bonannos had successfully avoided would reach them six weeks later.

23

O<small>N</small> J<small>UNE</small> 10, 1969, many of the inner secrets, intrigues, and events leading up to the Banana War—together with a preponderance of data and gossip about the Mafia in general—were revealed by the FBI, which between 1961 and 1965 had been recording private conversations through the use of hidden microphones placed in three locations frequented by alleged mafiosi. One of the mafiosi was a rather jaunty man of fifty-nine with wavy gray hair named Samuel Rizzo De Cavalcante, who was the boss of a sixty-man "family" in New Jersey and who, in the interest of peace and harmony in the underworld, served as the Mafia national commission's messenger in its troubled negotiations with the Bonanno organization between 1964 and 1965.

It was a thankless task at times, and Samuel De Cavalcante's frustrations in the 2,300-page FBI log testify to how his hopes were usually unfulfilled and how finally he himself realized the futility of his efforts. But it was also evident that De Cavalcante, an obscure New Jersey don who had limited prestige in the national society, truly enjoyed his mission, was challenged by its possibilities of success, liked to brag to his underlings about his being on the inside with the top dons, even as a courier, and did not mind shuttling back and forth between New York, New Jersey, and Pennsylvania to meet secretly with such commission members as Joseph Zerilli of Detroit and Angelo Bruno of Philadelphia as well as with Bill Bonanno and other representatives of the loyalist and separatist groups.

By all standards of the underworld, and even the larger world beyond, Samuel De Cavalcante was a patient, well-meaning man trying to do his duty, a man who listened for hours to the dictates of men whose words were really intended for someone else, someone who was never there, Joseph Bonanno; and yet De Cavalcante, responsive to the task, remained always available even after he knew he was wasting his time—time that he might otherwise have devoted to his plumbing business in New Jersey, to his numbers and loan-sharking and other enterprises, to the wife and children that he loved, and to the mistress that he frequently missed.

The romantic diversions of De Cavalcante, which he alluded to in the privacy of his office to confidantes or in telephone conversations, did not evade the sensitive microphones of the FBI any more than later did they evade the newspapers, the magazines, or the two paperback books that gave national circulation to his words after the FBI released them in June 1969. *The New York Times* for days gave as much space to the De Cavalcante dialogues as it did to the Ecumenical Council in Rome, gaining no doubt a higher rate of readership; and among the *Times*'s regular subscribers, none read with more interest than Joseph Bonanno, whose photograph had appeared with the first article (a rare photograph, for he was not smiling), and Bill Bonanno, who had learned for the first time what certain mafiosi were saying about him behind his back. The paperback books went into even greater detail, and it was also possible to obtain, as Bill later did, the full thirteen volumes of the FBI transcripts, which federal authorities gave to certain friends and reporters and which could be purchased for $95 at the federal courthouse in Newark.

One of the first admissions by De Cavalcante that difficulty existed in the Bonanno organization was recorded in August 31, 1964—two months before Joseph Bonanno's disappearance. The recording was made by an electronic device implanted somewhere on or near De Cavalcante's desk in his office in the one-story cinder block building in Kenilworth, New Jersey, where, with a Jewish partner with whom he could speak fairly fluent Yiddish, he operated an air-conditioning and plumbing supply business. Shortly before noon on August 31, De Cavalcante was visited by one of the captains in his "family," Joe Sferra, who was also the business agent for a hod carrier's union in Elizabeth, New Jersey.

"I've been busy with the commission," De Cavalcante complained.

"Who's giving you problems?" Sferra asked.

"It's nothing with us," De Cavalcante replied. "More lousy meetings!"

"Yeah?" Sferra asked.

"They don't want nobody to know about it," De Cavalcante said, and he paused momentarily, as if hesitant about saying anything more even to his captain. But Sferra's curiosity was aroused, and he asked, "So, what's new?"

"Oh," De Cavalcante said, "a little trouble over there, in New York."

"New York?"

"Yeah," De Cavalcante said. Then he told Sferra, "Close the door. Nobody's supposed to know."

After he closed the door, Sferra seemed to have second thoughts about wanting to pry into commission affairs, and he said, "Sam, if you don't want to tell me you don't have to tell me." But Sam De Cavalcante wanted to tell him.

"It's about Joe Bonanno's *borgata* [family]," he said. "The commission don't like the way he's comporting himself."

"The way he's conducting himself, you mean?"

"Well, he made his son *consigliere*," De Cavalcante explained, "and it's been reported, the son, that he don't show up. They [the commission] sent for him and he didn't show up. And they want to throw [Joe Bonanno] out of the commission. So—just now they figure that the coolest place is Rhode Island. You know what I mean? It's a pain in the neck. I feel sorry for the guy, you know. He's not a bad guy."

"How old is he?" Sferra asked.

"Sixty, sixty-two."

A month later, after De Cavalcante had had unsatisfactory meetings with Bill Bonanno, John Morale, and others, De Cavalcante sat in his office telling one of his subordinates, Frank Majuri, and unknowingly also telling the hidden microphone, how difficult it was to deal with Bill Bonanno, adding that he was more fearful of the younger Bonanno than the elder.

"His son is a bedbug," De Cavalcante said, continuing, "I had an appointment . . ."

"You went to see him?" Majuri cut in.

"Yeah," De Cavalcante said, adding that he had been accompanied by Joseph Zicarelli, a Bonanno member residing in New Jersey. "They got one car in front and one in the back. I said,

'What's going on here? Are were being followed?' He [Zicarelli] said, 'No, don't worry.' " But De Cavalcante realized that while en route to the meeting he was surrounded by Bonanno cars, and that Bill "made sure like I didn't have nobody to set him up."

Although not speaking personally to the elder Bonanno, De Cavalcante did talk to him by telephone, recalling how indignant Joseph Bonanno was that the commission was interfering in Bonanno's family affairs and was protecting Bonanno's disloyal captain, Gaspar Di Gregorio, from reprisals.

" 'Where do they come off protecting him?' " Bonanno is supposed to have demanded of De Cavalcante, as De Cavalcante recalled it in his office for Majuri. " 'This is a Cosa Nostra family!' he's telling me over the telephone. 'The commission told me not to try anything with this guy [Di Gregorio] because the commission is responsible for him!' He [Bonanno] don't care, he thinks nobody is responsible, [Di Gregorio] belongs to *his* family. . . . They [the Bonanno organization] took an attitude he was thrown out of their family and that nobody should have anything to do with him, and where are they coming off protecting him . . ."

"Maybe the guy wasn't wrong, right?" Majuri asked De Cavalcante.

"Who?"

"The guy they threw out," Majuri said, quickly asking what the Bonanno man in New Jersey, Zicarelli, thought about the situation.

"He don't think," De Cavalcante said, explaining that Joseph Bonanno was Zicarelli's boss. Then De Cavalcante, as if pondering the disastrous consequences that would befall the Mafia if this dispute were not settled, said, "That's all the government would want—a thing like this to happen!"

"It would be all over," Majuri agreed. "It wouldn't be like it was the Gallo boys. This would be an entirely different affair now."

"It would be," De Cavalcante said, conjuring up global visions, "like World War III!"

It was around this period, still a month before Joseph Bonanno's disappearance, that Sam De Cavalcante learned that the commission had lost all patience with Bonanno's independent

attitude and had voted to remove him from membership. While
the FBI transcripts contain no details on whether the vote was
unanimous or even whether all eight of the nine commissioners
(excluding Bonanno) participated in the voting, the FBI listed
as commission members in 1964 the following: Stefano Magaddino of Buffalo, Joseph Zerilli of Detroit, Angelo Bruno of
Philadelphia, Sam Giancana of Chicago, Joseph Colombo of
New York (who reportedly succeeded to the leadership of the
Profaci–Magliocco family), Carlo Gambino of New York,
Thomas Lucchese of New York, and the imprisoned Vito Genovese of New York.

While De Cavalcante was under no formal obligation to do
so, he decided to inform the New Jersey–based Bonanno member, Joseph Zicarelli, of the commission's edict mainly because
he liked Zicarelli personally and because he wanted Zicarelli to
start thinking quickly about his own interests.

"Joe," De Cavalcante began, after Zicarelli had entered his
office, "this is strictly between you and I."

"Yeah?" Zicarelli said.

"If I didn't do this," De Cavalcante confessed, "I'd feel like
a lousy bum." Then he said, "The commission doesn't recognize Joe Bonanno as the boss anymore." Zicarelli said nothing,
and De Cavalcante continued, "I don't know what's the matter
with this guy, Joe. I done everything possible."

As Joe Zicarelli continued to be speechless, De Cavalcante
said, "Well, Joe, I'd feel bad if I didn't tell you. Tomorrow I
don't want you to say, 'What the hell, we're so close and he
couldn't tell me!' . . . They [the commission] can't understand
why this guy's ducking them . . . They respect all your people
as friends of ours, but they will not recognize Joe, his son, and
Johnny [Morale]."

Zicarelli seemed incredulous, repeating, "Joe, his son, *and*
Johnny?"

"Yeah," De Cavalcante said, "when they don't recognize a
boss . . ."

"Then all three goes," Zicarelli finished the sentence.

"The whole three," said De Cavalcante, but on the brighter
side he explained that "the commission has no intention of hurt-
ing anybody, either. That's most important for me to tell you."
But Zicarelli countered that Joseph Bonanno also had no intention of harming anyone, "as far as I know."

"Well," De Cavalcante said, "he might hurt people in his own outfit to cover up some of his story," though he emphasized, "the commission is out to hurt no one—not even Joe Bonanno. But they don't want no one else hurt either."

"Who?" Zicarelli asked.

"Right in your own outfit," De Cavalcante said, meaning Gaspar Di Gregorio and anyone choosing to follow Di Gregorio. "When Joe defies the commission," Sam De Cavalcante went on, grandly, "he's defying the whole world."

It was not a simple matter for Zicarelli to suddenly accept the verdict about his boss; while Zicarelli had never been in a position to observe the Mafia hierarchy intimately, being merely a Bonanno soldier—or, as he described himself to De Cavalcante elsewhere on the FBI tape, "a lousy little peasant"—Zicarelli was aware that Joseph Bonanno had been a respected don since 1931, had been a member of the nine-man commission for several years, and it seemed odd that Bonanno would almost overnight be found unfit. Zicarelli also, though only a soldier, had been influenced by the independent style with which Bonanno had long presided as a "family" boss, being fair and personally close to the men but condoning no interference from other dons. From the formative days of the commission in 1931, following Maranzano's murder, Bonanno had defined the commission as a peace-keeping body that should not intrude into the internal affairs of a family, and since no one had challenged his concept for more than thirty years, why anyone was seeking to do so now confused Zicarelli.

When De Cavalcante sought to explain that the commission was justified in protecting Gaspar Di Gregorio and any other family members who had defected because of the elevation of Bill Bonanno, or for other reasons, Zicarelli kept insisting that all this was an internal matter and that Joseph Bonanno was not obliged to answer for his actions to the other dons on the commission. As to De Cavalcante's point about the elder Bonanno's not appearing before the commission or its representatives as requested, Zicarelli noted that Gaspar Di Gregorio had been boycotting meetings of the Bonanno organization, and Zicarelli asked, "Why didn't Gasparino [Di Gregorio] come in when all the captains assembled?"

"Well," De Cavalcante said, "he probably had his own right."

"Where does this make sense, Sam—where can he have his own rights?" Zicarelli asked, citing as an example, "You're my boss, you say 'Come in.' Where is my right? I don't have no rights!" Then Zicarelli, speculating darkly about Gaspar Di Gregorio's reasons for staying away, asked, "Is he afraid he's gonna get hit? This guy [Di Gregorio] gotta be guilty of something! Why didn't he come? . . . He was told! From what I understand, he was given all the extensions in the world, that nobody meant no harm or nothing. There was just some misunderstanding and they're holding a meeting. The guy's a captain! What kind of example is he?"

"Well," De Cavalcante said.

"Right or wrong, you go!" Zicarelli said, quickly. "I guarantee you one thing—this guy here is my boss. Right or wrong, if he calls me—I'm going! If I'm gonna get hit—the hell with it! I get hit and that's the end of it. It don't make no sense to me!"

"This guy refuses to go, right?" De Cavalcante asked, seeking to clarify Di Gregorio's position.

"Yeah."

"And he was put on the shelf."

"Temporarily," Zicarelli corrected.

"All right," De Cavalcante said, "so how about Joe? Joe knows better than this. This guy [Di Gregorio] is only a *capo*. Joe is supposed to be chief justice—one of the chief justices."

"Fine," Zicarelli said.

"Wait a minute," De Cavalcante cut in, "now he puts this guy on the shelf, so why shouldn't the commission put Joe Bonanno on the shelf!" Although De Cavalcante conceded that he had finally reached the elder Bonanno and had arranged to deliver the commission's message in person, De Cavalcante added that Bonanno, getting very technical, wanted *three* commission members to deliver the message.

"Why don't you use three people for it?" Zicarelli asked. "To make it *really* right?"

"What's the difference?" De Cavalcante said. "I'm a responsible person . . ." Anyway, De Cavalcante went on, as the commission was about to officially demote Bonanno, he, De Cavalcante, interceded and said, " 'Wait a minute, boys. Give me an opportunity. I want to see this man on my own. I'll take full responsibility.' That's when you took me over to New York, right?" he asked Zicarelli. "At that time I talked to him. For

an hour and a half he kept telling me what a nice guy he was!
'Well, why don't you do the right thing for your family? These
people are not looking to harm anybody. They're all embarrassed. You're putting them to a point where you're aggravating
the whole situation.' People will start to wonder what the hell
has this guy done? You understand what I mean?''

"Yeah," Zicarelli said, conceding, "maybe there's something here that you and I don't know about."

"I know a little more," De Cavalcante said. "There's a lot
of questions they want to ask. Some of them are pretty serious—
but the guy can either say yes or no, that's all. But now they
figure there's something in this that's not kosher. So they wanted
me to go back and tell him to tell these *caporegimas* in his
administration that 'We recognize you but not him. Don't let
this man lead you to where you're all involved. This man has
made a mistake.' It's a bad situation," De Cavalcante said, "and
I've stuck my neck out all the way."

"This is a rough one," Zicarelli said.

"You know this could smash up the whole country again,"
De Cavalcante said.

Zicarelli, while not disputing him, still did not understand
what, if anything, Joseph Bonanno had done that was a violation
of the brotherhood's rules. And it could also be that Bonanno
had been a good boss and that the membership wished to stay
behind him.

"I want to tell you something," De Cavalcante said. "You're
a soldier."

"That's all I am!"

"You see," De Cavalcante said, "these people [Bonanno's
officers], none of them want to open their mouths about him.
There isn't one man in that group that'll challenge him [except
Di Gregorio]." But, De Cavalcante said, he hoped disaster could
be avoided, pointing out to Zicarelli: ". . . there's nobody that
wants peace and harmony more than me, you know that."

"I'm with you."

"I'm telling you because tomorrow I don't want to see you
get involved in anything. I want you to know that the commission has nothing against any of you people."

"Sam, maybe I don't understand . . ."

"Cause this is strictly off the record," De Cavalcante continued. "It's between you and I, but tomorrow I don't want you to

say, 'Jesus Christ, I hold this guy as a friend and he don't let me know!' "

"I understand that, Sam," Zicarelli said. "But," he added, "you're only as good as the team you're on. You're with the team—win, lose, or draw! How can I go the other way?"

"Wait a minute," De Cavalcante said, "I'm not asking . . ."

"I know that! You say to me that in the event something happens I don't want to see you involved. How do I duck? What kind of jerk would I be to duck?"

"Well, you see," De Cavalcante said, "as long as nobody gets hurt . . ."

"See what I mean?" Zicarelli said. "Maybe I don't understand you!"

Undiscouraged, Sam De Cavalcante persisted with his view that Joseph Bonanno was unreasonable. "This guy don't want to listen to reason," De Cavalcante said, "he don't want to be kind. He's causing so much friction amongst everybody! They been looking for this man for over a year!"

"Over a year?"

"Yeah!" De Cavalcante cried. "He said he never got the message. Now they're gonna prove to him that messages were sent and that he received them."

"Well," Zicarelli said, "the man should be at least entitled to the chance to clear himself."

"Well, does he expect the commission to come to him, right or wrong? His own uncle, who is the most respected of the commission, has pleaded with him to come up and see him."

"Who's his uncle?" Joseph Zicarelli asked.

"Stefano Magaddino."

"He's Joe's uncle?"

"Yeah," De Cavalcante said, "there's a relationship. I think it's uncle. And they treated him like dirt! This guy was crying to me—the old guy [Magaddino]. He said, 'Sam, now you tell me this guy's a nice guy. I sent for him. He didn't know if I needed him to save my neck.' Understand what I mean? Joe, if I call you up in an emergency, and you don't show up—you don't know why I'm calling. There might be two guys out there looking to kill me, right? And your presence could save me."

"Yeah, right," Zicarelli said.

"You can't take it upon yourself to ignore these things," De Cavalcante said. "Joe, if you called me, no matter what time,

I'm gonna be down there. And if you're gonna go down, we'll go down together, right?''

"That's right," Zicarelli agreed. "But in the same sense—if your boss is your friend and you have committed yourself to him, right or wrong, where are you going?"

"That's why the commission feels bad," De Cavalcante said. "Because they know that he lied to them. The commission wants your people to know the truth. Then decide if you still want him."

Zicarelli said that the commission should convey this to the officers in the Bonanno family, which De Cavalcante acknowledged was the right thing to do except that the officers were still under Bonanno's control.

"That proves they still recognize him as the boss," Zicarelli deduced.

"I understand that!" De Cavalcante said. "Hey, I'm not saying they didn't do the right thing. The commission also knows that it's under Joe Bonanno's orders . . . But the commission supersedes any boss."

"He ought to know that," Zicarelli finally conceded.

"Better than anybody," said Sam De Cavalcante.

On October 16, 1964—five days before Joseph Bonanno disappeared on Park Avenue—Sam De Cavalcante was again in his office discussing developments with his own man, Majuri. De Cavalcante was upset about a meeting he said he had in Brooklyn with Joseph Colombo, who had somehow failed to impress him, and De Cavalcante wondered aloud at how Colombo could have been elevated to a place on the commission.

"What experience has he [Colombo] got?" De Cavalcante asked. "He was a bust-out guy all his life."

Majuri had no comment.

Despite his closeness to the situation, De Cavalcante seemed no less surprised than the average newspaper reader by the headlines concerning Bonanno's disappearance on October 22, 1964; and a month later the FBI recorded a conversation in which De Cavalcante was asked by one of his men, Joseph La Selva, to explain the Bonanno mystery.

"So what happened?" La Selva asked.

"He [Bonanno] pulled that off himself," De Cavalcante said.

"That figures," said La Selva.

"Well, who the hell is he kidding?" De Cavalcante asked. And then answered his question, "He kidded the government."

"Yeah," La Selva agreed.

"It was his own men," De Cavalcante said. "We figure it was his kid and Vito [possibly meaning Vito De Filippo, his captain with gambling concessions in Haiti]." De Cavalcante went on, "This guy [Bonanno] has got a lot of government appearances . . . but he left everybody in trouble."

"Yeah," said La Selva.

It was to La Selva that De Cavalcante also confided that Joseph Bonanno in 1963 had been the mastermind behind Joseph Magliocco's scheme to dispose of the two commission dons, Carlo Gambino and Thomas Lucchese, and that when the plot failed, the commission was convinced that Joseph Bonanno arranged for the murder of Magliocco.

"They feel that he poisoned Magliocco," De Cavalcante told La Selva. "Magliocco didn't die a natural death," he added, disregarding the medical report that Magliocco had died of a heart attack—Bonanno poisoned him because Magliocco was the only one who could accuse him of plotting against Gambino and Lucchese.

"See," De Cavalcante went on, "Magliocco confessed to it. But this Joe [Bonanno] didn't know how far he went. Understand? So they suspect he used a pill on him—that he's noted for it. So he knows the truth of all the damage he done . . ."

La Selva listened without comment as De Cavalcante continued to regale him with tales learned from the highest authorities in the secret society, tales that seemed right out of medieval Florence, but all that La Selva could finally express was a sense of remorse for the dishonored Bonanno.

"It's a shame," La Selva said. "What was he, fifty-eight, fifty-nine years old? And the prestige he had! What was he looking for anyway?"

De Cavalcante had no answer.

"It's really bad for the morale of our thing, you know?" La Selva continued. "When they make the rules and then break them themselves. He's been in twenty years."

"Thirty-three years he's been in," said De Cavalcante.

By December 30, 1964, with the elder Bonanno still vanished after five weeks, with many people believing him dead, and with the commission now applying increased pressure on certain labor unions to keep Bonanno followers out of work, it was apparent to Sam De Cavalcante that his friend, Zicarelli, had achieved a certain wisdom rather quickly. Zicarelli, who had during the previous month been so staunch in his loyalty to his boss, Joe Bonanno, was now on Gaspar Di Gregorio's side.

Entering De Cavalcante's office, Zicarelli said, "Gasparino sends you his regards."

"Yeah?" De Cavalcante said. "Did you tell him you saw me?"

"I told him, 'Sure, I see him three or four times a week!' "

While apparently pleased that Gaspar Di Gregorio was gaining additional support from such former Bonanno soldiers as Zicarelli, De Cavalcante could not resist reminding Zicarelli of his recently expressed pledge to die for Joseph Bonanno.

"I said until I see different!" Zicarelli corrected him. Zicarelli asked, "What do you mean, I want to die? I said if somebody looks to hurt him before I get a chance to see different, certainly I'm gonna help him." Then, switching the subject to Bill Bonanno, Zicarelli ventured that he thought Bill was a little crazy, or else "he's immature to a point where from being born with a silver spoon." And Bill "don't know what hardship is— he thinks he's running a cowboy camp here. A Wild West show!"

"You can't," Zicarelli went on, "take a kid out of a cradle and put him in a tuxedo and let him boss people in the gutter if he can't talk their language."

As De Cavalcante continued to listen, Zicarelli announced: "I told him one time to his face—I said, 'You got three strikes against you, kid.' He said, 'What are they?' I said, 'One, you can't talk to everybody on *their* level. Number two, you're the boss's son. And number three, you're too young and inexperienced. These are the three strikes that are gonna destroy you.' I told him this the day they made him *consigliere*. We were sitting in Westworth Restaurant.

"He went and told his father, and his father sent for me. [He said] 'What do you mean and this and that.' You know, it took me until five one morning to get out of that. I told him, 'This is the way I feel. Now if I can see this picture, you, who came up the hard way from all the wars you say you've been through, you should see it too. If it was my son, I'd never put him in—in a million years! I wouldn't make him a friend.' "

"That's right," De Cavalcante agreed.

"Unless the kid was a wayward kid," Zicarelli amended, "and I knew that he knew all the angles."

Near the end of February 1965, however, the luster that Gaspar Di Gregorio seemed to have as a leader of men was no longer so obvious to Sam De Cavalcante, who had been witness to complaints and who had himself noticed negative qualities about Di Gregorio in recent weeks.

"I think it's going to his head," De Cavalcante said, speaking with one of his underlings, Louie Larasso, in the plumber's office.

"Well," Larasso said, "he's no kid. What is he, sixty-two or sixty-three years old? He's been around a long time, that guy."

"He's been around as long as Peppino," De Cavalcante said. "He's done as much work for that outfit as Peppino did." But Larasso agreed with De Cavalcante's declining opinion of Di Gregorio.

"Gasparino looks . . . no good," Larasso said. "They should have waited a long time before they made a boss. Cause there's too much undercurrent."

These recorded revelations, which represent a small fraction of the tonnage of tape that the FBI has drawn from Mafia privacy, might have remained beyond the reach of public scrutiny had it not been for a strategic error on the part of De Cavalcante's attorney in 1969 before the trial of De Cavalcante and two co-defendants in an extortion-conspiracy case in federal court in Newark.

Contending that the indictments against De Cavalcante and the other defendants had been obtained illegally through wire-tapping, the defense attorney called for a bill of particulars and disclosure as to whether or not electronic eavesdropping had been used. The attorney, who had once served as an Assistant United States Attorney in New Jersey, believed that the government would, as usual, refuse to release the transcripts and thus be forced to drop the indictments. But the attorney, by his own admission, was astounded when the government turned over to the court the 2,300 typewritten pages of recorded conversations, which then became public property and accessible to the press and which by their circulation would produce repercussions and debates that went far beyond the issues in the case against De Cavalcante or even the Mafia. Many individuals with no connection with the Mafia were mentioned in certain tapes released in 1969 and 1970; dozens of politicians, businessmen, public entertainers, policemen, laborers, and even lawyers would be publicly linked to the Mafia because of the tapes—some justifiably, some only because of the boasting of small-time mafiosi, and some would protest. Among those who did complain were Mayor Thomas Dunn of Elizabeth, New Jersey, who, while admitting taking $100 or $200 from De Cavalcante during a 1964 mayoral campaign, insisted that he had no idea that De Cavalcante was a mafioso. Representative Cornelius E. Gallagher of Bayonne, New Jersey, issued a statement in Washington denying any connection with Zicarelli, claiming that he was merely a victim on tape of Zicarelli's name-dropping.

Arguing in support of publicizing the wiretap disclosures were editorial writers, law enforcement officials, and several members of the New Jersey legislature who believed that the tapes were a valuable weapon against organized crime and would prove to an otherwise skeptical or lethargic public that there was indeed a Mafia. And New Jersey, which was presently sponsoring one of the most enthusiastic anti-Mafia campaigns in the nation, permitted its state police to pursue a policy of harassment, which included such tactics as ticketing the cars of individuals who were visiting the homes or business offices of reputed mafiosi and dispatching state police to the home in Deal, New Jersey, of a mafioso, Anthony Russo, each night and turning their high-beam lights directly on Russo's bedroom.

While the disclosures revealed on the De Cavalcante tapes were said to be inadmissible evidence in court, the publicity surrounding them established Sam De Cavalcante as a national figure in crime—his face adorned the cover of a paperback entitled *The Mafia Talks*; and he was profiled in *The New York Times*'s "Man in the News" column on June 13, 1969. When his extortion-conspiracy case came up in court, he was convicted and received the maximum sentence permitted under law—fifteen years in prison.

He was visibly stunned by the decision, turning pale, his left cheek twitching uncontrollably as the federal judge, Lawrence A. Whipple, revoked the $50,000 bail and ordered him jailed immediately.

After the sentencing, De Cavalcante was interviewed by the press.

"What can I say?" he asked, still seemingly confused, shaken. "I don't know what happened. I tried to make things equal, and this is how it turned out."

24

ON READING THE transcripts in San Jose, Bill Bonanno was immediately angered at being described so unflatteringly; but he also felt, after a second and third reading, that the tapes clearly reconfirmed what he and his father had concluded—the brotherhood was now overpopulated with braggarts and mini-mafiosi, and if President Nixon needed $61 million from Congress to combat such insignificant characters it surely must represent the greatest example of law enforcement featherbedding in history.

There was also something sadly comical about the De Cavalcante dialogues, suggesting to Bill an outdated parody of *Guys and Dolls* by inferior actors, or the 1940s cartoons of "Willie and Joe," the two bedraggled GIs sitting in foxholes philosophizing about the war and the generals. It was no wonder that his father had become incompatible with the commission and had refused to be guided by the dictates of old men approaching senility and middle-aged men hardly competent.

And yet, long after Bill had put the transcripts aside, he sat in the living room alone after Rosalie and the children had gone to sleep, feeling embittered, thinking again about the situations that De Cavalcante had made reference to, remembering the years that he wanted to forget—1963, 1964, the time of friction in the organization after his elevation to *consigliere*. All of Bill's hostility toward De Cavalcante and Zicarelli after reading their comments, and all of Bill's self-justification and ego, did not belie the fact that the "trouble" had begun in 1963 after he had moved from Arizona to New York. And still Bill did not believe, as Zicarelli apparently did, that he was merely a product of nepotism, that he owed his position of leadership strictly to his father when in fact Bill had often felt when he looked back on it that what he had inherited from his father was a slowly sinking ship. His father had gone off to Canada in 1963, had disappeared entirely in 1964, leaving Bill with a crew of mutineers led by Di Gregorio. If the men had remained loyal, if Di Gregorio had not been so bitter and jealous, and if Stefano Magaddino had tended to his own business, they might all be better off today. Or maybe not. Bill was better off without them. Let them sink, he thought, the hell with them.

But the sensational publicity generated by the De Cavalcante tapes would undoubtedly keep the Mafia in the national head-lines throughout the summer and fall of 1969, and Bill antici-pated more subpoenas and visits from federal agents asking the same old questions, to which he would give the same old an-swers. He would say that he had played no role in his father's disappearance, that he had absolutely no idea where his father had been during those many months, and that he would make no effort to find out. When the case came to trial—if the gov-ernment could produce a witness claiming to have seen Joseph Bonanno during the period he was allegedly kidnaped—Bill Bonanno wanted nothing to do with the case. He had already told the grand jury everything he swore he knew about that situation, and he had enough court problems of his own to worry about.

The government in fact now claimed to know the elder Bo-nanno had been in Haiti during the months it was searching for him. *Life* magazine had already published this, and *True* mag-azine was about to report it in greater detail. According to *True*, the CIA and the Justice Department had gathered "hard" in-formation earlier in the year that Joseph Bonanno personally knew President François Duvalier of Haiti; he had had private talks at the palace in Port-au-Prince with Duvalier in 1963 when he had acquired the Haitian casino concession; and after he vanished on Park Avenue in October 1964, Bonanno reappeared in Port-au-Prince and lived there under Duvalier's protection for a full year. The kidnaping, according to *Life* and *The New York Times* and other publications, was legitimate and had been ex-ecuted by gunmen working for the commission who took Bo-nanno to a hideaway in the Catskills, where he met with other dons and talked his way out of his assassination by vowing that his death would start a national gangland war and also by prom-ising to relinquish his leadership in repayment for his life. He was believed to have been released under these conditions in December 1964, whereupon he traveled to Haiti, perhaps by ship, leaving unresolved the matter of his succession. Since the United States had poor diplomatic relations with Duvalier, who suspected the Americans of repeatedly attempting to overthrow his regime with guerrilla infiltrators trained by Special Forces and spies, Joseph Bonanno found Haiti ideal because it considered the CIA and FBI as archenemies.

Bill doubted that his father would ever confirm or deny these reports; he believed that the circumstances surrounding his father's disappearance, and the place and manner in which his father had lived during the nineteen-month period, were a dark fascinating secret that Joseph Bonanno would take to his grave.

What most surprised Bill Bonanno about the De Cavalcante tapes was the commission's theory that Joseph Bonanno had poisoned Magliocco, which Bill knew was absurd, having lived in Magliocco's house with Rosalie and the children at the time of his uncle's death. Nevertheless, on the basis of De Cavalcante's statement the government ordered Magliocco's body removed from the vault where it had been for more than five years, and a second autopsy was performed. It failed to show any trace of poison, and the Suffolk County District Attorney's office in Long Island announced that the inquiry into the death of Joseph Magliocco was closed.

The taped references to Magliocco, however, as well as to some of Magliocco's relatives in the Profaci family caused much discomfort among some of the second generation of that family—one such individual was Rosalie's older brother, Salvatore Profaci, a quiet, stout man in his mid-thirties who lived in New Jersey and was in the real estate business. The publicity that Profaci received in the New Jersey press, though not incriminating in a legal sense, disturbed him, and he was upset when he arrived in California on the second weekend in June to attend the wedding of his youngest sister, Josephine.

Slumped in a patio chair at the home of his sister Ann, where Sunday dinner was being prepared for a gathering of Josephine's family on the day before the wedding, Salvatore Profaci shook his head and said that the state of New Jersey was conducting an inquisition, and he repeated, slowly and sadly, that the association of his name with the De Cavalcante publicity would have a ruinous effect on his business opportunities. Bill Bo-

nanno, who sat casually, drink in hand, with Profaci and some
other men, disagreed, saying that his brother-in-law was overreacting, that things were not that bad, and that public clamor
over De Cavalcante would eventually subside as the FBI and the
media discovered something else to exploit. But Bill realized
that his attempt to comfort Sal Profaci was having little effect—
Profaci, unlike himself, was unaccustomed to having his surname in the national press in recent years. The decline of the
Profaci organization in the early 1960s and the ascension of
Joseph Colombo after the death of Magliocco in 1963 had taken
the focus off the nephews, uncles, cousins, nieces, wives, and
sons of the late Olive Oil King, Joseph Profaci, or The Fat Man,
Joseph Magliocco. Such people as Bill and his father had replaced the Profacis in the headlines, and there were times in
recent years, at family gatherings, when Bill sensed that a few
of Rosalie's close and distant relatives would have preferred to
disown him. It had little to do with his problem with Rosalie,
though they might have justified it for that reason, but rather
with "what he stood for." He could not prove this, he just felt
it, believing that he reminded them of a life-style that they would
prefer to forget. And so hearing the lamentations of his brother-
in-law Sal Profaci, on the patio, Bill felt along with sympathy a
slight perverse sense of delight in Sal's discomfort. It was nice,
for a change, not to be the house gangster; and he was strongly
tempted to gently poke fun at Sal, to mockingly complain at
dinner in front of the assembled Profaci clan that Sal was "giving us a bad name." While prudence triumphed in this instance,
Bill was later unable to resist saying teasingly to Josephine, the
bride-to-be, that the next day the FBI might be among the wedding guests. Josephine was repelled.

"They'd better not!" she snapped. She glared at him, and
was not amused.

The sprawling green lawns of the campus were almost abandoned at 6:00 P.M. except for the people moving up the stone
steps of the Stanford University Memorial Chapel. It was bright
and sunny at this hour, the air was clear and still. It was a perfect
day, a perfect time for a wedding.

Inside the high-ceilinged chapel the pews were empty row
upon row, and beyond the altar rail the wedding guests filed into
the choir stalls flanking the altar. On the left were the Profacis,

formal, dressed in dark suits and silk dresses. In the first pew, alone, was Mrs. Profaci, serene and maternal, wearing a well-tailored pink damask dress. Behind her was her younger son, an attorney, with his wife; her daughter Ann and her husband, Lou; Mrs. Joseph Bonanno and Catherine, whose hair was elaborately curled and carefully coiffed; other relatives, friends, children. As yet, Rosalie and Bill had not appeared, but since one of their children was ill, they were expected to be a few minutes late.

On the right were the Stantons—tweedy, bright flowered or print dresses, lean young women with long straight hair, long-haired college boys in sports jackets, including one youth who attended the tape recorder at the right of the altar from which the wedding music would come. The groom's parents, in the front row, were a handsome couple exuding the good health of the suburbs, and with them was the groom's grandmother, elegant in old age, looking very much the dowager.

In the center of the altar stood the chaplain, a tall, distinguished man with gray hair, blue eyes, an eagle's gaze. He stood waiting, eyes fixed on the long empty aisle stretching ahead of him, although once he flashed a quick look to his right at a noisy child on the Profaci side. It was not a sign of reproof but of awareness.

Standing in front of the altar was the groom, Tim Stanton, wearing a new tan suit, loafers, his long blond hair neatly combed, a pink carnation in his lapel. Next to him was his best man, wearing the blue cornflower that Josephine had intended for Tim.

As the music was turned on at the tape deck—it was the Latin American folk Mass, *Misa Criolla*—Josephine Profaci, on the arm of her brother Sal, walked slowly up the aisle, looking poised and lovely, her dark bright eyes and hair in sharp contrast to the white veil and Juliet cap she wore. Her long white gown was of silk organza, with single rows of lace running vertically, and while it seemed to have been specially designed for her, she had in fact selected it in twenty minutes, much to the dismay of her mother who had spent months with Rosalie and Ann searching for their gowns. Josephine's bouquet was of blue cornflowers, pink carnations, and white baby's breath, which she had made herself, disliking the ones usually produced by florists.

Continuing up the aisle, Josephine felt a warm, deep attach-

ment to her brother Sal, who, possibly even more than her
mother, had initially found it difficult to accept her break with
Catholicism; and if he had been part of the typical bull-headed
"over-thirty" crowd that she saw as abounding in America today, he would never have come to this nondenominational ceremony. But she felt at this moment that she was walking between
two traditions—her own family's on the left, with which she still
symbolically identified herself by wearing a white wedding
gown, and Tim Stanton's on the right, which she saw as closer
to the independent spirit she felt as a modern young woman.
Both of Tim's parents were democratic individuals in a suburban
community that revolved around the right school, the right
church, the right clubs; and while Tim's brothers and sisters
seemed to have accepted the more traditional values of that community, in the same way that Josephine's brothers and sisters
had accepted the values of theirs, Tim had somehow remained
remote from his surroundings as Josephine had from hers. Tim's
closest boyhood friends in suburban New York had not been the
sons of stockbrokers but rather the sons of an actor, a well-
driller, and a black garbage man who had since been driven out
of business by the Mafia. After Tim had gone West to attend
Stanford, he seemed to Josephine to be as lonely and as searching as she was herself; they shared, in a quiet and undramatic
way, a rebellion away from the values of their parents' societies,
and yet they also shared an abundance of love and acceptance
from their parents. And so while Josephine recognized her own
past as provincial and dull, she had never been tempted to turn
her back on her family or deny her origins, and the proof was
right here, as she on the arm of her brother Sal reached the altar,
approaching Tim Stanton.

   As the chaplain delivered a short sermon on the challenges
and meaning of marriage, Josephine looked at Tim, thought him
very handsome, admired his new tan suit, and noticed that he
was wearing the wrong boutonniere. After the vows and rings
were exchanged, and the young man at the side of the altar
pressed the button on the tape deck, the sound of "O Happy
Day," a Negro spiritual, was heard; and Mr. and Mrs. Tim
Stanton turned and walked down the aisle toward the vestibule
of the church.

   Outside, a photographer snapped pictures of the couple walking down the steps, and soon all the guests gathered in front of

the chapel, standing very close but not really mingling. They nodded toward one another, shifted awkwardly from foot to foot, but they continued to talk within their own circles along the sidewalk. Only the bridal couple and their parents moved freely between the two groups, kissing, shaking hands.

Mrs. Profaci appeared to be very much the mother of the wedding, a large smiling woman who had just married off the fifth of her five children; she seemed very comfortable in this situation, and she knew all the guests by name, including the couple's classmates from Berkeley and Stanford. Still, Mrs. Profaci saw no sign of Rosalie and Bill; and when the only explanation that she could get from one of Bill's friends was that Bill's home telephone did not answer, she became worried and mildly irritated.

An hour later the guests reassembled at the Los Altos Country Club, passing in the parking lot on their way to the reception a new Volkswagen camper that was Mrs. Profaci's gift to the couple. The reception was held on the lawn of the club's Tally Ho Restaurant, a picturesque setting surrounded by trees and rolling hills and echoing with music from the orchestra that played under a canopy. Waiters moved through the crowd carrying trays of food and champagne, and as it became darker and the outdoor lights were turned on, Mrs. Profaci could no longer contain her concern at Rosalie and Bill's absence, and finally she approached two men she knew to be close to Bill and demanded: ''Are you people holding something back from me?''

They said they were not, and one of the men excused himself to make another telephone call, although it was only a ploy—he knew, as did others, that Bill was boycotting the wedding and refused to let Rosalie attend because Josephine had failed to invite a cousin of his, a man from Castellammare who had recently moved to San Jose. When Bill had learned earlier in the day that his cousin was not on the guest list he regarded it as an insult, attaching more significance to this than to the fact that Josephine did not consider his cousin close enough to be included. But Bill preferred to believe that his cousin was not invited because, during the previous summer, while his cousin was in East Meadow helping Rosalie move the last of the furniture from the house, he had indiscreetly suggested in Josephine's presence that Rosalie's and Josephine's late father had been the ''brains'' behind the organization headed by the fa-

mous Joe Profaci, the Olive Oil King. This view had certainly
never been held by anyone in Rosalie's family, who believed
their father's association with Joseph Profaci was merely a relationship between brothers. Bill saw the exclusion of his cousin
at the wedding as a rebuff by Josephine to the expression of an
opinion that Bill himself shared, and he conveyed this to Rosalie
on the day of the wedding. And during the afternoon as no
invitation was extended, even belatedly, Bill's anger mounted
and he finally forbade Rosalie to appear at the church. Rosalie
protested, crying, it was her *sister's* wedding, but Bill was adamant.

By eight that night they were hardly speaking to each other
and the next day when Mrs. Profaci learned the truth about their
absence, she too became incensed and refused to answer the
phone when Rosalie tried to call to explain and apologize. For
days the hostility between Rosalie and Bill continued, and Bill
told friends that there might be a separation. But Rosalie's one
runaway summer in Long Island in 1967 seemed to have been
the limit of her capacity to rebel, and gradually the energy to
sustain the anger was too much and their life in San Jose drifted
back to its uneventful routine of household details, children,
waiting, and eventually forgiving.

25

On July 21, 1969, one year after Joseph Bonanno's home had been bombed, the Tucson police arrested a suspect—a lean, spectacled twenty-three-year-old electrical engineer employed in Tucson by the Hughes Aircraft Company. His name was Paul Mills Stevens, and he had acquired a knowledge of demolitions in the Marine Corps. At the time of his arrest, Stevens's right hand and arm still showed the effects of being hit by the shotgun blasts fired by Bill Bonanno seconds after he tossed the bombs into the Bonanno backyard and made his escape along a dark street where a getaway car was waiting.

But Stevens was not the only one involved in the bombings. Two days after his arrest, a second man, William John Dunbar, twenty-six, was surrounded by police at a trailer camp on the Gila River Indian Reservation, where he had been hiding out with a girl. He was returned to Tucson and, like Stevens, was held on $10,000 bond. Dunbar was once a professional auto racer, a skilled archer, a springboard diver; and though he was most recently employed in the accounting department of an auto specialty shop, he still identified himself as a car racer and kept in top physical condition through regular workouts at the local YMCA. He was suspected by the police of having assisted Stevens with the bombings, but both men were believed to have worked under the direction of someone else, an individual whose name neither man would reveal.

And when it finally did become known, it was not through Stevens or Dunbar but rather through a twenty-one-year-old girl who was a friend of theirs and had been privy to their plottings, a girl who had been engaged to marry Dunbar's brother before his death in a motorcycle accident. Her allegations in Superior Court caused sensational headlines in Arizona's newspapers as well as shock and disbelief in Tucson and embarrassment in Washington. The man who instigated the bombings, who picked the targets and drove the getaway car, she said, was an agent for the FBI.

While she did not give his full name, saying only that he was "an FBI agent named Dave," Bill Bonanno knew immediately who "Dave" was after the newspapers reported the story—David O. Hale, the FBI's Arizona expert on Mafia affairs, an agent who had regularly tailed Bill around Tucson and who, on the day that Hank Perrone was murdered in New York, had visited the elder Bonanno's Tucson home and told Bill, "Well, I see your friend got it." Bill recalled the angry exchange that had followed between Hale and himself, and he also remembered that it was David Hale who had tried to induce the friend of Joseph Jr., the young blond Texan who had been the Bonannos' houseguest, into informing the government on the routine of the Bonanno household.

When the press confronted David Hale with the charges against him, he refused to comment; nor would anyone from the Justice Department or FBI headquarters in Washington reveal any information. But as the press persisted in its investigative reporting, the Tucson police finally acknowledged that David Hale was a suspect, among other citizens, and before long Stevens and Dunbar pleaded guilty to the bombings in court and told most of the story.

They testified that the bombing raids had been planned by Hale in the early summer of 1968, which was an auspicious time for such a scheme in Tucson. Editorials had already advocated that the Bonannos and other underworld figures leave the city, and many influential citizens throughout the state were in agreement with the national crusade against the Mafia—which, having reached a peak under Attorney General Robert F. Kennedy, and having declined under Attorney General Ramsey Clark (who thought that the Mafia was overrated), had been revived by President Nixon and his Attorney General, John N. Mitchell. It was not difficult in the charged atmosphere that existed in Tucson in 1968 for David Hale to find citizens who shared his concern about Mafia infiltrators, and he was thus able to interest the president of the Southern Arizona Bank in sponsoring a series of crime seminars. He also received enthusiastic moral support from such respected businessmen as Walter I. Prideaux.

Prideaux, fifty years old, a graduate of the University of Wisconsin, had once taught school in Arizona and had briefly tutored Joseph Bonanno, Jr., so that he could pass the entrance requirements for the University of Arizona. Prideaux had been the general office manager of the Complete Auto Supply Company in Tucson in 1968 when he was approached by Hale with a plan to finally purge Tucson of the Mafia. Hale's plot was to explode bombs on the property of the Mafia leaders, which he hoped would provoke a feud by making them suspect that each was trying to eliminate the other. Since Hale's plan might at the very least drive mafiosi from Tucson, Prideaux agreed to help the FBI agent carry out his mission. David Hale then approached Dunbar, another employee of Complete Auto, whose participation was encouraged by Hale's promise that Dunbar's record of a 1963 theft conviction—Dunbar's only encounter with the law but one which prevented him from getting higher-paying jobs—would be cleared from his record. Dunbar then recruited Stevens, who he knew had had experience with explosives while serving in the marines. Stevens became an accomplice because, as his defense attorney later explained in court, Stevens "was in awe of law enforcement."

Stevens and Dunbar both testified that on the night of July 21, 1968, they drove to Peter Licavoli's ranch with David Hale and Walter Prideaux. Stevens said that he accompanied Hale over fences and across a field to the ranch house, but when Hale instructed him to bomb the house, which had a light burning that indicated someone might have been inside, he refused; so Hale settled for planting dynamite in the garage. They then hurried back to the car, and with Prideaux driving they raced to a point three miles from the ranch before the first two explosions could be heard, damaging four vehicles and knocking a hole into the roof of the carport.

On the following evening the four men drove to the Bonanno house, first passing the front of the home on East Elm Street, then turning onto Chauncey Lane, where Hale parked the car near a corner, leaving the motor running, and dispatched Dunbar and Stevens with the dynamite to blow up Bonanno's brick wall. After they placed the dynamite at the wall and after Dunbar tossed a small bomb over the wall, they turned to run; but Stevens was then hit by the shotgun blasts, and, confused, he proceeded to run, staggering, in the wrong direction—away from

the car. Hale became nervous and impatient, Dunbar later recalled in court, and wanted to drive off without Stevens; but
Dunbar insisted that they get Stevens, which they did, taking
him first to Prideaux's home and then to St. Mary's Hospital.

During the months that followed, Hale continuously assured
the other men that, since they were assisting the FBI and the
government, they would be protected from prosecution if they
were arrested. Convinced that it was Peter Notaro who had shot
at Stevens the night of the Bonanno bombing, Hale approached
Dunbar with a plan to avenge Stevens's injury by killing Notaro;
knowing that Dunbar was a skilled archer, Hale suggested that
death by crossbow would be an interesting method. Dunbar refused.

On August 16, Notaro's house was bombed, and by then Hale
had drawn up a list of other locations to be hit, still convincing
his accomplices that they were acting under government orders.
Stevens told the court that once Hale even visited him in the
hospital, carrying sticks of dynamite under his coat, asking Stevens to "crimp a cap into a fuse"; but Stevens, without the use
of one arm, was unable to oblige.

Dunbar, Prideaux, and Stevens, however, were not Hale's
total cadre against the Mafia, for he was sometimes joined on
other raids by a pretty blonde divorcee named Frances Angleman, who was completing her Ph.D. in anthropology at the
University of Arizona and who hoped to do an anthropological
study on the Tucson-based Mafia for her doctorate thesis. The
story about her relationship with Hale was revealed in an article
in the Arizona *Republic*, which obtained its information from
individuals in whom Frances Angleman had confided.

According to her friends, she was with Hale on the evening
of July 3, 1968, when he used a shotgun to blast out the large
picture window at the Oro Valley home of Anthony Tisci, son-
in-law of Chicago's Sam Giancana. She frequently wore a brunette wig when traveling with Hale, and she affected a Sicilian
accent while sitting with him in Tucson nightclubs she believed
were frequented by mafiosi. It had possibly been Frances Angleman seated in the cream-colored Chevrolet that Bill Bonanno
observed during the summer evening of 1968 cruising slowly
with its headlights off in front of his father's house when dynamite had been tossed out the car window, but had failed to
detonate.

But Bill would never be able to confirm this from her personally, because before the FBI plot became public knowledge, she was found dead in her apartment with a .22-caliber pistol in her right hand and a bullet in her head. The police called it a clear case of suicide, noting that before her death—she was discovered by her mother on May 14, 1969—she had left notes requesting that certain books and other items be returned to their owners and that she had also left a typewritten will and a diary. David Hale was mentioned in her will, a fact confirmed by her father, a retired lawyer for Hughes Aircraft; and while her friends believed that her diary contained notations about the bombings, her father was quoted in the Arizona *Republic* as saying that he had thrown the diary into the rubbish without reading it.

Not long before her death, she was reported to have been in an extremely nervous state, believing, according to her friends, that the Mafia was following her and was aware of her involvement in the bombings. She had also claimed to have found, on the floor outside her apartment door, an empty shotgun shell.

On August 12, 1969, three weeks after the arrest of Dunbar and Stevens, David Hale resigned from the FBI and quickly disappeared from town, unavailable for comment to the press. His attorney later stated that United States Attorney General John Mitchell had ordered Hale not to testify about anything he had learned in his official FBI capacity or to disclose anything contained in FBI records. Although the Arizona press was dissatisfied with this, it was unable to reach by telephone cooperative spokesmen in Washington for either the Justice Department or FBI. The editorial writers who had once been condemning the mafiosi were now condemning federal law enforcement authorities, and the columnist for the Arizona *Republic*, Paul Dean, expressed the sentiments of many citizens of Tucson in his "Open Letter" column to J. Edgar Hoover dated August 18, 1969:

Dear Mr. Hoover:

It has been some time since we traded letters. And time is too long. For I enjoy our exchanges, reaching back years to when you commended an article I wrote on the work of the FBI in Arizona.

Yours were kind words, expressing gratitude for my support

of your office and officers while hoping that the FBI's "future efforts will continue to merit" my approval.

That was June 1965. This is August 1969.

And today, a segment of the efforts of the FBI in Arizona no longer merits my approval.

It concerns that hand grenade in your in-basket; that allegation made in Tucson last week that your bureau, or at least one of its agents, attempted a CIA-type fait accompli and tried to foment a Mafia war between those local boys made bad, Pete Licavoli and Joe Bonanno.

Joe's place was bombed. Pete's ranch and trucks got blasted. Several restaurants and businesses allied to both mobs suddenly found business "booming." Finally, two men were picked up and charged with the attacks.

And now, commenting on testimony from the state's chief witness, you have personally confirmed an FBI man was "allegedly involved" in the bombing of Bonanno's home and that this agent is no longer with the bureau.

My God. This is like finding out that Eliot Ness was on Al Capone's payroll, that the Taj Mahal was built from an erector set and the Apollo 11 moon landing was actually a simulation in Meteor Crater.

Worse, like Teddy Kennedy who crossed a bridge before he came to it, your office is spreading the wound by offering no comment beyond empty mumbles that "yup, it may have happened and we're looking at it."

Your senior agents refuse to discuss even the basics of the issue, the name of the agent involved, the date his service ended, reasons for termination, and why, if his exit was clouded, it took you so long to get around to investigating him. Nobody under legal scrutiny, from traffic offender to accused mass murderer, gets that kind of police protection.

Tucson agents (apparently forgetting who pays the rent) have refused to allow a reporter for this newspaper into their front office. One has lied by saying he didn't know where the involved agent was or when he would be coming back.

Reticence in search of discretion; reluctance for fear of false condemnation; silence in the interests of national security. This has been the FBI way for years and is a formula understood by the news media.

But this is ridiculous. Suddenly, the FBI is tangoing with

the truth to save face. This is children at play and third-grade public relations.

While politicians are steaming, the U.S. Attorney is on tippytoe, and a police chief is promising a sensational trial with blue-ribbon scandal, the FBI is sitting back playing with its destruct button.

Strangely, Mr. Hoover, in this particular instance, I'm not kicking around old arguments involving freedom of information, freedom of the press, and the public's right to know. There's a more important issue at stake.

For, by this Tucson action, your fine, hand-crafted organization is playing to the subversive, militant, extreme elements we have been fighting together for years.

I'm a member of the establishment, right down to my mortgage, three-year-old auto and sta-prest pants. So I've heard long-haired yelps about my institution, my government, and my Federal Bureau of Investigation being hypocritical, immoral, corrupt, and sprinkled with collusion, dishonesty, and deceit. I haven't bought 'em because I've witnessed, even envied, the FBI as the world's finest crime-cracking machine. And I used to be a Scotland Yard man.

But now, with all this ducking, weaving, and swerving, there is some support for the rabid claims. Suddenly, I have to ask myself questions. Tragically, I can't get any answers.

How long before the angry young minds start asking questions? When they do, what do we tell them, Mr. Hoover?

Yours sincerely,
Paul Dean

P.S. I'd appreciate a reply of about column length.

The reply that Paul Dean received from J. Edgar Hoover was a few paragraphs of formalized evasiveness; and when Dean wrote a second private note to Hoover asking for something substantial, he received nothing at all.

Although David Hale was reported to have moved to Miami, where he was said to be a security officer for Giffen Industries, Inc., he was served with a subpoena to appear for the Superior Court trial of his involvement in the bombings. When Hale did appear, he refused to testify. Walter Prideaux invoked the Fifth Amendment. Neither man was held. The two who pleaded guilty, Stevens and Dunbar, were freed, after being fined $286 each on misdemeanor charges.

After the trial, the Bonannos had no comment to make to the press. That the FBI was on the defensive was no cause for rejoicing in the Bonanno household, where it was felt that the agents would retaliate like wounded lions, unrelenting in their pursuit of revenge. The elder Bonanno and Peter Notaro had already felt the backlash of the FBI shortly after the publication of the initial press reports linking David Hale to the bombings—a simultaneous FBI raid at 7:00 A.M. was directed at the Bonanno and Notaro homes in Tucson, arresting both men on charges of plotting to get Bonanno's *capo* Charles Battaglia out of jail through the use of bribes, blackmail, and threats of death.

Battaglia was then serving a ten-year sentence in Leavenworth, having been fined $10,000 because he was found guilty of threatening to force a Tucson bowling alley manager to install a coin-operated pool table that would be provided by a vending firm Battaglia represented. On the day of the arrest of Bonanno and Notaro, the FBI contended that the imprisoned Battaglia had sought to win a retrial on the basis of new evidence showing that his conviction had been obtained by the illegal use of electronic eavesdropping equipment. The FBI further alleged that Battaglia's plot to free himself had been outlined in a series of cryptic letters between himself and Bonanno, letters alluding to sums of money and certain rewards to be made to citizens who might support and assist Battaglia's campaign for freedom, and death threats to those who would not. On Bonanno's death list, according to the FBI, was David Hale.

The FBI's informant was a fellow prisoner of Battaglia's at Leavenworth, an inmate who worked as a clerk to a prison official and could send letters without censorship, and claimed to have done so on Battaglia's behalf. But when the conspiracy case against Bonanno and Notaro came to trial in Tucson, a third prisoner surprised the jury by testifying that the FBI's informer had admitted privately that he had lied—the government's conspiracy case was a hoax. The elder Bonanno and Notaro were acquitted—the FBI was embarrassed; and Bill Bonanno, who was then in a New York court facing the possibility of spending many years in jail, thought apprehensively to himself, *the gov-*

ernment will get me now. My father beat them in Arizona, but they'll get even in this case.

The case Bill was referring to was the credit card situation in federal court—his having taken Torrillo's Diners' Club card from Perrone, having signed Torrillo's name on more than fifty vouchers during the cross-country journey from New York to Arizona during the heat of the Banana War, a time when Bill seemed to be a most likely target in the East.

Now, almost two years after that misguided venture, he felt he was the government's target. Though he had stood before many judges and juries in recent years, this latest court appearance was unlike any other in that it filled him with a sense of impending doom. He knew that the government had Torrillo on its side, that teams of federal agents had joined forces to fortify the prosecution's case, and that their combined efforts could incarcerate him for years.

When he said good-bye to Rosalie and the children in San Jose prior to his flight, he was aware, and thought that they were also aware, though nothing was said, that it might be a long time before they would see one another again.

PART FOUR

THE JUDGMENT

26

THE CREDIT CARD case against Bill Bonanno began in federal court in downtown Manhattan on Monday afternoon, November 10, 1969, with the Honorable Walter R. Mansfield presiding. At fifty-seven, Judge Mansfield, a man with a full head of white hair, gentle blue eyes, and a smooth pinkish complexion, seemed so self-assured in his courtroom manner that one might have assumed that he had spent most of his life in magisterial robes; whereas, in fact, he had only become a judge three years before. It was true that he had been reared with the advantage of rank and position, and perhaps that contributed to his aura of command. His father, the late Frederick W. Mansfield, had been the mayor of Boston in the 1930s when the younger Mansfield was attending Harvard Law School; and during World War II, Walter Mansfield served as an officer in the Marine Corps, both in the European and Asiatic theaters, including duty with the OSS—parachuting behind enemy lines in Yugoslavia and working with guerrilla groups behind Japanese lines in China.

After the war, separated from the marines with the rank of major, he became an Assistant United States Attorney for the New York Southern District, where he prosecuted and tried a variety of criminal cases that included customs violations, crimes of theft on New York piers, bankruptcy frauds, narcotics activities, illicit still operations, counterfeiting, confidence swindles, and mail frauds. In 1948, a year after his marriage at the age of thirty-five, he went into private practice with the firm of Donovan Leisure Newton & Irwine, of 2 Wall Street, remaining there until becoming a federal judge in 1966.

A skier, golfer, tennis player, swimmer, and gardener, hobbies he pursues when he leaves his Park Avenue home on weekends for his residence in New Canaan or his travels into New

England, Walter Mansfield's sedentary existence as a judge has
not diminished his vital energy, a fact that was apparent in the
spry manner with which he strode into the courtroom on this
Monday in November. Climbing the steps to the bench, ac-
knowledging the assembled jury, Judge Mansfield seemed anxious to begin the proceedings that had been delayed the previous
Friday by the task of selecting a jury that would not be prejudiced by the notoriety of the Bonanno name. On that day, fifteen
of the first twenty-seven prospective jurors had been excused or
challenged. But now the twelve jurors were impaneled—eight
women, four men—and the judge leaned back in his chair waiting for the government prosecutor to walk to the rostrum to
deliver the opening statement. The judge momentarily looked
toward the rows of spectators, the reporters in the front row,
and he also observed with apparent satisfaction that the windows
were partially open to let the cool November breeze into his
courtroom on the eleventh floor overlooking Foley Square.
Mansfield, a New Englander, relished fresh air and ran a cool
courtroom.

The prosecutor, a tall, thin dark-haired man named Walter
Phillips, who was about forty and wore a gray suit and a thin
blue-striped tie, was about to speak. Bill Bonanno stopped whispering to his attorney, Albert Krieger. To Bill's right at the big
table that was behind the government's table, was the codefendant, Peter Notaro, a burly man in his mid-fifties; and on Notaro's right was his attorney, a soft-spoken sandy-haired man in
his forties named Leonard Sandler.

"May it please the Court, Mr. Foreman, ladies and gentlemen of the jury, Mr. Sandler, Mr. Krieger," Phillips began.
"As His Honor has already stated to you, my name is Walter
Phillips, and I am an Assistant United States Attorney, which
means that I am representing the government in the prosecution
of this case. I say prosecution because this is a criminal case.
There are criminal charges which have been brought against this
defendant or these defendants.

"What happened," he continued, looking at the jury seated
to his left, "is that a grand jury sitting in this courthouse made
up of people just like yourselves returned an indictment charging
these defendants"—he nodded toward Bonanno and Notaro—
"with certain crimes, and they have pleaded not guilty to this
indictment, which is the reason that we are here today, and you

have been chosen as the triers of the fact. It is your function to determine the facts of this case. How are facts proven? Facts are proven through witnesses, witnesses merely being a fancy name for human beings who come here, take the witness stand, and testify under oath to things that they have observed; that is, seen or heard.

"Facts are also proven by exhibits which are introduced into evidence and which you can see. Now, this particular case, the indictment charges the defendants with three separate crimes—conspiracy, mail fraud, and perjury.

"Now conspiracy merely, as His Honor will charge you in much more detail, is merely an agreement to do an unlawful act. It is an agreement between two or more people. In this case the agreement was to commit mail fraud by use of a Diners' Club credit card not belonging to either of these defendants, and not with the permission of the true cardholder, the person who actually owned the card. The mail fraud is the actual use of the Diners' Club credit card.

"Now you ask yourselves, what does mail fraud or what does the use of a credit card have to do with mail fraud? Well, the fraud is the scheme to defraud Diners' Club and/or other establishments who have contracts with Diners' Club out of money or property and that they do this by the use of the mails or that the mails are incidental thereto . . .

"Now what is perjury? Perjury is a very simple thing. Perjury is merely testifying willfully and falsely under oath before a competent tribunal such as in this case the grand jury. In this particular case the grand jury was investigating into the alleged fraudulent use of this particular credit card, and the two defendants appeared before the grand jury and as you will see, and as I will explain to you, they testified falsely when they did appear.

"Now the government, of course, has the burden of the proof, as it does in every criminal case. It is necessary for the government to come forward with the evidence, the proof. And what the government will prove in this particular case is that the defendant Bonanno went into a Mexican restaurant in Tucson, Arizona, and that he treated five other people, including Mr. Notaro, to a meal in that Mexican restaurant, and you will hear from the cashier of that Mexican restaurant. You will also hear that Mr. Bonanno went into a department store in Tucson, Arizona, and that he attempted to purchase almost two hundred dollars' worth of sweaters and clothes . . .

"You will hear that he was later called before the grand jury to testify concerning the use of this credit card, which was in the name of Don Torrillo, and he testified that he was given permission by a Mr. Samuel Hank Perrone to use this card that was given to him by Mr. Perrone, and he said as soon as he learned or immediately upon Mr. Perrone's death, he stopped using the card. You will hear testimony that this same Hank Perrone was killed, shot on March 11, 1968 . . .''

"Your Honor!'' cried Sandler, Notaro's lawyer, getting quickly to his feet, "I object to this statement and I move for a mistrial.''

"I join in that application, Your Honor,'' said Krieger, furious that within the first ten minutes of the trial, the prosecutor had suggested to the jury the vision of a gangland murder.

Judge Mansfield, frowning, said, "I didn't quite get the significance of it,'' and he permitted Krieger and Sandler to explain their objection to him at the sidebar, beyond the jury's hearing. "Your Honor,'' Krieger said, "this is totally irrelevant, this is just designed to prejudice these defendants before the jury.'' Mansfield paused, then agreed that the manner of Perrone's death had nothing to do with this credit card case, and so he instructed the jury to disregard Phillips's statement about the death. But the judge denied Sandler's motion of a mistrial, and asked Phillips to proceed.

"You will also hear,'' Phillips continued calmly, innocently, "that Mr. Bonanno testified that while he was in Tucson, Arizona, he asked certain attorneys out there about the propriety of his using this particular credit card. You will hear from each one of these attorneys that Mr. Bonanno didn't discuss this with them at all. And finally you will hear that Mr. Notaro also testified before the grand jury and that he said before the grand jury that a certain signature was not his, that he had not made the signature, and he had not seen certain airline ticket envelopes. You will hear that this was false, too, from one person who saw him make this signature.

"Now, finally, you will hear the testimony of Mr. Torrillo, Don Torrillo, the person who owned this credit card. You will hear that early in January he purchased airline tickets for Mr. Bonanno and Perrone to fly to the Coast and that he was never paid for these tickets and that sometime at the end of January of 1968 that Mr. Perrone came to his house and literally demanded from him the credit card and that he turned over the credit card and thereafter started incurring bills from all over the country.

"This is the government's proof. I have said to you what the government will intend to prove. In effect, in a way, I am indebted to you now—I owe you a debt because it will be your function to determine whether I have lived up to my word, whether I have in fact, whether the government has in fact, proved what they said they were intending to prove. . . . I am sure at the conclusion of the case you will be convinced not only beyond a reasonable doubt but beyond any shadow of a doubt that these defendants are guilty of the crimes that they are charged with. Thank you."

Krieger then stood and walked toward the rostrum next to the jury box. "As I am sure you recall," he said, "I represent the defendant Salvatore Bonanno, and my name is Albert J. Krieger." Krieger's head was still shaved bald in the manner made famous by Yul Brynner, and he spoke in a loud voice, his broad shoulders held firmly as he paced up and back in front of the jury. After expressing confidence in the jurors' capacity to render a fair verdict with regard to Bonanno, "to drive from your minds the prejudices which we may carry with us," Krieger assured the jury that the defense was "not interested in taking up the time of this court, in taking up your time, by engaging in any game of charades as to who signed what on such and such a date." Bonanno, he said, had already appeared before a grand jury and had admitted that he had signed the name "Don A. Torrillo" on numerous vouchers, having done so in the belief that the credit card had been obtained for his use through legitimate means. "The issue which you people will ultimately have to resolve," Krieger said, "is, number one, was the credit card extorted? A dirty word, extorted, but I think that it is what we are going to get down to here. Was the credit card extorted?

"Two, if it was extorted, did Mr. Bonanno have anything to do with the extortion? Number three: if it was extorted and he didn't know it was extorted by Perrone at the time that he started to use it, did he subsequently find out and use some kind of illegal means to prevent a complaint being made about the use of the card?

"This," Krieger said, still pacing slowly back and forth, "is what we are going to be dealing with, not whether he went to a restaurant some place in this country and treated four or five people to dinner. That means absolutely nothing. You will hear the stipulations in this court where he concedes use of the credit card because the use is meaningless insofar as this case is concerned unless the government can prove the fraudulent intent which we respectfully submit to you the government cannot.

"The perjury court is window dressing. The perjury counts arise from exactly the same circumstances as would come about if in the course of this trial I, as a lawyer, decide that it's pertinent and material for Salvatore Bonanno to get on that witness stand and tell what his recollection is as to certain pertinent facts here, and you reject that explanation. Is that perjury? I don't think that it is.

"Ladies and gentlemen, I am very anxious and I believe that you are, to start hearing the witnesses. I believe very, very strongly that any defendant who comes into an American courtroom wants one thing, and that is justice. The government never loses a case because whether the verdict is guilty or not guilty, justice has been done so long as the jury has fulfilled its function.

"I am going to sit down, and look forward to this evidence. Please evaluate the evidence as carefully and with the same attention, once again, to duplicate some phraseology of His Honor, as if you were one side or the other. Pay that same careful attention. Don't let a word go by. Judge these witnesses, judge Torrillo, because Torrillo is the keystone to the government's case, not a bill in a restaurant, not an airline ticket. Torrillo's credibility is going to mandate your verdict. Thank you."

Leonard Sandler then stood, speaking in behalf of Peter Notaro, and emphasized that when Notaro had taken the cross-country motor trip in February 1968 with Bonanno and Bill's elderly uncle, Di Pasquale, that Notaro had no knowledge of the credit card that Bonanno was using for gasoline, meals, and lodgings; Notaro had merely gone to Arizona to help Bonanno with the driving and to take a short vacation. Before the trip, Sandler said, Notaro had worked in a trucking business that was going bankrupt, and since he was inactive at the time, he welcomed the opportunity to accompany Bonanno to Arizona, which Notaro had never visited.

"The facts will show," Sandler said, "that [Notaro] did not

use the credit card on the trip, didn't use the credit card for a month, during which period he was in the company of Mr. Bonanno, who occasionally used the credit card with him, occasionally used it when he was not present. Nothing is done by him with regard to the credit card for virtually a month after its alleged original acquisition. Finally, in March of that year, his vacation has been extended and he is thinking of staying in Arizona and perhaps going into business there.

"Mr. Bonanno calls up the airport for a ticket for some other person who is coming from Canada and a kind of invoice, a preticket invoice, is prepared, and the name of Torrillo and the Torrillo credit card is given over the phone so it can be ready when it is picked up, and Mr. Bonanno asked Mr. Notaro to accompany him to the airport. When he gets to the airport he cannot park. He is a few feet away. Rather than take a parking space, he says to Mr. Notaro, 'Here, take this credit card, pick up the invoice, sign the name,' in substance. And he does so without any feeling he is doing anything illegal, without any feeling that this is so extraordinary a thing.

"This credit card is waiting, he signs the name. Maybe he looks at the two documents, the credit invoice and the receipt he gets for five seconds, maybe ten, maybe three, but surely no more than that, brings the credit invoice, brings the receipt to Mr. Bonanno and that's the end of it. A minor, insignificant detail in his life of no consequence, nothing to alert him.

"Eight months later he is brought before a grand jury, questioned by U.S. Attorneys, and they show him not the two slips separately in the form in which he may have seen them for three seconds, but together on a photostat, and he is asked whether he saw these tickets, which they are not, and he does not at that moment in time remember the occasion on which he signed Torrillo's name and he says he does not recall the tickets.

"That's the perjury. That is the wicked, dreadful perjury, and the government is going to say to you, 'It is impossible, it is impossible that he could have forgotten that episode seven, eight months before,' and that will be the issue as to perjury with regard to Mr. Notaro.

"Was it impossible for him to forget it eight months later? I submit that you will have little difficulty using your common sense and experience in understanding that a man could forget the episode, and if you see something you wrote which is not your signature but another name which you never used before and never used since, that you don't necessarily recognize it as something that you wrote, particularly if you are on the witness stand under oath confronted by a group of jurors and under considerable personal attention.

"That will be the issue. I don't think you will have any difficulty in acquitting Mr. Notaro of everything in this case. Thank you very much."

"All right," Judge Mansfield said. "Mr. Phillips, call your first witness."

"Jeanne Sands," said Phillips.

Miss Sands, the hostess at Pancho's Mexican Restaurant in Tucson, walked into the courtroom from the door in front of the jury box. A fast-stepping attractive woman in her thirties who seemed to have just been to a beauty parlor, Miss Sands was duly sworn and was shown by the prosecutor a Diners' Club receipt signed by Don A. Torrillo.

"Do you remember the circumstances under which you made that receipt out?" Phillips asked.

"Yes," she said.

"What were they?"

"We were pretty busy," Miss Sands recalled, "so the waitress who had served the table brought it to me at the register and asked me if I would take it back to the table for signature."

"Did you take it back to the table for signature?"

"Yes, sir."

"How many people were at that table?"

"Six."

"Did somebody sign that receipt?"

"Yes, sir."

"Do you see the person in the courtroom who signed that receipt?"

"Yes, sir."

"Would you point him out, please?"

"Yes," Miss Sands said, edging up on her chair, and looking toward the defendants' table. "The gentleman in the blue suit."

"At which table, the first table or the second table?" Judge Mansfield interrupted.

"The second table."

"And as you look at the second table, going from right to left, which person is it?" the judge asked.

"The second one."

"The second person," Judge Mansfield repeated, adding, "the record will show that the witness has identified the defendant Bonanno."

Bill Bonanno felt the eyes of nearly the entire courtroom focusing on him, but he continued to look straight ahead toward the judge's bench and the court stenographer's quick-tapping fingers. He was indeed in court, he thought, and he reminded himself that, if convicted and unable to get bail, he could be sent from this courtroom directly to a federal vehicle that would transport him to prison; and it would not, as in the past, be for thirty or ninety days. As he was thinking, half-listening to Miss Sands being cross-examined by Krieger, Bill could faintly hear the street traffic eleven floors below, the horns and trucks shifting gears, the drilling of a construction gang, the gongs from a distant clock or church tower. The gongs were loud, carrying into the courtroom, and the judge interrupted the witness's testimony to explain to the jury in a genteel manner: "We are listening to the melodic tones from the bell from St. Andrew's. Wait until it is completed. At least it is more palatable than some of the tones you may be hearing." The judge added, smiling, "That last remark was not intended to mean either counsel or the witnesses. I was speaking of the sounds from outside."

The procession of government witnesses continued through the day. There were the Diners' Club employees who explained the company billing procedures, its policy against nonholders using a card, and they also recalled the day when the debt-laden Torrillo card had been removed from circulation—March 11, 1968. There was the young salesman, the owner's son, from Bloom's shop in Tucson who had waited on Bill on March 11 when Bill attempted to pay for purchases worth $200 with Torrillo's card. And there was the lady cashier from Bloom's who, because the bill was more than $50, had telephoned the Diners' Club credit office in Los Angeles, which in turn had telephoned New York because Torrillo's card was registered there.

As Bill sat in court listening to the cashier's testimony he remembered that he had not really been worried while waiting in Bloom's that afternoon, overhearing the conversations on the telephone—first the cashier, then the manager talking to the Diners' Club official, and then Bill himself was called to the phone

and asked bait questions by the man on the other end, questions
intending to trick him, and they had. Bill remembered, after
admitting to the name "Torrillo," being asked if he still was
employed by a certain firm, if he still had a house at a certain
address, and—since Torrillo had been affiliated with several
firms and had several properties, being a realtor of some sort—
Bill replied affirmatively, which was a mistake.

After that conversation, the store manager confiscated the
card, cutting it into two pieces, and now Bill heard the cashier
telling the courtroom how he behaved at that moment: "He
didn't seem real angry at Diners'. . . . He seemed angry that a
man in his firm in New York had neglected to pay the bill." He
remembered calling Perrone, collect, from Bloom's, reaching
him at the warehouse in Brooklyn; and Perrone, apologizing,
assured him that there was nothing to worry about, Perrone
would talk to Torrillo, and Torrillo would take care of it right
away. Perrone had always presented himself to Bill as a kind of
partner of Torrillo's—they had deals going together, Perrone had
said, and so when Perrone told Bill that he would get Torrillo to
"take care of it," Bill assumed that he would and could. As
proof of Perrone's close relationship with Torrillo, Bill had only
to recall that it was Perrone who in 1966 had produced Torrillo
to take title to Bill's East Meadow home in order to satisfy the
Dime Savings Bank, which wanted someone less controversial
than Bill liable under the mortgage. The house was in Torrillo's
name during the period that Bill was using the credit card; and
Bill had even considered himself in a kind of remote partnership
with Torrillo, through Perrone, and thus he had no hesitancy
about taking the card and signing Torrillo's name after Perrone
said it was all right with Torrillo.

Then, hours after Bill had spoken with Hank Perrone from
Bloom's store, Perrone was dead. The next thing that Bill heard
about Torrillo was that he was in deep trouble with the law on
something other than the credit card issue; Torrillo was being
questioned by detectives, Bill had heard, and was possibly willing—in return for his own freedom—to become the government's key witness against Bill in a federal case alleging, among
other things, credit card theft.

And now on this Monday in November 1969 in federal court,
Don Torrillo represented the government's main hope in putting
Bill Bonanno behind bars. Since Bill would most likely not take

the stand, being in Krieger's view too vulnerable on many subjects that the government wanted to probe, the outcome of the case would undoubtedly depend on Torrillo's performance in front of the jury and on whether or not Krieger and Sandler could destroy Torrillo's credibility as a witness. Before Krieger and Sandler left the courtroom on the first day of testimony, they learned that they would soon have an opportunity to test that credibility, for the prosecutor informed Judge Mansfield that on the following day the government's witness would be Don A. Torrillo.

27

At 10:30 A.M. on November 11, the second day of testimony in the case of *United States of America* vs. *Salvatore V. Bonanno and Peter Notaro*, the government called its key witness, Don A. Torrillo. Torrillo was a thin, rather short dark-haired man in his thirties wearing horn-rimmed glasses, a dark suit, white shirt and striped tie; and as he took the stand he sat with his shoulders hunched slightly forward and his hands loosely clasped in his lap.

He seemed calm and relaxed; and after the prosecutor, Walter Phillips, began the questioning, Torrillo's responses were delivered in an unhesitating and polished manner, suggesting an above-average education and a facility with words.

After having established that Torrillo was aquainted with Hank Perrone, Phillips led Torrillo into describing a meeting that he had had in a barbershop with Perrone in January 1968. At the time of the meeting, the Banana War was very much in the headlines—it was two months after the triple murder in the Cypress Garden Restaurant in Queens, and two months before Perrone was killed; and the shop in which Don Torrillo met Perrone and Bonanno was in a neighborhood where the Bonanno organization had gambling and other interests. In the barbershop, Perrone asked Torrillo if he knew of a travel agent who would accept a personal check in payment for airline tickets; after Torrillo said he did not, Perrone asked if he knew of an agent who would accept a credit card. When Torrillo said that he did, Perrone asked if he could use Torrillo's card to charge two airline tickets to California. Torrillo agreed.

"Before you left the barbershop," Phillips asked, "did anything unusual occur?"

"There was an incident," Torrillo said, explaining that as he was leaving the shop with Perrone—Bonanno by this time having driven off in his own car—an old man in the shop said something to Perrone, causing him to turn in a violent rage and say, "You don't tell me anything . . ."

"I object to this," Krieger called out in the courtroom, "this is out of the presence of the defendant"—meaning that Bonanno, who had left the barbershop, was uninvolved with what Torrillo was now describing. But after the attorneys conferred with Judge Mansfield at the sidebar and after Phillips argued that the barbershop scene had a bearing on Torrillo's fear of Perrone, the judge allowed Phillips to pursue the questioning; and Torrillo, after recalling Perrone's anger, added that Perrone hit the old man and knocked him down.

Torrillo then testified that he proceeded to the travel agency, saying nothing to Perrone about the old man, and that Bonanno was waiting at the agency when they arrived. There the tickets were purchased with Torrillo's card, and Perrone promised to reimburse Torrillo after returning from California. Not only did Perrone never do so, Torrillo said, but Perrone not long after his return from California arrived at Torrillo's home in Elmhurst, Queens, early one evening, very angry, and said, "I have been calling you for a day and a half. What's the matter with you? Why don't you return my calls?" Then Perrone said that he needed the card again for two more tickets, demanding the card; and, Torrillo testified, he gave it to him. As Torrillo walked to the door with Perrone on that evening, Torrillo said he saw Peter Notaro sitting in the car parked in the driveway.

"Did you thereafter receive any bills or receipts from the Diners' Club?" Phillips asked.

"Yes."

"Where did they come from?"

"From all over the country," Torrillo said.

Krieger interrupted, asking, "May we have when he received these?"

"Yes," Judge Mansfield said, "fix the time."

Torrillo said he did not exactly know when he began to receive the bills, but that it was after Perrone had taken the card.

"Did you give Mr. Perrone permission to use your card or authorization?" Phillips asked.

"No, I didn't," said Torrillo, adding that he had also not

given permission or authorization to Bill Bonanno or Peter Notaro.

"Did you pay any of these bills?" Phillips asked.

"No, I didn't."

"When did you first tell Diners' Club that the card was being used without your authorization?"

"Approximately a month after Mr. Perrone's death."

Phillips later asked Torrillo if he had seen Perrone in a bar called the Posh Place, which was on Second Avenue some blocks from the barbershop, and was a hangout for members of the Bonanno organization.

"Yes, I did," Torrillo replied, and when asked by Phillips if he had noticed anything unusual at that time—this being before Perrone's visit to Torrillo's home to get the card—Torrillo recalled that in the Posh Place he had noticed that Perrone was carrying a gun.

As Torrillo continued to testify, Bill Bonanno sat listening, looking toward Torrillo but not directly at him, realizing that if he did he might suggest to the jury, through a facial expression or gesture, his private thoughts about Torrillo, which were not flattering, but which if sensed by the jury would certainly not favorably reflect upon his own image, such as it was. Bill was in a peculiar situation in the courtroom. While he was a defendant in an important case, and while the trial coverage in the press associated him with the Mafia (and was possibly being read or heard by the nonsequestered jury), he would not be speaking in his own behalf to these eight women and four men in the jury box who each day observed him, watched him sitting next to Krieger, noticed the way he was dressed, the way he combed his hair, saw him whispering to Krieger and occasionally writing notes on a yellow pad at the defense's table. He felt that he was on trial every second he sat in the courtroom—his every movement, every twitch, might be under observation, might confirm in a juror's mind what he was or was not. While Bill did not dress any more conservatively for this trial than he normally did, he kept reminding himself that his appearance was on trial, his face and eyes were on trial, and so he was careful not to look too directly at Don Torrillo.

After Phillips finished, Krieger stood to begin the cross-examination. Krieger began slowly and calmly, his tone becoming slightly more sharp and direct as he proceeded, and soon Bill became aware that Torrillo's voice had lost some of its steadiness and Torrillo's responses were not as quick as they had been when Phillips was asking the questions.

"Mr. Torrillo," Krieger asked, "when did you meet Mr. Perrone for the first time?"

"When did I meet him?" Torrillo repeated. "I met him approximately the beginning of 1967, I believe."

"1967?" Krieger asked, doubtfully.

"I believe," Torrillo said. "It could have been 1966. The time sequence I don't remember but I can pinpoint it by certain other items that happened."

"I see. Well, there was a certain real estate transaction, was there not, in which Mr. Bonanno was involved, and Mr. Perrone was involved, and you were involved?"

"Correct," Torrillo said, recognizing it as the time when he had taken title to Bill Bonanno's house in East Meadow.

"And I suggest to you that the date was approximately November of 1966," Krieger said. "Now, did you know Mr. Perrone prior to that transaction?"

"Yes. I had met him about two weeks prior to that transaction, two weeks to a month."

"And you became rather friendly with Mr. Perrone after meeting him, just taking a date arbitrarily, say October 1966?"

"Yes?"

"And you had some business relationships with him, did you not?"

"Yes."

"And those business relationships continued up until the time of his death?"

"Yes."

"Now, was Mr. Perrone in a trucking business, or warehousing?"

"Something like that," Torrillo said. "Trucking business, I believe."

"Well, you visited him from time to time at his place of business, did you not?"

"Yes, I visited him before he even bought the business because I wrote an appraisal up on the building for him."

Krieger asked Torrillo about a letter that Torrillo had written to the Diners' Club dated April 17, 1968—which was a month after Perrone's death—and in which Torrillo claimed to have lost his credit card. Krieger had a copy of the letter in his hand, and in it Torrillo also stated that he had written two previous letters to Diners' Club concerning the "loss" of the credit card, complaining that he had received no reply to those previous letters from Diners' Club. Krieger asked Torrillo if he had lied in the April 17 letter to Diners' Club about the card being lost and about having written twice previously. Torrillo, after lengthy exchanges with Krieger and objections by Phillips, finally admitted that, yes, he had lied in the letter.

The courtroom was intensely silent now as Torrillo, shifting in the chair and adjusting his glasses, saw Krieger holding other documents in his hand, other instances in which Torrillo had lied. There was a document of May 28, ten weeks after Perrone's death, which was an affidavit that Torrillo signed at the request of Diners' Club in which he said that he had lost the card. And there was Torrillo's testimony before a grand jury in July 1968—four months after Perrone's death—in which Torrillo held to the version that he had lost the card and repeated the false statements that he had made in the letter of April 17 to Diners' Club.

"And that wasn't true?" Krieger asked, referring to Torrillo's grand jury testimony.

"No," Torrillo said, quietly.

Krieger paused momentarily, giving the jury time to consider what had just been said—Torrillo had admitted to perjury.

Peter Notaro looked straight at Torrillo, as did Notaro's attorney, Sandler. Notaro had been indicted for perjury because he had not recognized the charge slip on which he had signed Torrillo's name for the plane tickets at the Tucson airport; whereas Torrillo's grand jury testimony had not resulted in a perjury indictment.

Bill Bonanno sat looking at the table, while Krieger continued, "Mr. Torrillo, let me go to something else for a moment. Did you tell us on your direct examination that you were a travel agent at the present time?"

"Yes."

"And how long have you been a travel agent?"

"Well, I have been in the travel business just about two years."

"Pardon? I'm sorry, please keep your voice up."

"I have been in the travel business about two years," Torrillo repeated.

"Two years?"

"Just about. Mainly it just started to take hold this year, the beginning of 1969."

"Well," Krieger said, "you weren't a travel agent back in January of '68, were you?"

"Beg your pardon?"

"Were you a travel agent in January of '68?"

"Yes."

"And you didn't have a place of business?"

"No," Torrillo said, explaining that he was not the type of agent who sold tickets but rather one who conducted travel tours, packaged the tours and sold them.

"Now, that was your business in January of 1968?"—the time Torrillo met in the barbershop with Perrone and Bonanno.

"Well," Torrillo clarified, "I was getting out of the real estate business, and I started picking up on this business."

"Prior to that you had been in the real estate business?"

"Yes."

"And what did your real estate business consist of?"

"I owned and operated rent-controlled apartment buildings."

"How many?"

"Five."

"Where?"

"Do you want the addresses?"

"Please."

"446 East 116th Street; 416 East 116th Street; and 7 and 23 East Third; and 536 East Thirteenth Street."

"These were all multiple dwellings?" Krieger asked.

"Yes."

"Basically railroad flats?"

"Yes."

"Now," Krieger went on, "were you ever employed by Western Electric?"

"Yes."

"When?"

"1960. In that area."

"And in what capacity?"

"As an engineering associate."

"What does that mean?"

Torrillo seemed confused.

"That means that I was an engineering associate," Torrillo said, finally, "whatever that means."

"Well," Krieger asked, "are you an engineer?"

"No."

"Are you a graduate engineer?"

"No."

"Did you ever go to college?"

"Yes."

"And what degree did you get?"

"I didn't finish."

"Now, were you also at one time in the stock market business?"

"Yes, I was."

"In what capacity?"

"Your Honor," Walter Phillips said, rising, "I'm going to object. I don't see any relevance to this testimony."

"I will tie it up, if Your Honor please," Krieger said.

Judge Mansfield overruled Phillips's objection, and Krieger asked Torrillo: "What were you doing in the stock market?"

"I started in the Research Department and then as a salesman."

"Now, you first got a Diners' Club card in 1963, isn't that so?"

"I believe so, yes."

"And what was your income in 1963?"

"Oh, approximately $30,000. Thirty and change."

"Pardon?"

"Approximately $30,000."

"And in 1962?"

"It is hard for me to remember because there was a transition period between Western Electric and the stock market, and I was in the army for a time in 1962. So I don't remember."

"You didn't make any $60,000 in 1962, did you?"

"No."

"And did you make an application to Diners' Club in 1963 where you represented yourself to be—well, have an annual income of $60,000?"

"Yes."

"And characterized yourself as being the head of research of a brokerage house?"

"I was at the time."

"You weren't making any $60,000, were you?"

"No."

"What did you make?"

"I made thirty, I think, for a year, but that sixty was projected earnings. That's what I felt I would have made if I had finished it out."

When Krieger asked Torrillo if he had any unpaid debts of his own in the Diners' Club account before receiving bills that were incurred by Perrone and Bonanno, Torrillo admitted that he had—approximately $1,500 in bills, which included monies due on a monthly installment plan he had with Diners' Club in addition to bills for Christmas gifts he had bought in 1967, and also one business trip he had made.

"You didn't clean up your account with Diners' in January of 1968?" Krieger asked, which was when Perrone had taken his card.

"No, not at all," Torrillo admitted.

"Now the trip to which you just made reference, was that a trip that you had arranged in your travel business?"

"Yes."

"And to where was that?"

"To Haiti."

"And was that a gambling junket?"

"Well," Torrillo said, "no. It was more or less of a business trip in the sense that we were thinking of going into that business. Instead of me being in the travel tour business, I was thinking of going to the other side of the fence and getting involved with the hotels and casino aspect, so I had four or five friends of mine that were thinking of getting involved in that aspect of it and we went down and came back with that in mind."

"And that was the money that you owed at the time?"

"Yes."

"And you found it difficult to pay that money, isn't that so?"

"No."

"Well, did you ever pay Diners'?"

"No."

"So you did find it difficult to pay that money, isn't that so?"

"Objection!" shouted Walter Phillips.

"Sustained," said Judge Mansfield.

* * *

Torrillo remained on the stand through the entire morning, and as Bill listened he thought that Krieger had scored decisively with the jury. Krieger had not only impeached the government's witness but he raised doubt about Torrillo's explanation that Torrillo's relinquishing of the Diners' Club card to Perrone had been motivated by fear, and fear alone—a motivation presumably inspired by having seen the gun in Perrone's shoulder holster in the Posh Place, by seeing Perrone knock down the old man in the barbershop, and by Perrone's publicized affiliation with the Mafia. If Torrillo was guided by fear of Perrone, how did he explain his persistence in saying that his card was lost weeks and months after Perrone's death? Why had Torrillo lied to the grand jury in July—four months after Perrone's death—and then, at some unspecified date later, why had he changed his whole story to assert that the card had been forcibly taken? Bill Bonanno had his theories, of course, and these were based on his and Krieger's knowledge that Torrillo had been involved, quite apart from the credit card situation, with some unrelated legal entanglement, and perhaps the government agents had made a deal with Torrillo—if he would help them nail Bonanno they would help Torrillo with his other case, whatever that case was. At this point in the trial, Krieger did not know precisely what the government had on Torrillo. Krieger knew that Torrillo had been arrested three days after Perrone's death, and had been interrogated about the Perrone murder. But that was all Krieger knew, and whether he could find out more through cross-examination depended largely on Judge Mansfield's rulings—if the judge supported Phillips's attempts to block Krieger from probing into Torrillo's other legal difficulties, then Krieger would be unable to exploit what he believed was a vulnerable witness. Meanwhile, Krieger continued in the courtroom to concentrate on the evidence that he had at his disposal against Torrillo, seeking to establish before the jury that Torrillo was a man whose word could not be trusted.

Krieger held up for the jury to see a small white business card. It was Torrillo's, and on it Torrillo had represented himself as possessing illustrious degrees in a formal education. Handing the card to Torrillo, Krieger asked: "Is it your business card?"

"Yes," said Torrillo, sheepishly.

"And it was a business card which you had in 1966 and 1967, is that not so?"

"Well, it is approximately correct."

"Your Honor," Phillips interrupted, "again I am going to object. I don't see any relevance to this at all."

"I don't see any relevance yet," Judge Mansfield said, "but maybe he is leading to something."

"What does BSEE mean?" Krieger asked Torrillo.

"Beg your pardon?"

"BSEE, does that mean anything?"

"To me, yes," said Torrillo. "Bachelor of Science, Electrical Engineering."

"And MSEE?"

"Master of Science, Electrical Engineering."

"And Ph.D.?"

"Doctorate."

"Doctor of what?"

"It's an educational term," Torrillo said, "doctor of whatever it may be."

"Well," Krieger said, "did you represent yourself to be a Ph.D.?"

"Objection!" shouted Phillips.

"In 1966 or 1967," Krieger continued, ignoring Phillips, "when you met Bonanno?"

"Objection!" Phillips repeated.

"Overruled," said the judge.

"Did I—beg pardon?" asked Torrillo, looking at Krieger, then toward Phillips, then up to the judge.

"Yes, you may answer," said the judge, nodding.

"Did you represent—"

"I didn't represent myself as anything to Bonanno," Torrillo replied, with irritation.

"Did you give Bonanno Defendant's Exhibit F for identification?" Krieger asked, meaning the business card.

"I didn't give Bonanno anything," Torrillo said, "I don't know where he got it, but—"

"This is your card?" Krieger asked quickly.

"Yes."

"I offer it—"

"Your Honor," Phillips said, "I object to this offer on the same basis as I objected to the others as irrelevant."

"Overruled," said the judge.

"On your business card," Krieger continued, "did you represent yourself to be a Master of Science in Electrical Engineering?"

"Yes, sir," Torrillo said, quietly.

"A Bachelor of Science in Electrical Engineering?"

"Yes."

"A Ph.D.?"

"Yes."

"What does the Ph.D. mean that you were representing yourself to be?"

"I don't see where it makes any . . ." Torrillo said. "I told you it was a doctorate, doctorate title."

"In what?"

"I don't see where it makes any . . ." Torrillo caught himself, and said, "I didn't have any specific goal in mind. I didn't give out any cards, by the way. I thought it was a bad ploy to use. I had them with me, but I never represented myself as anything."

"Did you have offices in 1966 and 1967 at 15 Park Row?"

Phillips stood to say, "In view of the witness's last answer, I again object to the admission into evidence of this."

"Overruled."

"Did you have offices in 1966 and 1967 in 15 Park Row?" Krieger repeated.

"I had an office in a suite of offices."

"Did you have an office at the San Jeronimo Hilton at San Juan, Puerto Rico?"

"Well, I had set up temporary—I had set up a temporary room in a hotel in San Juan."

"When?"

"In '66 and '67."

"For how long?"

"Oh, on and off for a period of about four or five months."

"Do you recall when?"

"Do I recall—I beg your pardon?"

"Do you recall when you had this office in Puerto Rico?"

"In the early part of '66, the middle six months."

"The early part of '66?"

"Yes."

"And that was when you were in syndications and real estate and mortgages and so forth?"

"Trying to get into that. I was involved with it, but I wanted to go in on my own."

"And you felt representing yourself to be an electrical engineer and a doctor of something or other would help you?"

"Yes."

Soon Krieger decided that the time had come to see what he could learn about the circumstances surrounding Torrillo's arrest on March 14, 1968, right after Perrone's murder.

"Now Mr. Torrillo, the first law enforcement officials to whom you spoke about the matters concerning which you have given testimony on direct examination were the New York police, isn't that so?"

"Yes."

"And that was after March 14, 1968, was it not?"

"After March 14," Torrillo repeated, seeming somewhat confused.

"March 14, 1968," Krieger said.

"Well, I didn't hear the first part of your question, Mr. Krieger."

"That was after March 14, 1968?"

"What was after March 14?"

"That you spoke to law enforcement officials for the first time concerning the matters about which you have given testimony here on direct examination."

"Yes."

"And those law enforcement officials were New York City police?"

"Yes."

"And you were speaking to them in relation to a problem that you had?"

"Objection, Your Honor," said Phillips.

"Sustained," said the judge.

Krieger shook his head and, turning toward the judge, said, softly, "I make an offer here on motive, Your Honor, and bias."

"All right," said the judge.

But Phillips said, "Your Honor, I object to these remarks of Mr. Krieger's."

"Don't make statements in the presence of the jury," Judge

Mansfield said. "If you wish to take it up you may take it up at the sidebar."

- Krieger and Phillips, together with Notaro's lawyer, Leonard Sandler, gathered at the side of Judge Mansfield's bench.

"Yes," said the judge to Krieger, "what is your offer?"

"On March 14, 1968, Your Honor, this witness was arrested, I believe, at his home in the County of Queens by police officers from the New York City Police Department. That after his arrest he was interviewed at length by the CIB [Central Intelligence Bureau of the New York City Police Department], officers from the CIB; that those officers turned over the results of the interview to the postal inspectors or to various officials of the United States government; and that his position in regard to the credit card came about through those interviews. And I would like to show to this jury, that he [Torrillo] was motivated by his own sense of self-preservation for the criminal charges brought against him and so he testified as to these events."

"I don't quite see any motivation," Judge Mansfield said. "How can there be any connection between the two?"

Krieger, not wishing to be too accusatory at this point, said, "There doesn't have to be a connection."

"No, but what would motivate him to lie about this?" asked the judge. "How could it help him in connection with the charges that were against him then?"

"To get the charges dismissed," Krieger said, in a manner implying simple logic.

"The charges that were against him, Your Honor," interjected Phillips, "were trumped-up charges. About twenty police officers came to Mr. Torrillo's home the day after Mr. Perrone was killed and they arrested him on three phony charges, such as possession of heroin on the basis of some white powder that he had in his garage, and I am going to ask the court for a ruling directing Mr. Krieger not to ask any questions with respect to that particular arrest because the charges were dismissed. They were trumped-up charges, and the police came in because of all the confusion about Perrone."

"Came in as a result of *what*?" Krieger asked, suspiciously.

"Let me say this," Judge Mansfield cut in. "I think that you are going too far afield into collateral matters. You may bring out anything that has to do with a prior conviction, but I don't think that I'm going to get off on a wild-goose chase as to whether or not a charge that was ultimately dismissed against him was dismissed because he had furnished the police information that incriminated Bonanno and Notaro. It seems to me that this is too remote, too flimsy, inadequate, and, in the absence of a greater showing than what you made here, I sustain the objection.''

''Your Honor,'' Krieger persisted, ''I have an application to the court, and in the interest of that application let me rephrase or restate my offer because I think that Your Honor may make a ruling partially upon a misapprehension of the trust of my argument. Number one, Your Honor, particularly in light of what Mr. Phillips has just said, at least twenty officers came to this man's apartment, and apparently he has no prior criminal record, I have no knowledge of any prior criminal record, and he is put into the most fantastically pressured situation in regard to trumped-up charges, as Mr. Phillips categorized this. These charges were dismissed, according to the transcript in Queens County, in October [seven months after Perrone's death], after he had testified before the grand jury. If, as a result of the pressure of these trumped-up charges, he testified in this fashion, I am, I respectfully submit, under Wigmore, under McCormak, under Gratheks, under Lester, entitled to bring out circumstances which might have motivated him to testify in a fashion favorable to one side or to the other. The test, Your Honor, which Your Honor has indicated in your previous ruling, is a much more stringent test than the one which the cases indicate.''

''You have the right,'' the judge said, ''to ask the witness the straight question whether or not, in making any statements with respect to any of the defendants or Perrone, he was motivated by any desire to escape any prosecution by any law enforcement authority. I will permit that, but what I will not permit is to go into the collateral issue of whether the dismissal of the other charges was due to the inadequacies of the government's evidence in those charges or because he furnished some useful information. If he went into that I would end up by trying the other cases, so I have ruled, and that's my ruling.''

''But, Your Honor,'' Krieger continued, ''I don't intend to go into that portion of it.''

''The government will then want to go into it in order to show that those charges couldn't possibly have been sustained, and then we get into the trial of those charges, and whether the witness could have possibly been motivated by what are called specious charges. So, I have ruled.''

Krieger turned and walked slowly back to the witness stand, and Bill Bonanno could tell from Krieger's expression that he was disappointed and dissatisfied. After five more minutes of cross-examination, Krieger told the judge that he had nothing further to ask Torrillo at this time, but he reserved the right to cross-examine him later in the trial on questions that might arise if Krieger could obtain the written notes or tape recordings that had been made by the police during their interviews with Torrillo after his arrest. While Phillips said he was uncertain that such material existed, the judge agreed that Krieger was within his rights to seek it if it did exist, and subpoenas were served on various individuals who had talked to Torrillo.

As the court recessed for lunch, Judge Mansfield directed that Torrillo return on the following day at 10:00 A.M. The remainder of the day's session would be devoted to other government witnesses, several of whom had been flown in from Arizona to testify against Bill Bonanno.

During the lunch recess Bill went to a telephone booth in the corridor and called his father in Arizona, saying that Krieger had done well but that it was impossible at this point to know how the jury was reacting. He spoke for only a few minutes, explaining that Krieger was waiting and that they were due back in court in one hour.

On the way out of the federal courthouse, several reporters greeted Bill by name and stopped to exchange a few words. Some of the reporters had come to court on that day to cover the bribery trial of the city's former water commissioner, James L. Marcus, which was being heard on the ninth floor, two floors below Judge Mansfield's courtroom; and as they talked to Bill they wanted to know how his case was going, and they smiled and seemed conciliatory. The press is friendly in person, Bill thought, but they kill you in print.

The restaurant, a few blocks from the courthouse, was crowded, as were all the restaurants in the area at this hour, and Bill and Krieger had to wait standing for several moments. At various tables Bill recognized a few judges, defense attorneys, prosecutors, FBI agents, alleged mafiosi, convicts, court stenographers, bail bondsmen. They were all having lunch in the same big room—the accused and the accusers. They were co-workers in the crime industry, they kept the wheels turning in the big gray court buildings in Foley Square where decisions were hammered out five days a week, supplying jobs for jail keepers and magistrates, barristers and bondsmen, providing news for the press and customers for restaurants—they all fed off one another.

After lunch, which was barely digestible, Bill returned to the courtroom; and soon there was the rap of the gavel, the arrival of the judge, and the first of a half dozen witnesses who would testify during the afternoon. The first witness, a co-owner of a cocktail lounge in Tucson, testified that he had accompanied Peter Notaro to a Tucson travel agency where Notaro, at Bill Bonanno's request, ordered five Montreal–Tucson airplane tickets to be billed to Torrillo's card. The second witness was the travel agent who booked the reservations with American Airlines, and the third witness was the man behind the counter at the Tucson airport who identified Peter Notaro as the individual who signed for the tickets in Torrillo's name. The government's witnesses also included a secretary from the Southern Arizona Bank, who testified that Notaro had opened an account there under the name of Peter Joseph; and a Long Island mailman who said that he had delivered letters in the past to the Bonannos' East Meadow home that were addressed to Carl Simari and also to William Levine. Among the mail addressed to Levine, who had occupied and owned the East Meadow house before selling it to Bill Bonanno, was a Mobil Oil credit card that Bill had occasionally used at gas stations, paying the charges through 1967 until July 1968, by which time Bill had left New York and had moved West. Since July 1968, according to another government witness—a Mobil Oil credit representative who had been flown in from Missouri—the Levine account was currently $329.90 in arrears. But the next witness, William Levine himself, a genial middle-aged man, testified under cross-examination that he had no qualms about Bill's using the Mobil Oil card because Levine had never requested the card, did not know it had been sent to the East Meadow home, and felt no responsibility for its use—the card had apparently been mailed by Mobil, unsolicited, to many people in the hopes of luring them to Mobil gas stations. Levine also admitted that when he sold the East Meadow property to Bill that the mortgage pay-

ments continued to be made under the name of Levine, with
Bill's money; and Levine had also allowed the lighting and heating to be paid by Bonanno under Levine's existing account.
Bill's home telephone number during those years, which was
unlisted, was under the name of William Levine.

The government's parade of witnesses continued to appear
during the next day, and among them were three Tucson attorneys who handled legal matters for Bill in the past but who now
were in New York for the government to refute statements that
Bill previously made to the grand jury—statements contending
that, after he obtained Torrillo's card from Perrone, he consulted
with the Tucson attorneys about the legality of using it since he
was then having some second thoughts; and, according to Bill's
grand jury testimony, the attorneys told him in substance that as
long as Torrillo knew that Bill was using the card and had given
his permission, there was nothing illegal about it.

One after another, the attorneys took the stand, were sworn
in, and were questioned by Assistant United States Attorney
Phillips. The first attorney, Garven W. Videen, who had represented Bill on two tax cases in Arizona, told Phillips emphatically that Bill had not consulted with him about Torrillo's card.
The second attorney, William E. Netherton, who was Bill Bonanno's representative in 1968 when Bill was charged and convicted with exceeding the speed limit by five miles, conceded
that Bill may have asked him about Torrillo's card. "It strikes a
chord," Netherton recalled, during cross-examination, "it
strikes a chord." But Netherton, when further questioned by
Judge Mansfield, said he could not "recall specifically" a conversation in which he had told Bill Bonanno that it was all right
to use a card in another man's name.

The third attorney, Joseph Soble, who had represented Bill in
various matters in Arizona beginning in 1961, admitted to having met with Bill and Hank Perrone in Tucson in February
1968—a month before Perrone's death—and having told Bill at
that time to be careful about using Torrillo's card because "it
could be a forgery problem," to which Bill had replied in es-
sence, according to Soble, that there was nothing to worry about
because Torrillo owed Bonanno approximately $3,000, and
"that was the way it was going to be taken care of." Soble also
testified that Bonanno later in 1968 charged about $500 in air-

plane tickets to the account of Soble's law firm, which Bonanno
had attributed to an office mix-up, but which had nevertheless
angered Soble, had caused "strong language" between the two
men, and had ended their long social relationship. Soble added
in court that while no one in his firm had paid for those tickets,
and while he was not sure that the tickets had ever been totally
paid for, he did admit to hearing about a partial payment.

As Bill Bonanno sat listening to his former attorneys testifying
against him, his reactions varied between bitterness and frustration, dejection and a sense of betrayal. He was most frustrated
because now in court he could not defend himself against their
versions of the past, could not differ with them, remind them of
things that they had not told the court. He was forced to sit
silently, revealing no emotion, as the government sought to prove
its perjury counts against him with the help of Tucson men who
had once been his defenders and friends. Bill found it extremely
difficult to appear unemotional at this point in the trial—he felt
somehow that he had been deceived, used, sold out, and he
suddenly had a vision of himself as the star of a sardonic and
satirical showing of *This Is Your Life*, a production in which his
old friends and associates were assembled to tell him in public
what an abominable person he was.

Later in the afternoon, in response to a subpoena issued on
behalf of Krieger requesting the right to read the tape recordings
or written notes on the interviews that the police had with Torrillo following his arrest, three members of the New York City
Police Department appeared in court with transcripts of two
lengthy sessions with Torrillo—the first was conducted on
June 25, 1968, the second on July 9, 1968. While the police
department was initially reluctant to release the transcripts of
the two taped interviews, Judge Mansfield determined that the
defense attorneys had a right to read those portions relating to
this case; and immediately after the material was made available, Krieger and Sandler quickly read it, reread it, and under-
lined those paragraphs that they would use in their continuing
cross-examination of Don Torrillo.

What they hoped to prove to the jury was that Torrillo had
somehow been intimidated by the police into changing his story
about the card being lost to its being stolen by Perrone and
Bonanno; and in return for his cooperation, Torrillo would be

spared the legal penalties of harassment that he could otherwise
anticipate from law enforcement authorities. If the defense could
prove this or even if it could suggest this to the jury, it still might
not help the cause of Bonanno or Notaro; and yet Krieger and
Sandler were as convinced now as they had been before the trial
began that their only chance of success was in destroying Torrillo's credibility as a witness.

So Torrillo was called back to the witness stand, and Krieger,
reading from the transcripts of Torrillo's interviews with the
police, proceeded to question the witness about what he said
and what had been said to him. Torrillo appeared timid on the
stand now, his hands clasped tightly in his lap; and among the
spectators in the courtroom, he could see Detective Frank Goggins and Sergeant Robert J. O'Neil, two of the men who were
quoted in these transcripts. Detective Goggins and Sergeant
O'Neil sat grim-faced in the second row.

"Do you remember this?" Krieger asked, pacing slowly before the jury, holding a copy of the transcript in his right hand,
"do you remember making this statement?"

"Which page?" demanded Phillips, who had a duplicate copy
at his table.

"Thirty-nine," said Krieger, who then quoted from a passage
in which Torrillo was being interrogated by Sergeant O'Neil.

SERGEANT: I realize your position, see, but don't feel that I
don't know what your role is. Naturally, you don't want to get
involved.

TORRILLO: Well, see, when you tell me that you are not going
to see the Diners', that's what I'm worried about because I signed
an affidavit that I . . .

SERGEANT: Let me be very basic. We could arrest you right
now. Do you understand what I'm saying to you? There is a
report in . . . that it's stolen or lost. I'm not interested in that,
that is a very small part in the fiction. I want those people . . .
I want to put them in jail. I want to send them away. Do you
understand what I mean? Now, I'm not saying you are going to
get on a stand. I told you this before . . . but maybe there is
something you can do for me, you can tell me and put me in an
area where I can get these guys? Right? Do you understand what
I'm trying to say to you? Enough of your hedging here.

TORRILLO: The only thing that I hedged about was the Diners' Club card. You know that involves a lot of money.

SERGEANT: Allow us for knowing a little bit, will you please, because there is a couple of things you said here, and I'm not coming back at you and finding fault with a couple of your statements. But I know you haven't told me the whole truth. And you are either putting yourself in a good light or you don't want to deviate from your blank relationship with them. . . .

"Your Honor!" Phillips said, standing in court, "I object at this point. I don't see any inconsistency whatsoever."

"Yes," Judge Mansfield agreed, turning to Krieger, "I fail to see that you have established any relevancy of this on cross-examination. It fails to show anything inconsistent with what the witness has previously testified. I'm referring to this last question and answer."

"Well," Krieger said, "if Your Honor please, I respectfully submit that this shows the motive of the witness to fabricate the story."

"I object to the speeches by Mr. Krieger," Phillips said quickly.

"Well, it is in before the jury now," the judge said, mildly piqued. "I will allow it to stay."

Krieger continued to question Torrillo and to quote from the transcripts for nearly a full hour; and in one transcript Sergeant O'Neil was quoted as telling Torrillo, at the end of a day's interrogation: "We'll see you at another date. . . . As a matter of fact, to show that it is not one-sided, if we can do you a favor, and maybe we can . . ." And Torrillo responded: "Look, I will tell you anything, Mr. O'Neil, anything, because I haven't committed any crime, so I'm not worried. Do you understand?" The sergeant concluded: "As a matter of fact, I have you on the credit card, you realize that?"

"Your Honor," Phillips said, "I object to that statement by the sergeant. That's no question. There has been no answer in response to that."

"Let's see whether there is a response," Judge Mansfield said. And nodding to Krieger he added, "All right, read the response."

"I am going to, Your Honor," Krieger said, and turning back to Torrillo he continued, "And you are responding, ' . . . that was the only thing I was worried about, but I leveled with you because you put it to me in such a way that I had to level with you, you see. I didn't know from'—something inaudible—'if they come all I can do is pay. I'm trying not to, you know.' ''

Krieger stopped reading, and asked Torrillo: "Do you recall that?"

"Yes," Torrillo said.

"Was it true?"

"Yes."

Krieger began to read again, quoting Sergeant O'Neil as saying, " 'Well, you don't want to pay.' And you are saying, 'Well, if I can pay I will.' And the sergeant saying to you, '. . . if you pay them what you are doing is rebutting your original statement. Like I say I am not particularly interested in that end of it.' ''

Krieger asked Torrillo: "Do you recall that?"

"Yes."

After Krieger completed his cross-examination, Leonard Sandler stood to ask Torrillo additional questions, concentrating on a discussion that Torrillo had had with another detective, named Doherty.

DOHERTY: Don, let me interrupt you a minute. Now you said that they sort of bullied you into giving them the card, right?

TORRILLO: Right.

DOHERTY: Now why were you so willing to give them the card? Why didn't you just tell them that you didn't want to get involved in that business?

TORRILLO: Well, I told them that. You know what I mean? But he had a nice way about him, you know, and I was reading about what was going on, and he [Perrone] says, look this is important now, don't worry, we'll give you the money, you know, as soon as he [Bonanno] comes back, it's only two separate tickets, right, so as soon as he comes back we'll give you the money and we'll—I'll give you the card back and everything will be all right, that's the way they, you know they told me to do and he says, don't worry, he says, look, we might be a little short of cash now but we're going to get money from something or other and I'll give you back the money. He says, I don't want to hurt you in any way; so he conned me, but then I was—it's easy for me to go and do something and get them out of the way, you know what I mean, or anything like that you know it's always the easy way out. It's stupid, you know, but . . .

Sandler stopped reading, and asked Torrillo: "The 'he' in this answer—was that Mr. Perrone?"

"Mr. Sandler, to be perfectly honest with you," Torrillo replied, "I got lost."

"I am reading *your answer*, Mr. Torrillo," Sandler said.

"Oh," Torrillo said, "could you pick out . . ."

"Didn't I make that clear?" Sandler asked.

"I think," Phillips said, "the witness should be permitted to look at the answer."

"Fine," Sandler said, "I agree with you. I think Mr. Phillips made a very good point." After handing Torrillo a copy of the transcript and pointing to the place where the long quotation appeared, Sandler asked Torrillo who the "he" was in the statement "he had a nice way about him."

"Perrone," Torrillo answered, after handing the transcript back to Sandler.

"And did Mr. Perrone have a nice way about him?" Sandler asked.

"In a derogatory sense, yes," Torrillo replied.

"I am sorry?" Sandler said, surprised. "Oh, you were being sarcastic when you said that?"

"Yes," Torrillo said.

"And the transcript does not reflect that, does it?" Sandler asked.

"Exactly," said Torrillo, in a voice suddenly sharp and aggressive, revealing an attitude that Torrillo had until now concealed from the jury.

28

On the following morning, Sandler called his client Peter Notaro to the stand. Notaro, heavily built, thick-armed, with a workman's rugged features but soft brown eyes and thinning gray hair, sat straight-spined in the chair. His dark suit, white shirt and tie seemed almost too tightly drawn around his thick neck and broad shoulders, and he was so soft-spoken as he began to testify that the judge and Sandler both urged him to speak more forcefully—he could not be heard in the courtroom, they said, and it was apparent by the manner in which the spectators leaned forward that they wanted to hear what he had to say. It was not often that a man identified in the press as a Mafia soldier, a don's bodyguard, appeared in court to testify. The spectators wanted to hear every word; and from the way that Sandler began his examination, he too seemed interested, for whatever reason, in documenting Notaro's biographical background in the courtroom record.

"How old are you?" Sandler began.

"Fifty-six."

"Are you married?"

"Yes."

"When were you married?"

"1948."

"And where do you live with your wife?"

"Tucson, Arizona."

"You have a child?"

"Yes."

"And is that a girl or a boy?"

"Girl."

"How old is she?"

"Eighteen."

"Does she go to college?"

"Yes."

"Where?"

"State University."

"In Arizona?"

"That's right."

"Does your wife work for a living?"

"Yes, she does."

"How does she work for a living?"

"Waitress work."

"And has she worked for a living all of her life?"

"Yes, she has."

"Where were you born, Mr. Notaro?"

"New York City."

"Where in New York City?"

"The Lower East Side."

"And where did you go to school in New York City?"

"P.S. 114 on the East Side."

"How far did you get in school?"

"Eighth grade."

"What did you do when you left school?"

"I went to work for my father."

"What kind of work did he do?"

"Wholesale and retail produce."

"How long did you work for your father?"

"About three, four years."

"Did you then do something else?"

"Yes."

Walter Phillips, who had been displaying signs of impatience for several seconds, finally stood and said, "Your Honor, I am going to object at this time, I think we ought to get to the point here rather than going through the entire life . . ."

"Overruled," Judge Mansfield said. "This is just background."

Sandler continued, "What did you then do?"

"I bought a truck off my father."

"How much did you pay for it?"

"One hundred dollars."

"Thereafter, were you in the trucking business for a number of years?"

"Yes, I was."

"How long?"

"Thirty-seven years."

"And is that your own business?"

"That's right, yes."

"And what did you do yourself in connection with your business?"

"I drove a truck."

"Did there come a time when you had more than one truck?"

"Yes, there was."

"What was the most you ever had?"

"Six."

"And do you recall about when you had six trucks?"

"Oh, around 1950, '51."

"Did there come a time when your business began to recede, contract?"

"Yes."

"Do you understand that?"

"Yes."

"About when was that?"

"Oh, about '60, '61. The year of '60 or '61."

"Did there come a time when the business was reduced to two trucks?"

"Yes, there was."

"Do you recall when that was?"

"That's around '62, the year of '62."

"And thereafter, did it require less of your time?"

"Yes."

The questioning continued in this manner for several minutes, with Phillips barely containing his impatience. The judge, leaning back in his chair, rocking softly, listened without comment. Bill Bonanno also listened, becoming more interested when Notaro reached the year 1964 and Notaro testified that he had been introduced to the Bonannos through a cousin, the late Joseph Notaro. Then, after admitting to the court that his trucking business had declined in 1968, Peter Notaro told of the trip to Tucson that he had taken with Bill Bonanno in February 1968, adding that as he left New York he had no idea that Bill carried Torrillo's card, that he had never heard of Torrillo at that point, and that he certainly had not—contrary to Torrillo's previous testimony—gone to Torrillo's home with Perrone to procure the credit card. Notaro told the court that he first became aware of the card after Bonanno, who had been driving all day and wanted to rest, asked Notaro to take over for a while, and to use the card which was in the sun visor, "in case you need gas . . ."

"I object to this as being hearsay," Phillips said.

"Overruled," Judge Mansfield said. "I will allow it."

"Did you see the name on the card at that time?" Sandler asked.

"Yes," Notaro said.

"What was the name on the card?"

"Don Torrillo."

"Did you speak to Mr. Bonanno about that?"

"Yes, yes, I did."

"Objection to what Mr. Bonanno said," Phillips called in a loud voice, "anything Mr. Bonanno said, Your Honor."

"It seems to me that we are getting into an area here of hearsay," the judge agreed.

"I thought I was questioning the man about his criminal intent, Your Honor," Sandler explained.

"Yes," Judge Mansfield said, adding, "I will instruct the jury as follows: I am going to admit this evidence not to prove the truth of what Mr. Bonanno said, but simply to prove the fact that it was said to this witness. I think you ought to grasp the difference there," the judge continued, now turning toward the jury. "It is not being received in evidence to prove that what Mr. Bonanno said was true, because Mr. Bonanno would have to be cross-examined on that. It is being offered simply to prove that it was said to this witness."

"If Your Honor please," Krieger said, standing, seeming almost indignant. "I would like to make an objection at the sidebar. May I?"

"Yes."

With Sandler and Phillips standing next to him at the side of the judge's bench, Krieger said, "If Your Honor please, I have no quarrel with the instruction as given in that it is, in my understanding, a correct statement of the law. But what bothers me here is that it may well be construed as a comment upon the failure of the defendant Bonanno to testify and to expose himself to cross-examination here. I think that my obligation requires me to move for a mistrial under these circumstances, Your Honor."

"It certainly is not intended as any such comment," Judge

Mansfield said. "If you desire in the instructions or at this time
an instruction to the effect that the failure of the defendant Bonanno to take the stand does not constitute a basis for any inference or presumption against him, I will give it."

"Well," Krieger said, "I had assumed, Your Honor, that you
would so charge in the main body of your charge. I think, Your
Honor, at this time I would request that you instruct this jury
now that in their consideration of the charges against Salvatore
Bonanno that they are to specifically exclude from their consideration—they are to draw no inference one way or the other as
to the fact of his failure to testify and not to construe any of your
remarks as a comment on that, etc., without waiving any rights
which may have accrued as a result of the original statement."

"I am not going to add that last," said the judge.

"No, I am adding that as far as the record is concerned,"
Krieger said.

The judge turned to the jury, and said, "Ladies and gentlemen, the defendant Bonanno has rested without taking the witness stand. Under the law he has the right to do that and I think
I will instruct you more completely when the time comes. At
the present time, however, I give you this statement which will
be repeated in my instructions to you. No inference or presumption whatsoever is to be drawn against the defendant Bonanno because of his failure to take the witness stand or to testify
in his own defense. He is not required to do that and any comment made by me with respect to an evidentiary question here
was not intended to imply that any such inference should be
drawn."

With a nod from the judge, Sandler resumed his examination
of his client, and Peter Notaro told of his first months in Arizona
during which he resided at the elder Bonanno's home, dined
often with Bill Bonanno in restaurants where Bill occasionally
used the card, and Notaro also described the day that he had
accompanied Bill to the Tucson airport and, because Bill could
not find a parking place, Notaro had gone to the ticket counter
to sign Torrillo's name to a voucher, doing as Bill had asked,
and Notaro told the court that he had no idea at that time that
he was committing fraud.

Finally, Walter Phillips had his chance to cross-examine Peter
Notaro, holding in his left hand a pack of Diners' Club receipts
signed in the name of Don Torrillo.

"Are you familiar with the Statler Hilton in Tucson, Arizona?" Phillips asked.

"Yes."

"Have you ever been to the Statler Hilton, have you ever stayed there or had dinner there?"

"I have had dinner there."

"Did you have dinner there with Mr. Bonanno?"

"Yes."

"And at that time was the Don Torrillo credit card used to pay for the dinner?"

"This I don't remember."

"I show you Government Exhibit 14A in evidence," Phillips said, handing a piece of paper to Notaro. "Does that refresh your memory?"

"No, I don't remember how he paid it."

"Are you familiar with the Tucson Desert Inn in Tucson?"

"No, I don't remember it."

"You don't remember the Tucson Desert Inn?" Phillips repeated, seeming surprised.

"No."

"You don't remember ever going there?"

"I can truthfully say no, I don't remember going there."

"I show you Government Exhibit 15 in evidence," Phillips said, handing it to Notaro. "Would you look at that and see if that refreshes your memory at all."

"No," Notaro said, "I don't remember this."

Reverting back to the New York–Tucson trip of February 1968 Phillips asked, "Do you remember if you stayed at the Catalina Motel in Indianapolis, Indiana?"

"No, I don't remember the name of the motel, no."

"I show you Government's Exhibit 17 in evidence. Would you look at that for a minute."

Notaro squinted at the small piece of paper, saying finally, "No, I don't remember the hotel."

"Do you remember eating at a place called the Zeno's Steak House in Rolla, Missouri?"

No, said Notaro.

The Imperial Motel in Las Cruces, New Mexico?

No.

The Airport Travel Lodge in San Diego?

No.

"When you went over to the travel agency [in Tucson] to purchase those tickets from Montreal to Tucson, you went at Mr. Bonanno's direction, is that correct?" Phillips asked.

"He told me if I would do him a favor to go and get them for him."

"And he gave you the Don Torrillo credit card, is that right?"

"He did," said Notaro.

"When you arrived—you went over there with Mr. Pasley, is that right?" Pasley, co-owner of a cocktail lounge, was a friend of Bill Bonanno's.

Notaro admitted going with Pasley, saying that it was Pasley who had asked the travel agent, Ruben Serna, for the tickets.

"And Mr. Serna then made a telephone call, did he not?" Phillips asked.

"Yes, he did."

"And while he was on the telephone, did he turn to you and ask you, 'How do you spell your name?' "

"Yes."

"And you pulled out the credit card and you spelled Torrillo?"

"No, sir, I didn't spell it. I showed him the card."

"You showed Mr. Serna the card?"

"That's right."

"Did you hear Mr. Serna testify here that you spelled the name for him?"

"But I didn't spell the name for him," Notaro insisted.

"You have a distinct recollection of that event, is that right?" Phillips asked.

"That's right."

Judge Mansfield turned toward Notaro and asked, for clarification, "When you showed him [Serna] the card, you were indicating that you were Torrillo, isn't that what . . ."

"He introduced me as Don, Your Honor."

"Well, when you were introduced by Mr. Pasley to Mr. Serna, the travel agent, in March of 1968, you were introduced as Mr. Torrillo, weren't you?" asked the judge.

"Not to him I wasn't," Notaro said. "I was introduced to Ruben [Serna] as Don. Then when he says, 'Which credit card,' that's when I gave him the card and that's when he knew I was Don Torrillo. I was introduced to him as Don and that's all."

"But you understood, did you not," Judge Mansfield asked,

"that you were being introduced as the person Torrillo shown on the card, whether or not the word Torrillo was used?"

"Yes, this I know," said Notaro.

"Well now," the judge said, "when that happened, you knew, did you not, that you were not Don Torrillo?"

"Yes," Notaro said, "I knew that."

"Did you turn around and say to Mr. Pasley or anybody, 'Look, I'm not Torrillo'?" asked the judge.

"Mr. Pasley knew that because he knew me," Notaro said.

There was laughter in the court, but Judge Mansfield, unsmiling, continued: "Had you prior to the entry of Mr. Ruben Serna's office discussed this matter with anyone?"

"No," Notaro said, "because there was nothing to fear. The card was good. There was nothing to fear."

29

THAT AFTERNOON, THE fourth day of testimony, after minor procedural matters had been resolved by the judge, the jury heard the final arguments from Krieger, Sandler, and Phillips.

Krieger, who spoke first, reminded the jury that at the start of the trial he had said that the "credibility of Torrillo will mandate your verdict"; and now, at the completion of testimony, Krieger said he would not retreat from that position. If anyone had engaged in fraud in this trial, Krieger said, it was not Bonanno— it was Torrillo, whom he characterized as a deceiver, an exaggerator, and finally a tool of the prosecution. After signing an affidavit that he had lost the credit card, he changed his story, Krieger said, when the detectives began to visit him. "In June of 1968 he is interviewed by the detectives, and then," Krieger said, "I believe we started to see the truth. The light comes out, the candle in the darkness comes out—Torrillo is behind terribly in his bills, he can't pay the accumulated charges. He is worried. He had a house in his own name which suddenly had gone over into his father's name, and I think that you can draw an inference there that he was seeking to conceal his assets from creditors such as the various credit card agencies. He knows, because the detectives tell him, 'You are in trouble in this Diners' Club thing. We could arrest you right now. You are in trouble. You are in trouble. You are in trouble.' "

If Bonanno did not think that it was permissible to use Torrillo's card, he would surely have behaved in a more surreptitious manner than he did, Krieger reasoned, and he would not have been so open and casual in displaying the card in his hometown, Tucson, where he was so well known. When the card was confiscated in Bloom's store, Krieger continued, Bonanno had not reacted in a violent manner, he had not run from the store and fled to the hills, which would have been the predictable reaction of a man wishing to conceal what he believed to be a serious crime. Bonanno had paid for the merchandise at Bloom's, Krieger reminded the jury, and later on his Tucson attorney, Netherton, had called Bloom's seeking without success the return of the card.

The government's perjury charges against Bonanno were also unfounded, Krieger said, being partly based on the issue of whether or not he had discussed the matter of the credit card with his attorneys in Tucson. Quoting from Bonanno's grand jury testimony of October 24, 1968, which Krieger conceded was not sufficiently clear and precise—Bonanno had said: "I may have mentioned it to a few attorneys."—Krieger nonetheless recalled that one of the attorneys, Netherton, had admitted on the witness stand that the question of Bonanno's discussing the card with him "strikes a chord." While Videen denied that the subject had been discussed, a third attorney, Soble, had said, "Yes, there was a discussion about a credit card," cautioning Bonanno on that occasion that "there might be a forgery."

When Sandler stood to deliver his summation, he also focused on the exaggerations, inconsistencies, and the admitted lies in Torrillo's testimony, adding: "He is a kind of a person who pretends to be a big shot when he is not, who pretends to be more important than he is, to have more affluence, more resources, more credit. Such a person met people who seemed to him important, whether they were or not. And he was trying very hard to impress them with how important he was so that he could use them ultimately for his interests. And a time came when his bluff was called, when they said—when Perrone said, 'We are short of cash, we need help, can we use a credit card,' and he says consistent with the image he had presented, 'Of course, I have twenty credit cards. Don't worry about it, we will straighten it out.'

"I suggest to you that he is the kind of person who could have done that. You know he is the kind of person who could have lied about doing that and that there is at least at the beginning a substantial possibility that this is what occurred, that he led them to believe that it was all right with him, the bills would be taken care of. I suggest that, at least, that is a reasonable possibility, perhaps more."

In conclusion, Sandler said: "I have no apologies whatever

to offer to Mr. Notaro, none whatever. He's a man who has worked all of his life, and at the age of fifty-six he has a wife whom he's had for twenty years and a young daughter who is going to school, to college in Arizona, and his wife is not ashamed to work as a waitress, and when he buys a house in a new area of this country, a $16,000 house, and he puts down a down payment by borrowing against an insurance policy and borrowing money from his daughter's savings account, this is not a man who has to be afraid to look anybody here in the eye. He is a man, he is a decent worthwhile man. He is ten times in decency the man Torrillo is, ten times. I think I am using a very small numeral when I make that kind of comparison.

"We do not ask for sympathy. We do not ask for mercy. We ask for justice. We ask you to do that which you were sworn to do. Apply your experience and your common sense and your feeling for life to what happened in terms of the court's charge. If you do that you will acquit Peter Notaro. Thank you very much."

When it came Phillips's turn to speak he quickly refuted Krieger's contention that the keystone of the government's case was Don A. Torrillo; the government's case rests simply on the crimes that had been committed, Phillips said, specifically the crimes of perjury, conspiracy, and fraudulent use of the mail. Each and every time that Bonanno or Notaro were representing themselves as Torrillo in a restaurant, a motel, or at an airlines counter, they were guilty of fraud, and Phillips refused to accept the notion that Bonanno or Notaro were so naïve as to think otherwise. Phillips also dismissed as absurd the defendant's explanation that Torrillo had given his card willingly to Perrone and had agreed to its use by Bonanno.

"Now, ask yourselves," Phillips appealed to the jury, "applying your common sense, would Mr. Torrillo have given permission to Mr. Bonanno, or *anybody* for that matter, to take five people into Pancho's Steak House and treat them to a meal and pay for it on his credit card? Would Mr. Torrillo have given Mr. Bonanno, or anybody, for that matter, permission to go into Bloom's store, charge up almost two hundred dollars' worth of clothes on his credit card? Does your common sense tell you that Mr. Torrillo would have given Mr. Bonanno, or anybody, for that matter, permission to purchase airline tickets, two parties, first-class, one way, San Francisco to John F. Kennedy, to

New York? Two parties, first-class, Phoenix to New York City? $300. Tucson to New York? $259. And so it goes. Los Angeles, San Francisco–Phoenix, San Francisco–Phoenix? Do you think that Mr. Torrillo would have, in his right mind, given him permission, or anybody permission, to purchase these tickets on his credit card? Does your common sense tell you that Mr. Torrillo would have given Mr. Bonanno, or anybody, permission to charge up almost $2,500 in just over one month on this card?

"But let's look at what else we have. The bills weren't paid. Not one single bill that Mr. Bonanno used on this credit card was paid. If Mr. Torrillo had given him permission why wouldn't he at least have paid a bill or two? But this shows you, that fact alone . . . that he didn't give him permission."

Recalling Torrillo's admitted fear of Hank Perrone, Torrillo's having seen Perrone carrying a gun and also hitting an elderly man in a barbershop, Phillips asked the jury to put itself in Torrillo's place on the evening in January 1968 when Perrone had come to Torrillo's home and asserted his need for the card. "What would you have done under those circumstances?" Phillips asked. "Would you have denied him the credit card? I hardly think so. I think your common sense tells you go get the credit card and you give it to him."

On the following morning, Friday, November 14, a week after the trial had begun, Judge Mansfield greeted the jury and explained that the time had come to perform the final function in the administration of justice in this case.

"We have three kinds of charges here against the defendants," the judge explained. "The first is in count 1 charging a conspiracy to violate the federal statute that prohibits mail frauds and use of a fictitious name or address in furtherance of a scheme to defraud.

"Counts 2 through 52, inclusive, charge violation of the mail fraud statute. Count 53 charges violation of the statute prohibiting use of a fictitious name in furtherance of a mail fraud scheme. Counts 54 and 55 charge perjury against the defendant Bonanno, and count 56 charges perjury against the defendant Notaro.

"Each of these counts must be considered by you separately and made the subject of a separate verdict as to each defendant named in the count . . ."

Bill Bonanno sat next to Krieger listening as the judge continued with his instructions to the jury, which within the hour would
begin their deliberation and attempt to reach a verdict. Bill could
see that Notaro seemed tense, his fingers lightly on the table,
but Bill now felt calm and thought that he was psychologically
prepared for the worst. He had talked to Krieger the night before
about his chances for an acquittal, and Krieger had said candidly
that his chances were slim. The government's case was strong,
and Phillips's summation yesterday afternoon had seemed effectively presented and damaging to the defense. If convicted, Bill
thought he could expect at least a ten-year sentence; and, even
with time off for good behavior and other concessions, he would
have to serve about seven years, meaning that he would probably
be in his mid-forties when he got out. His children would then
be in their teens: Charles nearly twenty, Joseph sixteen, Tory
fourteen, Felippa thirteen. Bill doubted that his father would be
alive. What was most sickening about this whole credit card
episode to Bill was the amount of money involved—$2,400,
which would have seemed a paltry sum to him at one time. On
his wedding day in 1956, as he checked out of the Astor Hotel
carrying a suitcase with $100,000 in cash gifts, he would never
have dreamed that he could be imprisoned for *years* in an alleged
fraud totaling $2,400.

Bill continued to listen to Judge Mansfield's instructions to
the jury. ". . . an act is done willfully if it is done knowingly
. . . an act is done knowingly if it is done voluntarily and pur-
posefully and not because of negligence . . ." Then Bill's mind
drifted again, and he heard noises coming from Foley Square
below. He could hear a crowd of anti–Vietnam War protestors
shouting in the square, could hear a policeman with a bullhorn
warning the protesters to remain behind the barricades. Bill had
seen the group forming when he entered the courtroom earlier,
a few of them carrying signs announcing MORATORIUM II and
denouncing NIXON'S WAR. The shouting now became louder,
and finally Judge Mansfield turned and asked that the window
be closed. After this was done, the judge resumed with his instructions.

The jury retired at 11:30 A.M., and it took three hours and
twenty-five minutes to conclude the deliberations. At 3:00 P.M.
the jurors returned to the courtroom, and, after a roll call, the
clerk asked: "Mr. Foreman, have you arrived at a verdict?"

"Yes, we have."

Notaro edged up in his chair now, but Bill was lounging with his left arm draped over the back of Krieger's chair.

"As to the defendant Bonanno, what is your verdict as to count 1?" asked the clerk, meaning the conspiracy charge.

"Count 1," the foreman announced, "we find the defendant guilty."

"As to counts 2 through 53, what is your verdict?" asked the clerk, referring to the violations of the mail fraud statute.

"Guilty."

Bill removed his arm from the back of Krieger's chair and rested his left hand under his chin. He still seemed calm, relaxed, but within him he felt a sinking sensation and perspiration along his back and neck.

"Counts 54 and 55, what is your verdict?"

"Guilty."

"As to the defendant Notaro," the clerk continued, "what is your verdict as to count 1?"

"Guilty."

"Counts 2 through 53?"

"Guilty."

Bill was stunned and further depressed on hearing Notaro's verdict, and he did not look at Notaro, who had been rubbing his hand back and forth across his mouth.

"And count 56?" the clerk asked, meaning the perjury charge against Notaro.

"Not guilty."

Well, Bill thought, at least they gave him one small break. Notaro remained still, his face glistened with perspiration.

"Members of the jury," the clerk said, "listen to your verdict as it stands recorded. You say you find the defendant Bonanno guilty on count 1, guilty on counts 2 through 53, and guilty on counts 54 and 55. You also say you find the defendant Notaro guilty on count 1, guilty on counts 2 through 53, and not guilty on count 56, so say you all."

Krieger spoke up. "Could we have the jury polled, Your Honor?"

"Yes," said the judge. "Will you poll the jury?"

The clerk, facing each of the eight women and four men, asked them individually: "Is that your verdict?" Each answered affirmatively.

"Ladies and gentlemen," the judge said, "this has been a fairly long week for all of you and I know you paid most careful attention to the evidence and have given it conscientious, thoughtful consideration. It is never a pleasant duty to render a verdict finding anyone guilty of anything. On the other hand, under our system of justice it is a most important and, I think I said earlier, probably the most important singular function of citizenship besides voting, and that is to serve on a jury and to make the decision fearlessly and objectively on the basis of the evidence . . ."

After thanking the jury, Judge Mansfield excused them, and they filed out of the jury box and walked in tandem past the table where Bill and Notaro sat quietly with their attorneys.

Bill watched them, looked each one in the face. He noticed that ten of the jurors looked away as they passed; but two women momentarily returned his glance, and, seemingly as self-conscious and embarrassed as the others, quickly walked on.

30

Aᴀꜰᴛᴇʀ ᴛʜᴇ ᴊᴜʀʏ left the courtroom, Phillips made application to the judge that Bonanno and Notaro be held in custody until the day of sentencing.

"The basis of the government's application in this particular case is as follows," Phillips said. "Mr. Salvatore Bonanno is the son of Joseph Bonanno, who is the leader of the well-known family, the Bonanno family. Approximately two or three years ago there was an intermural war within this family. As a result of this war, there were twelve public shootings and of those twelve shootings, six people were killed, six people were wounded. In addition to which, during that time and subsequent to that time in Tucson, Arizona, where Mr. Joseph Bonanno lives and where Mr. Salvatore Bonanno had been living, there were a number of bombings, explosions of TNT in business establishments, residences, and other places, other buildings.

"It is the government's information that this was also a direct effect or cause of this Bonanno war," Phillips continued, as Krieger shook his head, amazed at the outdated and incorrect information that the prosecutor was quoting. "The fear that the people in Tucson live in of the Bonannos could have been reflected on each of the witnesses' faces," Phillips went on, insistently, as the judge listened. "Mr. Walters, for example [the ticket counter employee for American Airlines in Tucson]. I submit that in addition to which Mr. Don Torrillo, who was a witness here, will also be a witness in a case here the defendant Bonanno is under indictment in the Eastern District for income tax evasion and that his safety is endangered. Mr. Notaro was the bodyguard for Mr. Joseph Bonanno and is presently or had been the bodyguard for his son, Salvatore Bonanno, and is directly linked with these shootings as is Mr. Salvatore Bonanno.''

Krieger wanted to interrupt, but Judge Mansfield held up his hand signaling Krieger to wait. And Phillips went on: "I submit that under all the circumstances it would be in the best interests of justice and the best interests of the public and society at large that Mr. Salvatore Bonanno and Mr. Notaro be remanded. I have not mentioned the fact that Mr. Bonanno lives in California and Tucson and has no roots whatsoever here in New York and neither does Mr. Notaro, as his home is in Tucson, Arizona, at the present time.''

"I am not quite clear from what you said," Judge Mansfield cut in, "how you attribute any of this danger that you say exists to the community or to persons to the defendants here.''

"The fact is of the bombings out in Tucson, Arizona," Phillips replied, "Mr. Joe Bonanno's house was bombed at one time, there were other business establishments which were bombed.''

"You think his son bombed his house?" the judge asked, facetiously.

"The government has information," Phillips said, "that some of the business establishments that were bombed were bombed on orders of either Mr. Salvatore Bonanno or Mr. Joe Bonanno, Jr., or Mr. Bonanno, Sr.''

Krieger and Bill Bonanno were both shaking their heads now, and Krieger finally appealed to the judge loudly, "May I respond to something of my own knowledge, Your Honor?''

"Yes.''

"As far as this Tucson, Arizona, situation is concerned, an FBI agent by the name of Hale has been relieved of service as a result of charges leveled against him by two people who were arrested and indicted in Tucson, Arizona, who have also been charged with committing the bombings which Mr. Phillips just lavishly lays at the door of the Bonannos.'' Phillips seemed puzzled by the remark, having heard nothing about the FBI's involvement—that story, unlike the previous bomb reports from Tucson that held the Mafia responsible, had not been featured in *The New York Times* or other New York papers. Phillips was hearing this now for the first time, and he did not interrupt as Krieger explained, "Mr. Bonanno was home and Salvatore Bonanno was home when the Bonanno home was bombed. It just does not stand to reason that he is planting bombs in his own house to blow himself up.''

The judge listened patiently, though without great interest, to the story about the Tucson bombings; he had already made up his mind to free Bonanno and Notaro on bail until the day of sentencing, and merely wished to warn them that this temporary freedom would be reconsidered ''if there comes to the attention of the court the slightest indication of any violence or harm to the community or threatening or intimidation or tampering with witnesses who are likely to appear in any other criminal proceeding.''

Bill Bonanno was released on $15,000 bail, Notaro on $10,000, and the day of sentencing was put off until after the Christmas holidays.

Before Bill and Notaro turned to leave the courtroom, which was now nearly empty, the judge turned to them and said, reassuringly, ''Your counsel did everything that could possibly have been done on your behalf. I just think the government had a very strong case from what I see with respect particularly as to the defendant Bonanno. So I don't think when you start second-guessing this you can say that your counsel moved the wrong way at some stage. They didn't.''

The defendants nodded in agreement, and then, with Krieger and Sandler, they left the courtroom. Bill and Notaro, excited and relieved that they were out on bail, went directly toward telephone booths to relay the news of their conviction to their families, and then to check out of the hotel and fly home for the weekend. The attorneys planned to appeal the conviction and to remain alert for new evidence that might benefit their clients' cause, although they did not anticipate anything specific, and they were both disappointed and dejected by the jury's decision.

Then suddenly and unexpectedly, on the following Monday, their hopes were revived. Leonard Sandler, walking through the criminal courthouse on Monday morning, met a friend of his, a lawyer, who during a brief conversation about the Bonanno case asked if the witness, Don A. Torrillo, was the same individual who was a codefendant in another case in which this lawyer's client was also involved. Sandler was surprised to hear that Torrillo had another case pending, and when he asked what Torrillo's indictment was about, his friend said it concerned a ''bucket shop''—a fraudulent brokerage house. Sandler quickly left to check the records, and he soon discovered that Torrillo had been named a year and a half ago in a ninety-nine-count indictment. The date on the indictment was May 25, 1968, which was a little more than two months after Perrone's death; and it was obvious from the docket entries that little legal action had been taken on Torrillo's case. If Sandler was prone to jumping to conclusions, which he was not, he might assume that the government had exhibited considerably less enthusiasm in prosecuting Torrillo than it had demonstrated in the Bonanno–Notaro case. Bonanno had been indicted for the credit card episode in early December 1968, six months after Torrillo had been indicted for federal securities violations; and, if nothing else, it meant that when the government was interrogating Torrillo during 1968–1969 about his credit card, it had more on him than the mere fact of his arrest by twenty policemen immediately after Perrone's death—an arrest on the "trumped-up charges" of heroin possession that Phillips had referred to the previous week in the courtroom.

Sandler called Krieger and also asked for an appointment with Judge Mansfield. The request was granted, and at 5:00 P.M. on Wednesday, November 19, the two defense attorneys met with the judge and were joined by Walter Phillips.

"What can I do for you gentlemen?" the judge asked after they had assembled.

Sandler replied: "Your Honor, I asked your clerk if we could have a conference as a result of something I learned on Monday morning, and the purpose of the conference, as I see it, is not for me to make any motions but simply tell the court, in the presence of Mr. Phillips, what came to my attention which will, I assume, be the subject of a subsequent motion."

After relating what he had learned, Sandler said that he wanted to be certain before proceeding further that his information was factually correct.

"Well, what do you know about this?" the judge asked, looking at Phillips.

"I can verify, Your Honor," Phillips said, "that this Mr. Torrillo, the same Torrillo who testified in the trial last week, is under indictment in the Southern District for a security violation, and so I don't think that we need to go any further. It is the same man. I gather that the reason that Mr. Sandler is bringing this up is because he would have liked to have had that information last week in order to cross-examine Mr. Torrillo about it. I would naturally have objected to it since it would not be a felony conviction and therefore not proper to be brought up for impeachment purposes in cross-examination. It is only an indictment and it has not been brought to trial.''

''Well,'' asked the judge, ''what is the status of that other case?''

''I think motions have been decided in the case,'' Phillips said. ''It is awaiting trial. That is the status of the case.''

''Your Honor,'' Sandler said, ''I don't think that argument is appropriate at this point, and having said that, I throw in one spear if Your Honor will indulge me. In a fairly extensive experience, both as a prosecutor and as a defense lawyer, I have never ever heard of a situation in which a witness is under indictment and it was for the office where he is under indictment, in which there was not discussion between that office and himself or his attorney with regard to the effect on his case of his testimony, and I would find it hard to believe that that did not exist in this case, that it was not something which ought to have been furnished to us under the *Brady* v. *Maryland* rule, if no other rule.''

''I don't know about Brady–Maryland,'' said Judge Mansfield, ''but it seems to me—am I wrong?—that there was some questioning of some witness with respect to whether he didn't have an indictment pending?''

''I recall, Your Honor,'' Sandler said, ''because we had a misunderstanding about it, and I was very perplexed at the time, having . . .''

''Oh, I remember,'' the judge interrupted, ''you started to ask about whether a fellow had been indicted for perjury.''

''Right,'' said Sandler.

''And I thought you were just going to try to bring out an indictment which I do not consider subject matter for impeachment. Then your twist was that you were going to, in effect, imply that because he had not been indicted for perjury, therefore certain inferences could be drawn. So then I said all right.''

''Yes,'' Sandler agreed, ''it was a misunderstanding between us.''

''You could put it in,'' the judge continued. ''But on this one, I will wait until I see your motion. I can't comment until I see it, I suppose.''

''For whatever informational value, Your Honor,'' Krieger

said, "my recollection of that indictment number is 68 CR.471. Do you recall that, Mr. Sandler?" Sandler confirmed it.

"Well," said the judge, "we will check. If I have that indictment, it is unbeknownst to me because I wouldn't have, I haven't any recollection of seeing an indictment against a fellow named Torrillo. The only time I ever heard of the name Torrillo was in this case." The judge turned toward his clerk, a tweedy young man with a red moustache, and asked, "Isn't that right?"

"No, I haven't been here long enough, but we have never . . ."

The judge cut him off, saying "No, I don't remember. I'd know if I had, I would think, unless I got it by some curious quirk unbeknownst to me. So, we will check." Turning to his clerk again, the judge asked, "You have got the number?"

"Yes."

"I will await your papers," the judge said to Sandler and Krieger. They thanked him and left.

Judge Mansfield received the papers and reviewed them during the next two months, with the day of sentencing meanwhile postponed from January 1970 until March. On February 3, a posttrial hearing was held in which, among other people, Sergeant Robert J. O'Neil was called to testify about Torrillo's indictment, O'Neil being one of the police officers who had interviewed Torrillo after Perrone's death.

"At the time when you participated in those interviews," Judge Mansfield asked O'Neil at the posttrial hearing, "did you have any knowledge regarding an indictment that had been filed in this court in late May naming Don A. Torrillo and various others in connection with charges of alleged violations of the federal securities laws?"

"Did I have knowledge of an indictment at that time? No, sir," O'Neil said. "No, I did not."

Another witness, however, a postal inspector named William O'Keefe who had participated prominently in the credit card case against Bonanno and Notaro, testified that the subject of Torrillo's pending indictment had once been discussed in Phillips's office before the Bonanno trial.

The subject had been raised by Torrillo himself, O'Keefe recalled, adding that Torrillo had inquired about what could be done about his indictment. But Phillips had "shut off" Torrillo,

O'Keefe testified, explaining that "Phillips simply told him [Torrillo] he didn't want to know nothing about that trial until after the [Bonanno] case." Sandler received permission to question the witness, and he asked O'Keefe: "At this conversation when Mr. Phillips said he didn't want to hear anything about the other indictment until after the trial, did he say until after the Bonanno trial?"

"I may have phrased it incorrectly," O'Keefe replied. "I believe he said that. He said he would check with the attorney and find out about it, who had it, and that he didn't want to know anything about it. It was a very short conversation where he shut him off and there was very little to it."

"Did he say anything about possibly talking to Mr. Torrillo about the indictment after the Bonanno trial?" Sandler asked.

"Negative, sir."

"Never said that?"

"No, sir," O'Keefe repeated.

"In your presence?"

"No, sir, he did not."

"Did Mr. Phillips ever discuss with you the Torrillo indictment in the absence of Mr. Torrillo?"

"He may have asked me if I knew anything about it or something in that context," O'Keefe said. "But beyond that, no, sir."

"Did he ever say to you that he didn't want to have any conversation about it because it would become the subject of cross-examination?"

"No, sir."

"Nothing of that nature?"

"No, sir."

"That's all," Sandler said, and then Phillips received permission to ask O'Keefe one question.

"When the matter was brought up, did Mr. Torrillo bring it up in the context of what his status was concerning traveling subsequent to the Bonanno trial in view of the fact that his bail limits were confined to the Southern District of New York and the Eastern District of New York?"

"Yes, he did, sir," said O'Keefe.

"That's all I have, sir," Phillips said.

The day of sentencing for Bill Bonanno and Peter Notaro was Monday, March 9, 1970. They arrived in Judge Mansfield's courtroom shortly before 10:00 A.M. with their attorneys, took their places at the defense's table, and remained seated as the clerk called out, "Government ready?"

"The government is ready for sentencing, Your Honor," said Phillips.

"Defendant ready?"

"Defendant Bonanno is ready, Your Honor," said Krieger.

"Defendant Notaro is ready, Your Honor," said Robert Kasanof, a large dark-haired man who was filling in for Sandler.

"Is there anything the government wishes to say with respect to sentence before sentence is imposed?" asked Judge Mansfield.

"No, Your Honor," said Phillips. "I am sure Your Honor has a full presentence report in this matter and the government has nothing to add to that report, Your Honor."

"All right," said the judge, "let me take the two defendants seriatim." Nodding toward Bill, the judge said, "Mr. Bonanno, will you please stand."

Bill stood, smoothing out the back of his jacket, seeming calm, unconcerned. He appeared considerably overweight, perhaps 235 pounds, and his face was round and full. His dark wavy hair, as always, was carefully combed, precisely parted.

"Is there anything that you wish to say or that you wish to have your attorney, Mr. Krieger say, or both of you want to say before sentence is imposed by the court?" asked the judge.

"No, I haven't anything to say," Bill answered. "Mr. Krieger has something."

"Do you know of any reason whatsoever," the judge asked, "why sentence should not be imposed at this time?"

"None that I know of, Your Honor," said Krieger, standing. Then, after he had confirmed that the judge had denied all the postverdict motions made by the defense, Krieger said: "Your Honor, I wish that Salvatore Bonanno could appear before you today in reality facing a sentence which would be unaffected or uncolored by really a life which has been stark. I know that the pretrial applications and various relief which was afforded to the defendant during the course of this trial had disclosed a rather unhappy and unfortunate history, at least over the last ten years, Your Honor, concerning this defendant. On the one hand there has been publicity of his allegedly running a criminal empire where he is dealing in untold fortunes, and yet the government has through its investigations, both legal and illegal, found out that there were times when he could not pay his own telephone bill. The government knows that the roof over his family's home was lost from just nonpayment, foreclosure. The government knows that he is living basically on the largesse of other members of his family.

"The government also knows, and I don't know if this has ever turned up in a presentence report, but it cannot really be contradicted—at the time of his father's kidnaping, alleged kidnaping, the government, in an effort to locate his father, placed IRS liens in a comparatively large amount against both the father and the son. Joe Bonanno at that time owned a piece of property in Tucson, Arizona—it was income property, it was paying him a good few thousand dollars a year in income up until that time. The government liened it, took the proceeds; and despite repeated applications to apply the proceeds to the payment of the mortgage to prevent a foreclosure, so that if the government's lien was upheld the government could at least obtain the value of the property rather than just see the property go through foreclosure and have both the defendant and the government ousted of any benefits of the property, the government stubbornly saw to it that foreclosure was had and neither the government was paid the taxes due, nor did the defendant receive any income from that property. The property was subsequently obtained by the city of Tucson through eminent domain, and it is my understanding that the amount received by the fortunate mortgagee would have been sufficient to pay off a considerable portion, if not all, of the tax lien levied against the defendant.

"Your Honor," Krieger said, "this is the sort of thing which has haunted him. His family—I am referring to now his wife and his four children—have paid an enormous amount just through their blood association with Salvatore Bonanno and I don't think that the price which has been exacted from them is truly founded upon criminal activity as such. It has been founded upon reputation. Salvatore Bonanno, realistically, appears before the court as the dog who has been given a bad name and has been beaten for it.

"I do not think—and I say this most advisedly—that the problem which faces the defendant today is one necessarily of his own design and his making. In the eavesdropping logs which Your Honor permitted me to hear prior to trial, there was one

statement made there by an uncle [Labruzzo] which I think best
sums up the situation insofar as Salvatore Bonanno is concerned.
His uncle, who is now dead, is quoted by the Federal Bureau of
Investigation as saying, in substance, 'This poor kid, Bill, he
was going to college, he was making something out of himself,
and they destroyed him.'

"I don't know, Your Honor, as to whom the 'they' attaches,
but I do know that Salvatore Bonanno is a person of intelligence
and of attainment and a person whose life has literally been
destroyed for one reason or the other. I don't think that the real
reason which attaches to his own self-destruction is one of criminal propensity as such.

"This credit card situation of which he stands convicted before the court—and I think that it would be most advised to say
that the indictment was obtained in large measure as a result of
the rejection of Salvatore Bonanno's explanation of the circumstances which gave rise to the possession and the use of the
credit card, the indictment does not speak of the type of criminal
activity which demands a quarantine of the defendant from the
community.

"It does not speak of the sort of activity where the public
screams for protection, Your Honor," Krieger said, his voice
rising. "I think that in the vernacular the defendant stands before
you convicted of having committed a white-collar crime and,
having been convicted of a white-collar crime, Your Honor, I
most respectfully state to the court—and I suggest to the court
that he should be sentenced—in conformity with people who
have been convicted of white-collar crimes, and not be sentenced on the basis of his being Salvatore Bonanno."

The judge interrupted, saying, "Let me check a few facts that
are in this presentence report prepared by the Probation Department." Turning to Bill, the judge said, "Mr. Bonanno, this
report shows that you are thirty-seven years old, is that right?"

"Yes, sir," Bill said.

"And that you have had three years of college—I think it was
Tucson University or the University of Arizona?"

"That is correct," Bill said.

"Now it also shows a prior record," the judge said. "First,
a three-year suspended sentence in January of '62, and restitution, jury fees totaling $2,248 on a charge of bad checks, I guess
insufficient funds on checks."

"One check, Your Honor," Bill said.

"One check?"

"Yes, sir."

"It also shows," Judge Mansfield went on, "upon your refusal to testify as to the disappearance of your father here in the Southern District of New York, you were held in civil contempt for a period of from March 2 to June 8, 1965, and that you later testified and were released."

"That is correct, Your Honor," said Krieger.

"It also shows," the judge said, scanning the document, "that in November—the end of November of 1966, in Montreal, Canada, you were picked up in a car charged with driving without registration, and that there were two cars—in one of the other cars were Louis Greco, Vito De Filippo, and [Peter] Magaddino, and in the other car were Carl Simari, Peter Notaro, and Pat De Filippo, and that revolvers were found in Simari's car and that Notaro and the others pleaded guilty to possession of weapons and were sentenced to two days and deported, and you were ordered deported on December 1, 1966."

"That is not quite correct, Your Honor," said Bill.

"In what respect then is it inaccurate?"

"In the matter of the detention—my detention—I was picked up in a restaurant and that is all I know about it. After that I pleaded in the court in Montreal for failing to have a valid registration card, which was in the glove compartment of the car, but in order to facilitate the deportation I agreed to plead guilty so that we could facilitate the deportation."

"The next charge," the judge continued, without commenting on Bill's response, "is that on September 21, 1968, you took a rifle out of the trunk of an automobile, loaded it, and pointed it at a police officer who apparently had been following you. This apparently was done on more than one occasion and you were with Peter Notaro and one Tony Mustakas at the time. You were charged with possession of a deady weapon with an attempt to assault and were fined $150."

"That is a rather odd one, Your Honor," Krieger interjected, "because the defendant was tried in absentia on a misdemeanor and it is impossible to really explain the legal circumstances behind that, but certainly if anyone points a rifle at a police officer he is going to be fined more than $150—that is, if the court believes it."

"Well," the judge said, skeptically, "I don't know what happens down in Arizona when you do that. Maybe you don't get as stiff punishment as you would in some other urban communities. Is there any basic dispute about the substance of the facts and the fine?"

"No," Krieger said, "the fine is correct, Your Honor. The defendant has always denied doing that. The issue as to whether it was done was, as far as this defendant is concerned, an absolute falsehood."

"All right," the judge said, looking down at the document again, "there is also a statement here to the effect that in 1968 when you went to Arizona, using the credit card that is the subject of the present prosecution, you rented a car in New York, reregistered the car in Arizona, after it was repainted, new plates and new ignition were put into the automobile. You then stopped paying the rental bills, disposed of the car, rented another car, and never paid the bills on that car."

"That is not true, Your Honor," Bill said quickly. Then, amending his statement, said, "Part of it is not true."

"Well, what part is not true?"

"The automobile that was leased here in New York was leased by the company that I was associated with," Bill said. "I drove it to Arizona and the car was never repainted, the keys were never changed on it, and I was advised in Arizona that you could interstate the car. By that I mean that the state of Arizona would allow you to have Arizona plates. In fact, they preferred that you have Arizona plates, and that is all that was done. The bills were being paid from the New York office. The person who leased the car, I believe Your Honor will remember, Mr. Sam Perrone, is now deceased. That was an unfortunate accident," Bill said, pausing. "That is all I know about the car. The leasing company also, by the way, Your Honor, was notified as to where the car was and they were also notified as to what they wanted done with the car."

"Well," the judge said, "before I pass sentence in the case of the defendant Bonanno, I think I will first hear from Mr. Notaro and his counsel. Let me state that in this report with respect to Mr. Bonanno there is a reference to the fact that his father is reputed to be a former Mafia chief in charge of one of the Mafia families, and I in passing sentence give no consideration whatsoever to that statement. As far as I am concerned, guilt is personal and I do not take into consideration the charges or rumors with respect to people or their parents, relatives, wives, or the like.''

"Yes, Your Honor," said Krieger.

Then focusing on Peter Notaro, who stood erect with his gray hair slicked back, Judge Mansfield asked, "Mr. Notaro, do you know of any reason why sentence should not be passed on you at this time?''

"No, Your Honor."

"Is there anything you wish to say or you wish to have your counsel—your counsel is changed, I see—Mr. Kasanof say, or both of you want to say at this time before sentence is imposed by the court?''

"I have nothing to say, Your Honor," Notaro said.

"Mr. Kasanof?"

"If Your Honor please," Kasanof said, "Your Honor is in a position, actually, of having a clearer picture of the trial, which I did not try, Your Honor, than I do. Mr. Notaro testified and I am quite confident that having observed him as a witness Your Honor will have come to some conclusions about him, what sort of person he is, about his capacity, about his relationship to the offense charged, his relationship to the codefendant and what relative roles, assuming, as I must at this point, that the jury's verdict—addressing myself entirely to the question of clemency—their relative roles, their relative culpability. And if guilt is personal, and I am sure it is, Your Honor, Mr. Notaro has suffered because of things that have been said about him, things said about people who he knows.

"He now lives in Arizona. He is not employed, Your Honor. His wife is employed. She works two jobs. He has a young daughter attending the University of Arizona. His wife is required to work as a waitress at two different jobs because he has found himself virtually unemployable because of things that have been said about him.

"I think, Your Honor," Kasanof continued, "judging him in the context of this case and having an opportunity to have seen and heard him, I would prefer then to reserve further remarks to anything that Your Honor would have to say. I would make a motion similar to that made by counsel for the codefendant that if there is any material in the probation report on which Your Honor is to rely, that it either be disclosed to counsel in camera or, following Your Honor's practice with the codefendant, to give us an opportunity to meet it."

"Is there anything you want to add to that, Mr. Notaro?" asked the judge.

"No, Your Honor."

"Let me ask a few questions. The presentence report shows that you are fifty-six years of age, is that right?"

Before Notaro could reply, Kasanof remembered something he had forgotten a moment before, and he said: "Your Honor, let me say that there was some significant question about who was in which car and where what weapons were recovered [in Montreal, November 1966], and that case was disposed of by a plea with the anticipation of a prompt deportation from Canada."

"Well, that may be," said the judge. Then, turning to Notaro, he asked, "But are you now saying you were not guilty of the charge, but that you pleaded guilty in order to be deported in a hurry? Is that about what you are saying?"

"It is not fair," Kasanof interjected. "There was a close question there, Your Honor. I don't think that it is a major matter. I am trying to give Your Honor a fair picture of what had transpired."

"I am only trying to make sure that in passing sentence I am not being influenced by any misinformation, that is all," said Judge Mansfield. "I don't think—let me add quickly—that the Probation Department would ever consciously put anything in that was a misstatement, but I want to make absolutely sure."

"I am sure they wouldn't," Kasanof quickly agreed, "and that is not the thrust of my remarks. The defendant tells me that the car in which he was there were no weapons. In the other car, which was in proximity, there were, apparently, some weapons. All of the participants were charged together and they all pleaded guilty and were promptly thereafter deported."

"Now I also see," the judge said, looking at the document, "that it shows as pending this case down in Tucson charging conspiracy to obstruct justice, but I understand that has ended with an acquittal?"

"Yes, Your Honor," said Notaro.

"Is that the same case?" the judge asked, referring to the one in which Notaro and the elder Bonanno had been charged by the FBI with plotting to get Battaglia's sentence reduced in Leavenworth prison.

"That is the same case," Kasanof said. "That was a jury acquittal on the direct merits."

"All right," the judge said, putting the document aside, and looking at the men who stood before him and also at the spectators in the courtroom. "I have given quite a lot of thought to this. And with respect to the defendant Bonanno you stand convicted on fifty-five counts of three different crimes, conspiracy, and then the use of the Diners' Club card, and, finally, perjury before the grand jury. With all due respect to what your counsel has so eloquently said on your behalf, I don't think that you are a victim of circumstances.

"You have had a relatively good education," the judge said, speaking slowly, directly at Bill. "You have had comforts provided you in your youth and there is hardly any excuse for the type of conduct of which you were found guilty here. This was a case where you didn't just yield to a passing temptation but over a period of time engaged in pretty extensive fraudulent use of this card. There is no indication of any economic compulsion. You are not the product of a ghetto. I don't see that because of the family relationships to which Mr. Krieger referred you were under any great handicap that required you to use these cards. You could have gotten a job. There was no need to do what you did.

"Furthermore," the judge continued, as Bill stood thinking that the sentence was going to be a long one, "the record shows that this, apparently, is not exactly an isolated use. You have used another card of Levine, the evidence in the case showed, and then there is this reference to the use of the rental car, which you say was paid for, but I don't know whether it was completely paid for. You also have a prior record of passing a bad check and your conduct in the use of a weapon as charged and of which you were found guilty, as well as the circumstances surrounding your being in Montreal, all indicate a proclivity toward antisocial conduct.

"I have given a lot of thought to it," the judge repeated, as the tension was building within Bill, his mind racing with anticipation, though his face showed nothing, "and I have decided, after listening to counsel, that the sentence in the case of the defendant Salvatore V. Bonanno is that it is adjudged that he be committed to the custody of the Attorney General or his authorized representative for a term of four years on counts 1 through 55, the sentences to run concurrently. In addition it is adjudged that the defendant pay a fine to the United States pursuant to his conviction on count 1 of $10,000. That is the sentence of the court. The fine is a committed fine.''

Bill, almost breathless, had been waiting for more years to be added on, and when the judge turned to Notaro, Bill could barely conceal the sense of relief that he felt, the ecstatic and grateful realization that it would be *four* years and not *ten* as he had almost become resigned to and not the lifetime in prison that had been predicted for him by some people he knew. Four years!—he thought, trying to concentrate on what Judge Mansfield was saying to Notaro: ''. . . it seems to me that there are different influences in your case. You didn't have the advantages that the defendant Bonanno had. You have had a fairly hard life. You haven't had the education, and the part you played in these crimes was, without minimizing the crimes, a relatively minor part. You were going along—and I have no doubt well aware of what was being done. You, as I recall the evidence, participated in obtaining airline tickets at the Tucson Airport from the American Airlines representative there by signing the name of Torrillo, and using his card. . . . There was evidence that you had opened up an account under 'Peter Joseph,' as I recall it. After considering the whole picture and the fact that your record is limited to this one instance in Quebec, the sentence of the court will be that you are committed to the custody of the Attorney General or his duly authorized representative for a term of one year, and you are adjudged to pay a fine to the United States in the sum of $1,000.'' Notaro lowered his head slightly. He was neither pleased nor disappointed; he had thought that there was a chance of an acquittal, but he accepted the judge's verdict and was relieved that the situation, the suspense, was finally over.

''Your Honor,'' Krieger said, ''I have a notice of appeal here in the courtroom which I would request my client file immediately upon leaving Your Honor's presence. I would also ask on his behalf, Your Honor, for a fixation of bail pending appeal. The defendant presently is at large on a surety bond in the sum of $15,000, I believe it is, Your Honor. There has never been any problem whatsoever in the defendant's appearance here in response to the court's directions and in response to the mandates of the court and, needless to say, he was here for sentence, Your Honor."

"Your Honor," said Phillips, "I take it that the same application is made on behalf of Mr. Notaro?"

"Yes, sir," said Kasanof.

"I would like to address myself to both applications at this time," Phillips said. "The government opposes the applications for the following reasons: Your Honor has just imposed a substantial prison sentence on Mr. Bonanno and also, Your Honor, on Mr. Notaro. Although Mr. Bonanno has appeared every time he was required to do so, this prison sentence does substantially increase the likelihood that he will not appear at the time that he is required to start serving the sentence . . ."

The judge, however, disagreed and he said he would continue the defendants in their present bail on two conditions: "First, if there comes to the attention of the court any indication whatsoever that they are threatening, expressly or impliedly, any third persons or witnesses, the government may immediately apply for an increase in bail pending appeal; secondly, I do so on the condition that there will be a diligent prosecution of the appeal so that we do not find, as I have found in some cases, that years go by before the adjudication of the court ever becomes effective."

The defendants and their attorneys expressed agreement, and after the judge dismissed them, they thanked him and left the courtroom. In the corridor, newspaper reporters asked Bill what he thought of the sentence, but before he could reply Krieger stepped in to say that there would be no comment and that the decision would be appealed. While they questioned Krieger further, Bill pressed the elevator button and stood waiting with Notaro. Notaro smiled and seemed satisfied, and although he said nothing, Bill was sure that Notaro held no ill feelings toward him because of the credit card case. Notaro was not a complainer. As the judge said in the final remarks, Notaro's life had not been easy; and Notaro, who had long ago adjusted to that fact, was not the sort of man who would be shattered or disillusioned by a higher authority's verdict that he should spend a year in jail.

As the elevator arrived, Krieger quickly left the reporters and departed behind Bill, Notaro, and Kasanof. It was after one o'clock, and they decided to have a leisurely lunch and a few drinks, and as they walked down the stone steps of the federal courthouse they were almost in a festive mood. It was over, the dreaded case was over, and Bill admitted to Krieger that the judge's sentence could have been a lot worse. Krieger quickly agreed and was pleased that Bill was looking at the brighter side of the situation. Krieger was also appreciative of Bill's expressed gratitude for the legal efforts that had been made; Krieger was fond of Bill personally, and while he knew that the sentence could have been harsher, he still felt that four years was a heavy price to pay for what he considered a $2,400 misunderstanding. While the case might be reversed on appeal, Krieger was not optimistic, and so he was relieved that Bill seemed prepared for jail.

In the restaurant Bill called Rosalie from a telephone booth, and after he had relayed the news and had emphasized that the decision could have been worse, she seemed more cheerful—although as she listened she was crying. She was free to release her emotions now because the children were in school, it was midmorning in California. He said that he had a few legal details to complete with Krieger later in the evening and that he would return home on the following morning. Rosalie said that she would call Catherine and others and that they would have a large family dinner after he returned. She also said, reflecting further on the prison term, that he would be only forty when released and that all the children would most likely still be living at home then. He agreed, and he was about to add that there was the pending appeal to consider, and that he might also be free to spend the entire summer at home before having to surrender— but he withheld these comments; his conversation was undoubtedly being recorded, and he thought that perhaps one bonus accompanying his imprisonment was that the FBI would stop tapping his phone.

Saying good-bye to Rosalie, he returned to the table, where the men were laughing and finishing their first round of drinks. Bill picked up the Scotch that had been ordered for him, held it up in a sign of toast, finished it in two swallows, and ordered another.

He had dinner that evening in Brooklyn with the Di Pasquales, and on the following morning boarded a plane for San Francisco, pleased that the flight was not crowded. He preferred sitting by himself and not having to converse with anyone who might recognize him because his photograph had been in the morning editions of the *News* and the *Times*. He thought that he looked better in the *News*—his face was thinner, it was an older picture, and he was not wearing a hat as he was in the *Times*'s photograph. The *Times*'s picture had obviously been taken by a cameraman bending low, and it emphasized his jowly look, heavier face, and the shadows under his eyes. The *News* also gave him a better play, a five-column headline reading COURT SLIPS YOUNG BONANNO A FOUR-YEAR TERM; while the *Times*'s was a one-column head written from a more patriarchal viewpoint BONANNO SON GETS FOUR YEARS IN PRISON. As the stewardess hung up his jacket, Bill sat against the window in the front row, alone, flipping through the pages of the *Times*, reading the international news, the financial section, the theater reviews, the sports page; but then he again folded the paper back and reread what had been written about him.

Salvatore V. (Bill) Bonanno, the thirty-seven-year-old son of Joseph (Joe Bananas) Bonanno, reputed to be a former head of a Mafia family here, was sentenced yesterday to four years in federal prison for his part in a scheme involving a stolen credit card. . . .

31

SPRING AND SUMMER came and went quickly, followed by a melancholy autumn during which Bill expected at any moment to be told that he had two weeks left in which to surrender. His appeal had been rejected by the higher court—and he was not surprised to learn that Torrillo, after pleading guilty to the ninety-nine-count securities indictment, received a suspended sentence. Such were the vagaries of justice—Torrillo was a free man; David Hale, the FBI's bomber, was free; the Green Beret's assassin in Songmy was free; and Tucson's Charles Battaglia, who had allegedly tried to force a bowling alley manager into installing a vending machine, received ten years. It was a bizarre period, a time when the nation seemed pulled between its twin forces of violence and puritanism, balanced by hypocrisy, and perhaps that was one reason why Bill was unable to explain during the summer to his children, and to himself, why he was going to be spending four years in jail.

He was in one sense going to jail because, desperate for cash in 1968, and with the Banana War going badly and his life in danger (excuses he could hardly offer in his own behalf in federal court) he had done the expedient thing and not the wise thing in using Torrillo's credit card; but that did not fully explain why he would be going away for four years or why he had already been in and out of jails: there were other important, complex factors that had shaped him, had influenced what he had done and what had been done to him, and in order to explain these to his children he would want to explain his whole life, beginning with his birth in 1932 and the beat of the different drum to which he had marched during most of his maturity. He would want to explain his father's life, the spirit of that loving and destructive father-son relationship, the period and place in which it was set, beginning with his father's arrival in America during Prohibition, that glamorous, lush, lawless era in which fortunes had been made by men who might otherwise have labored all their lives digging ditches or driving trucks.

Bill remembered the story of how his father—shortly after being chased out of Sicily by Mussolini and after sailing from Marseilles to Cuba—had settled in Brooklyn and was offered a job as a barber by an uncle named Bonventre, an offer that Joseph Bonanno politely refused. If he had accepted it, the recent history of the Bonannos would doubtless be quite different today—Bill almost certainly would not now be going to jail; but if his father had accepted the job, he would not have been Joseph Bonanno, the vain, proud, unusual man that Bill had tried without success to emulate. Bill saw his father as a misplaced masterpiece of a man who had been forged in a feudalistic tradition but had been flexible enough to survive and prosper in mid-twentieth-century America, albeit not in the manner of which Judge Mansfield would approve.

Judge Mansfield, the Harvard-educated son of a former mayor of Boston, saw the world through different eyes than did Joseph Bonanno of Castellammare del Golfo; and Bill remembered from his own recent trial in federal court the judge's words on the day of sentencing: *There is hardly any excuse for the type of conduct of which you were found guilty. . . . You are not the product of a ghetto. . . . I don't see that because of family relationships you were under any great handicap. . . . You could have gotten a job . . .*

Yes, Bill thought, I could have gotten a job—but doing what? After all the publicity that had been attached to the Bonanno name since the Kefauver hearings twenty years ago—a time in which Bill himself had been called out of a high school classroom to be questioned by the FBI about the Mangano murder—he doubted that he could have gotten a job worthy of his intelligence; doubted, for example, that he could have joined the training program of a large American corporation and risen within the structure unless he had changed his name or had disowned his father. And, if he had done that, he would not have been Bill Bonanno, a son who deeply loved his father although recognizing that the relationship had been destructive; curiously, more destructive to him than it had been to his father, who had not spent time in jail, who had fewer legal problems than Bill, and was no doubt more cunning, more careful, stronger, more selfish perhaps, and less loving.

Joseph Bonanno, an orphan at fifteen, had been independent and self-reliant and had never had a father to answer to except in a mystical sense—his father, dead at thirty-seven, became an idealized figure preserved in a dozen sepia photographs and religious cards and in the exalted, reverential recollections of Joseph Bonanno, recollections that were all part of his dated, idealized world rife with ritual and rigidity. Bill Bonanno had been lured into that world through the magnetism of his father, realizing too late that his father was a rare natural inhabitant of that demanding state of mind; and it was not surprising now, in the fall of 1970, that his father was one of that world's few survivors. Most of the powerful dons who had immigrated during the 1920s were now dead, decrepit, or very old, and their Americanized sons were too smart, or not smart enough, to replace them. Bill Bonanno was among the last of his generation to make the attempt, and he would not have tried had his father not been so successful and awesome, offering to Bill what appeared to be great opportunities and advantages, a status at birth that had seemed almost regal.

But now those times were past; and the government, continuing its crime-busting crusade reminiscent of Mussolini's successful anti-Mafia campaign in Sicily, disregarding civil rights as it invaded privacy and relied on shady informers, recorded a series of highly publicized arrests of mafiosi and reputed mafiosi, incarcerating many men who seemed ready for an old-age home. Before his own conviction, Bill had read in the newspapers that sixty-eight-year-old Gerardo Catena, alleged successor to the late Vito Genovese, was sent to jail for an indefinite term for refusing to answer questions about organized crime; and the sixty-seven-year-old New Jersey *capo*, Angelo De Carlo, a victim of FBI eavesdropping, received a two-year sentence and $20,000 fine for conspiracy and extortion. On his way to a federal penitentiary in Danbury, Connecticut, De Carlo shrugged his shoulders at reporters and said, "I've got to die sometime, so I might as well go this way."

Carlo Gambino, a sixty-seven-year-old don of one of New York's five "families," was surrounded and seized by FBI agents as he was with his wife and daughter-in-law in a car in Brooklyn, and he was charged with conspiracy to hijack an armored car carrying $3 million to $5 million in cash belonging to the Chase Manhattan Bank. The FBI's informant against Gambino was a veteran bank robber from Boston, John Kelley, who had been arrested in May 1969 for the $542,000 robbery of a Brinks truck in 1968 and who was awaiting trial in that case. Gambino was furious over the FBI's allegations, and after bail was set at $75,000 Gambino refused to let a waiting bondsman post bail, declaring: "I'll stay in jail—I'm innocent from this accusation and I won't put up five cents for bail." But after twenty minutes of persuasion by his son and his lawyer and after the tiny white-haired don popped a heart-stimulant pill into his mouth, he reluctantly signed the bail application.

In Miami, customs agents arrested Meyer Lansky, sixty-seven, the most prominent Jewish gangster in organized crime, for carrying in his suitcase, as he returned from Mexico, a quantity of Donnatal that he used for his nervous indigestion, but for which he did not have a prescription. Angelo Bruno, sixty-year-old don of Philadelphia and South Jersey, was jailed for an indefinite term for refusing to testify before the New Jersey State Commission of Investigation, and in New York it was reported, though not confirmed, that seventy-nine-year-old Frank Costello was forced out of retirement to help fill the Mafia's leadership vacuum.

Bill Bonanno also read, as he awaited his notification to surrender, of the arrest in New York of thirty-five underworld figures that had been carried out as early as 6:00 A.M. by 100 men from the police department and the Brooklyn District Attorney's office. The arrested men, charged with refusing to testify after they had been granted immunity from prosecution by the Kings County grand jury, included the leaders of the dwindling dozen or so members still linked to what was once the 350-member Bonanno organization: Natale Evola, sixty-three, who had been associated with the elder Bonanno for thirty years, and the ailing Paul Sciacca, who had recently relinquished the leadership of the faction he inherited from Gaspar Di Gregorio—who, on the day after the raid, died of lung cancer, at sixty-five. Some of those sought in the raid could not be found—among them was Frank Mari, the man believed to have murdered Hank Perrone and to have led the Troutman Street ambush against Bill and who had been listed as missing and probably dead since September 1968.

Perhaps the individual who received the most attention from the police, the FBI, and the press during the summer and fall of 1970, and continued to receive it in 1971, was an affable, neatly dressed, short dark-haired man named Joseph Colombo, who, after being indicted by a federal grand jury in Brooklyn for income tax evasion (in the total amount of $19,168 between 1963–1967), was charged with criminal contempt by a Nassau County grand jury in Long Island for refusing to answer questions about organized crime. At the same time, one of his four sons, twenty-three-year-old Joseph Colombo, Jr., was arrested by federal agents on charges of conspiring with other young men to melt United States silver coins, profiting because the face value of the coins was less than the intrinsic value of the metal. The government's case against the younger Colombo, which was again based on evidence from an opportunistic informer with whom the FBI had made a deal, may have been one of the more imprudent moves made by the government in its years of vigilant anticrime crusading: the case suddenly boomeranged against the FBI, as the elder Colombo, who regarded his son as a legitimate young businessman who was being framed, organized a group of protesters to picket FBI headquarters at Sixty-ninth Street and Third Avenue in Manhattan, protesters who carried signs and shouted slogans claiming that law enforcement authorities were waging a vendetta against Italo-Americans, defaming an entire ethnic group of patriotic, law-abiding Italo-Americans by using such words as "Mafia" or "Cosa Nostra." Spokesmen for the FBI countered by saying that the protest was a Mafia-inspired ploy designed to weaken the government's attack on organized crime, and the press quoted from government data in several articles identifying Joseph Colombo, Sr., as a member of the Mafia commission and as the head of the "family" once ruled by Joseph Profaci and Joseph Magliocco. Colombo had been a subordinate officer in the Profaci organization, the articles said, when the Gallo brothers led a revolt in 1960–61 and it was Colombo who had later arranged the concessions with the Gallos that had ended the feuding.

The press also cited Colombo as the man who in 1963 tipped off Carlo Gambino and Thomas Lucchese to Magliocco's murder plot against them, a plot that some reports stated was Joseph Bonanno's idea; and while it had not been carried out, Magliocco's position was in jeopardy, and after his fatal heart attack in December 1963 the Profaci "family" was taken over by Joseph Colombo, Sr. The elder Colombo's father, who was killed in 1938, was also described in the press as a onetime member of the Profaci organization.

Little was known about Joseph Colombo's boyhood except that he was born in Brooklyn forty-eight years ago—making him by far the youngest don of any importance—that he had attended two years of school at New Utrecht High, and that from 1942 to 1945 he had served as an enlisted man in the Coast Guard, being discharged with a disability allowance of $11.50 a month for a service-connected nervous disorder. After the war, he was arrested on several occasions on charges ranging from running crap games to consorting with known criminals, and in 1966 he was among those arrested in the so-called Little Apalachin Meeting held at La Stella Restaurant in Forest Hills. He was also arrested later for dining in the House of Chan Restaurant in Manhattan in the company of Carlo Gambino and Angelo Bruno.

Colombo was connected with several legitimate businesses, the principal among them being his listed occupation as a real estate broker, with estimated annual earnings of between $30,000 and $40,000. But because he had allegedly lied about his criminal record when applying for his real estate broker's license, the government in 1970 brought a perjury indictment against him; this charge, however, together with the many others that were widely publicized, did not seem to hurt his popularity with hundreds of Italo-Americans who joined him and his sons on the picket lines night after night outside FBI headquarters in the summer of 1970. These protesters were the nucleus of a much larger organization that Colombo was helping to form, a militant pressure group called the Italian-American Civil Rights League.

The league, which hoped to do for Italo-Americans what the Jewish Anti-Defamation League had done for Jews and similar organizations had done for other minorities, was conceived as a national body that would appeal to a large percentage of the estimated twenty-two million Americans of Italian ancestry, an assumption that was initially greeted with skepticism by many Italo-American politicians and leading citizens. They recalled that previous attempts to unify Italo-Americans had failed or had proven to be ineffective, and they suggested that Italians were inherently individualistic, were not group-oriented, were so far removed from the melting pot and so integrated into the American mainstream that they no longer identified with, or wished to be reminded of, their ethnic past. Many of the Little Italys in large cities were disintegrating in the wake of modern construction, a new mobile society, the flight to the suburbs; and it was also pointed out that second-generation Italians were marrying non-Italians and that what remained of the traditional clannishness and what Lampedusa in *The Leopard* referred to as a "terrifying insularity of mind" was now dying with the aging immigrants who had passed through Ellis Island a half century ago, was dying with the Mafia.

It was therefore astonishing to such theorists to read on June 29, 1970, that approximately 40,000 people gathered in New York's Columbus Circle on Italian-American Unity Day to proclaim their pride in their Italian heritage and express deep resentment at the press and law enforcement authorities that concentrated on the Mafia. The Mafia, some protesters said, was only a small part of organized crime, while other protesters said there was no Mafia at all—it was merely a creation of the media and the FBI. The gathering was attended largely, but not exclusively, by Italo-Americans; in the crowd were representatives from Jewish groups, black groups, who shared the view that the government's crime busters had gone too far with their harassing, their eavesdropping and stereotyping. Representative Allard K. Lowenstein of Nassau County, Long Island, was cheered when he said, "Anyone who doesn't understand what America owes to Italy doesn't understand America." Harlem's Adam Clayton Powell told the crowd, "This nation is for all, not just the Wasps," and former New York Controller Mario A. Procaccino said, "Don't let anyone imagine that when looters, arsonists, and bombers are being coddled and treated like heroes, we are going to stand by and permit the smearing and harassment of innocent people whose sole crime is that they are related, friends, or neighbors, or just happen to be Italian-American." But the greatest applause came near the end of the program when the five-foot-six-inch, round-faced, unprepossessing figure of Joseph Colombo stood to tell the crowd: "This day belongs to you—to you the people." Then he added, with a simple directness that struck a responsive chord and loud cheering: "You are organized now, you are one. And nobody can take you apart anymore."

Colombo was not talking to people who necessarily justified the Mafia and loathed the FBI—in fact Colombo himself said he respected the FBI, called it "the greatest organization in the country" except when "they're framing our children and harassing our pregnant women"; Colombo's audience was rather part of America's silent majority, its hardhats, and World War II veterans, its civil servants, small-home owners, middle-class housewives who had apparently felt, more than was previously realized, acute embarrassment and humiliation during the last decade over the enormous publicity given to gangsters with Italian names. And so, quite apart from any self-interest that Colombo may have had in turning the spotlight off the Mafia, he was expressing a desire shared by many thousands of citizens who had no personal stake in the Mafia, who had no relatives connected with it, but who also felt unconnected from the larger America that was the focus of their aspirations and identity. They were voiceless, powerless, frustrated; most of them felt that they had been playing by the rules and losing. They were unrecognized by the thousands of Italo-Americans who had made it in America and who were climbing the social ladder behind the Irish; and the media, which was largely influenced by Jews and was very sensitive to anti-Semitism, was not nearly so sensitive to issues that the lower-middle-class and middle-class Italians considered prejudicial.

In Washington, there was only one senator of Italian origin; in the House of Representatives, only eleven of 435 members. There was not an influential Italo-American in the Cabinet or White House, and among the protesters in Columbus Circle listening to Colombo was one man carrying a sign announcing that there were no Italians on the city's board of education. While the federal government passed laws to help the urban blacks escape substandard schools and ghetto housing, it would not be the legislators or newspaper publishers or network executives who would be personally affected by such legislation—the blacks would never move in large numbers into the white legislators' segregated neighborhoods or into their children's private schools or their country clubs. After the son of New Jersey Governor William T. Cahill—who had campaigned hard against organized crime—was twice arrested on marijuana charges, the governor

supported a bill reducing the penalty for possessors of small
amounts of marijuana, and this bill was passed by the New
Jersey legislature into law. But crimes committed by the sons of
alleged mafiosi were vigorously prosecuted, and it was this belief that caused many people to sympathize with Joseph Colombo and to support his protest after his son had been arrested
in what the elder Colombo denounced as an "FBI frame-up."
And Colombo's characterization would eventually be substan-
tiated in a Brooklyn federal court when, on the fifth day of the
trial in which his son was accused of plotting to melt down silver
coins into more valuable ingots, the government's chief witness—a former coin dealer named Richard W. Salamone—
admitted that he had falsely accused the younger Colombo.
Salamone told a startled courtroom that he had implicated him
because the FBI, which was anxious to "get" the son, had
promised to help Salamone recover $50,000 that he had lost in
a business transaction, would help him find a job, and would
return to him his confiscated pistol permit. The FBI's failure to
back these promises influenced Salamone in recanting his previous testimony, although it would quickly lead to his arrest,
and that of another government witness, after the jury acquitted
Joseph Colombo, Jr.

One month after the Columbus Circle rally, with the growing
Italian-American Civil Rights League showing promise of political influence, Attorney General John N. Mitchell sent a confidential memorandum to all agency heads, including the FBI
director, instructing them to stop using the words "Mafia" and
"Cosa Nostra" because the terms offended "decent Italian-
Americans." Encouraged by this decision, officers of the
league—the elder Colombo was not an officer but his eldest son,
Anthony, was the vice-president—received similar assurance after writing to the Ford Motor Company, which was one of the
sponsors of ABC's television series, "The F.B.I." The league
also gained concessions from advertising agencies whose commercials, in the league's opinion, portrayed Italians in a de-
meaning way. When a Staten Island newspaper, the *Advance*,
published a series of articles on mafiosi residing on Staten Island, noisy picketers from the league appeared outside the newspaper building, interfered with delivery trucks, and urged that
the author of the series be dismissed and that future references
to "Mafia" or "Cosa Nostra" be banned. The *Advance*, which

did not comply with either demand, obtained an injunction against the picketing, but not before a fracas had occurred between league members and the police. Among those arrested was the league's president, Natale Marcone, a fifty-seven-year-old former union official who lives on Staten Island.

The New York Times's plant on the West Side was also picketed, and spokesmen for the league later met with the *Times*'s executives to complain about certain articles and the use of Italian "labels" to describe a portion of organized crime. While the league's representatives were told that under no circumstances would the *Times* respond to pressure tactics, the managing editor, A. M. Rosenthal, said that the newspaper was sensitive to all aspects of discrimination in America and that it would review its performance with reference to Italo-Americans to see if there were deficiencies.

In the months that followed, while "Mafia" still appeared in the *Times*'s news columns, it did so with somewhat less frequency than before, being alternated with such terms as "organized crime 'family.' " The *Times* also published certain articles that Joseph Colombo, Sr., approved of, one being a lengthy article about the league itself. The article, though not ignoring the criminal charges against Colombo, concentrated on the league's growth, its aims, and its fund-raising charity drives, hospital construction, its contributions to black neighborhood groups, Spanish-speaking groups, antinarcotics education programs, and its close liaison with the Jewish Defense League. It was estimated to have 45,000 dues-paying members around the nation, and the most active members in its various chapters were called "captains": of the 2,000 captains, 200 were said to be Jewish and 90 were black. The league had raised about $400,000 from members' dues, and $500,000 from a charity show at which Frank Sinatra and several other show business personalities entertained the audience of 5,000 at the Felt Forum in New York. The audience included New York's deputy mayor, Richard R. Aurelio; Paul O'Dwyer, a prominent Democrat; Ed McMahon, the television personality; and several hundred league members among whom, of course, was Joseph Colombo, Sr. The joke that received perhaps the biggest laugh was delivered by the black comedian Godfrey Cambridge who told the crowd: "I got a strange invitation to this thing—a rock came through my window."

A few months after the show Joseph Colombo was named "Man of the Year for 1970" by *The Tri-Boro Post*, a weekly newspaper that circulates in Queens, Brooklyn, and Staten Island. At a dinner marking the occasion—a $125-a-plate affair that netted the league $101,000—Colombo received a bronze plaque honoring him as the "guiding spirit of Italian-American unity."

But despite such awards and the progress of the league, law enforcement authorities continued to pursue Joseph Colombo; and Colombo believed that the growth of the league and its persistent picketing of FBI headquarters had so offended federal agents that they were more determined than ever to win a conviction against him and to remove him from the scene by a long term in prison. After the announcement of his Man of the Year award, he was arrested in connection with a jewel theft that had occurred three years before in Garden City, Long Island; he was accused of "mediating" between quarreling participants in the $750,000 jewel robbery, and, for his services, he supposedly received a fee of $75,000. Colombo was also arrested with several other men by the FBI on charges of operating a $5-million-a-year gambling business. After he was released on $25,000 bail, Colombo left the court and went directly to FBI headquarters to join the picket line. While walking, he spoke with newspapermen, repeating his often-expressed opinion that he was innocent of all accusations, that there was no such thing as a Mafia in America, and that the government's law enforcement authorities were prejudiced against Italo-Americans. In an interview he gave to a reporter from the *Times*, he pointed out that when General Electric was proven guilty of price-fixing, its bosses were merely fined; but when the government was dealing with Italo-Americans, it was far less genteel.

Such pleas of persecution, which Colombo repeated on radio programs and also on television on the "Dick Cavett Show," were considered ridiculous by many Italo-Americans around the nation, and among this group was State Senator John J. Marchi, a Republican of Staten Island. He criticized the producer of *The Godfather* for agreeing to delete "Mafia" and "Cosa Nostra" from the movie script, adding: "Apparently you are a ready market for the league's preposterous theory that we can exorcise devils by reading them out of the English language." Even some of the "devils" were said to be disconcerted by Colombo's campaign, although they were possibly envious of the publicity he was receiving and the money that the league was accumulating. Carlo Gambino was one of those rumored to be upset by Colombo's tactics, seeing no wisdom in publicly berating law enforcement authorities, without whose cooperation organized crime could not exist. Gambino was of the old school, and like many ancient Sicilians he was something of a stoic, a believer in patient suffering, acting quietly, saying nothing. *Omertà*. Colombo, American-born and relatively young, was suddenly breaking with tradition. Colombo had adopted the style of the civil rights movement, was staging his campaign in the street in front of television cameras; and Gambino, who had seen many young men come and go in his lifetime, wondered.

Bill Bonnano, 3,000 miles away in California, carefully followed the newspaper reports of Colombo's pickets, but as yet he had no opinion, waiting to see the final results. So far the lawyers had managed to keep Colombo free on bail, except for two short terms in jail, and no one could doubt that Colombo's publicity had brought national attention and donations to the league, and perhaps picketing FBI headquarters had not been a bad idea—for years the federal agents had played a ruthless game, and, regardless of the manner in which the agents might retaliate, they could not do much that they had not already done. Bill recalled David Hale's bombing escapades in Tucson, remembered Hale's plan to have Notaro killed with a crossbow, and Bill wondered what David Hale's counterparts in the FBI were planning in New York.

32

WHEN BILL BONANNO finally received official word that he was to report to prison on the following Monday—January 18, 1971—he was relieved and even pleased. The waiting had been almost unbearable during the last months of 1970. To make matters worse, he had received during that period several calls from New York indicating an approximate date of surrender, then later calls delaying that date *after* he had already been given farewell parties by relatives and friends in California. There was nothing more embarrassing than to be the central attraction in a crowded room laden with laughter, tension, and sadness, a scene that culminated after dinner with toasting and tearful farewells and embraces; and then, days later, to see many of those same people again.

This had occurred three times during the winter of 1970, and after the third party and prison delay he told Rosalie to tell friends who might call that he had already gone to jail; and for days afterward, he sat in the house with the shades down watching television with the children, not coming to the phone, which Rosalie answered, not venturing outdoors even at night. These had been the most humiliating hours of his final weeks of freedom, a time when he had truly withdrawn from the world, feeling useless and worthless, an emotional drain on everyone close to him. He had long ago turned in the Cadillac that he had leased for his final month, had solved every problem that he was capable of solving, had said everything that he was going to say to Rosalie and the children. He was psychologically ready for life behind bars; still, from September through December, week by week, he had been inexplicably detained, tortured by time, and it was slowly eroding the pleasant memories that he had planned to carry into confinement.

He hoped to remember most of all the previous summer, during which he, Rosalie, and the children had taken several long motor trips sightseeing through California. They had also spent a week cruising on a large houseboat, accompanied by his sister Catherine, his sister-in-law Ann and their families. He had driven down to Arizona to visit the elder Bonannos, and though his father was restricted to the Tucson area, he assured Bill that he would look after Rosalie and the children during Bill's absence. Bill's brother, Joseph, had meanwhile moved from Tucson to an apartment in San Jose, and Rosalie's mother planned to fly to California for an extended stay as soon as Bill had gone to jail.

Fortunately, with help from family and friends, Bill and Rosalie managed to buy a ranch-style home in a new development near San Jose; it was a four-bedroom house on a street with many children and friendly neighbors, and Rosalie was as contented as she could be under the circumstances.

In the fall, the children returned to school and became more preoccupied with their own activities. Bill's oldest son, Charles, nearly thirteen, the most ingratiating of the Bonanno boys, quickly made friends in the neighborhood and he seemed to be doing better in the present school than he had in the last one. Charles continued to build cages for the endless number of pets under his custody, and he still collected Blue Chip stamps toward the acquisition of new gadgets, having already gotten the electric lawnmower that he had saved for during the previous year.

Joseph, almost ten, was as studious as ever, and his asthma had improved somewhat since undergoing hypnotic treatments from a physician and since Rosalie had asked that guests not smoke in the house. But Joseph was still fundamentally a loner, and recently while playing in the garage he had discovered a bullet, had tinkered with it until it exploded, burning his fingers.

Tory, seven, was becoming huskier and bolder, and Bill continued to see his own boyhood image through Tory's manner and appearance. Tory, like Charles, had quickly made new friends, seemed adept at sports, and he had made his debut on the block by hitting a baseball through a neighbor's window. Felippa, six, was becoming taller and thinner; she was no less attached to Bill, and he was painfully aware in advance of how much he would miss her.

Though Rosalie was now qualified to work as a computer programmer, she had been unable to find a job in the San Jose area that paid enough to cover the expenses of full-time help at home. She also did not want the children to be without her the first year Bill was away, and so she concluded, after awkward discussions with Bill, that she would apply for welfare. Bill was unhappy at first, but he was beyond such vanity at this point. The government claimed all his assets, his car, his landholdings in Arizona; he was bankrupt, could not earn a dime that was not subject to back taxes, and so he soon accepted the idea that, since the government was taking him out of circulation, it could at least help support his family while he was away.

He had several times planned to explain to the children why he was going to jail, but during the entire summer and fall he managed to avoid it, partly because the children never questioned him about it and partly because there seemed no way of discussing the subject without degrading himself in their eyes. Bill's dilemma was that while he wanted his children to respect the law, he did not want them to disrespect him.

He wanted them to understand that the law was created for the majority of people, and that there were those who committed acts that the law opposed and so those people were penalized; but he also wanted them to know that the law often changed, that what was disallowed now might be permitted a few years from now. He thought of how radically things had changed in his own lifetime with reference to social mores and customs, marriage and sex, literature, films. He remembered that once he had been expelled from boarding school because he led a group of students into *Forever Amber*, a film that now, in a period of permissiveness and nudity, was mild indeed. He had been born near the end of Prohibition when moralists were still condemning the vices of alcohol, yet now liquor was not only legal and acceptable but was a substantial source of income to the government that prior to 1933 had opposed it. And Bill had just read that New York State was going into the off-track betting business, attempting to eliminate bookmakers and absorb the profits from this enterprise that generations of district attorneys had called a racket, an exploiter of working men, a source of deprivation to their families. Next, Bill was sure, the government would try to take over the numbers game, and the drug market—it was already pushing methadone as a heroin cure—

and the point was not that lawmakers were unjustified in doing what they deemed socially beneficial, but rather that they were endorsing the very items that they had not long ago abhorred. They were changing the laws with regard to acts that thousands of men long dead had been arrested for doing—it was all a matter of timing, Bill thought morosely, sitting behind lowered shades in his living room, it was a matter of being at the right place, the right time, and being on the winning side of wars, and having enough money to avoid using a credit card offered by Perrone, and having enough sense to not sign the name "Don A. Torrillo."

Bill had no quarrel with the jury that had convicted him. It had concentrated on those months when he had carried Torrillo's card, had weighed the evidence against him during that time of retreat from New York with a "contract" on his life, and his thoughts at that time had not been overly concerned with the judiciousness of signing another man's name on Diners' Club charge slips. But his acts during those months were related to the pressures of the Banana War, which had its origins and sources of conflict years before he had moved to New York, years before he had even been born—his whole life was interwoven with the past, and for this past he would spend four years in prison; but there was no simple way to explain all this to his children. The only thing for him to do was to begin serving the sentence so that he could be done with it. And after his release in 1974, he would hopefully begin again in another direction. He had no idea what he would do when he got out of jail at forty-one, but he had plenty of time ahead to think about that.

And so after the many delays in the fall and winter of 1970, he was relieved to learn that he was to surrender on Monday, January 18, to the federal marshal's office in downtown Los Angeles. It was finally definite, precise, real. He told Rosalie, and she reacted quietly and made plans for a final family gathering on the Sunday before his Monday flight to Los Angeles. Bill's mother was then staying at Catherine's house, and the only person who would be unable to attend the dinner would be Bill's father in Arizona, which was why Bill flew to Tucson on Thursday to say good-bye.

Bill was accompanied by his brother, and they were met at the Tucson airport by Peter Notaro, who was driving the elder Bonanno's 1970 Buick Riviera. Notaro would also be surrendering in a few days, having been directed to report to a prison in Texarkana, Texas. Notaro seemed casual and resigned; it was only a year, and Bill kidded him about it, saying that if *he* had gotten only a year he could have done it standing on his head.

At the Bonanno home on East Elm Street at the patio gate, Bill was embraced by his father, who seemed thinner, somewhat drawn, but his tanned face was still strong and handsome, and he wore trimly tailored Western pants, a bright shirt, and cowboy boots. After a light lunch with wine, they drove to the elder Bonanno's government-liened 1,110-acre cotton farm beyond the town, where they walked slowly and did not have to concern themselves with the possibility of electronic bugging. Bill told his father of Rosalie's plans to remain at home with the children, and the elder Bonanno again assured him not to worry about any problems that might arise. Bill explained that after surrendering in Los Angeles he would probably be flown to New York to the federal prison on West Street, where he would be available to stand trial on charges of having fraudulently transferred the ownership of the East Meadow house. Bill would plead guilty, and he thought that possibly more time would be added to his term but that soon after the trial he might be shipped back to California to complete his term at the federal prison on Terminal Island, in San Pedro. There he could be visited regularly by Rosalie and the children, perhaps as regularly as twice a month, and his separation from them and from the outside world would not seem so distant and decisive.

The more Bill talked, the less depressing it all seemed, although he noticed that his father was not saying much as they walked through the fields, with Notaro and his brother walking a few paces behind. His father made general comments, nodded often as Bill talked, but Bill had no idea what his father was thinking or feeling until after they returned to the house. The sun was fading then, the late-afternoon wind was blowing harder through the trees, kicking up dust in the patio where they were sitting. Then, turning to his father, Bill said that he had better begin packing certain things that he wanted to take with him; it was getting close to the hour when Bill was due at the airport.

His father followed him into the hall and stood silently in the doorway of what had once been Bill's bedroom, watching Bill opening and closing drawers, tying his necktie in front of the mirror, then putting on his jacket. His father suddenly seemed shaken and pale as he watched, and Bill said finally, "Look, I can cancel this plane, I can get a later reservation . . ." But the elder Bonanno quickly shook his head.

"Then, let's say good-bye here," Bill said, not wanting to do so in front of his brother and Notaro.

Joseph Bonanno stepped forward, put his arms around Bill and kissed him. Then the elder Bonanno quickly turned with tears in his eyes; he walked into the bathroom, closing the door gently. Bill stood in the middle of the room, feeling numb and unsteady. He picked up the suitcase and, from the hall, told Notaro to start up the car. After Notaro and Joseph Jr. left the house, Bill walked toward the door, but stopped when he heard his father behind him crying softly, *Dio ti binidici*, God should bless you, *Dio ti binidici*.

Bill paused but he did not look at his father. He left the house and walked toward the car.

It was foggy and damp at daybreak on Monday, and the children had breakfast with Bill and did not go to school. They knew that they would not be seeing him again for a long time, but only Felippa cried. She had had nightmares during the weekend and was so sick that Rosalie put her back to bed.

Though Rosalie pleaded with Bill to let her go with him to Los Angeles, or to at least accompany him to the airport in San Francisco, Bill insisted that she remain at home. After breakfast, his brother Joseph arrived, remaining in the car as Bill said good-bye, kissing each of the children quickly, then kissing Rosalie, who burst into tears as he left the house.

At the airport, because of the fog, his plane was delayed. Bill was wearing a new yellow shirt, a silk tie, and his best suit, a well-tailored gray pin-stripe which partially concealed his excessive weight; and, as he sat in the plane after saying good-bye to Joseph, he would have passed for one of the many executives flying to Los Angeles for a Monday-morning conference. It was a commuter plane and the passengers had an easy familiarity with the stewardesses, the plane, and each other, nodding and smiling as they sat down, but Bill was grim and depressed, which he had never remembered himself being on an airplane, and he ignored the man next to him who in a jovial way was trying to discuss the Super Bowl football game played on the previous day.

Landing in Los Angeles, Bill walked through the terminal carrying one suitcase and took a taxi to the federal building at North Spring Street in downtown Los Angeles. A guard stood at the door, and Bill asked directions to the federal marshal's office; arriving, he saw two signs, one marked "civil" and pointing to the left, another marked "criminal" and pointing to the right. Bill headed to the right, stopping when he came to the desk of a deputy marshal on whose uniform was a name tag reading "Ernest Newman."

"I'm Salvatore Bonanno," Bill said, and Newman nodded, unsmiling; he was expecting him. Newman picked up the phone, and placed a call to New York. Bill stood waiting. He heard Ernest Newman asking to speak to Walter Phillips, the Assistant United States Attorney; and when Phillips came to the phone, Bill heard Newman say, in a very official manner, "Salvatore Bonanno has surrendered."

AUTHOR'S NOTE

THE RESEARCH ON this book was begun on the afternoon of January 7, 1965, the day I first met Bill Bonanno. He was standing with his back to the wall in a dimly lit corridor of the federal court building in Manhattan talking to one of his attorneys during a recess. Though he seemed deeply engrossed in private conversation, nodding with his head bent low as he listened, he also seemed to be watching through the corner of his eye everyone who came along through the marble-floored corridor, and he seemed very aware of the detectives and newsmen who stood talking in a circle near the door to the jury room. At one point he noticed that I was watching him. And, as if he knew me, he smiled.

I was then a reporter on *The New York Times* and was close to Bill Bonanno's age, and I wondered, not for the first time, what it must be like to be a young man in the Mafia. Most of what I had read about organized crime in newspapers and books was obtained through sources in the federal government and the police, and this data, which focused largely on gangland slayings and grotesque portraits of men with Runyonesque nicknames, did not satisfy my curiosity about life within the secret society. I was more interested in how the men passed the idle hours that no doubt dominated their days, about the role of their wives, about their relationships with their children.

I continued to listen to the reporters and detectives huddled in the corridor, but my mind was wandering. Almost impulsively, I detached myself and walked toward Bill Bonanno and his lawyer. As I introduced myself, the lawyer said quickly that his client had nothing to say. I responded that I wanted no statement, conceding that it was an inappropriate time for an interview—Bill Bonanno had recently been arrested by the FBI in

Arizona after a long chase and now he was being questioned by a federal grand jury about his father's disappearance—but some-day, I said, months or years from now, I would like to sit down with him and discuss the possibility of writing a book about his boyhood. The lawyer again said that his client had no comment, and Bill Bonanno remained absolutely silent. But I sensed from his expression that he was responding. Perhaps the idea in-trigued him.

I called his lawyer's office several times after that, trying with-out success or encouragement to arrange a private meeting. But later in the winter, after I had written to Bill Bonanno, had continued to call, and had sent him a book that I had written, which he read and liked, I received word that he would see me at a restaurant in Manhattan.

At dinner, although he was noncommittal about being the subject of a book, we talked for several hours and got along extremely well. He seemed to enjoy recalling details from his boyhood, his school days in Arizona, the double life he had led as a university student, escorting pretty co-eds to parties on football weekends and then driving alone to the Tucson airport to meet one of his father's men arriving from the East. Undoubt-edly he had never discussed such things with anyone before, so lonely and remote had his life been. In the restaurant I felt that we were both hearing his story for the first time.

Nearly everything in Bill Bonanno's life had left a sharp, last-ing impression. He had almost total recall. He could remember minor incidents in precise detail, could recreate past scenes and dialogue, could describe the places he had seen, what he had felt. Yet he possessed a rare quality of detachment—it was as if a part of him had remained outside of everything he had ever experienced. He would have made a marvelous reporter.

Before our discussion ended that night, I asked if he would soon bring his wife to my home for dinner. He said that he would, and he did. After that, sometimes with our wives and children, we met on several occasions, gradually establishing the rapport and trust necessary in friendship and essential to the book I hoped to write, a book that would suggest the complexity of being a Bonanno, the special atmosphere within the home, the pull of the past upon the present.

A year after we met, Bill Bonanno appeared unexpectedly at my place during an afternoon, unshaven, wearing a dark suit and black shirt without a tie. Apologizing for the manner of his arrival, he explained with remarkable calm that gunmen had been trying to kill him. He had been "set up" on Troutman Street in Brooklyn three nights before—Friday, January 28, 1966—by a rival faction. Although the entire neighborhood must have been awakened by the several gun blasts, there had not been a line about it in the newspapers. He was surprised and disappointed; he actually wanted press coverage of the incident, for reasons that I have discussed in this book in Chapter 10. I was no longer with the *Times* then, but I volunteered to call an editor friend of mine, and it was this tip that broke the story. It also brought me closer to Bill Bonanno.

Hearing that I was leaving that week for California on an *Esquire* assignment, Bill wrote a letter of introduction for me to his sister, Catherine, saying that it was all right for her to discuss personal aspects of his life with me. From Catherine I gained valuable insights not only into Bill's character but also into their father, who was still missing at this time—he was never discussed in the present tense. Catherine was also perceptive in her analyses of herself, her mother, and her mother's family, the Labruzzos.

Later, returning to New York, I was able to meet other family relatives and friends through Bill, and they soon became vaguely aware that I hoped to someday write a book touching on their lives. But if they were suspicious and skeptical—and they undoubtedly were—they nevertheless accepted me as a friend of Bill's and did not question me too closely. Nor did I question them: I was sensitive to the situation, and at this juncture I was far more interested in the domestic atmosphere and the style of the people than in any specific information. I was content to observe, pleased to be accepted. At night, after I returned home, I described on paper what I had seen and heard, my impressions of the people. Soon, as I reread certain scenes, I could see the book taking shape. It seemed to suggest fiction, but each detail was true.

In May 1966 Joseph Bonanno made his dramatic reappearance. While I was able to meet him and dine with him, resulting in such scenes as described in Chapter 13, I felt that he had reservations about the book. Consequently Bill Bonanno began to reconsider the project at this time: tension was now building in the underworld, the so-called Banana War was expanding in

Brooklyn and Queens, and Bill was perhaps also concerned about my welfare, a concern that I was beginning to share.

The feud intensified in 1967, with shootings and murders reported in the press, and I lost touch with Bill for months at a time. His wife and four young children were often living in tight security in their home on Long Island. The telephone, when answered at all, was answered by bodyguards who had little to say. I was no longer able to visit.

I was then also concentrating on a book that I had begun in 1966, a history of *The New York Times* entitled *The Kingdom and the Power*. I worked on this through 1967, 1968, and into 1969. Occasionally, when I least expected it, I would hear from Bill, who called from a telephone booth to chat briefly and say that he was all right. Once I met him for a drink, and he was then in an angry mood, embittered by the disloyalty and fence-straddling of certain men in his world. He was willing to concede that the great leaders from his father's era were either dead or now too old and that the younger men who remained could neither lead nor follow.

The Banana War was essentially over in 1969. The feuding factions had become so splintered that nobody knew who was on which side. Disillusioned, the elder Bonanno retired to his winter home in Arizona and Bill settled his family in San Jose. During the winter of 1969, after the Tucson bombings had subsided and the federal agent who had allegedly organized them had retired from government service, I flew out to San Jose and spent much of the winter and spring there. I saw various members of the family and their children every day. I also spent time with Bill in New York when he made brief court appearances before his conviction on the credit card case.

Although I had read several books about Sicily—profiting most from the splendid volumes by the English author Denis Mack Smith—I found very little useful information about the region where the Bonanno family came from; so, after accepting an offer of family assistance, I flew to Palermo and then drove in a rented car to Castellammare del Golfo.

There I was greeted by a handsome, gray-haired gentleman who looked like the Italian movie director Vittorio De Sica. This man, among others, escorted me through the town, took me to visit the grave where the elder Bonanno's parents are buried, arranged for me to enter the Bonanno family home on Corso

Garibaldi, and accompanied me to the ancient castle on the gulf that gives the town its name. I returned on the following three days to the town, driving from Palermo less than two hours away, and each time when in town I was in the company of the gray-haired man who arranged for me to speak with anyone I wished.

Back in the United States, in addition to other visits to California, I also drove with Bill to Arizona, where I dined in his father's home. His father, courtly and hospitable in my presence, was no doubt still mildly confused by my relationship with his son, but I do not think he attempted to interfere. Bill was his own man now, no longer merely "JB's son," and in many ways the deterioration of the organization had freed Bill, although sometimes I still saw flashes of bitterness. Bill still felt betrayed, but I believe that deep within himself he harbored no great rancor toward the Mafia rivals who had tried to kill him or the government agents who possibly had tried to frame him. I think that the sources of conflict within Bill Bonanno were much closer to home, and this might explain why I was able to become his friend and companion and to write about him intimately. He was feeling a tremendous need to communicate when I first met him. While my initial proposal to write about him might have been flattering, particularly since he then felt so misunderstood and had gone through life being his father's son, I do believe that later I served as an instrument through which he could communicate to those closest to him. He could reveal through me, who respected and understood him, thoughts and attitudes that he did not wish to personally express to his family, to his father.

I sensed, later, that Rosalie also confided to me thoughts that she wished to convey to Bill or to her father-in-law; and Catherine, too, and other members of the family as well had told me what they wished others to know. I had become a source of communication within a family that had long been repressed by a tradition of silence.

INDEX

ABOUT THE AUTHOR

Gay Talese joined the reportorial staff of *The New York Times* in 1955, and remained there for a decade. During the 1960s and 1970s he contributed many articles to magazines, principally *Esquire*. He is the author of eight other books. His latest, UNTO THE SONS, was published by Alfred A. Knopf in February 1992. He was born in Ocean City, New Jersey, in 1932, and now lives in New York City and Ocean City with his wife, Nan A. Talese, an editor and publisher, and their daughters, Pamela and Catherine.